FASHIONS IN
CHURCH FURNISHINGS

FASHIONS IN CHURCH FURNISHINGS

1840–1940

BY

PETER F. ANSON

STUDIO VISTA LONDON

First edition published by The Faith Press 1960
Second edition published 1965 by Studio Vista Ltd
Blue Star House, Highgate Hill, London, N19
Printed in Holland by
N.V. Grafische Industrie Haarlem

FOREWORD

AS was explained in the Foreword to the first edition, published in 1960, this book was not meant to be a definitive history of church art in the period 1840–1940. What I tried to do was to make a pattern of both art and life, constructed from the specimens, extracts and fugitive pieces collected since the far-off days of my youth. I remarked that the apparent paradoxes and inconsistencies of church furnishings and decorations are an illustration of Cecil Beaton's dictum: 'Fashion, ever re-creating the past, usually takes two to four decades to view a period with that distance which lends enchantment and makes it possible to utilize again its better innovations. . . . Just as, in nature, new growth springs up from old roots, so the present is only a variation of the past.' [1]

The majority of the church furnishings described and illustrated here are nothing else but a side-line of the archaistic 'Gothic Revival'—a movement which, starting as a hobby of the nobility and landed gentry who erected sham 'ruins' in their parks and built residences in styles supposed to reproduce the effect of medieval monasteries, soon spread to church design and restoration. Here it secured a potent ally in the Oxford Movement on its archaistic side, and finally found riotous expression in factories, gas-works, hospitals, hotels, railway stations, schools, villas and viaducts.

As was inevitable, the time came when archaistic church furnishings—like archaistic architecture and much else—ceased to be fashionable. Then began the so-called 'Art Nouveau' movement of the eighteen-nineties. This was part of a sort of back-to-nature movement, trying to lead what was called 'the simple life.' It had been preceded by and, to a certain degree overlapped, the Arts and Crafts movement. Yet so strong was the hold of Gothic in ecclesiastical circles that churches went on being built and furnished in the medieval manner even until after the first world war, as I have related in these pages. Few people saw anything inconsistent or illogical in this divorce between secular and religious life.

By 1910 Gothic Revival was quite *demodé* with the *avant garde*. So there followed a riotous and Rococo–Baroque revival that found its leading exponents among the more papalist-minded Anglo-Catholic clergy in Britain. It was great fun while it lasted, but the so-called 'Liturgical Movement,' which started in Belgium during the first decade of the present century, eventually spreading to Austria, Germany, France and Holland, and thence to the United States of America, gained momentum.

It will be noticed that I entitled the last chapter of this book 'Chaotic Eclecticism—The End of an Era,' and so were the ten years that preceded World War Two. Fashions in church furnishings became more and more chaotic. When I was collecting my material during the nineteen-fifties there was very little evidence that

[1] *The Face of the World* (1957), p. 226.

7

church architects and craftsmen in Britain realized that archaism was dead. Most of them were still amusing themselves with variations of the fashions of former centuries, or trying desperately to be clever and original. Within a month or two of the publication of my book, Peter Hammond's *Liturgy and Architecture* appeared. I feel I must draw special attention to this volume because its influence during the past five years has been far-reaching. Mr. Hammond explained in his Preface:

> 'The unsatisfactory character of so much recent writing on church architecture, particularly in this country, is due to the authors' reluctance to face fundamental issues. The really basic problems are rarely so much as hinted at. . . . I hope that this book may go some way towards meeting the needs of the many thoughtful people who share my concern at the present state of church architecture on this side of the Channel, and who can find no satisfaction in the modish and gimmick-ridden pavilions of religious art which are constantly being held up to us as the precursors of a genuine renewal of sacred building: a church architecture for our time. I believe that they are nothing of the kind: that it is worse than useless to worry about introducing more modern art into churches so long as we continue to ignore the fundamental, if unfashionable, questions of theology, liturgy and sociology which are raised by the very act of setting apart a special building for the service of God; and that it is supremely irrational to labour *ad nauseam* the point that architects must make full use of modern building materials and techniques while refusing to face the fact that the one thing that gives a certain coherence to all the serious architecture of the last ten years is its emphasis on the *programme.*' [2]

As far back as 1946 the German Liturgical Commission had published what was entitled *Directives for the Shaping of the House of God, according to the Spirit of the Roman Liturgy*.[3] These directives embodied the results of unofficial research for more than a quarter of a century, and as Peter Hammond points out, 'the results can be seen to-day in every city of western Germany. A comparison between these German directives and the brief which was supplied to the architects who took part in the Coventry cathedral competition underlines the reasons for the Church of England's failure to seize an opportunity which was exploited to the full in the bombed cities of the Rhineland.' [4]

What may have finally sounded the death knell of the particular 'modish and gimmick-ridden pavilions of religious art' that form the subject-matter of this book is the *Constitution on the Sacred Liturgy,* promulgated on December 4th, 1963, at the closing of the second session of Vatican Council II. At long last the Roman Church has formally approved of almost all the details of church planning, furnishing and decoration advocated by the leaders of the Liturgical Movement, which I mentioned briefly in my epilogue. They have ceased to be revolutionary, and have

[2] op. cit., p. xiii.
[3] English translation in *Documents for Sacred Architecture* (Collegeville, Minn., 1957).
[4] *Liturgy and Architecture* (1960), p. 33.

been made obligatory. Yet in a sense they are 'archaistic,' because the ideal set before us is a return to fourth or fifth century modes of public worship. Once again, distance lends enchantment, and (in the words of Cecil Beaton) 'new growth springs up from old roots, so the present is only a variation of the past.'

The *Constitution* lays down that 'the church edifice should be so arranged that the very position of all its elements and places should be a clear and faithful echo of the sacred liturgy, which is the assemblage of God's people hierarchically constituted and duly organized from His 'servants' and His 'holy people.' One wonders what Augustus Welby Pugin and the leaders of the Ecclesiological Movement in the eighteen-forties would have felt about the directive that the main altar should be separated from the wall so that the ministers can easily walk round it; fittingly be erected midway between the seats of the clergy and those of the laity, 'that is to say in the middle of the church, although this is to be taken in a broad and not mathematical sense.' It is recommended that behind the main altar there should be 'a simple chair for the pastor or officiating priest in the name of the bishop, whose collaborator he is. However any suggestion of a throne should be avoided in those cases where the episcopal throne is not permitted.' A *ciborium* or *baldachino* should be provided as a covering for this altar 'so far as the nature of the building will allow.' The urge to get back to the fashions of the Christian Roman Empire was so strong during the second session of Vatican Council II that the compilers of this Constitution laid down that 'the crucifix and candlesticks, required according to the liturgical quality of the Mass, should be placed either upon the altar, or even adjacent (around) the altar according to the earliest ecclesiastical usage.'[5] Such is the latest expression of 'archaism' and the yearning to revive ancient modes of church furnishings.

Side altars are definitely *demodé*. We are told that 'they are better placed in special chapels rather than in the main body of the church.' The administration of the Lord's Supper facing the people is to be encouraged wherever possible, even though 'there may be a small tabernacle in the middle of the altar (one, however, which is of good material and dignified) where the Blessed Sacrament is reserved.' On the other hand, it is recommended that in larger churches the Eucharist should be reserved in a special chapel, 'closed to mere spectators but open to worshippers.' Lecterns or reading stands for the recitation or singing of the Epistle and Gospel are now obligatory in churches of the Roman Rite. It is laid down that they must express 'the majesty and dignity of the sacred Scriptures' proclaimed at them. A special place of honour must be found for the baptistery in both cathedrals and parish churches—if possible 'arranged for the instruction of the faithful like a small room.' The confessionals must be 'in a dignified spot, open and plain to see.' Last but not least there is the ruling that 'without serious reasons images of the saints should not be multiplied within the same church building,' and that 'the multiplication of such images behind the main altar is altogether disapproved of.'

The same wind of austerity is blowing in other Christian denominations, and is not confined to the Church of Rome. What was the *dernier cri* of ecclesiastical

---

[5] See drawing reproduced on p. 367.

fashions in the eighteen-sixties is completely *vieux jeu* in the nineteen-sixties. It is impossible to say at the moment what will be the next swing of the pendulum.

Having reached the age of seventy-five I can confirm from the close observation and love of a lifetime Mr. Beaton's remark: 'Thus we are perpetually coming full circle in our notions of the beautiful, the amusing, the useful. And some of us may at times admit that *"Plus ça change, plus c'est la même chose"."* [6] Fashions in church furnishings and decorations seem to follow a policy not unlike rotation of crops in agriculture. After periods of rigorous rationing and austerity they burst forth into opulence. The pendulum swings backwards and forwards all the time.

PETER F. ANSON

Lady Day, 1965

Ferryden
Montrose
Angus

[6] *The Face of the World*, p. 226.

'This is a fearsome place: it is the house of God, the gate of heaven: it shall be named the palace of God.'   *Genesis* 28: 17

'Lord of hosts, how I love thy dwelling place! For the courts of the Lord's house, my soul faints with longing.' *Psalm* 82: 2–3
(Douai version)

'I saw in my vision that holy city which is the new Jerusalem, being sent down by God from heaven, all clothed in readiness, like a bride who has adorned herself to meet her husband. . . . Here is God's tabernacle pitched among men; he will dwell with them, and they will be his own people, and he will be among them, their God. . . . And he who sat on the throne said, Behold, I make all things new.'   *Apocalypse* 21: 2–5

'For the fashion of this world passeth away.'
First Epistle of S. Paul to the Corinthians 7: 31

ACKNOWLEDGMENTS

M Y thanks are due to the following persons who have supplied information, given advice, or made criticisms of chapters in this book: Right Revd. David Colin Dunlop, Dean of Lincoln; Right Revd. Dom David Parry, O.S.B., Abbot of Ramsgate; Very Revd. Provost George J. C. Douglas; Revd. Canon R. R. Martin; Revd. Canon J. L. Cartwright; Revd. Canon A. Hopkins; Revd. Basil F. L. Clarke; Revd. C. M. L. Bough; Revd. Frank Harwood; Revd. A. G. Cooke; Revd. Frank White; Rev. Dr. Geoffrey Soden; Revd. Henry S. Hutchinson; Revd. Dr. A. L. Drummond; Revd. Eric G. Ogden; Revd. J. S. B. Wallis; Revd. D. N. Chamberlin; Revd. C. St. M. B. MacFarlane; Revd. H. C. Butler; Revd. R. Corbet-Milward; Revd. E. A. Grey; Revd. Harold E. George; Revd. V. G. Davies; Revd. W. R. Corbould; Revd. Geoffrey Heald; Revd. Mark Taylor, Cong. Orat.; Revd. R. P. Griffiths; the Earl of Wicklow; Dr. Nikolaus Pevsner; Mr. H. S. Goodhart-Rendel, P.P.R.I.B.A.; Mr. Ian G. Lindsay, O.B.E., A.R.S.A.; Mr. George Hay, A.R.I.B.A.; Mr. John Betjeman; Mr. Colin E. Beswick; Mr. A. J. Bryant (A. R. Mowbray & Co.); Mr. A. W. Campbell; Mr. W. I. Croome; Mr. Samuel Gurney; Mr. G. V. Hoare (Watts and Co.); Mr. Francis Stephens (The Faith Craft-Works); Mr. John H. Hutchinson; Mr. Louis Billaux (Louis Grossé Ltd.); Mr. Patrick A. Feeny (John Hardman Studios); Mr. Edward J. H. Burnett; Mr. Edmund D. Esdaile; Mr. Gerald W. Spink; Mr. N. Cecil Wright; Mr. L. B. Broon; Mr. C. Clarkson; Mr. Peter Eden; Mr. Peter Floud (Victoria and Albert Museum); Mr. J. W. Shaw; Mr. Alan Rome; Mr. Patrick Nuttgens; Mr. Philip Lindsey Clark, D.S.O.; Miss Judith Scott, F.S.A. and Miss Joan Petersen (Central Council for the Care of Churches); Miss M. Alexander (The Warham Guild); Miss Edith Cooper; Miss Dorothy Sedding; Miss Ursula Radford; the Incorporated Church Building Society; R. Bridgeman and Sons Ltd.; Campbell Smith Ltd.; L. Oppenheimer Ltd.; Gunning and Co.; The London Library; the Librarians of Buckfast Abbey, Fort Augustus Abbey, Prinknash Abbey, Quarr Abbey, Ramsgate Abbey, Pluscarden Priory, the House of the Resurrection, Mirfield, and the Royal Institute of British Architects; and others whose names may have been omitted.

My thanks are likewise due to the authors and publishers of several books or articles quoted in various places; and to all those who have lent me material, especially Mr. John Betjeman, whose interest, advice and guidance have been a constant encouragement. Lastly there is Mr. Robin Denniston of the Faith Press who spent so much time on the revision of the manuscript, and whose suggestions were so helpful.

CONTENTS

ILLUSTRATIONS

IN TEXT

PLATES

EARLY VICTORIAN BACKGROUND

WHEN Queen Victoria ascended the throne in 1837, two hundred and seventy-eight years since *Ecclesia Anglicana* finally decided to use a vernacular liturgy in its public services, and ceased to be an integral part of the Western Patriarchate, there still remained countless examples of pre-Reformation church furnishings in England and Wales; probably more than in any other country in Europe.[1]

Many of the medieval cathedrals and parish churches had preserved their screens and galleries, fonts and font-covers, choir-stalls, pulpits, lecterns, bench-ends, etc. Although almost every stone altar had been destroyed by the end of the sixteenth century, and a 'Lord's Board,' in the form of an honest table, decently covered, set up in some convenient part of the chancel of every cathedral and parish church; nevertheless there remained a fair number of carved stone reredoses, their statues having been removed or mutilated for fear of encouraging idolatry.

Here and there could be found examples of post-Reformation rails before or around the communion tables, which were ordered by the early seventeenth century Caroline bishops. Some chancels retained their medieval stone piscina, credence and sedilia, although no longer used. In parts of Scotland there were a number of early sixteenth century desecrated stone aumbries, known as 'Sacrament Houses'; in England a few ancient Easter Sepulchres and holy water stoups.

There was a greater wealth of post-Reformation furnishings and ornaments, especially in the churches designed by Sir Christopher Wren after the Great Fire of London in 1666, and in other Anglican places of worship planned by eighteenth century architects.[2] Most of them were of very good quality and admirably suited to the type of Reformed worship for which they were intended. Both from the æsthetic and liturgical points of view, there was not much wrong with the fonts, reading-desks, pulpits, pews, communion-tables, reredoses, organs, etc., which were erected roughly between 1670 and 1800. On the other hand, the conduct of public worship often left much to be desired. When Victoria came to the throne in 1837 a large number of cathedrals and parish churches badly needed restoration and refurnishing.

[1] All these medieval furnishings are dealt with by Francis Bond in *Screens and Galleries in English Churches* (Oxford, 1908); *The Chancel of English Churches* (Oxford, 1916) and *Fonts and Font Covers* (Oxford, 1908). Reference should be made also to J. Charles Cox, *Pulpits, Lecterns and Organs* and *Bench Ends in English Churches*. Both these books appeared in the series edited by Francis Bond on Church Art in England, published by the Oxford University Press; likewise his two volumes on *Wood Carving in English Churches*. Other sources of reference are Frederick Bligh Bond and Dom Bede Camm, o.s.b. *Rood Screens and Rood Lofts* (2 vols., 1909); and Aylmer Vallance, *English Chancel Screens* (1936).

[2] Cf. G. W. O. Addleshaw and Frederick Etchells, *The Architectural Setting of Anglican Worship* (1948).

Early Victorian church furnishings and decorations need to be studied in relation to the social conditions which (like those of every period) they indirectly reflect. They were influenced by an increase in the population of towns, romantic literature, a revived interest in medieval archeology, philanthropy, religion (Catholic, Tractarian and Evangelical), likewise by changes in the structure of society and in the distribution of wealth.

We must try to think of Early Victorian ecclesiastical fashions going with the paintings of William Etty, J. M. W. Turner, J. S. Cotman, Sir Edwin Landseer, and some of the later portraits by Sir Thomas Lawrence or the landscapes by John Constable. The music of Mendelssohn, William Sterndale Bennett and Henry Bishop belongs to the same period. So does the sculpture of Sir Richard Westmacott and Sir Francis Chantry. Among living authors, Dickens, Tennyson and Thackeray were beginning to be talked about. William Wordsworth was still writing poetry.

A new middle-class of society was being evolved during the eighteen-forties. Some business men were making fortunes. 'Like the buccaneers of Queen Elizabeth's reign they wanted comfort, warmth, ornament and richness in their homes. They wanted them for their own sakes, for the impression they would make on other people, as symbols of success, and for themselves, to help them to believe that it was all worth while. As the century went on the desire for luxury, ostentation and comfort increased.' [3]

In towns most of the new houses built for the richer middle-classes were in dull terraces, so the display of wealth had to be confined to the interior furnishings and decoration, which was generally eclectic in inspiration. The windows were draped with curtains of muslin or lace, reinforced in addition with serge, plush or velvet. There were crystal chandeliers, and a great use of brass in ornaments. Rugs were replaced with carpets of loud and garish patterns. English firms were turning out pretty wallpapers. The furniture was of many styles and periods, a good deal of it reproductions of old work.

In new churches the furnishings tended to be austere compared with those of houses, and it was seldom that so much money was spent on them. Since weekday services were very uncommon except in cathedrals and in the still comparatively few Roman Catholic chapels, the realistic minded Early Victorian church builder or benefactor cannot be blamed for being economical, unless it so happened that he had begun to be influenced by Tractarian teaching, and started to look back wistfully to the Middle Ages.

Jane Austen's novel *Emma,* published in 1815, supplies us with a good description of the furnishings in a typical parish church of a country town in England, as they existed in many places for long after. 'Highbury' church—and many others at the same date—had a galleried interior, and white-washed walls adorned by memorial tablets and texts. The plain communion table, where the Sacrament was administered about four times in the year, was hidden by the three-decker pulpit. The upper classes had their comfortable box-like pews. Those belonging to the

[3] Bruce Allsopp, *Decoration and Furniture* (1952), Vol. I, The English Tradition, p. 137.

nobility were quite likely to be furnished with small tables and stoves. The middle classes probably had seats in the front rows of the galleries, while the lower orders were relegated to benches or forms in the side aisles or in the central passage. In the west gallery would be the singers, supported by a few instruments. In respectable Anglican churches hymns were still frowned on as tainted with Methodism. So the music consisted of anthems and metrical psalms. Before the sermon the preacher would retire to the vestry to change his voluminous linen surplice for a black silk gown. Black or grey silk gloves were regarded as correct vesture while preaching.

Church interiors and furnishings are mentioned in other novels by Jane Austen, especially *Mansfield Park,* which is a valuable ecclesiastical source-book for the early nineteenth century. In 1816 the Revd. J. W. Cunningham of Harrow published the autobiography of a then popular article of church furniture, and entitled it *The Velvet Cushion,* showing how it had been used as the basis for sermons of the most diverse doctrines. Mr. Cunningham wrote from the evangelical standpoint. The atmosphere, if not the details of liturgical furnishings, of many an Anglican place of worship in the eighteen-thirties is also to be found in some of George Eliot's novels, in particular *Scenes of Clerical Life, Adam Bede,* and *The Sad Fortunes of Amos Barton.*

For a perfect description of a typical 'proprietary chapel' such as flourished in the West End of London, and in most fashionable resorts like Brighton, Bath and Cheltenham, there is Thackeray's *The Newcomes* (1835). As Dr. A. L. Drummond remarks in his *Churches in English Fiction,* 'Lady Whittlesea's Chapel had many a counterpart in real life. . . . They were extra parochial, and were often run on a commercial basis, supported by pew-rents and sometimes built over wine vaults. . . . An ingratiating preacher ("for women like a consumptive parson"), a well-nourished verger and genteel pew-opener did their best to attract the quality.' [4]

From the point of view of contemporary fashions, the best ecclesiastical furnishings and decorations during the first decade of the reign of Queen Victoria were those of the typical English Nonconformist chapel or meeting-house. They were both functional and dignified, honest and unpretentious. It is curious how both the planning and furnishing of most Baptist, Congregational and Methodist meeting-houses of that period, solve the problems which face Roman Catholic and Anglican architects at the present time, when trying to achieve a closer participation of the laity in public worship.

The majority of these small buildings of a Cistercian-like austerity had white-washed walls and ceilings, which contrasted with the wood panelling of the gallery fronts and pews. Some of the pulpits were richly carved, and provided with sounding-boards. The communion tables were invariably well designed, and stood in front of the pulpit, so that every worshipper had an unbroken view when the Lord's Supper was administered. Some of these chapels were adorned with brass

[4] op. cit. (1950), p. 30.

candelabra, often of Dutch workmanship. Organs were of later introduction, and the singing was unaccompanied by any musical instrument.

In the New England states of North America, Calvinism had evolved its own style of ecclesiastical *décor* by the close of the eighteenth century, based on classic architecture. Some of the meeting-houses had achieved a very high standard, as had many of the Episcopal churches farther south, the planning and furnishing of which owed much to the typical Anglican place of worship in the early eighteenth century.

Some Presbyterian kirks in Scotland were more attractive from the æsthetic point of view than an average Anglican church in England. Sometimes the former were far from being drab and repellent places. 'If they lacked the sumptuous furnishings and representational art of earlier times, no longer admissible, medieval colourfulness was in some measure continued in the form of whitewashed walls as a background for painted pews and lofts displaying carved details and armorial and trade devices brightly blazoned in appropriate tinctures. Again, in the carved and decorated pulpits, patrician pews and magistrates' lofts, there were rich cushions, velvets and other hangings. . . . In fact the drabness which is usually represented as inseparable from Reformed tradition originated very largely among Victorian and later ecclesiastical specialists.' [5]

[5] George Hay, *The Architecture of Scottish Post-Reformation Churches, 1560–1843* (Oxford, 1957), p. 27. For further details of non-Anglican church furnishings see Martin S. Briggs, *Puritan Architecture* (1946), pp. 11–36; and A. L. Drummond, *The Church Architecture of Protestantism* (Edinburgh, 1934), pp. 19–62.

CHAPTER I

AUGUSTUS WELBY PUGIN
A VOICE CRYING IN THE WILDERNESS'

I

B Y the end of the third decade of the nineteenth century there was more than enough evidence that persons of good taste were growing a little tired of Classical art, which had retained its hold for more than three hundred years. 'Gothick' was becoming fashionable among the *avant garde,* and regarded as revolutionary. Several churches had been designed and furnished in what was then supposed to be correct 'Gothick,' but it was a far cry from anything that had ever existed before the Reformation. England was waiting for the voice of one crying in the wilderness, so that all mankind could see the saving power of true Christian architecture, i.e. medieval Gothic. This new John the Baptist, Augustus Welby Pugin, was born in 1812 and died in 1852. He was the son of a French architect who had fled to England at the time of the Revolution. Augustus Pugin senior married an English woman of rigid Calvinist opinions, who later became a disciple of Edward Irving. At the age of twenty-six their son took the then most unusual step of becoming a Catholic. In after years he explained: 'I learned the truths of the Catholic religion in the crypts of the old cathedrals of Europe. I sought for those truths in the modern churches of England, and found that since her separation from the centre of Catholic unity she had little unity and life; so, without being acquainted with a single priest, through God's mercy, I resolved to enter His Church.' [1]

Young Pugin's reconciliation with the Church of his French ancestors took place only five years after Catholic Emancipation in England. He found nothing attractive about the ritual and ceremonial in the chapels of the persecuted minority that had just emerged from the shadow of the Penal Laws. 'He expected austerity, but found slovenliness. Priests "would administer Baptism out of an old physick phial; reserve the Blessed Sacrament in dirty cupboards; burn gas on the altar; have everything as mean, as pitiful, as shabby as you please." What enraged him more than anything else, however, was tawdry pretentiousness. "Going into Catholic chapels (there were no 'churches' then) what did I see? The very taber-

[1] *The Tablet,* September 25th, 1852.

21

SS. MARY AND JOSEPH, HEDON, YORKS (1803)
A typical Catholic 'chapel' before the Gothic Revival with furnishings dismissed by Pugin as 'purely pagan'

nacle, a Pagan Temple; the altar, a deal Sarcophagus; over which a colossal eye with rays looked down from a flat ceiling, artificial flowers under glass shades between the altar candlesticks, costly marbles produced in cheap paper, brackets painted with sham shadows supporting nothing." Even where Gothic was used, it was a miserable travesty of the ancient cathedrals and parish churches of England.' [2]

Pugin was convinced that only by drastic changes in the externals of worship could Catholicism in England be revived. 'The clock must be put back; the usages of pre-Reformation England must be restored, and those of modern Tridentine Romanism rejected.' [3]

[2] A. L. Drumond, Augustus Welby Pugin, Art and Vocation, article in *The Church Quarterly Review,* July 1952, p. 338.
[3] ibid., p. 339.

He immediately became very unpopular among his newly-found brethren. But it was not long before he gained the support of several wealthy patrons, including Lord Shrewsbury, the premier Catholic Earl of England. Another rich friend was Ambrose Philipps de Lisle, the convert squire of Grace-Dieu and Garendon in Leicestershire.

In 1835, after the death of his first wife, Pugin started to build himself a very medieval-looking house near Salisbury, which he called S. Marie's Grange. It included a small private oratory. On Sundays, however, he had no choice but to worship in the humble little chapel at Salisbury, erected by a French *emigré* priest about fifty years before.

The few Roman Catholic chapels in London would have had little to attract Pugin. They were, as Archbishop David Mathew remarks, 'rectangular buildings with plain windows and a gallery supported by iron pillars; beadles walked the centre aisle in their gold lace and three-cornered hats; the members of the Italian Opera House sang in the Sardinian Chapel on the great festivals.' [4] Besides the Sardinian Chapel in Lincoln's Inn Fields (1762), there was the choice of the Bavarian Embassy Chapel in Warwick Street (1788), a Portuguese Chapel in Mayfair, and the Spanish, Belgian and French Embassy Chapels. Neither the cosy little Baroque chapel in Somers Town (1808), nor the far more grandiose Italianate furnishings of the Moorfields chapel (1820) would have made any appeal to this young protagonist of Gothic. In the other chapels around London in the eighteen-thirties, the fittings were what Pugin dismissed as pure paganism.

As the result of several tours made on the continent of Europe during his youth, Pugin had acquired an encyclopædic knowledge of church furnishings by the time he was reconciled with the Roman Church. In 1835 he brought out a book entitled *Gothic Furniture in the style of the 15th Century*, with twenty-five plates etched by himself. The following year saw the publication of his *Designs for Iron and Brass work in the style of the XV and XVI centuries*, containing twenty-seven etched plates. A few months later appeared his *Designs for gold and silver-smiths*. The second part was devoted to church plate. Several other books helped to encourage the new fashion for medieval art forms; including *Contrasts; or a parallel between the noble edifices of the 14th and 15th centuries, and similar buildings of the present day, showing the present decay of taste*, which was published in the year of Queen Victoria's accession to the throne. Pugin did not waste time in replying to the critics who had attacked this book. He did his best to encourage popular taste by bringing out Sheet Almanacks, embellished with devotional engravings, also a *Ladies' and Gentlemen's Annual Catholic Pocket-Book and Diary*, with engravings by himself and other artists. In 1839 he published *Illustrations to the Missal*. But it was his articles in the *Dublin Review* between 1840 and 1842 that did most to win a larger circle of friends and enemies.

All these illustrated articles were reprinted in book form in 1843, under the title of *The Present State of Ecclesiastical Architecture in England*.

[4] *Catholicism in England* (1936), p. 176.

The second article, 'Elevation of the Cathedral Church of S. Chad, Birmingham,' written in 1840, contains the very clear ideas formed by Pugin on the furnishing and decoration of churches by the time he had reached the age of twenty-eight. Here is a summary of them.

Every Catholic church should have a stone font, with a wooden cover, fastened with a lock, and near it an aumbry in a wall for the holy oils. The chancel ought to be separated from the nave by an open screen, supporting a rood loft, the latter ascended by a staircase in the wall. Wooden seats, with low backs, placed wide enough to admit kneeling, may be fixed in the nave and aisles. The pulpit may be of stone or wood, but sufficiently elevated, and placed in any convenient position in the nave. Every chancel should be raised at least one step above the nave, and the altar on three steps above the level of the chancel. The altar must consist of a solid slab of stone, encised with five crosses, with a cavity for relics; raised on solid masonry or on stone pillars. On the epistle side of the altar there ought to be a sacrarium, i.e. a basin with a wall pipe, and a stone shelf for the cruets. On the same side, and farther west, there should be three niches, partly in the thickness of the walls, but partly projecting, with canopies, as convenient seats for the priest, deacon and sub-deacon at High Mass.

Opposite, on the gospel side of the chancel, there should be an open tomb for use as a sepulchre during Holy Week. If the church were too small to permit the erection of a sacristy, then an 'almery' should be provided on the gospel side of the altar, within the chancel. All side altars ought to be protected by open screen work.

Such were the basic functional furnishings which Pugin regarded as essential. They may seem antiquated to-day, but in 1840 they were revolutionary, above all the insistence on a screened-in chancel. Pugin regarded the chancel as the place of sacrifice, the most sacred part of a church. He wrote: 'Well may we exclaim, when passing beneath the image of our Redeemer, and through the separating screen of mystic import, into this holy place, "*O quam terribile est locus iste.*" The ancient chancels were truly solemn and impressive, and those who have souls to appreciate the intentions of the old Catholic builders must have been edified with their wisdom and propriety, in keeping the seat of the holy mysteries at a reverential distance from the people, and in setting forth the dignity and privilege of the priestly office, by separating the ministers who are offering up the holy sacrifice from the worshippers.' [5]

He went on to say: 'Of all lamentable innovations, the wretched recesses substituted for chancels in modern churches are the most horrible: the altars are not only crowded up by seats, but *actually overlooked,* and the sanctity of the sacrifice itself partially disregarded. If these barriers round the holy place were considered necessary in the days of faith, how doubly are they wanted at the present time. Churches are now built on exactly the same principle as theatres, to hold the greatest number of persons in the smallest possible space; and the only difference

[5] *The Present State of Ecclesiastical Architecture in England* (1843), p. 34.

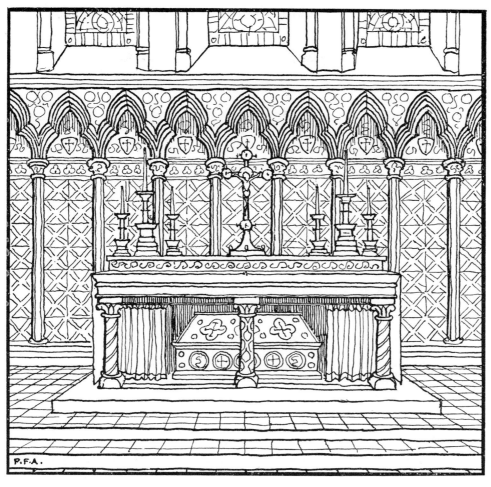

S. WILFRID'S, HULME, MANCHESTER (A. W. Pugin, 1839–42)

in the arrangement is the substitution of an altar-piece for the proscenium and drop-scene. What is the consequence? Catholic feeling is soon lost among the people: there is not even a corner for holy meditation or retired reflection; they are filled and emptied like dissenting meeting houses. The worshipper is either in a mob, or in the odious and Protestant distinction of a private pew. The humblest old Catholic church, mutilated as it may have been, is ten times more impressive than these staring assembly-rooms, which some persons, in these days, consider the most appropriate erections for Catholic worship.' [6]

The present generation would regard all this vituperation as mock medievalism, but in the early forties of the last century it sounded far more like dangerous modernism. The new fashions shocked all but the bright young things, who lapped

[6] ibid., pp. 34–5.

up Mr. Pugin's principle. Soon nobody could be regarded as a sincere Christian unless they believed that the only orthodox way to worship God was against a background of 'Pointed' architecture. To admit that it might be possible to enter heaven by way of a Renaissance route was sheer heresy.

Some of these Gothic settings were described by Pugin in his second *Dublin Review* article. He explained that a font ought to have a decent cover, which should rise to a great height, with canopies and pinnacles. It could either be suspended from the roof by a counterweight, or a portion of the tabernacle work made to open at the side. He had inserted fonts of this type at S. Mary's, Derby; S. Chad's, Birmingham; S. Giles', Cheadle, and at Stafford. He felt that it was most important to have a 'Doom' or Last Judgment painted on the wall above the chancel arch. Side altars should never be exposed to the gaze of worshippers, but always hidden by open screens, called parcloses. He described some of the chancel screens, roods and rood lofts designed by himself; mentioning that the first had been set up in the chapel at Grace Dieu Manor. 'In this chapel,' he wrote, 'most solemn service is performed on Sundays and festivals, the Gradual chaunted from the "Lettern," and the whole Office sung by men and choristers in the devotional and sublime plain chant, the only music sanctioned by the Church.' In parish churches chancel screens could be of wood, with open tracery, ranging from eight to fifteen feet in height. The entrance should be fitted with doors, capable of being kept locked.

The rood loft had its functional purposes, so he pointed out. The Gospel at High Mass ought to be sung there, also the Passion at Tenebrae during Holy Week. A small organ could be placed in the loft. There should always be lighted candles on the great festivals. He laid down that besides a central crucifix, there should be carved figures of our Lady and S. John. He recommended that the cross should be floriated, terminating at the extremities with quatrefoils, with emblems of the four Evangelists on one side, and on the reverse those of the four Doctors of the Church.

Pugin's powers of design and his vivid imagination were revealed in the engravings of some of his rood lofts, for instance S. Mary's, Southport, which showed a very small church, complete with the correct type of screen, diapered and painted from ancient examples. At S. Alban's, Macclesfield, he had erected a much larger rood-loft with a wide gallery, twelve feet from the nave floor, and approached by a staircase leading from the south chapel. In the engraving of S. George's, Southwark, the very massive open stone screen had two staircases terminating in pinnacled turrets.

Never had altars been seen like those illustrating this fascinating book: they were nothing if not daring. Many an old-fashioned priest must have held up his hands in horror as he studied the engravings or read the descriptions.

Did Mr. Pugin really expect him to pull down his sarcophagus shaped altar, backed by a stately reredos in the Classic style, several gradines and many tall candlesticks, and substitute an altar like that at S. Wilfrid's, Hulme, Manchester? For here was a strange looking stone table, supported on three stone pillars,

S. MARY'S, UTTOXETER (A. W. Pugin, 1839–40)
'The first Catholic structure erected in this country, in strict
accordance with the rules of ancient ecclesiastical architecture since
the days of the pretended Reformation' (A. W. Pugin in
Orthodox Journal, 20 July 1839)

with a reliquary beneath it. Why was it considered correct to hide the reliquary
with velvet curtains? This stone table stood well away from the east wall, and there
was no proper reredos—merely a series of lancet stone arches, the panels of which
were richly diapered, and ornamented with Christian emblems. And what was
wrong with ordinary chairs for the sacred ministers to sit on at High Mass?
Mr. Pugin's sedilia looked very uncomfortable. A decent table would be far more
convenient than a silly stone sacrarium.

If one must be in the fashion and adopt Gothic furnishings, then the altar at
S. Mary's, Uttoxeter, with its reredos of the 'ancient triptic form' was less objectionable than some of the others depicted. Mr. Pugin said that the doors would
have to be closed during the latter part of Lent, which would be very awkward,

just as were the two silk damask curtains, hung on cords at the sides of the altar. And what authority had he for saying that the two large standard candlesticks to hold tapers must be lit from the Sanctus to the Communion? That rood supported on an arched beam, with angels bearing tapers, could only be described as highly eccentric. What reason could this dictatorial architect give for his statement that one of the three hanging lamps must always be kept burning, and the other two lit only during Mass?

As to S. Giles', Cheadle, it helped to confirm the widespread opinion that Lord Shrewsbury was a mad millionaire, who was squandering his money on fantastically decorated churches, instead of assisting many more deserving charitable objects. Who would take the trouble to look up at that chancel ceiling richly painted with gilt stars, or the string course supporting the ribs charged with shields and armorial escutcheons? Take that ridiculous rood screen—what useful purpose did it serve? It merely prevented the congregation from getting a good view of the high altar, and blocked up the building. Then there was that fussy Gothic reredos composed of nine niches, filled with images of the saints, and surmounted with elaborate tabernacle work—*why* must Mr. Pugin add curtains hung on rods at the sides? *Why* must he place his pair of candlesticks and crucifix on the mensa of the altar? *Why* could he not be satisfied with the usual 'Altar of Repose' to which people were accustomed in Holy Week, instead of wasting Lord Shrewsbury's money on that richly decorated Easter Sepulchre? As to trying to combine a credence table with seats for the ministers at High Mass under four Gothic arches. Really! It was high time that the Vicars Apostolic put a stop to all this nonsense.

It was quite clear that Mr. Pugin held opinions that were heterodox if not actually heretical. Clerical critics noticed none of the plans of his churches showed confessional boxes. He appeared to disapprove of them, because they were not medieval. He informed his readers that confessions used to be heard in church by priests. They sat on chairs whilst the penitents knelt beside them. 'Even on the continent,' he explained, 'confessionals cannot be found older than the last century, and this is alone sufficient to prove the extreme absurdity of the stories circulated by vergers and others, respecting confessionals in the ancient churches.'

Moreover he made some very disrespectful statements about flowers being incorrect decorations for altars, though he admitted that 'the custom of hanging garlands and branches, on the great feasts, to decorate the church, is of the highest antiquity; even the whole pavement was not unfrequently sprinkled with flowers and aromatic herbs.' [7] As a layman and a mere convert, what right had he to say that 'every reflecting mind must be both struck and pained at the incongruous decorations of most modern altars; the chief aim of those who arrange them appears to be merely a great show. All mystical reason, all ancient discipline, all dignity and solemnity are utterly lost sight of; everything is overdone. Candlesticks are piled on candlesticks as if arranged for sale; whole rows of flower pots mingled with reliquaries, images and not unfrequently profane ornaments; festoons of upholsterers' drapery; even distorting and distracting looking-glasses are introduced

[7] ibid., p. 41.

28

in this medley display; the effect of which upon persons who are conversant with ancient discipline and practice is not easy to describe.'

'Of all decoration, that of ecclesiastical buildings is the most difficult; to unite *richness* with *severity,* to produce *splendour* without *gaudiness,* and to erect a temple somewhat worthy of the holy sacrifice, is a wonderful effort for the human mind: but when decoration is attempted in honour of the victim there offered— the Blessed Sacrament itself—art drops unequal, and genius fails. Who is there that can set forth the glory of God, or add lustre to His majesty? The attempt is simply profane. Hence the ancient churchmen veiled the sacred host in mystery, and like Moses before the burning bush, bowed themselves to the ground. If the faithful are required to adore in silence, during the elevation of the host, as being too solemn a moment for even the psalmody of praise, *"Sileat omnis caro a facie Domini quia consurrexit de habitaculo Sancto suo,"* what forms can be embodied to honour so great a mystery?'

So, like a new John the Baptist, Augustus Welby Pugin was the voice of one crying in the wilderness in the first decade of the reign of Queen Victoria. This tough little architect, with dark hair and flashing eyes, dressed like a common seaman, aroused the enmity of most conservative Catholics, yet by 1842 he was making more and more disciples, even among those who were outside his Church.

II

For the new chapel of S. Marie's College, Oscott, near Birmingham, which had been opened on May 29th, 1838, had set the fashion already for many other Catholic places of worship in England. Bishop Ullathorne recorded his impressions of the ceremony 'at which all the bishops were present, as well as a hundred priests. On that occasion the more ample form of vestments was first introduced in place of the old form derived from France. Pugin, with his dark eyes flashing and tears on his cheeks, superintended the procession of the clergy, and declared that it was the greatest day for the Church in England since the Reformation.' [8]

How this chapel struck people of taste more than a hundred years ago is difficult for us to appreciate. One can see what Pugin himself felt about it from one of his drawings, reproduced in *The Oscotian* (1888), and thus described by Mr. Trappes-Lomax. 'In the foreground is the heavily ornamented rail dividing the choir from the remainder of the building. The floor of the choir is slightly raised, and over it is spread a panelled ceiling supported on massive beams. Beyond it the floor-level rises again to the apsidal sanctuary, where High Mass is in progress at a tall and minutely decorated altar. Beyond and on either side of the altar, tall perpendicular-traceried windows fill the spaces between the piers which support the roof. The whole thing is grey and dim. Light strikes obliquely on the backs of the priests and servers at the altar. The clergy in the choir-stalls on the epistle side are almost invisible in shadow; those on the gospel side are pallid against the light. But in reality the whole scene was gorgeous with colour. Poly-

[8] Dom Cuthbert Butler, *The Life and Times of Bishop Ullathorne* (1926), vol. II, p. 60; quoting Bishop Ullathorne's *Autobiography* (1891), p. 142.

chrome decoration had been revived and had been applied by a master. There was 'something of eastern splendour, mingled with simplicity, at once rich and quiet, in the exuberant mixture of gold and colour which this great artist reintroduced into England after a century and a half of whitewash and false marbling.' [9]

Then there were the richly coloured stained glass windows which added to the gorgeousness of this alarmingly 'modern' place of worship; the like of which nobody had ever seen in England, and which took away their breath. 'On that May morning the paintwork was untouched by time, and the light passed enriched with colour through the windows as yet unclouded by the blown grime of Birmingham. The flames of the candles on the altar were palely aspirant in that glowing light. Jewels and points of metal glinted like spurts of flame. Incense rose in whorls of grey and palest blue; the air was heavy with it. Before the altar, the splendour of ritual proceeded like a slow dance of exquisite restraint. The light touched to more glowing colours the robes of the celebrant and his assistants —the Bishop of Cambysopolis and Vicar Apostolic of the Midland District, his assistant priest, the deacon and sub-deacon, the two assistant deacons at the throne —moving slowly about their sacrifice; lay like a wash of colour over the white cottas of the servers, and dimmed the candle-flames of the two acolytes; shone on the magnificence of the two attending prelates; glinted on the ambient incense motes. And enriching it all was the fact that Catholicism was displayed in its glory for the first time in England for two hundred years. Long night had chastened the Church in England; there had been the wan grey twilight of approaching dawn; the commencement of the Pontifical High Mass at Oscott was as the first appearance of the sun's rays above the horizon. Or so it must have seemed to Pugin, who loved the splendour and panoply of worship. . . . For his was the passionate love which had made so much of that beauty possible; his was the decoration of God's sanctuary; his the windows which shed their added colour upon the Mass; his the reredos on the altar; his the organization of the ceremonies.' [10]

Benjamin Ferrey tells us that from about 1839 'Pugin seems to have been more than ordinarily annoyed by observing that in all the accessories connected with the Catholic worship where art should be apparent, there had been a sad declension since the period of the Reformation; and having exposed in no sparing manner all the abominations as he was accustomed to call them, of the Reformed Church, he now sought, by the influence which his genius gave him, to effect an improvement in ecclesiastical vestments, furniture, holy vessels, and other objects connected with the ritualism of the Roman Catholic Church. His intimacy with many learned ecclesiastics enabled him to obtain such an amount of historical information in reference to these matters, that, aided by them, he produced the most elaborate and beautiful work which had hitherto been attempted, under the title of

[9] *Pugin, A Mediæval Victorian* (1932), p. 245.
[10] ibid., pp. 146–7. This gem of a college chapel has been redecorated on several occasions in the past hundred years, but it still retains its glamour and romantic beauty. Most of its furnishings and ornaments are those which were used on the day of its opening in 1838.

Requiem aeternam dona eis, Domine!
A Puginesque vision of perfect Christian worship
(from a *Glossary of Ecclesiastical Ornament and Costume*, 1845)

A Glossary of Ecclesiastical Ornament and Costume . . . with extracts from the works of Durandus, etc. Faithfully translated by the Rev. Bernard Smith, of S. Marie's College, Oscott.' [11]

The first edition of this magnificently illustrated volume appeared in 1844. A second and enlarged edition was brought out two years later, and a third edition in 1868. Even to-day Pugin's *Glossary* remains the *locus classicus* for the furnishings of churches. No other book published in the past hundred years has actually superseded it.

To style it a 'Glossary' was an understatement, for it is a veritable encyclopædia. It deals with the origin, history, and significance of the various emblems, devices,

[11] *Recollections of A. Welby Pugin* (1861), p. 148.

and symbolic colours peculiar to Christian design of the Middle Ages. There are many pages devoted to the decoration of vestments and altar furnishings. Among the eighty plates which, as the prospectus truly said, were 'splendidly printed in gold and colours by the new Lithochromotographic process,' are examples of the ecclesiastical costumes of the Roman, English, French and German bishops, priests and deacons; altar furniture, embroidery, diaperings, bordures, powderings, floriated crosses, holy emblems, holy monograms, examples of the nimbus, conventional forms of animals and flowers for heraldic and church decoration, funeral palls, also a variety of ornamental alphabets of Church texts of various dates. The details of many of the ornaments are given in full size. There are countless line blocks besides the coloured plates.

'It is almost incredible,' Mr. Trappes-Lomax writes, 'when one examines this bulky volume, with its multiplicity of crafts and its exquisiteness of details, its boldness of design and exactness of execution, that it is the work of one who was already an overburdened architect. There must have been a secret behind that power; and that secret Pugin's secret. In his buildings, and in his other books, it is elusive, as though spoken in a key to which modern ears are not quite attuned. But in the richly coloured pages of this book it lies open for any one to read.' [12]

Pugin was indeed 'one of nature's athletes,' in Mr. Trappes-Lomax's phrase, who 'seem to achieve victory by natural genius.' But just how far the achievement of the *Glossary* was due to hidden labour, or to his natural quickness in co-ordinating actions, it is impossible to tell. Benjamin Ferrey remarks that its 'subject was one so entirely congenial to [Pugin's] taste that he seems to have exhausted all the resources of art bearing upon the sacred furniture and decoration of the Church.' [13] Had Pugin never produced anything else than this book as his contribution towards the better furnishing of places of worship, he would still have his own particular niche and be remembered more than a hundred years after his death.

It is becoming increasingly difficult to find specimens of Pugin's ecclesiastical furnishings and decorations. Several of his smaller churches were either demolished or enlarged after his death. S. George's Cathedral, Southwark, and S. Mary's, Highfield Street, Liverpool, were laid waste by enemy action in the Second World War.[14] Elsewhere new altars or decorations have replaced those he designed. Some of Pugin's romantic dreams of gorgeous interiors got no farther than paper.

It is still possible, however, to study his work in the Chapel of S. John's Hospital, Alton, Staffordshire, which remains in almost the same state as when it was completed about 1844. The drawing which appears in his *Present State of Ecclesiastical Architecture in England* (facing page 93) conveys a good impression of what it looks like to-day. His own description of the interior contains very few details which need to be changed.

'The whole floor is laid with figured tiles, charged with the Talbot arms and

[12] op. cit., p. 285.
[13] *Recollections*, p. 148.
[14] The former has been rebuilt, but the original design much changed.

1. S. Augustine's, Ramsgate (1847–52), designed by and paid for by A. W. Pugin, is a treasure house of Victorian ecclesiastical art. Seen through the oak rood-screen is the tabernacle on the high altar, which came from the Great Exhibition in Hyde Park (1851). The east window is filled with John Hardman stained glass. The wrought iron gates of the Lady Chapel are splendid examples of period metalwork

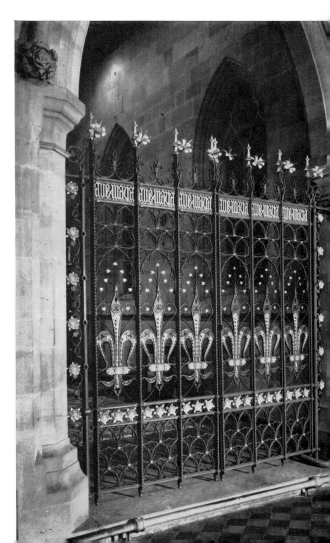

2. Extremes meet! There is not much difference between the furnishings of S. Mary's Catholic Chapel, Edinburgh, as designed by James Gillespie Graham in 1814, and those of S. James's Proprietary Chapel, Ryde, Isle of Wight, which date from about 1829. The latter remain almost unchanged after more than a century

An ideal altar, with overhanging dais, side curtains, frontal
and dossal (A. W. Pugin, n. 70, *Glossary*)

other devices. The benches are precisely similar to those remaining in some ancient
parish churches in Norfolk, with low backs filled with perforated tracery of various
patterns; the poppy-heads are all carved, representing oak and vine leaves, roses,
lions, angels and other emblems. The chancel is divided off by a rich screen,
surmounted with a rood and images. The shields in the breastsummer are all
charged with sacred emblems in gold and colours. The rood is also richly gilt.
Each principal of the roof springs from an angel corbel, bearing each a shield
or a scripture; the braces, tiebeams, rafters and purloins of this roof are moulded,
and the spandrils filled in with open tracery. On each side of the east window is a
niche with images of S. Katherine and S. Barbara. The reredos and altar are both

33

worked in alabaster; the former consists of a series of richly canopied niches surmounted by an open brattishing; images of the apostles holding the emblems of their martyrdom, with our blessed Lord in the centre, occupy these niches. The altar itself consists of three large and three lesser compartments, with images of our blessed Lady, S. John the Baptist and S. Alban, with two angels seated on thrones bearing the lamb and cross. The sunk work is picked out in azure; the raised mouldings and carved ornaments gilt, and the remainder in polished alabaster, similar to some of the costly tombs yet remaining in Westminster and other churches. On each side of this altar silk curtains are suspended on rods. The cross is an exquisite specimen of ancient silver work of the fifteenth century, made as the inscription round the foot relates, by one Peter, for a German bishop, who bore the charge for the love of Christ crucified. This precious relic of Christian art is parcel-gilt, and covered with ornaments and images of wonderful execution. A pair of parcel-gilt silver candlesticks have been made to correspond in style with this cross; they are richly chased, engraven and ornamented with enamels.

'On the gospel side of the chancel is a small chapel, containing an altar for the reservation of the most holy sacrament, which is placed within a gilt tower surmounted by a cross. This chapel communicates with the chancel by a richly moulded and panelled doorway, and also by an arcaded opening of the same description, containing a high tomb with a tracery and emblems, to serve for the sepulchre at Easter.

'On the north side of the chapel is a three-light window, and in every light an angel bearing the cross, the pillar and the holy name, with the scripture, "By thy cross and passion, O Lord deliver us." In the east window are also three lights, with an image of our blessed Lady with our Lord in the centre, S. John the Baptist, with the lamb on the right and S. Nicholas, vested as he used to say mass, with the three children, on the left, all under rich canopies; and in the upper part of the window angels with labels and scriptures. The side windows are filled with ornamental quarries and rich bordures and quatrefoils, containing the emblems of the four evangelists, the annunciation of our Blessed Lady, the pot of lilies with the angelical salutation entwined, and the holy name of our Lord.

'The sacristy is fitted with oak almeries for vestments, and furnished with such sacred vessels and ornaments as are required for the solemn celebration of the divine office. The cloister is paved with figured tiles, and the windows contain many arms and emblems in stained glass; while the walls are enriched with niches containing sculptured representations of our Lord's passion, and other edifying mysteries of the Christian faith.' [15]

Such then is the small chapel designed by Pugin and paid for by Lord Shrewsbury, intended to be the place of worship for 'twelve poor brethren, a schoolmaster and an unlimited number of poor scholars.' The hospital was to be administered by 'a warden and confrater, both in priest's orders; six chaplains or decayed priests, and a sacrist.' [16]

[15] ibid., pp. 93–4.
[16] ibid., p. 92, S. John's Hospital is now occupied by Sisters of Mercy.

Pugin would hardly recognize the interior of the church at Mount S. Bernard Abbey, Leicestershire, if he could revisit it to-day. For very practical reasons the Cistercian monks decided to reverse the original plan when the church was completed in 1945, so what Pugin intended to be the nave has become the choir. The massive stone rood loft supported on three open arches, with two altars on either side of the entrance to the choir, depicted in the engraving in *Ecclesiastical Architecture* (facing page 99), was never built. To-day the high altar stands beneath the central tower, and the layfolk who occupy the east end of the church, facing west, can get an unobstructed view of it. Poor Pugin! the 'screens party' did not win the day, and the abbey church of Mount S. Bernard shows how the 'all-seeing' principle in church arrangement gained the final victory.

The chapel at Grace-Dieu Manor, now used as a preparatory school for boys, run by the Rosminian Fathers, still retains its Pugin furnishings, including the stone ciborium in the chapel of the Blessed Sacrament, erected in 1848.[17]

III

It was not until 1846 that Pugin managed to decorate and furnish a parish church in strict conformity with his ideals; hitherto there had always been limited funds or difficult clients, who interfered with him. Thanks to the reckless generosity of Lord Shrewsbury, S. Giles', Cheadle, Staffordshire, was transformed into the most gorgeous church in England at that date. Many authors have tried to convey the impression of its interior, but none has surpassed Mr. Henry-Russell Hitchcock, who writes: 'The warm darkness of the interior is the most notable first impression. This effect is only partly due to the rather feeble coloured glass of the aisle windows, through which the daylight seeps into the unlighted nave; for here is a magnificent coloured darkness not unlike that of S. Mark's in Venice or other Byzantine churches lined with mosaics. Every square inch of the interior is painted either with gold or with colour chiefly in repeating patterns—diapers, chevrons and brocaded effects—which are infinitely various in design, and yet consistently harmonious in scale. Least happy is the figural painting over the chancel arch; but so perfect is the evenness of tone in all the decorations that the mural does not offend as do the garish windows, certainly among the poorest that Pugin ever designed.

'The overall tonality is brownish grey high lighted with gold; and time has only slightly darkened the general effect. The combination of colours in the various areas of pattern is bolder and richer than the general effect would at first suggest: the floors, for example, are of red and cream tiles, and a dado of yellow and deep grey-blue figured tiles lines the aisle walls. The chancel screen is brown, red and gold, while around the font in the south-west corner is a screen of bright polished brass.

[17] Other places where his furnishings and decorations can be studied include S. Barnabas's Cathedral, Nottingham (1844); S. Chad's Cathedral, Birmingham (1840); The Convent of the Sisters of Mercy, Handsworth, Birmingham (1840–7); S. Augustine's, Solihull (1839); S. Mary's, Dudley (1842); S. Osmund's, Salisbury (1842); S. Thomas's, Fulham, London (1847), besides those churches mentioned already, and others in Ireland.

'There are many, undoubtedly far too many, accessories. But the darkness tends to merge them in the total effect of subdued richness. One is reminded forcibly by the sumptuous quality of patterned tone on patterned tone, of form dissolved in drenched colour, of a Baxter print—or even of the orchestration of the great Romantic composers. . . . A major monument of late Romanticism; for it recalls, among contemporary works in other arts, not the music of Queen Victoria's favourite Mendelssohn, but rather that of Berlioz; it may even be compared not unjustly with the coloristic painting of Turner and Delacroix.' [18]

It is impossible to mention all the interesting and original accessories in this unique church. The chancel screen, with its lofty rood is perhaps the best that Pugin ever designed. The engraving in his *Present State of Ecclesiastical Architecture in England* (Plate XVI) enables us to study the details of the chancel furnishings. The high altar, backed by a reredos composed of ten niches, each containing the statue of a saint, has riddel curtains on either side. The cross and six candlesticks stand directly on the mensa. There is no tabernacle, because Pugin had provided a Blessed Sacrament chapel enclosed by screens within the eastern bay of the south aisle. Two standard candlesticks stand at the north and south ends of the footpace. Needless to say there is a triple sedilia and a double stone credence. An aumbry for the holy oils is in the north wall of the sanctuary, and west of it is an Easter Sepulchre of ornate Decorated Gothic design. The ceiling of the chancel, divided into square panels, is covered with painted decorations. The five-light east window with flowing tracery is filled with obviously Hardman glass.

Mr. Trappes-Lomax writes that the curious beauty of S. Giles', 'heavily decorated, overladen with choice richness, sombre and gorgeous, close compact, is similar in effect to a piece of old brocaded stuff, or to one of the more intricately woven passages of Huysman's prose. . . . The church stands, strange monument of the religious ardour of two wholehearted men who never attained to perfection in achievement.' [19] The year of its opening also saw the height of the railway building mania in England, the repeal of the Corn Laws, the aftermath of the potato famine in Ireland and the coronation of Pope Pius IX.

It is extremely doubtful if any of Pugin's churches recreated the atmosphere of those erected in the later Middle Ages. Like Victor Hugo, who made himself familiar with every nook and cranny of the cathedral, and spent over three years accumulating material from chronicles, charters and inventories before he began writing *Notre-Dame de Paris,* Pugin was too much of a natural genius to produce a dead copy. The sole merit of Pugin's ecclesiastical furnishings and decorations, like Victor Hugo's novel, lies in the fact that they are works of imagination, whim and fancy.[20] His best work possesses the quality of a medieval miniature painting. At a first glance one is only conscious of the composition as a whole. Then, if one studies it through a magnifying glass, one is amazed at the consummate perfection of tiny details. The mystery is how he managed to find the

[18] *Early Victorian Architecture in Britain* (New Haven, 1954), Vol. I, pp. 82–3.
[19] op. cit., pp. 118–19.
[20] Cf. André Maurois, *Victor Hugo* (English translation, 1956), p. 166.

craftsmen to produce these works of art in the first decade of the reign of Queen Victoria. They prove that the tradition of sound craftsmanship was far from dead in the forties of the last century.

It is impossible for us to realize how startling young Pugin's churches must have been to those who visited them or worshipped at their altars unless we can visualize the typical upper-middle class domestic environment of the eighteen-forties. This is how Osbert Lancaster describes an average Early Victorian home.

'Painted walls vanished beneath a variety of patterned papers; striped, spotted and flowered. Mahogany reigned almost supreme as the popular wood for furniture, though both birch and rosewood maintained a certain vogue. Carpets, whether elaborately floral in pink and white or severely patterned in billiard-cloth green or scarlet. Fireplaces were comparatively plain marble. The room assumed the function of a museum of *objets d'art*. The mantelpiece was transformed into a parade ground for the perpetual marshalling of rows of Bristol glass candlesticks, Sèvres vases, Bohemian lustres around the glass-protected focal point of the massively allegorical clock.

'For the better display of whole cavalry divisions of plunging bronze equestrians, Covent Gardens of wax fruit, bales of Berlin woolwork, the drawing-room, the library and the boudoir were forced to accommodate innumerable cupboards, consoles and occasional tables. The large family portrait loses none of its popularity, but the fashion for miniatures and silhouettes enables the range of visible reminders of the importance of family ties to be extended to the third and fourth generation of uncles, aunts and cousins of every degree.' [21]

Mr. Lancaster points out that there was something curiously surrealist in this Early Victorian passion for souvenirs and the aggressively personal note in the fashion of house furnishing. The variety of objects might include 'a sand-filled paper-weight from Alum Bay, a lock of little Willy's hair, and dear Fido stuffed and mounted.'

Interior decoration by 1840 had been taken over by the upholsterer from the cabinet-maker. Upholstery, tassels, fringes, bobbins, braids, etc. did their best to conceal the basic shape of most furniture.

The men and women who made up the congregations of Pugin's churches which did not happen to be situated in the poorer parts of towns were almost as upholstered as their homes. There was little or nothing Gothic in their appearance. The male costume out of doors usually consisted of a very tight fitting overcoat with a shaped waist. A top-hat was obligatory, but by 1848 the once almost universal beaver had given way to the silk-hat. Some men, who tried to be fashionable, sported trousers with oblique stripes or blue and white checks. Their jackets and waistcoats might be of any colour, but dark blue was popular. Round their necks were tight 'chokers.' Hair was worn long, with curls round the head. Beards

---

[21] *Homes Sweet Homes* (1939), no. 36.

S. BARNABAS' CATHEDRAL, NOTTINGHAM (A. W. Pugin, 1842–4)
High altar on eight shafts of Petworth marble, with gilt caps and bases.
Perforated oak screen, with standards for wax tapers, Lady Chapel
behind. Pavement of 'incrusted tiles of various colours, similar in design
and composition to those used in ancient churches'

tended to form a fringe round the face. About the middle of the 'forties side
whiskers, moustaches and an 'Imperial' became the vogue.

Almost every well-to-do lady had a tea-cosy silhouette. The upper part of her
body rested on a dome-shaped pedestal. The bell-like skirts were distended by
many petticoats, worn one over the other. First came a flannel one; then another

38

padded with horsehair stiffened with braid; a third had flounces of horsehair; and on top of these were one or two starched muslin petticoats under the dress. A fashionable lady was so well padded in the eighteen-forties that there was really no need for cushions in pews or benches. Loose cloaks were worn over the tight waisted bodices. Poke bonnets hid the hair, worn in short ringlets. Bonnets were of all colours. In summer shawls were draped over the shoulders, and the cloaks discarded.

Such were the sort of people who would have been *seen* in any church of this decade; very different from the congregations that Pugin would have *chosen* to complete his *décor*. Subconsciously at least, he and his disciples pictured their churches filled with men and women in thirteenth century costumes. The men ought to have worn two long tunics the outer one sleeveless. In the front pews there should have been a few knights in chain-mail, with surcoats decorated with coats of arms. How much more picturesque hooded cloaks than frock-coats. The women who worshipped in Pugin's churches, or those which the Cambridge Camden Society pronounced as correct for Anglican rites, ought to have worn loose fitting robes with long trains. The parti-colour costumes of the early Middle Ages would have been far more in keeping with the vestments of the clergy than even the often gay shades fancied by the ladies of the eighteen-forties.

IV

It was the Oratorians and their wholehearted zeal for Italian fashions of church furnishing that drove Pugin to take up the line that a church without a chancel screen and rood loft is hardly worthy to be described as Christian. By 1848 screens had become an obsession. From July to December that year, he continued to write letters in their defence in almost every issue of *The Rambler,* in answer to his many opponents. As Mr. Trappes-Lomax points out: 'the idea of the sacrosanct quality of rood screens had developed in Pugin's mind in the course of his studies of ancient examples. They do not appear in his earlier churches. As soon as he started to build them, opposition arose.' [22]

Faber, even more than Newman, was determined that modern Rome must be the source of inspiration for the furnishing and decoration of churches erected in England. In Pugin's eyes he was the arch enemy who must be attacked and defeated. In 1849 Fr. Faber and his five companions started work in London in an improvised chapel situated in King William Street, off the Strand. Pugin wrote to Lord Shrewsbury: 'Has your lordship heard that the Oratorians have opened the Lowther Rooms as a chapel!!—a place for the vilest debauchery, masquerades, etc. —one night a MASKED BALL, next BENEDICTUS. This appears to me perfectly monstrous, and I give the whole order up for ever. What a degradation for religion! Why, it is worse than the Socialists. What a place to celebrate the mysteries of religion in! I cannot conceive how it is allowed. It cannot even be licensed or protected by law, since they only have it for a time. It is the greatest blow we have

[22] ibid., p. 222.

VESPERS IN THE ORATORIANS' CHAPEL, LOWTHER ROOMS (1850)
'What a degradation for religion!' (A. W. Pugin)
'Fitted up in a horrible manner, with a sort of Anglo-Roman
altar. These things are very sad, and the mischief they do is
inconceivable'

had for a long time; no men have been so disappointing as these. Conceive the poet
Faber coming down to the Lowther Rooms! The man who wrote *Thoughts and
Sights in Foreign Churches!!!* hiring the Lowther Rooms! Well may they cry
out against screens or anything else. I always said they wanted rooms, not churches,
and now they have got them. Sad times! I cannot imagine what the world will
come to, if it goes on much longer.' [23]

Pugin also wrote to Ambrose Phillipps in the same strain saying that the whole

[23] Benjamin Ferrey, *Recollections of A. Welby Pugin* (1861), p. 127.

thing was 'really quite lamentable,' and telling him that the Oratorians had 'got the most disgusting place possible for the Oratory in London, and fitted up in a horrible manner, with a sort of Anglo-Roman altar.' [24] Pugin did not stop at writing letters. He and his friend Phillipps arranged to meet Faber, but the interview did not help to pour oil on the troubled waters. Newman tried his best to restore peace by tactful letters written from Maryvale near Oscott, reminding his correspondents of 'that so good and true maxim, *In necessariis Unitas, in dubiis libertas.*' [25]

The real point at issue, as Mr. Trappes-Lomax stresses, was 'whether Renaissance Italian or Medieval English ideas were to prevail in Catholicism in England. Screens were, so to say, a strong point, the possession of which would give the final victory. If the screens party won the day, the "all-seeing" principle in church architecture, as exemplified by the Oratorians, would remain as but an occasional alien extravagance. If the anti-screens party won, the "all-seeing" principle would become the normal, and Gothic would be tolerated only in so far as it could be made to fit in with Roman ideas. For the leaders on either side there could be neither weakening nor compromise.' [26]

Driven almost to desperation, Pugin started work on another book, which was published in 1851, and entitled *A Treatise on Chancel Screens and Rood Lofts, Their Antiquity, Use, and Symbolic Signification.* The purpose of the book was to prove 'that the idea of room-worship, and the all-seeing principles is a perfect novelty.' Pugin was determined to impress on the minds of his readers 'that the very *vitals* of Catholic architecture are assailed by the opponents of screens.' He maintained that if the 'all-seeing principles of worship' are accepted, and 'if religious ceremonies are to be regarded as spectacles they should be celebrated in regular theatres, which have been expressly invented for the purpose of accommodating great assemblages of persons to hear and see as well.' He ended up his defence of screens with the words: 'there is no legitimate halting-place between Catholic doctrine and positive infidelity, and I am quite certain that there is none between a church built on Christian tradition and symbolism and Covent Garden theatre with its pit, boxes and gallery.' He tried his best to explain that 'screens arose from a natural as well as a symbolical intention—it is a natural principle to enclose any portion of a building or space which is set apart from public use and access, and when such a boundary is erected round the place of sacrifice in a church, it teaches the faithful to reverence the seat of the holy mysteries, and to worship in humility.'

The 'Conclusion' to this vigorously written *apologia* for mystery in worship was obviously inspired by the tawdry furnishings of the Oratory in King William Street. 'Bad as was the Paganism of the fifteenth and sixteenth centuries, it was dressed out in much external majesty and richness; but now nothing is left but the fag end of this system; bronze and marble are replaced by calico and trimmings; the works of the sculptor and the goldsmith are succeeded by the milliner

[24] E. S. Purcell, *Life and Letters of Ambrose Phillips de Lisle* (1900), Vol. II, p. 218.
[25] ibid., Vol. II, p. 204.
[26] op. cit., p. 226.

and the toyshop; and the rottenness of the Pagan movement is thinly concealed by gilt paper and ribands—the nineteenth century apeings of the dazzling innovations of the Medician era. Cheap magnificence, meretricious show, is the order of the day; something pretty, something novel, calico hangings, sparkling lustres, paper pots, wax dolls, flounces and furbelows, glass cases, ribands and lace, are the ornaments and materials usually employed to decorate, or rather disfigure, the altar of sacrifice and the holy place. It is impossible for church furniture and decoration to attain a lower depth of degradation, and it is one of the greatest impediments to the revival of Catholic truth. It is scarcely possible for men to realize the awful doctrines and the majestic ritual of the Church under such a form; and yet these wretched novelties are found on the altars of some of the most venerable temples, equally in the abortions of modern erection.'

But the finest bits of Puginesque invective are to be found in the four sketches which end the book, entitled 'The Calvinistic Ambonoclast,' 'The Pagan Ambonoclast,' 'The Revolutionary Ambonoclast' and 'The Modern Ambonoclast.' Here we have some of the most dramatic pieces of descriptive writing ever perpetrated by Pugin, depicting the destruction of a rood screen, which ends with the words: 'Nearly three hundred years have elapsed and the rood was again raised in glory in this very city, and the cry "Away with it" was again heard. Came it from the blaspheming Jews? No. Came it from the bitter Calvinists? No. Came it from the incarnate fiends? No. It procceded from a modern Catholic ambonoclast!!!'

Mr. Trappes-Lomax is of the opinion that 'Pugin loved screens before he understood them, and that his arguments were worked out to justify this liking; and that it was only then that he realized that if screens would once be shown to be an essential of Catholic art the whole position of his opponents would become untenable. Screens, in fact, started as a strong predilection, developed into an argument, and ended up as a principle which the argument was not strong enough to support.' [27] True enough, but it has to be remembered that Pugin's arguments influenced fashions in church furnishing for the rest of the nineteenth century. The 'battle of the screens' went on for nearly a hundred years. To-day opinion is just as strongly divided in favour of the 'all-seeing' type of church and 'room-worship' as against it. Bishops and priests are still engaged in pulling down screens and rood lofts. There are 'Modern Ambonoclasts' in the 'fifties of this century just as there were in the 'fifties of the last! [28] Though the present generation may smile at Pugin's arguments and feel they are hopelessly out of date, nobody could deny that the engravings which illustrate his book are works of art.

[27] op. cit., p. 243.

[28] The present-day conviction that communal participation in worship, with a greater use of the vernacular, often tempts priests and layfolk to make statements which will hardly stand examination. On August 2, 1957 it was reported in the *Catholic Herald* that a certain ardent liturgist had informed his audience at a congress that a 'final cleavage, stifling the participation of the Holy People of God, with the erection of rood screens, and the last of all horrors: the western gallery in the churches,' had been achieved 'by the fourteenth century,' when 'the death-knell had been sounded, and the laity were silenced for all time at the worship of the altar.' Such liturgical enthusiasts seem to forget that the solid *ikonastatis*, an invariable furnishing in churches of most Eastern rites, has never prevented the active participation of the laity in divine worship. Again, there are some authorities on congregational singing who are of the opinion that the best place for a choir is at the west end of a church, not in the chancel.

V

To understand Pugin's ideals of church furnishing it is essential to study those he designed for S. Augustine's, Ramsgate, for here he was his own master from start to finish, never worried by exasperating clients. The church was begun in 1847, and not fully completed until after his death. S. Augustine's is an almost unique museum of early Victorian ecclesiastical art. It remains very much as Pugin designed it, and most of the furnishings are his own inspiration. The nave is divided from the chancel by a typical Pugin rood screen in dark stained oak. The crucifix leans forward over the nave. Pugin believed that this was in accordance with the correct medieval custom. Within the chancel, laid with Minton's encaustic tiles, are returned choir stalls. The high altar is vested with rich frontals, which Pugin would have admired. The centre of the stone reredos (now hidden by a dorsal) is filled by the lofty brass tabernacle, with many crockets and buttresses on its sixteen feet high stone spire. It had been made for the Great Exhibition of 1851, and was afterwards presented to the church. The great east window of five lights glows with superb Hardman stained glass; the colours of which it would be difficult if not impossible to improve. The Lady Chapel on the south side of the chancel is divided from it by dark oak screens. The stone altar and reredos have blue silk curtains hanging on iron brackets at the sides. The pair of wrought iron gates through which the chapel is entered were designed by John Hardman Powell, and inserted after Pugin's death. Hanging on the wall outside the chapel is a silver lamp, in the shape of a medieval ship, before a stone statue of 'Our Lady Star of the Sea,' within a much decorated niche.

The carved stone font, raised on steps, with its loft oak cover, at the west end of the aisle, is the one shown at the Great Exhibition of 1851. The Chapel of S. Lawrence fills up the greater part of the transept on the south side of the church, from which it is divided by an oak screen. In a vault beneath the chapel lie the mortal remains of the founder. Under the south window is his recumbent effigy, very realistic. 'Here one sees Pugin as a saintly pilot, navigating his Gothic ark through the tempest of industrial protestantism—the tempest which destroyed him.' [29] Here his tired body has rested for over a hunderd years, within sight and sound of the sea which, with Christian architecture, was the love of his life. There was always something flame-like about his best work, both in his writings and in his architectural designs. And the flame burnt itself out in forty quick years. The over-stimulated brain and overworked body collapsed under the strain. But the influence of this strange character persisted in the fashions of church furnishings for more than a century.

[29] John Summerson, article 'Pugin at Ramsgate' in the *Architectural Review*, April 1945.

CHAPTER II

THE ECCLESIOLOGICAL MOVEMENT

I

AUGUSTUS WELBY PUGIN must be given the place of honour as the protagonist of the revival of medieval inspired church furnishings and decorations. There existed in his time another movement in favour of improving the furnishings and decorations of Anglican places of worship. It is doubtful if Pugin was influenced by the so-called 'ecclesiologists,' but it is certain that his ideals were adapted or imitated by his numerous Anglican disciples.

Throughout the next half a dozen chapters almost every description of church furnishings has been quoted directly or paraphrased from contemporary sources, the magazine entitled *The Ecclesiologist* in particular. In no other way was it possible to convey the effect produced at the time on those interested in ecclesiastical *décor*. Very few of the churches erected or restored a century ago retain their period furnishings now, and it is hard for us to visualize them as they were in the eighteen-forties and fifties. Again, if the furnishings and decorations have not been removed or obliterated, more often than not they have acquired a mellow patina, which gives them the flavour of antiques. The reader must try to form a mental picture of what these objects looked like when they were new and, if possible, to recapture the reactions produced on those who saw them for the first time.

On the continent of Europe men were looking back to the Middle Ages, hoping to revive the glories of medieval religious worship, as well as architecture and painting. In France there were, among others, Charles Forbes René, Comte de Montalembert, whose *Life of S. Elizabeth of Hungary* had appeared in 1836; and Dom Prosper Guéranger, who in 1837 restored Benedictine monastic life at the Abbey of Solesmes. The first of the sixteen volumes of his *Année Liturgique* was published in 1841. Eugène Viollet-le-Duc had begun to restore the Sainte Chapelle in Paris the previous year, and had started to collect the material for the ten volumes of his *Dictionnaire raisonné de l'architecture française du onzième au seizième siècle,* the first of which came out in 1854. For the next half century this encyclopædic work of reference became the chief inspiration for church furnishers and decorators across the Channel.

Pugin was known already to a limited circle of medievalists in France and

Belgium. In 1850 a French translation of his *True Principles of Pointed or Christian Architecture* was published at Bruges. Bruges thus became one of the chief centres for supplying church furnishings according to Pugin's principles.

Since 1810 Friedrich Overbeck and his disciples (known as 'Nazarites') had been striving to form a true Christian school of painting, fitted for the decoration of churches. From this group, whose headquarters was in Rome, evolved the Düsseldorf school of artists, including Edward von Steinle, who covered the walls of many a church in Germany with paintings, most of which were a combination of austerity, sternness, shallowness and sweet insipidity. The early Gothic Revival in Germany was closely bound up with the Romantic Movement. Its chief prophet was J. A. Moehler (1796–1838), still remembered by his once widely read book on Christian Symbolism. Church furnishings and decorations, as well as church architecture in Germany were affected indirectly by the principles laid down by these apostles of a reversal to medievalism, as opposed to classicism. Hirscher (1788–1865) was another writer who influenced liturgical reform, such as it was, in Germany.

II

The change of outlook in regard to the furnishing and decoration of Anglican churches which began about 1840 was due to the influence of the so-called 'ecclesiologists,' whose united front was helped by societies, each with its own periodical to spread propaganda. As Mr. Henry-Russell Hitchcock puts it: 'the simple solution of providing a large unified auditorium, from all parts of which the congregation would see and hear the preacher, was soon outdated. Ecclesiology prescribed a new method of assembling characteristic elements borrowed from medieval English churches into a complex shell within which various sacramental rites could be 'rubrickally' performed.

'The rubrics, or regulations for worship of the Anglican Church, were open to various interpretations, but more and more a High Church party found sanction in them for a ritual of considerable elaboration that seemed distinctly un-Protestant to their evangelical opponents. Thus the new attitude was not consciously æsthetic but rather, in a special if rather metaphorical sense, functional. Even to talk in purely visual terms of proportion and of other objective qualities in church architecture was in certain circles soon castigated as pagan; just as to-day some "Functionalists" condemn considerations of purely æsthetic values as antisocial.' [1] Thus the interest of Early Victorian churches lies far more in their furnishings than in their architecture. The pity is that so few are now left as they were designed.

No organization wielded greater influence on the fashions in church furnishings between 1840 and 1850 than the Ecclesiological Society. Founded in 1839 as the Cambridge Camden Society, with the object of promoting the study of Ecclesiastical Architecture and the restoration of mutilated architectural remains, its activities

[1] *Early Victorian Architecture in Britain*, 2 vols. (New Haven, U.S.A., 1954), Vol. I, p. 57.

were confined to Anglican places of worship, although its influence spread later on to those of other religious bodies. The actual founders were two Cambridge undergraduates, John Mason Neale and Benjamin Webb, both of whom became clergymen. It was not long before the Society started to set forth its ideals in a series of pamphlets; among the first of which were *Hints for the Practical Study of Ecclesiastical Antiquities* (1839); *A Few Words to Church Builders* and *A Few Words to Churchwardens on Churches and Church Ornaments* (1841); and *Church Enlargement and Church Arrangement* (1842). Several practical leaflets were issued at the same time, including *Twenty-three Reasons for Getting Rid of Church Pues* [*sic*], and *Hints to Workmen Engaged on Churches*.

The new word 'ecclesiology' soon became fashionable. Nobody was quite sure what it meant, although it is now defined in the *Concise Oxford Dictionary* as 'the science of churches, especially of church building and decoration.' A better meaning is given in the *Century Dictionary,* where we are told that ecclesiology 'treats of all the details of church furniture, ornament, etc., and their symbolism, and is cultivated especially by the High Church party in the Church of England.'

Writing in 1879, Mr. Beresford Hope, who was one of the pioneers of the ecclesiological movement explained that 'it embraced within its scope the buildings which were erected for worship, and all the accessories and adjuncts pertaining to such buildings, as well as the service of worship itself. It was the vehicle whereby many arts were made subservient to one great end, and the greatness of the end demanded the employment of the highest art. . . . The science of ecclesiology, too, included one of the most recondite branches of archæology, viz. liturgiology. It also included the study of church music, hymnody, organs, etc.'

The way had been prepared for the Cambridge Camden Society by the publication of several books during the 'thirties. Among the best known were J. H. Parker's *Introduction to the Study of Gothic Architecture* and M. H. Bloxam's *Principles of Gothic Architecture elucidated by Question and Answer*. Both these books went through many editions. More serious treatises were *The Analysis of Gothic Architecture* and *Parish Churches,* both written and illustrated by John Raphael and his brother Joshua Brandon.

The year 1841 saw the publication of the first number of *The Ecclesiologist,* a magazine in which the Camden Society planned to make known its aims and objects. It continued until 1868. One needs a considerable effort now to plough through all the musty volumes of this magazine, but if one has the time and patience to do so, one is rewarded by some priceless gems of dogmatic statements on what constitutes ecclesiastical good taste. In no other way is it possible to recapture the atmosphere of the period, or to realize how strong feelings ran a hundred years ago.

III

In 1845 there was a split in the ranks of the Cambridge Camden Society. The more progressive members broke away and formed themselves into the Ecclesiological Society (late Cambridge Camden) and the headquarters were moved to

London. The magazine continued to be published, but in a new form. Meantime other societies with similar aims had been founded—at Oxford, Exeter, Lichfield, Bristol and Northampton. The Committee of the Exeter Diocesan Architectural Society had no hesitation in setting forth that they 'willingly sanction and, as far as their calling will permit, heartily abet every effort to make men good ritualists, sound Churchmen, and true men; and they think that they need not be careful, after that, nor will have long to wait to find also, good, sound and true architects.' The movement spread overseas, first to North America, where a *New York Ecclesiologist* started publication; then it penetrated to India, Ceylon, Canada, Newfoundland, and even to Australia.

The condition of many places of worship up and down England was a standing disgrace to the authorities of the Established Church. Reference to this neglect was made again and again in the early numbers of *The Ecclesiologist*. For instance, in 1842 the chancel at Long Stanton in Cambridgeshire was used as a school. Green curtains were drawn across the chancel arch. A 'common kitchen-fire grate' had been inserted in the north wall, with 'a huge red brick chimney behind it, for the comfort and accommodation of the teacher (who sits within the altar rails with his chair against the holy table).' [2] Then at Long Shelford in the same county, the chancel was filled with deal  forms and straw mats. The Holy Table was 'a wretched deal frame, painted red.' The so-called altar at Hardwick was a 'rude frame of rough pieces of deal hammered together and painted red. It was covered with a dirty and torn rag of the very coarsest green baize.'

Even worse reports came from Yorkshire. At Scarborough there was an old font lying in a dark hole, covered with lumber. The font in use was 'a kind of wash-hand bason on a frame of painted deal.' All the woodwork in this medieval parish church was of 'the roughest and most barn-like description; each occupant has followed his own taste in fancy-painting. The whole structure exhibits a variety of shades and tinctures which might be expected rather in a play-house of mounte-banks than in a Christian Church. The pens on the floor are in a vile state; more like the cages at Smithfield than anything else.' [3]

Many chancels were being used as schoolrooms. Much ancient stained glass had been destroyed wantonly. At Ashton by Malton the 'holy table had the follow-ing furnishings upon it—20 writing and copy books, 7 slates, master's cane and sundry pens. Within the walls was the schoolmaster's desk; a jug of ink, covered with a rag, was in the sedilia.' [4] But even worse, so the ecclesiologists pointed out, was the 'desecration of the Lord's Table' in new churches, for instance at Lenton

[2] op. cit., Vol. II, p. 171.
[3] ibid., p. 174.
[4] ibid., p. 175.

in Nottinghamshire. Here was 'a W.C. contiguous to the holy Altar itself, nay, occupying the place where the Altar ought to stand.' The writer of the report said: 'we cannot trust ourselves to speak in sufficiently strong terms against this desecration of GOD'S House. . . . We have always spoken against the practice of building any sort of vestry behind the Altar; we now see what such a departure from ancient usage can lead to.' [5]

The state of ecclesiology in the Channel Islands was particularly bad. There

PROPRIETARY CHAPEL IN FASHIONABLE WATERING PLACE (from the *Ecclesiologist,* 1845)

were very few fonts. In some churches a coffee-pot and a small basin were used for baptisms. The holy tables lay neglected, and were seldom where they ought to be—at the east end of the church.[6]

The refurnishing of Mr. Richard Waldo Sibthorp's S. James' Proprietary Chapel at Ryde, Isle of Wight, which was a stronghold of extreme evangelicalism in the 'forties just as it is to-day, led to some abusive criticism in *The Ecclesiologist.* We read that the chapel had been 'brought back to its original state, or to a condition even worse. The pulpit, etc. have been replaced before the Altar, the east window made to open, so as to communicate with a schoolroom adjoining, and to render the church itself useful in accommodating an audience to listen to religious speakers who occupy a platform in the said schoolroom.' At All Hallows and S. Petrock, Exeter, the altars were furnished with drawers, wherein parish papers

[5] ibid., p. 176.
[6] Cf. Vol. II, p. 16.

3. In these four cartoons, reproduced from *The Reformation and the Deformation*, published by Mr. Mowbray of Oxford in 1868, we see what the Ecclesiologists found in many English parish churches, and how they strove to make them both 'correct' and devotional

Bristol Cathedral (J. L. Pearson, 1899)   S. Margaret's Convent, East Grinstead (G. E. Street, 186

4. Four typical Gothic Revival Anglican high altars and reredoses

Gloucester Cathedral (Sir George Gilbert Scott, 1873)   Salisbury Cathedral (Sir George Gilbert Scott, c. 1875)

were kept.[7] The presence of W.C.s close to the altar was mentioned again and again. At S. James', Bermondsey, there were two—one for the clergy, the other for the congregation, on either side of the chancel.[8]

Then we find a fascinating description (together with an illustration) of an 'Actual Arrangement of the Altar, Pulpit, and Reading Place, of a Proprietary Chapel in a fashionable watering place.' Here 'the architect fixed over the Altar twin boxes or tubs for the desk and pulpit, precisely alike in size and shape, and in the very closest alliance, indeed you pass from No. 1 into No. 2. These boxes are fastened to the wall; but have no visible support, and the wall itself, from its flimsy texture, must prove but a frail guardian. Should the preacher be weighty in person, and vehement in action, he will in falling cause these deformities to break from their moorings, and both he and his brother minister will be precipitated forwards at the risk of their necks and limbs.' [9] At All Saints', Spitalfields, 'the pulpit, reading-pue, and clerk's pue, ranging one under the other, stood exactly in front of the Altar.' As to the font, it was merely a shallow square basin, like a frying-tin.[10]

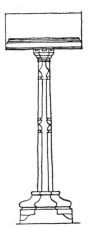

Still, there were hopes of better times ahead. A few churches did resemble churches, even in 1842. Llangorwen, Cardiganshire, was about the last place in Britain where one would expect to find perfect interior furnishings —'low open stalls of oak and chestnut (all free); a carved eagle and litany desk; a rood screen, an altar of Bath stone, with an arcaded reredos behind it, and a table of Prothesis; and a small raised platform railed off at the north side of the chancel arch for a reading pew.' Imagine the delight of the ecclesiological explorers in West Wales when they found a chancel paved with Painswick stone, raised on one step above the nave, with the altar raised on three steps to symbolize the Holy Trinity. They were informed that the planning and furnishing had been inspired by the new church Mr. Newman had built at Littlemore, near Oxford, in 1836.

Roused to action by the *Tracts for the Times,* published at Oxford, the members of the Cambridge Camden Society had developed very definite opinions about the planning and furnishing of churches by the time that Mr. Newman had retired to his monastery at Littlemore. Writing as if with the authority of the Roman Congregation of Rites, they laid down that the Lord's Table should be raised on two or more steps from the floor of the chancel, which itself should have a step

[7] ibid., p. 31.
[8] Vol. I, p. 211.
[9] ibid., Vol. II, p. 26.
[10] ibid., Vol. I, p. 195.

D

or two up from the nave. No seats must be placed between the altar rails and the north and south walls, so that as much room as possible be left for the access of communicants. The font must be at the west end of the building, or as near as convenient to its principal entrance, but not under a gallery. There must be sufficient space around the font for the sponsors to kneel. The font must be of stone, and large enough to admit the immersion of infants. A water drain was essential. Great care must be taken that the reading-pew does not resemble a second pulpit, and both must be placed at the side of the church. Provision for kneeling must be made in all seats. Hassocks were recommended in preference

TWO ALTAR CANDLESTICKS (approved by the Ecclesiological Society, 1847) Designed by Mr. Willement from 'ancient examples'

to kneeling boards. Galleries were taboo. 'None can be permitted in any part of the church,' we are told. Moreover it was stated that 'The Society will not sanction any plan involving a gallery, unless in cases where it is distinctly shown that no room is unnecessarily sacrificed, by inconvenient arrangements on the floor.' [11]

It was a hopeful sign of the improvement in ecclesiastical taste that a new church, in the Early English style, had been built at Hanham in Gloucestershire. Among its furnishings were two sedilia and a 'fenestrella' with a credence shelf. Much embroidered work had been contributed by devout ladies. Christian emblems had been liberally used in all the internal decorations, also on the holy vessels. Yet what could be said of S. Mary's, Penzance, where one found 'two huge pulpits

[11] ibid., Vol. I, p. 152.

of Gothick frippery, standing before the Altar, adjoining to that on the north side, the clerk's desk, on six Gothick legs.' The poor reredos of great pretence was flanked by two enormous pinnacled turrets.[12]

The Camden Society waged war on what were called 'altar chairs,' some of which seem to have been very luxurious, and placed on either side of the communion table, facing the congregation. Thus the faithful had no choice but to stare at the two clergymen's faces, and 'devotional feelings' were 'almost necessarily extinguished' by 'this most offensively publick situation by making the Holy Table

TWO ALTAR CANDLESTICKS (authorized by the Ecclesiological Society, 1847)
'In these, as in chalices, a knop is not to be dispensed with. They must have a pricket or spike.'

itself, with scarcely less decorum, a place to lean upon, and a book rest, during portions of the service which have nothing to do with the Communion Office.' [13] The only cure for this abuse was to erect proper sedilia.

Towards the close of the year 1842 the Camden Society felt bold enough to publish its recommendations on church plate and ornaments, including altar

[12] ibid., Vol. II, pp. 56–7.
[13] ibid., p. 91.

candlesticks. All those 'which are mostly in use are very tall, of gilt wood, in the arabesque style, and of foreign workmanship, of these we highly disapprove. Plain Altar candlesticks may be of *latten,* low, and with broad bases and basons: they ought also to have a *pricket* or spoke, and the serges whould taper from the base upwards.' [14] The Society was of the opinion that most church ornaments then in use were unbecoming, and that steps must be taken to improve general taste on this subject, and to afford facilities for the imitation of ancient models. The Society proposed to receive orders for church plate and ornaments through its secretaries. The objects commissioned 'would be executed in good taste and with the right spirit by workmen in the respective branches of art.' William Butterfield, Esq., Architect of 4 Adam Street, London, had agreed to accept the 'laborious and responsible office of Agent.'

The third volume of *The Ecclesiologist* (1843) went into the subject of the design of altars and altar screens, i.e. reredoses. 'When a clergyman sets to work in earnest at the restoration of his church, the Altar is the first thing which demands and receives his attention. That he should be indignant at, and at once seek to remedy, its disgraceful condition, is only natural; but the means adopted to obtain this end are generally wanting in taste as they are excellent in spirit. We propose to offer a few remarks on this important subject.' [15]

The 'few remarks' help us to realize how clear-cut the beliefs of the Camden Society had become after four years since it was founded. They start with the statement. *'An altar screen or reredos is neither necessary, nor (except in some peculiar instances) a fitting ornament for a small church.'*

The writer continues: 'Let us be content to have a plain east wall. We shall not exceed our ancestors; in the attempt we run the risk of falling into an absurdity. Look for instance at the ludicrous effect of niches for sedilia in the east end; or at the still more absurd arrangement of a Reredos of more *pretension* than our ancestors would have thought necessary for a minister—and which was raised at the expense of £100—and the deal table, value (second-hand) 3s. 6d., which stands before it!'

It seems that a taste for gorgeous reredoses in the early 'forties of the last century went with elaborately panelled wooden altars. The Camden Society maintained that if circumstances did not permit a fixed stone altar, a simple table of wood was much better. Detailed directions were given for the design of stone altars, including the five crosses which must be incised on the top slab or *mensa.* Either a solid mass of masonry, or a stone table resting on four or more legs were approved. Then follows some advice on altar furniture. 'We will conclude with one word on the arrangement of the Altar during the time of the Holy Eucharist. The frontal (scarlet, green or purple, as may be) is to hang down in front, touching the ground and visible; for the "fair linen cloth" is to be a strip, hanging down at the sides only. Altar carpets are not wanted, except one strip in front of the Altar; one down the middle of the chancel, and one for the use of the Priests who occupy the sedilia.' [16]

[14] ibid., p. 117.   [15] op. cit., p. 5.   [16] ibid., pp. 5, 6.

In the November issue of *The Ecclesiologist* for 1843 we find further details concerning altar screens or reredoses. The Camden Society was strongly against their introduction in general, but favoured the revival of triptychs, to stand behind the altar. A suitable framed picture would form a sufficient background; given 'hangings on each side, plain or embroidered, and of moderate height.' These would 'hide the rough wall, with no disguise, and add beauty and colour to the whole. ... What might not be hoped for, if the Church would once again make Painting her handmaid?' [17]

Mr. Henry-Russell Hitchcock points out that the Camdenians, like Pugin, had been riding high since 1843. 'The proscriptions in the new editions of their pamphlets had grown stricter, and their authority was widely accepted. Protests there were from both architects and laymen, but the protestant (and Protestant) party was fighting a losing battle. Their utilitarian arguments were admittedly mundane; moreover, the compromise solutions they continued to propose did not offer such satisfying, visual effects as the churches approved by the ecclesiologists. That fact was probably more important than any one cared to admit at the time.' [18]

In 1843 John Mason Neale and Benjamin Webb brought out a translation of the first volume of a medieval treatise on Christian symbolism, the *Rationale Divinorum Officiorum*. Its publication more or less coincided with that of Dickens' *Martin Chuzzlewit* and Thackeray's *Irish Sketch Book*. The author of the *Rationale* was a certain William Durandus, who was Bishop of Mende (a suffragan see of Bourges) between 1285 and 1296. For a long time to come the English version of this strange book, slightly adapted to mid-nineteenth century Anglican mentality by two of the most active members of the Cambridge Camden Society, would exercise a strong influence on church furnishings, ornaments and decorations.

In the very long introduction to *The Symbolism of Churches and Church Ornaments* more than sufficient evidence was produced to show that the reason why no good churches were being built at that date was that architects were ignorant of Christian symbolism. Architecture, so Neale and Webb explained, had 'become too much of a profession ... instead of being the study of the devout ecclesiastic. ... We are not prepared to say that none but monks should design churches, or that it is impossible for a professional architect to build with the devotion and faith of an earlier time. But we do protest against the merely business-like spirit of the modern profession, and demand from them a more elevated and directly religious habit of mind.'

No architect should design a church unless he were a practising Churchman; and it was even worse that he should fall into the temptation to prostitute his craft by designing a Nonconformist meeting-house. 'Conceive a Churchman designing a triple window, admitted emblem of the MOST HOLY TRINITY, for a congregation of Socinians!' The designers of assembly rooms, prisons and workhouses should never be allowed to plan churches. Such would be almost blasphemy and sacrilege.

[17] ibid., p. 33.　　　　　　[18] op. cit., p. 131.

'CORRECT' ALTAR (Cambridge Camden Society, 1847)
Details combined from *Instrumenta Ecclesiastica*

As clergymen of the Church of England, Neale and Webb were convinced that
most contemporary architects needed 'the deeply religious habits of the builders of
old,' and that they had been perverted by 'worldliness, vanity and dissipation.'
First of all, what was required was a thorough mastery of Christian Symbolism or
Sacramentality, so that 'the material fabric symbolizes, embodies, figures, represents,
expresses, answers to, some abstract meaning.' The Tractarian ideal of a return to
the world of medieval guilds can here be seen to be busily at work.

Not only the building itself, but also its furnishings and decorations must show forth the allegorical meaning of numbers. Full use must be made everywhere of such sacred symbols as the cross, the fish, the lamb, the dove, and the ark. Scatter them on every fitting, and the result would be a truly Christian place of worship. The translators of this thirteenth century treatise by the Bishop of Mende produced every possible argument, historical, philosophical, analytical and inductive, for the use of symbolism in a nineteenth century church—far too involved to quote verbatim.

Pages were devoted to such details as gable crosses symbolizing the Atonement;

ALTAR CROSS (approved by the Ecclesiological Society, 1847)

windows setting forth the Light of the World; a circle over three lancets revealing the crown of the King of kings; and a hood-mould above three windows symbolizing the unity of the Trinity. We are reminded that two-light windows are helpful as a symbol of the two Natures of Christ. It is quite wrong to suppose that doors are intended merely to keep out draughts or to prevent a church from being robbed of its treasures; they have a far greater value as symbols of Christ being the way through whom we enter the Kingdom of God after much tribulation. Of course there must be a chancel screen, otherwise how can we fully appreciate the separation between the Church Militant and Triumphant? Even the intricate tracery of the Gothic screen typifies the dim vision we have of the Church in Glory. The locked gateway keeping layfolk out of the chancel is a reminder of the difficulties of getting into heaven.

The two Cambridge Ecclesiologists, having described a typical Protestant place of worship, symbolical of 'spiritual pride, luxury, self-sufficiency and bigotry,' then give us a vision of the Anglican place of worship which they hope will result from architects studying the *Rationale Divinorum Officiorum.*

'Far away, and long ere we catch our first view of the city itself, the three

STANDARD LIGHTS
Recommended by the Ecclesiological Society for daily
evening services in country parishes. The single lights
'may be used in the sacraria.' (Candle-light was considered more 'correct' than oil-lamps or gas)

spires of its cathedral, rising high above its din and turmoil, preach to us of the most Holy and Undivided Trinity.' We reach the building, where 'Lessons of holy wisdom are written in the delicate tracery of the windows: the unity of many members is shadowed forth by the multiplex arcade; the duty of letting our light shine before men, by the pierced and flowered parapet that crowns the whole.' Passing through the door we 'are met with a luxuriance of Symbolism. Everything symbolizes something: the font symbolizes Baptism, and is of stone because Christ is the Rock.'

Bishop Durandus, as paraphrased by Neale and Webb, rambles on page after page, dealing with every detail of furnishing and decoration, the wood now hopelessly lost in the trees. Nothing is put into a church merely for functional purposes

—it is always there to represent something else. For instance: the purpose of a roof is to set forth charity, 'which covereth a multitude of sins. . . . The four side walls, the four cardinal virtues, justice, fortitude, temperance, prudence. . . . The windows are hospitality with cheerfulness, and tenderness with charity. . . . The piers of the church are bishops and doctors. . . . The bases of the columns are the apostolic bishops, and the capitals of the piers are the opinions of the bishops and doctors. . . . The ornaments of the capitals are the words of Sacred Scripture, to the meditation and observance of which we are bound.'

Ostrich eggs are appropriate symbols in churches if hung in the chancels, because they 'signify that man being left by God on account of his sins, if at length he be illuminated by the divine Light, remembereth his faults and returneth to Him, Who by looking on him with His mercy cherisheth him.' However, as Mr. Basil F. L. Clarke points out, 'in spite of its valuable Symbolism, the ecclesiologists do not seem to have adopted this custom.'[19] No Tractarian churches appear to have been furnished with symbolic ostrich eggs.[19a]

So, having dealt at great length with the symbolism of bells and bell-ringing; dedication and consecration ceremonies, and much else, the two clergymen editors managed to find space in their book for a translation of the first and second chapters of the *Mystical Mirror of the Church* by Hugh of S. Victor, a Canon Regular of S. Augustine who died at Paris in 1141. One of the characteristics of Victorine theology and mysticism was a strong emphasis on the symbolistic conception of the universe. Hugh of S. Victor provided Mr. Neale and Mr. Webb with a rich harvest of such symbolism.

It is hardly necessary to say that Protestant minded Anglicans grew alarmed at the increasing influence of the ecclesiologists and the opinions stated in their publications. By 1844 the time was ripe for exposing the obviously Popish nature of the Cambridge Camden Society. The first shot was fired at Cheltenham—always a stronghold of the Low Church party. The Rev. Mr. Close, a militant Evangelical who later on became Dean of Carlisle Cathedral, brought out a book entitled *Church Architecture, Scripturally Considered, from the Earliest Ages to the Present Time.* The reader was left in no doubt that 'Superstition and Church Architecture were coeval from the beginning.' Mr. Close was convinced that 'all temples, altars, churches and religious ceremonies are the badges and proofs of the fallen, guilty state of man. On the Vigil of Guy Fawkes' Day, 1844, he preached a powerful sermon at the parish church in Cheltenham, which was printed with the title of *The 'Restoration of Churches' is the Restoration of Popery: proved and illustrated from the Authentic Publications of the 'Cambridge Camden Society.'* The author-preacher proved conclusively that 'such Restoration of churches not only tends to, but actually is, POPERY.' Many conservative-minded

---

[19] *Church Builders of the Nineteenth Century* (1938), p. 94.

[19a] In more recent times ostrich eggs were placed on the cresting of the rood screen in S. Benedict's, Stratton-on-the-Fosse, Somerset; probably by Abbot Horne of Downside Abbey. Ostrich eggs were also used by Henry Wilson as part of the hanging lamps in Bodley's chapel at Welbeck Abbey (see p. 233).

members of the Church of England, who were nervous already of the novel and daring fashions encouraged by those young men at Cambridge and their disciples at Oxford, were grateful to Mr. Close for having laid bare their superstitious implication, and rallied round him.

The Ecclesiologist replied in two very long articles, maintaining that Mr. Close has badly misrepresented the aims and objects of the Society. From almost every part of England people defended or denounced the ecclesiologists. One writer hinted that the Cambridge Camden Society 'will in all probability lead to great and violent political commotions, and it may be to distress and bloodshed.' Another enemy described the magazine as 'a mischievous tissue of imbecility and fanaticism,' while the *Eclectic Review* maintained that 'this party, indeed, has been characterized as much by its petty pedantry, its arrogance and ill-considered positiveness of assertion, as by its love of ancient art.' But all this, and much more similar abuse, did not deter the Society from propagating its ideals, because the members were sure that their cause was that of the Catholic Church in its external manifestation, and they knew that truth would triumph in the long run. They continued to defend themselves, confident of divine protection.

It must be admitted that the Ecclesiologists were in a difficult position, because the *Constitutions and Canons Ecclesiastical* of 1604 gave little or no support for the novelties which they were trying to introduce into church furnishings. The more militant Protestants, like Mr. Close of Cheltenham, had only to refer to the Canons dealing with 'Things appertaining to Churches' to prove that the Cambridge Camden Society was doing its best to transform places of worship into something very different to that visualized by Parliament and Convocations in the first year of the reign of James I.

Every church and chapel had to be provided with copies of the Book of Common Prayer, a Bible of the largest size and the Book of Homilies 'allowed by authority.' A font of stone had to be 'set in the ancient usual places; in which only font the Minister shall baptize publicly.' A 'decent communion-table' was ordered; and 'covered in time of Divine Service with a carpet of silk or other decent stuff, thought meet by the Ordinary of the place, if any question be made of it, and with a fair linen cloth at the time of the Ministration, as becometh the Table, and to stand, saving when the said holy Communion is to be administered: at which time the same shall be placed in so good sort within the Church or Chancel, as thereby the Minister may be more conveniently heard of the Communicants in his Prayer and Ministration, and the Communicants also more conveniently, and in more number, may communicate with the said Minister.'

As to the mural decorations permitted in Anglican churches, all that the Canons and Constitutions mentioned were the Ten Commandments 'set up on the East end . . . where the people may best see and read the same, and other chosen sentences written on the walls . . . in places convenient.' A 'convenient seat' had to be made 'for the Minister to read service in'; and a 'comely and decent Pulpit' must be set 'in a convenient place' . . . 'and be there seemly kept for the preaching of God's Word.' The only other article of church furniture specified was a strong chest 'with a hole in the upper part thereof, having three keys . . . to the intent the Parishioners may put into it their alms for their poor neighbours.' Although Canon LXXXV laid down that the Churchwardens or 'Questmen' should take care that churches be well and sufficiently repaired; their windows glazed, their floors paved, plain and even, 'and that all things there in such an orderly and decent sort, without dust, or any thing that may be either noisome or unseemly, as best becometh the House of God,' nevertheless the Evangelical Anglicans had sufficient reason to maintain that the ideal aimed at by the Cambridge Camden Society was a menace to the Church of England, by law established under the Queen's Majesty— 'a true and Apostolical Church, teaching and maintaining the doctrine of the Apostles' (Canon III). Moreover, if the Camdenians continued in their efforts to undermine the Rites and Ceremonies, established in the Church of England; then they deserved to be excommunicated *ipso facto,* as was laid down in Canon VI.

Undeterred by such threats, the Camdenians informed the clergy and laity that it was most improper to erect niches, 'or any permanent construction *behind the Altar,* to receive the tablets' on which (in accordance with Canon 82) the Ten Commandments must be inscribed. In fact, they were inclined to think that this post-Reformation Canon had 'lost its meaning.' They pointed out that if the Ten Commandments were displayed on the east wall of the chancel as ordered, the laity in the nave would still be unable to read them, even if painted in large plain Roman type.

In March 1844 the reviewer in *The Ecclesiologist* had much to say about Miss Lambert's recently published book, entitled *Church Needlework.* 'We entirely object to flowing Altar cloths, and prefer a framed frontal, or at least a tightly stretched antependium.' He denounced the custom of the clergyman standing at the north end of the altar when celebrating the communion service, and said that, in order to be correct, he should read the epistle and gospel close to the rood screen. Every church ought to have a chest for frontals and vestments, ornamented with emblematic devices. The sacred vessels should be kept in 'an aumbrye with an iron clamped door or padlock.' [20]

We find more directions on church needlework and altar hangings in the May 1845 issue of the magazine. The author writes: 'a few years ago the only covering [for the altar] ever thought of was a large pall of baize or velvet, which hung down over the sides like a table cloth. But lately there have been many examples of more becoming ornament, though no fixed rule has been followed. In some cases the panelled front of the altar has been left exposed, which we must regard as quite wrong. In other cases a frontal stretched on a frame, or an antependium suspended over the face of the altar (if we may so distinguish these two words) gave occasion, by their presenting a plain surface, for what was less suitable to a loose hanging, namely a considerable display of embroidered ornament. The antependium (we may remark) seems to be the most fitting where the altar is in the form of a table.' [21]

[20] ibid., Vol. III, p. 44.   [21] p. 99.

In the 'forties of the last century there seems to have been a great difficulty in procuring appropriate patterns, for want of precedents, even if Mr. Pugin appeared to 'have invented for himself the kind of design which is to be seen in most of his published views of altars; as for example, in Nos. XX and XXIII of the *Dublin Review* (1841–2) and the patterns given in his *Glossary of Ecclesiastical Ornament.*' The first edition of this sumptuously illustrated book appeared in 1844. Nevertheless it was dangerous to follow Mr. Pugin too closely, because the ornaments he showed were intended for the worship of the Church of Rome, and not altogether suitable for imitation in 'the English branch of the Church.' In fact, the writer strongly disapproved of some of Mr. Pugin's designs for frontals. He referred to one design in particular which showed 'a large cross dividing the frontal into four parts, with an *Agnus Dei* at the intersection, and the four Evangelist symbols,' commenting: 'now we do not remember to have seen a frontal of this sort in actual use in any diocese of Europe, or in any ancient drawing or illuminations. Unfortunately, in our own communion, this example has been very generally followed.'

There were many problems connected with the decent vesting of the altar which needed to be solved. The writer went on to say, 'we conclude then that we ought to have hangings for the front and sides of our altars, either framed as frontals, or unframed as antependia; and that the top should be covered with a pall overhanging the three sides. We do not suppose it would be wrong either to attach, by lacings or otherwise, all these four hangings together so as to form a kind of case; or to keep them separate, fastening them as may be found most convenient. These questions need more deliberation. The latter plan seems the best; especially since only the colour of the frontal needs change, not necessarily that of the superfrontal.'

The High Church clergymen, also their wives and daughters, had more than enough to discuss when they were considering the improvement of the furnishings of places of worship more than a century ago. Indeed, there was an urgent need to beautify churches, because, as Mr. W. Percival Ward, the rector of Compton Valence, Dorset, pointed out to Dr. Pusey in February 1840, 'the simple truth, from which we cannot escape, is that thousands of souls, the care of the Church of England, are, year by year, allowed to perish, because we dare not make ventures beyond our old and, for these times, inefficient machinery. Surely at such a time everything but principle is to be risked?' [22]

The ladies in many a country parsonage, so Dr. Pusey had made clear to Dr. Hook, the Vicar of Leeds, as early as 1839, badly needed 'a holy employment' in their spare time. It was essential to direct their zeal, 'which will otherwise go off in some irregular way, or go over to Rome.' Not every young lady would be able to find an outlet for her zeal by joining a Sisterhood—if such bodies could be established in communion with Canterbury, when the time was ripe. What could be done for the moment? As Dr. Pusey pointed out, the Romanists were

[22] H. P. Liddon, *Life of Edward Bouverie Pusey* (1894), Vol. III, pp. 5, 6.

making great use of the appeal of their Sisterhoods to entice innocent Anglican gentlewomen. He feared that the Church of England might lose those whom it could least spare, above all those who 'are calculated to draw a blessing on the Church in which they are found, as the Fathers always speak of the virgins.' [23]

No holier employment could be found for the early Victorian virgins than the making of altar frontals and church embroidery. The practical advice given in *The Ecclesiologist* was all that they needed. The rectory ladies devoured the magazine published by the Cambridge Camden Society as a sort of early Victorian ecclesiastical equivalent of *Vogue*. Sometimes the latest fashions seemed almost too daring for a rural parish church.

Just as to-day, so in the 'forties of the last century, there were very strong views for and against what were styled 'super-altars,' i.e. gradines. *The Ecclesiologist* maintained that a super altar, otherwise a raised step at the back of the holy table or in the reredos, was 'desirable to hold the candlesticks.' This Tractarian Congregation of Rites also laid down that 'the super-altar may have a hanging.' [24] Letters asking advice must have been received by the editors, because once again they insisted that 'no richness of ornament on the face of the altar itself can justify the omission of a frontal.' They took the line that 'stoles' ought to hang down on every frontal to make it in accordance with 'strict propriety,' since they always 'occur in what has always seemed to us the model altar, i.e. as depicted in Van Eyck's sublime picture of the Adoration of the Lamb.'

Mr. Beresford Hope, who has been described as 'the Nestor of Ecclesiology,' had developed very ambitious ideas by 1845. He wrote to Mr. Benjamin Webb that new Anglican churches 'must have a foreign character, lofty and apsidal, and domineer by their elevations over the haughty and Protestantized shopocracy of their respective towns.' He felt that they ought to 'have a boundless area of nave to hold as many as possible of the adjacent all but heathen population. The windows should be lofty and space be afforded for mural painting, window tracery and painted glass being also developed to perfection. . . . The sermons would, of course, be preached from the rood-loft, which feature such a kind of church would be the most likely to reproduce. The stalls would rise loftily in two or three rows unless there were returns, when there would be only one row. . . . Towers and spires should be used wherever possible, but a lofty apsidal chancel, itself a quasi-church, domineers over the neighbouring buildings as a square-ended church with a low chancel never can.' [25] It is fairly obvious that these dream-churches and their furnishings were inspired by Pugin's writings and drawings. The mental picture of the congregation craning their necks at the preacher perched up in the rood loft, is in itself enough to prove the impractical mentality of this rich Anglican layman on whom the impact of the Ecclesiological Movement had proved too much.

[23] ibid., Vol. III, p. 6.
[24] *The Ecclesiologist*, 1845, p. 102.
[25] *Book of the Beresford Hopes*, p. 161.

Throughout the year 1846 *The Ecclesiologist* continued to deplore the absence of rood-screens in new churches, and to criticize their 'ritual arrangements.' Restorations of churches were going on everywhere; some good, but mostly bad. Altar-chairs were still being inserted instead of medieval sedilia. Despite the frequent denunciations of galleries, new ones were being erected.

High praise was given to the new stone altar at Bussage in Gloucestershire, resting on six legs. In this same church, designed by J. P. Harrison, and later on enlarged by G. F. Bodley, there were returned choir stalls, an 'oak lettern,' encaustic tiles 'of very good pattern,' and the window sill serving as a sedilia.

The ecclesiologists seem to have been puzzled over T. H. Wyatt's new church at Wilton, near Salisbury, above all by its 'ritual arrangements.' We are told that the seats for the clergy had been ranged round the apse 'according to Byzantine use,' and that this was 'an attempt to accommodate Basilican forms to English ritual.' The whole thing disturbed the arbiters of ecclesiastical fashions, and cut across their path. They disapproved of the 'cancelli' being reduced to the functions of altar rails, but had to admire the richly decorated mosaic pulpit, also the wooden gilt eagle from which the lessons were read, and the prayer desk at the foot of the chancel steps. In fact, the whole church produced a 'grand dazzling effect.' [26]
Nothing like this church had ever been seen in England, and the furnishings were a great novelty in the eighteen-forties. Most of the marbles and Cosmati mosaic work had been brought from Italy by the Dowager Countess of Pembroke. Dr. Denison, the Bishop of Salisbury, felt he must interfere, and forbade all this rich decoration on the communion table, so fragments were incorporated into the pulpit.

Equally astonishing things had been done at Kilndown in Kent, where the wealthy Mr. Beresford Hope spent vast sums on the re-furnishing of his parish church between 1840 and 1845. Mr. Salvin designed a stone altar, copied from the altar-tomb of William of Wykeham in Winchester Cathedral. Mr. Carpenter supplied a chancel-screen and a stone pulpit, the latter copied from that of the refectory at Beaulieu Abbey, Hampshire. Mr. Butterfield ensured that the design of the brass lectern and two coronas was correct from the ecclesiological point of view. The walls of the chancel were decorated with polychrome paintings by Messrs. Roos and Williment. Most of the lancet windows were filled with extremely colourful glass from Munich. Except for some of the mural decorations, the interior of this church still retains its Tractarian character.

When Mr. W. C. Yonge, the squire of Otterbourne, near Winchester, refurnished S. Matthew's in 1841, people said that everything was 'most elaborate,' but it is doubtful if the Tractarian altar and pulpit were really startling.

Terrible 'indecencies,' however, had been noticed in Liverpool. In one church the incumbent had moved the organ from the west to the east end, and placed it, along with the singers, in a gallery beneath the east window. Under the gallery was a vestry. The result was that the altar had been placed in front of this pulpit

[26] New Series, III, p. 171.

pile; the font ranged in close proximity to it, so as with the pulpit, reading desk and clerk's desk, to form one group approached by a sort of avenue from the vestry. 'Other indecencies' found in Liverpool included an altar and font in front of a pulpit, with an organ standing over the altar. In another church the ecclesiological investigators were horrified to find that the pulpit had been moved to the west end, and that the congregation sat with their back to the altar. Even worse—at S. Peter's, the parish church—on the occasion of the anniversary of the National School Board, a gallery had been erected over the holy table.

It was reported that the churches of the Roman Communion in this same city were far more correctly furnished. High praise was given to the three designed by Mr. Pugin and one by Mr. Hansom. The writer of the article said: 'Great is the mortification in this thriving town, which he, who desires to see his own beloved Communion clothed in the beauty of holiness, has to undergo.' Even the Irvingite 'meeting house' was better than most Anglican churches. Here the altar at the chord of the apse was furnished with a tabernacle and candlesticks, and daily worship was maintained.[27]

Still, there were signs of a revival of good taste. At S. Martin's the choir extended into the nave, and was fenced with parclose screens. The service was intoned from the western stall, the rest of the choir being filled with surpliced choristers. Moreover there were nice encaustic tiles, even a cross and candlesticks on the 'considerably elevated altar.'

A new crusade began to be preached in 1847—a holy war against whitewash— the old enemy which had to be attacked and defeated. In the February number of *The Ecclesiologist* a suggestion was made: 'If several parishes were everywhere to combine together towards purchasing sufficient Manchester card for their joint use, all the churches of England might in an incredibly short space of time be rid of the noxious intruder, at an expense which would be almost nominal, and with the advantages of employing during the process the idle lads of the village, without expecting very enormous wages, and we trust also, many an industrious poor man, who might be pining for want of work.' [28]

Very strongly commended was a new book by H. L. Jenner of S. Columb, Corn-wall, entitled *Of Flowers as employed in the Adornment of Churches*. It contained a complete list of flowers for all festivals of the Book of Common Prayer kalendar, which had the liturgically correct colours.

Here are two feasts which show how this useful book was compiled. Nothing of the kind can be procured to-day.

March 25. Lady Day. WHITE.

Flowers—Black Thorn, White Arabis, Camellia, Primula, Sinensis, Hyacinth, White Violets, White Azalea.

[27] Cf. ibid., pp. 201–2.
[28] p. 41.

June 29. S. Peter. RED.
Flowers—Roses, Poppies, Scarlet Lychnis, Geranium, Verbena, Kalma, Potentilla, Mallow, Red Valerian, Antirrhinum, Salvia, Heath, Phlox Drummondi.

Ecclesiastical horticulture of this kind would provide more than enough work for rectory and vicarage gardeners. The suggestion was made that 'flowers of the proper colours might be forced *on purpose* at almost any time in the hothouses of a rich parishioner.' [29]

Altogether the fashions in church furnishings were improving. At Lavington in Sussex, ever since 1833, the young rector, Mr. Henry Edward Manning, vested in a linen surplice had rung the bell himself for daily Mattins and Evensong. By 1840 he had been appointed Archdeacon of Chichester, and had shown great zeal in encouraging the incumbents of the one hundred and thirty parishes in his archdeaconry to restore and beautify their churches. He was greatly distressed in May 1846 when his sister-in-law, Sophie Ryder, her husband George and their family followed John Henry Newman and others on the road to Rome. Although the Archdeacon wrote in his private journal, 'Though not Roman, I cease to be Anglican,' he decided to call in Mr. Harrison to restore and refurnish the little church at Lavington. *The Ecclesiologist* praised the work, above all the rood-screen, copied from the one at Old Shoreham, the returned stalls with rich misericordes, the encaustic tiles in the chancel, the two steps to the 'sacrarium'; and above all 'the altar dressed with a super-altar and candlesticks.' Granted that there were a few 'trifling blemishes,' yet 'the general aspect is truly Catholic.' [30] But the poor Archdeacon himself was all the time being drawn farther from the Church of England and finding himself nearer Rome, in spite of the 'truly Catholic aspect' of his restored church.

Across the Atlantic there were definite signs of better taste in the furnishings of the places of worship of the Protestant Episcopal Church, so it was reported in *The Ecclesiologist*. The Chapel of the Holy Innocents at S. Mary's Hall, Burlington, New Jersey, was 'the first instance, we imagine, of an *exclusively* female community sitting in choir found in the communion of Canterbury for the last three centuries.' The woodwork was painted to represent old oak. The windows were filled with stained glass. A richly bound Bible stood on the lectern. Mattins was said at 6 a.m., Vespers at 7.30 p.m., and there was 'a short voluntary service at noon,' attended by the mostly female members of these almshouses.

A 'Catholic idea of worship' was discovered at Holy Cross Church, Troy, New York. Here had been erected a 'goodly font of stone and an altar covered with a crimson velvet cloth, embellished with sacred monograms.' The altar piece was a painting of the Crucifixion. The psalms were chanted antiphonally.[31] S. Mark's, Philadelphia, was commended for its screen, six stalls on either side of the chancel,

[29] ibid., p. 102.
[30] ibid., p. 117.
[31] Vol. VIII, New Series V, p. 67.

the three sedilia, and the altar on a foot-pace. The Church of the Advent, Boston, was also noticed favourably.

For the next two years there is more than enough material in this magazine to enable us to form mental pictures of the furnishings in new churches erected in Britain, and those which had been restored. The ecclesiologists did not wholly approve of S. Saviour's, Leeds, built at the cost of Dr. Pusey, and designed by John Macduff Derick, which had been opened in 1845. Granted that the altar was properly vested, the oaken screen was dismissed as 'sadly too heavy.' The lantern beneath the central tower had been 'fitted up as a sort of *chorus,*' bcause of objections to holding the services within the ritual choir.[32]

Mr. Henry-Russell Hitchcock describes S. Saviour's as 'in some ways a primitive of the High Victorian—not in obvious ways, but in its more intense emotional conviction. Even Pugin had hardly achieved so churchy a church, and it is therefore not quite typical of the period in which it was begun.'[33] Dr. Pusey did not see eye to eye with the Camdenians in some respects. We are told that he did not attach much importance to images, pictures and tapestries, and insisted that the Ten Commandments must be affixed to the east wall of this exceptionally lofty cruciform church, which, as was remarked at the time of its opening, had 'something of the proportions of a foreign cathedral.'

It is interesting to compare this church in Leeds with Holy Trinity, Rusholme, Manchester, designed by Mr. Edmund Sharpe (1809–77) about 1845. To-day its furnishings as first installed seem almost evangelical, but in the eighteen-forties they were considered quite Puseyite. They included a seventeenth century communion table; a feature which met with the approval of the majority of the ecclesiologists at that date.

From time to time the ecclesiologists made scornful comments on the laxity of Roman Catholics in matters of ritual and ceremonial. Here is a typical pronouncement in 1848: 'We have insisted upon the universality of the triple division of all Catholic churches, and upon the symbolical meaning and practical use of the sacrarium, chancel and nave, till we apprehend we have wearied our readers as much as we have ourselves.' The writer was really shocked that so many Romanist clergymen 'read Vespers' in the sedilia. To his way of thinking it was as 'incorrect as reading it westward from a centrically placed pulpit.'[34]

It was encouraging to find that ecclesiological good taste was making such progress in Scotland. At Drumlithie, Kincardineshire, a new Episcopal church had been built. Both the architect, Mr. Charles Brand, and the rector, Mr. Thom, deserved commendation for the rood screen of wrought iron, painted and gilt; the two sedilia, the stone altar, and the correctly furnished chancel with a lectern in its centre.

[32] ibid., p. 130.
[33] *Early Victorian Architecture in Britain* (1954), Vol. I, p. 122.
[34] ibid., p. 262.

E

S. Columba's, Edinburgh, which had been dedicated and opened for worship in 1848, was another proof that Tractarian ideals of worship were taking root in Scotland. Here Mr. John Henderson had inserted an oak rood screen with 'holy doors,' surmounted by 'a bold and handsome cross.' The stone altar was richly vested and adorned with candlesticks made at the direction of the late Society, so they were absolutely correct. But it was a pity that the reading desk had been placed outside the chancel. In this unassuming little Gothic church near the Castle there were daily morning and evening services—something quite unique in Edinburgh at that date. Moreover there was a weekly celebration of the Holy Eucharist, at which the rector, Dr. Alexander, used the Scottish Liturgy. Mr. John Henderson had designed another Episcopalian church—S. Mary's, Hamilton—where everything was correct according to Camdenian standards. Here could be found a stone altar, decorated with sacred emblems, not to mention a sedilia and piscina.

'Spreading altar cloths'—which have become so fashionable in recent years in

ALTAR CLOTH (from *Practical Remarks on Minor Accessories of the Church* by Gilbert J. French, 1844)

certain Anglican circles—were often denounced by *The Ecclesiologist*. Examples of them were discovered at S. John's Hackney, and in the chapel of Radley College —both in 1848. The writer said: 'There is no authority for this. It confuses the idea of an altar, which should be one of severity and dignity; and at the Holy Communion, we should think it must be productive of inconvenience.' [35]

Encaustic tiles were looked upon as an essential feature of a correctly furnished church. Various firms made them—Chamberlain's of Worcester, Minton's of Stafford, and Gambling's of Chichester. Mr. Minton's were said to be the best. They could be supplied in black, red, white, flowered and patterned. Detailed directions were given for their use.[36]

Ever since the foundation stone of S. George's Roman Catholic Chapel in Southwark had been laid on September 8th, 1840, the members of the Cambridge Camden Society had been keeping an eye on what, so they heard, was going to be Mr. Pugin's masterpiece. By the autumn of 1848 the moment had arrived to say something about this large church in *The Ecclesiologist*. The first things that were

[35] ibid., Vol. IX, New Series VI, p. 60.
[36] ibid., October 1848, p. 81.

noticed were the 'ingenious confessionals'—placed between buttresses, and approached by doors in the aisles. These confessionals were compared with those in Mr. Scoles' Jesuit chapel in Farm Street, which were 'absolute rooms containing fireplaces.' High praise was given to the double stone rood-screen and rood-loft, reached by a turret stair, with the rood painted and gilt. There was little wrong with the brass eagle lectern. The richly carved high altar was commended, but the tower-like tabernacle in its midst created a 'confusion of ideas.' 'When a tabernacle stands on an altar,' said the writer, 'great care should be taken not to render it so large as to crush the altar itself. The high altar there looks absolutely as if it were the base of this huge superstructure. Moreover the tabernacle encroaches very much upon the area of the mensa in the central part. The super-altars stretch beyond the ends of the altar in a very unsightly manner.' [37] Reference was made to the encaustic tiles used for the pavements, the two *coronae lucis,* and the two large brass standard candlesticks of many lights. The writer approved of the diapered painted decorations in the side chapels and on their screens.

With but few exceptions, the ecclesiologists were favourably impressed by most of the churches erected by their Roman brethren during the 'forties. They seemed bitterly to regret that Mr. Pugin had ceased to be in communion with Canterbury. Mr. Hadfield's church at Salford, begun in 1844, was mentioned in their magazine. The chantries, altar-tombs and rich furnishings, above all the brass lectern and the *corona lucis,* were singled out for praise.

Then there was Mr. J. J. Scoles' church of S. Francis Xavier, Liverpool, which had been begun in 1844. The nave columns were made of iron instead of stone, and the chancel was too shallow, but altars and pulpit, designed by young Mr. Nicholl, were very richly decorated with Gothic carving. Mr. Hadfield's church of S. Marie, Sheffield, not yet completed, had altars of very striking Gothic design, and so did his new church at Burnley in Lancashire.

The ecclesiologists envied their Roman brethren, who were not faced with anything like the same difficulties. As Sir Charles Eastlake puts it: 'A tamely-carved reredos, generally arranged in panels to hold the Commandments, a group of sedilia and a piscina, with perhaps a few empty niches in the clerestory, were, as a rule, all the internal features which distinguished an Anglican church from a meeting house. The sumptuously sculptured dossels, the marble altars inlaid with mosaic, the elaborate rood-screens and decorative painting, which private munificence has since provided for many of our national churches, with the approval of the clergy and to the delight of many a devout congregation, were then rare, and would, in nine cases out of ten, have created a scandal, even among the supporters of the Revival. But no scruples on this score prevented the introduction of such features in the Roman Church, where the worst innovation that could be feared was an exchange of good taste for bad. The ritual of Rome had always aimed at effect, though her priests might be robed in copes of miserable design. Her altars were meant to be attractive, though they were decked with tawdry artificial flowers. Her shrines and niches were never empty, though they were often

[37] ibid., p. 155.

filled with imagery from the toy-shop. Pugin had raised his voice long and loudly against these artistic heresies, and in course of time his denunciations had had their effect. . . .' [38]

The Cambridge Camden Society hardly knew how and where to carry on its crusade for the improvement in ecclesiastical fashions. Once again the most 'un-Catholick' furnishings of churches in the Channel Islands were brought to the notice of readers of *The Ecclesiologist* in its issue of August 1849. At S. Laurence's, Jersey, the so-called altar was a long narrow board, placed on a raised platform at the west end of the aisle. The church at S. Helier had no communion table at all. An 'oyster board' was kept in the porch, and only brought in on the rare 'Communion Sundays.' The writer said: 'When I saw it, turned upside down, dusters and brooms were lying on it.'

Neither at S. Ouen's nor at S. Mary's was there any sign of a permanent altar—merely rough tables, stored away in odd corners. Common wooden tables, with no coverings, served as altars at S. Mary's and S. Brelade's. In some of the churches on the Isle of Jersey the pews were arranged on inclined planes—east, west, north and south. Many had earthen floors and galleries.[39] What was the Bishop of Winchester doing to allow the continuance of the lack of ordinary decencies of worship in the insular parts of his diocese? The state of the churches in Jersey must create a very bad impression on Catholics coming over from France. England, however, was little better. At All Saints', Poplar, the altar served as a cupboard for parish registers. At S. George's, Ramsgate, the communion table was made of jointed deal, panelled to look like stone.

Reports received from North America indicated that the ecclesiological movement was making progress. Mr. Upjohn had designed Trinity Church in New York in the best Gothic style. Its sanctuary was paved with coloured marble, and contained an altar of panelled oak, backed by an elaborate oak reredos, the panels of which were painted with the Lord's Prayer, the Creed and the Ten Commandments. The 'Catholick' appearance of this Episcopalian church was stressed by the credence table. Unfortunately there was no sedilia, and the font lacked a drain.[40]

During the 'fifties many so-called 'Puseyite' churches were erected, and their furnishings, then regarded as dangerous novelties, attracted much attention, sometimes ending up with riots.

The most notorious of all was S. Barnabas', Pimlico, consecrated on June 18th, 1850. It was a simple little church, designed by Thomas Cundy, Jnr., in the First Pointed or Early English style, this, so he maintained, being best suited for a poor man's church. *The Ecclesiologist* took exception to his point of view, and asked: 'Why is the poor man's church to be of the plainest style? We should have taken the opposite tone, and argued that, of all men he, whose own dwelling is mean

[38] *A History of the Gothic Revival* (1872), pp. 244–5.
[39] p. 177ff.
[40] ibid., p. 194.

and poor, has the greatest claim to richness and magnificence in the temple of the LORD. The wealthy and luxurious can better afford to leave their carpets and arm-chairs for a few hours in a plain church, than the inmate of a garret who has such scanty opportunity of drinking in the beauties of external art.'

In the June 1850 issue of the magazine the furnishings of S. Barnabas' were described in detail, conveying the impression that they were rich enough even if their setting was simple. There was a lofty wooden rood-screen of four bays, picked out with colour and surmounted by a plain foliated cross. The choir stalls were not 'returned' which would have been more correct, but they had solid desk fronts and 'miserere seats' which folded back with a hinge in the middle.

Both the chancel and the sanctuary were paved with rich encaustic tiles. A grace-ful brass *corona lucis,* designed by Mr. Hardman was suspended over the choir. The sanctuary was raised on three steps. The front of the altar was composed of three pointed arches. On the low super-altar stood two silver candlesticks and a cross. The three graded sedilia were highly commended, so too the piscina and the credence; likewise the simple reredos of nine trefoiled arches with Purbeck marble shafts. The walls of the chancel were 'brilliant with diaper work,' creating 'richness and a religious effect.' The pipes of the powerful organ were also diapered. Over the chancel arch Mr. Bulmer had painted a full length figure of our Lord. 'Legends' in Latin were painted round the nave arches—one wonders how many of the poor for whom the church was intended could translate these texts? Mr. Potter's brass eagle lectern was regarded as a real work of art and the delicate colours of Mr. Wailes' stained glass were singled out for praise, likewise the small litany desk and the font of Purbeck marble. The sexes were separated. The men occupied the north side of the church, and the women the south. The oak benches were described as 'peculiarly felicitous, having flat boards of wood midway between them, so placed that the descending knee comes true to (the boards).' Finally, there were the striking brass gas standards placed in the centre of each bay. Mattins and Evensong were sung daily. There was also the great novelty of a daily celebration of the Holy Communion.[41] It was the rich, however, rather than the poor, who found their way to this church in the slums of Pimlico during the 'fifties. The new fashions in furnishings made a strong appeal to some of the younger aristocracy in Belgravia. At S. Barnabas' they felt they were in a spiritual world evocative of Mr. Tennyson. It was all very romantic, and to attend this church involved defying conventions. There was something rather naughty about S. Barnabas'. But how dull the services and the furnishings would seem to Anglo-Catholics to-day. No vestments other than the surplice and stole were worn at first. Many years elapsed before the interior became misty with incense at High Mass or Solemn Evensong. There was more dignified austerity than sensuous glamour about the services in the early days.

Another London church whose furnishings attracted attention in the early 'fifties was S. Stephen's, Rochester Row, Westminster. The architect was Benjamin

[41] ibid., pp. 110–15.

S. BARNABAS', PIMLICO (1850)
'The most complete and, with completeness, the most sumptuous church
which had been dedicated to the use of the Anglican Communion since
the Reformation' (T. Francis Bumpus, *London Churches Ancient &
Modern,* p. 185)

Ferrey, and the total cost was defrayed by Miss Burdett Coutts, who as the Camden
Society remarked, was not previously known to have 'given her adhesion to the
principles of archeology.' The style of this church was English Decorated Gothic.
The June 1850 issue of *The Ecclesiologist* devoted several pages to the furnishings.
The reredos was painted in diaper work. The three sedilia were lined with dark
red velvet embroidered with yellow silk, so it must have been no great penance
to the clergy to sit in them. The rich sanctuary carpet was adorned with patterns

70

of Berlin wool. The brass rails though elegant were merely a substitute for a rood-screen. The encaustic tiles were 'pretty,' but the choir stalls, painted blue and gilt, were dismissed as 'unsubstantial.' Mr. Potter had designed a corona for this church, similar to the one at S. Barnabas', Pimlico. It was illumined by both gas and candles. The oak 'lettern' was 'small and feeble.' More praiseworthy was the chancel roof, powdered with gold stars on blue. The Ten Commandments were painted on either side of the east window. Most of the stained glass was the work of Mr. Wailes and Mr. Powell. Above the chancel arch were some very ornate painted decorations by Mr. Hudson. The fanciful brass gas standards on either side of the nave must have helped to create a cheerful effect when they were lit. The tone of the services at S. Stephen's was much lower than those at S. Barnabas', even though daily Mattins and Evensong were provided. The writer had to confess that it was 'a great and real disappointment' that the Holy Communion had not been administered on the day of the consecration.[42]

Another church which began to set the tone in ecclesiastical fashions about 1850 was S. Mary's, Crown Street, hidden away in the slums of Seven Dials. Built in the eighteenth century as a place of worship for the small Greek Orthodox community in London, the interior had been refurnished and decorated by Mr. Hardwick. The devotional atmosphere attracted many well-known people whom their friends termed 'Puseyites.' Among them were young Mr. Gladstone and Lady Herbert of Lea. They found at S. Mary's a correctly vested altar, a credence table and two sedilia. Behind and above the altar was a red velvet dossal, with a large cross of yellow silk in the centre. The walls of the chancel were hung with a rich red fabric. The font was simple and graceful. The roof, as in most 'correct' churches of that period, was adorned with gold and colour. Although the daily services took place at the 'unfashionably practical hours of 6.15 a.m. and 8.30 p.m.,' the open seats were thronged by the poor, as well as by a few of the aristocracy from Mayfair and distant Belgravia. The Holy Communion was celebrated only on Sundays.

As we turn the pages of *The Ecclesiologist* we find more and more new churches or restored ones; most of them furnished with choir stalls, screens, encaustic tiles, sedilia, credence tables and richly decorated sanctuaries. In some of them there was a correctly vested altar, invariably a super-altar, and occasionally a cross and candle-sticks.

Anglicans as a whole had been afraid to employ Pugin because he was a Roman Catholic. Tubey, Berkshire, appears to be the only new church he designed, but he was often invited to advise on restorations or furnishings. 'But Anglicans could now console themselves with the belief that designs could be obtained from such young men as Benjamin Ferrey or Gilbert Scott that would equal in correctness those of their revered but Romish master; very soon sophisticated Camdenians began to feel that from Carpenter and Butterfield they were getting an even better brand of Gothic.'[43] The ecclesiologists held very strong opinions that the builders

[42] ibid., p. 115.   [43] Hitchcock, op. cit., Vol. I, p. 130.

of churches planned for Anglo-Catholic modes of worship must be communicant members of the Church of England; in fact 'only architects who were good churchmen should build Anglican churches at all.' [44]

A comprehensive idea of the church furnishings in at least one English diocese a hundred years ago is to be found in the notes on the churches in the Archdeaconry of Lincoln by H. K. Bonney, who was appointed archdeacon in 1845. [45]

In several churches there were no fonts; elsewhere they were not in 'the ancient usual place' as ordered in Canon 81. This energetic archdeacon visited 526 churches; in eleven of them the altar was not covered 'with a carpet of silk or other decent stuff' as directed in Canon 82. Many varieties of colours were noted. Bonney saw sixty-eight crimson, sixty-seven blue, sixty-seven green, seventeen red, twelve purple, ten scarlet, also velvet, drab, puce, maroon, brown and black. In several churches baize was the covering. Some of the frontals were dirty or moth-eaten. In one church the holy table was covered with oilcloth; but in another with a Persian carpet. Three of the communion tables had drawers in them: another had a shelf for books. At Kirmington the organ was over the altar. At Kirkby Green it was movable and set at the north-east corner of the nave; the east end of the chancel being occupied by charity seats. Eight altars mentioned were of stone. Three wooden ones were on brackets. The archdeacon took care to mention that a new stone altar at Gedney had been erected 'with no superstitious intentions.' At Waddington the Tenth, Eleventh, Twelfth and Thirteenth Articles of Religion formed part of the decorations on the ledges of the communion table. It is significant that he never uses the word 'altar'; although he sometimes refers to the decorations at the east end of the church as the 'altar-piece.'

He had a great eye for colour and noted the hues of cushions and hangings. He saw pulpit hangings seventy-seven crimson, twenty purple, thirty-eight blue, fifteen red, seven green, two puce, eleven scarlet, one drab, one pink, one white, one maroon, two black, one velvet and four were said to be faded. A good number of the Lincolnshire churches had funeral palls, but none of them candlesticks or altar crosses; at least, the observant archdeacon makes no reference to them.

If Archdeacon Bonney's inventory can be taken as typical of those in other counties of England at the same date, then it can be understood why the Warden of Sackville College, East Grinstead, felt that he must continue his crusade for the promotion of Christian Symbolism. In 1850, J. M. Neale read a paper in which he mentioned the names of innumerable medieval mystical writers who had dealt with this divine revelation, about which Anglican clergymen and layfolk appeared to be so ignorant. [46] But even the most ardent ecclesiologists had grown somewhat confused about what was meant by Christian Symbolism. They were certain that

[44] ibid., p. 130.
[45] *Bonney's Church Notes,* edited by N. S. Harding, Lincoln, 1937.
[46] Mr. Basil F. L. Clarke gives a list of these writers in his *Church Builders of the Nineteenth Century* (p. 95). They are enough to show that Neale's knowledge of the Middle Ages was encyclopædic, even if superficial.

the only style which was 'correct' was Decorated Gothic, but unfortunately Durandus had never known it, and when he was alive churches were being built in the French version of the 'First Pointed' style, otherwise known as 'Early English.' So was this late thirteenth century Bishop of Mende a really safe guide to Christian Symbolism? It must be admitted that many of Neale's arguments are more original and entertaining than convincing. Moreover they were dangerous, since they resulted in the destruction of many interesting articles of church furnishing and decoration that had a real historic value, merely because the ancient specimens did not feature correct symbolism, for which reason something new had to be substituted.

It is often forgotten that the Cambridge ecclesiologists, under the leadership of John Mason Neale and Benjamin Webb, were not the only people who were trying to improve the furnishings of Anglican churches in the eighteen-forties, and to achieve a greater dignity of worship. Inspired by the same ideals, but looking back to the primitive rather than to medieval religion for inspiration, was another group of Tractarians, led by Dr. Theodore Farquhar Hook, the Vicar of Leeds, and Dr. John Jebb, the nephew of the Bishop of Limerick. This party had no use for rood-screens. Jebb maintained that 'in the constitution of her choirs the Church of England has made the nearest possible approach to the primitive and heavenly pattern. Her white-robed companies of men and boys, stationed at either side of her chancels, midway between the porch and the altar, stand daily ministering the service of praise and thanksgiving.' [47] What Dr. Jebb and Dr. Hook tried to revive was what they supposed was the plan and furnishing of the Early Christian basilica. However 'the validity of Jebb's argument depends on the assumption that the basilican arrangement is the only proper one for a Christian church, and that cathedral naves were built for congregations, which the blindness of the Middle Ages had prevented from taking much share in divine worship by the erection of solid screens between the choir and nave, an assumption which to a large extent is a misunderstanding of the intentions of the original builders of our cathedrals.' [48]

Sir George Gilbert Scott's replanning and refurnishing of English cathedrals (see pp. 144–60) owed much to what Dr. Jebb wrote about choirs, and what Dr. Hook put into practice in the parish church at Leeds, after it had been reopened in 1841. Here the ideal aimed at was rather a reversal to the early seventeenth century ritual and ceremonial of the Caroline divines, which stressed that 'different parts of the church were allotted to different services for both priest and people alike.' [49] In the replanned interior of Leeds Parish Church, and other churches of the same mildly Tractarian level, the prayers were read from a desk in the chancel, the lessons from a lectern, the litany from a litany-desk. The flowing white surplices of the choristers symbolized the sacred duty of the laymen to help

---

[47] *Three Lectures on the Cathedral Service of the Church of England* (Leeds, 1845), p. 109.
[48] Addleshaw and Etchells, op. cit., p. 214.
[49] ibid., p. 218.

the clergy in public worship. But not every Anglican bishop in the eighteen-forties approved of surpliced choirs in parish churches. Bishop Blomfield of London felt that a fully choral service prevented the laity from taking its lawful share in public worship. The internal arrangements of Leeds Parish Church, designed by R. D. Chantrell, are well worth studying, even if modified since 1841. Dr. Hook insisted on a wide step below the communion rail where the communicants could kneel from the Invitation onwards. The altar, covered by a crimson velvet loose frontal, given by the dowager Queen Adelaide, had a reredos with a painting ascribed to Corregio. On the altar were two crimson velvet cushions and two candlesticks.[50] Altogether the 1840s saw a great advance in the theorizing between Anglican church furnishing. Where Pugin had shown the way, others as talented if not so original, less idiosyncratic but equally hard-working, were preparing, in the wake of the Tractarian movement, to transform the face of ecclesiastical Britain.

WALL DEVICE (*Christmas Decoration of Churches*)

[50] Cf. R. W. Moore, *A History of the Parish Church of Leeds* (1877), pp. 24, 29–30, 53.

CHAPTER III

RICHARD CROMWELL CARPENTER

BORN in the same year as A. W. Pugin was Richard Cromwell Carpenter (1812–55), an architect who had a great influence on the furnishings of Anglican churches during his brief but busy life. He died three years after his Roman Catholic contemporary. After his death in 1855 an obituary article appeared in *The Ecclesiologist,* in which the writer stressed that Mr. Carpenter was not merely an architect. His acquaintance with symbolism and the *instrumenta* of worship was great, his eye for colour exquisite, 'We think he was superior even to Pugin—safer and more equable.' He took a keen interest in stained glass, and personally supervised the execution of windows in churches of his own building. He trained Mr. Clayton of the firm of Hardman and Co.

Carpenter's first church was S. Stephen's, Birmingham, erected in 1840. It was soon followed by S. Andrew's in the same city. Then came the restoration of numerous medieval churches, starting with Hatfield Broad Oak, Essex, in 1843. As his reputation increased, so did his work. It is not difficult to understand why Carpenter got on with the early Tractarian clergy of the eighteen-forties. As was pointed out in his obituary: 'he never seemed to dream of producing a sudden or startling effect, and yet his works all tell, and are all eminently original and varied, and peculiarly devoid of mannerism. His success lay in the perfect keeping of everything which he did—the harmony of parts and general unity of proportion running through the entire building. The entire mass is broad and manly, and every detail beautiful, as a single study, and thoroughly finished, but never frittered into inanity.' Carpenter was closely associated with the Cambridge Camden Society, and was friendly with A. W. Pugin, whose ideas he often borrowed and adapted to Anglican modes of worship.

It was not until 1846 that Carpenter got his first real opportunity to design a church based on sound ecclesiological principles. This came when the Revd. Arthur Douglas Wagner asked him to prepare plans for a new church, dedicated to S. Paul, which his father, the Vicar of Brighton, wanted to erect at his own expense. When it was opened two years later this church was regarded as the last word of medieval modernism. *The Ecclesiologist* devoted much space to a critical description of its unusual features. The painted diapered decorations on the walls of the chancel were highly praised, also the ceiling adorned with gold stars on a blue ground. The dark-stained oak rood screen was 'elegant' but the choir stalls were regrettably not 'returned.' The writer wondered why most of the pews had doors—'so low that one might step over them.' He dismissed the pulpit as 'sorry,' in spite of its rich carving. The 'very rich' brass lectern, with figures of the four evangelists, compensated for the pulpit. Painted glass was needed obviously to create a dim religious light.

A hundred years ago the interior of S. Paul's must have looked very cold and austere in comparison with its present-day feeling, which is one of intense richness and colour. It glows like a page of an illuminated medieval manuscript. The glass in the great east window, designed by A. W. Pugin and carried out by Hardman, was not inserted until after the death of the architect. Neither had young Mr. Burne-Jones been invited to paint a reredos for the altar. For some years after S. Paul's was opened, what *The Ecclesiologist* described as an 'offensive' dossal hung on the east wall between the altar and the base of the window. It was divided into four parts by a cross, of which the side arms were much longer than the vertical ones, and gave the effect of a frontal. The services in this Brighton church were regarded as dangerously 'advanced,' and obtained much notoriety. But even as late as 1867 Mr. Wagner dared not burn incense, and at the request of the Bishop of Chichester he soon gave up wearing vestments. Sudden and startling effects were too risky in the eighteen-fifties. The more curious residents and visitors to Brighton; the gentlemen in frock coats and top hats; the ladies in crinolines, mantles, muffs and coal-scuttle bonnets who attended the new church in West Street, found plenty enough that was unlike anything they had ever seen in an Anglican place of worship, without Mr. Wagner scandalizing them more than was necessary in the effort to ensure correctness.

Shortly after S. Paul's, Brighton, had been opened, Carpenter was asked to design a new church in Munster Square, St. Pancras. The Revd. Edward Stuart, a clergyman of strong Tractarian views, wanted this church to be 'as nearly perfection as the handicraft of man, the skill of architects and the experience and ingenuity of ecclesiastical art could make it.' The dedication chosen was S. Mary Magdalene. The building as a whole is reminiscent of Carpenter's church of S. Peter the Great at Chichester, and is based on fourteenth century English Gothic.

Most of the furnishings and decorations within S. Mary Magdalene's, Munster Square, which are so admired by present day visitors, were inserted after the death of the architect, including the superb stained glass by Hardman in the seven-light east window with its flowing tracery. He never lived to see his church dim, dark and mysterious, fragrant with the faint odour of incense; the sense of mystery being increased by the rood-beam and the many hanging lamps. When the church was consecrated on April 19th, 1852, the fittings were correct according to Camdenian standards, but there was nothing particularly original about them. The nave was divided from the chancel by a low stone screen. The altar, raised on three steps above the chancel, was vested with a frontal and super-frontal, but it displayed no candlesticks. Above the altar, up to the level of the richly carved, painted and

S. MARY MAGDALENE, MUNSTER SQUARE (R. C. Carpenter, 1851)
'A church as nearly perfection as the handicraft of man, the skill of
architects, and the experience and ingenuity of ecclesiastical art could
make it' (Revd. Edward Stuart)

gilded cornice which ran along the whole of the east wall at the level of the
bottom of the window, was a dossal, with a large plain cross in its midst. On either
side of the altar were two panels of Decorated Gothic style, filled with diapered
painting. A credence, piscina and canopied sedilia took up the whole length of the
wall on the south side of the sanctuary. The pulpit was adorned with a fringed
'fall.' A massive wooden desk was provided for the chanting of the Litany. The
Gothic gas standards were of novel design, the upper part of foliated brass, resting

on clustered stone columns. There was more rich diaper work on the ceiling of the chancel.

The services at S. Mary Magdalene's in the eighteen-fifties were regarded as extremely advanced. There were processions of choristers in white surplices—even a midnight celebration of the Holy Communion at Christmas, which was a great novelty. By 1859 Mr. Stuart ventured to burn incense in procession on Easter Day. It is usually said that this was the first Anglican church in London in which eucharistic vestments were adopted, the date being Easter 1864.

At S. Nicholas, Kemerton, Gloucestershire, Carpenter had a free hand in the furnishings and decorations of the chancel shortly before his death. Mr. Goodhart-Rendel has described this church 'the Tractarian paragon,' and with good reason. There are ultra-medieval choir stalls; the returned ones being adorned with poppy-heads. Around the windows are diapered decorations. The whole of the east wall, surrounding the five-light window, is covered with painted figures of saints, legends in Gothic lettering, and most intricate patterns, obviously inspired by Pugin's *Glossary*. The altar is raised on three steps; vested with a richly embroidered frontal and super-frontal. Two brass candlesticks of Puginesque style stand on a low super-altar, but there is no cross. The credence table is coloured and gilt. A typical Hardman brass *corona lucis,* fitted for candles, is suspended on a chain from the riotously decorated panelled ceiling. Judging from a contemporary engraving, this church must have been almost unique when it was opened.[1]

Several of Carpenter's designs got no further than paper, including a wonderful church for Burntisland in Scotland and cathedrals for Kingston, Jamaica, and Colombo, Ceylon. The furnishings in the chapel of S. John's College, Hurstpierpoint, Sussex, were designed after his death by his pupil and assistant, William Slater (1819–72). The stately chapel at Lancing College, begun in 1868, was designed by his son, R. H. Carpenter (1841–93), but it was not opened until 1911, so the furnishings are of a later generation, by Temple Moore, W. E. Tower and Sir Ninian Comper.

---

[1] See illustration on p. 98, *English Architecture since the Regency* (1953).

CHAPTER IV

THE GREAT EXHIBITION, 1851

'GOTHIC'
MODERATOR
LAMP
From Catalogue
of International
Exhibition, 1862

I T was on May 1st, 1851, about the same time as the publication of Pugin's *Treatise on Chancel Screens,* that Queen Victoria opened the Great Exhibition in Hyde Park, and the Prince Albert was able to see that his anxious desire had been fulfilled: 'to promote among nations the cultivation of all those arts which are fostered by peace, and which in their turn contribute to maintain the peace of the world.' More than 25,000 persons assembled in Paxton's vast glass-house for this solemn occasion. The elegant proportions of the building were enhanced by the richness and tastefulness of the costumes worn by the well-dressed ladies and gentlemen. The Archbishop of Canterbury invoked the blessing of the Almighty on the undertaking, and the ceremony concluded with the performance of the 'Hallelujah Chorus' by a massed choir, and a solemn procession of the royal and foreign commissioners, Her Majesty's ministers, the whole of the lords and ladies of the court in waiting, and the foreign ambassadors. Every one was impressed by the rich variety of hues which burst upon the eye on all sides. The magnificent glass fountain, and the groups of sculpture and tropical plants and trees, that were intermixed throughout, flashed on the eye more like the fabled palace of Vathek than a structure reared in a few months by mortal hands. Everywhere were reflected the marvels of the age and the perfection of good taste as understood by Queen Victoria and her Consort.

In the Medieval Court visitors were able to study the quaint and beautiful works designed by Mr. Pugin and executed by Messrs. Hardman and Co. of Birmingham. Critics maintained that the Gothic chalices, candlesticks, flower-vases, cruets, croziers and monstrances fully realized the style and feeling of the best works of the Middle Ages. But not many people were eager to buy any of the Gothic cabinets, richly carved in oak, exhibited by Mr. Crace of London and Mr. Myers of Lambeth. The elegant prie-dieu, enriched with painting and gilding, may have been too Popish for insertion in even a Puseyite bedroom. Granted that Messrs. Hardman's bronze eagle lectern was a beautiful rendering of the best antique style in all its varied enrichments, it might have caused a revolution if presented to an Anglican place of worship at that date. Even at S. Barnabas', Pimlico, or at S. Paul's, Brighton, it would have been a risk to have hung up any of the brass sanctuary lamps; even more so to have adorned any Tractarian church with the canopied statue of the Virgin and Child, carved by Mr. Myers. This same

craftsman was responsible for the very beautiful font which formed the centre of the group of ecclesiastical objects in the Medieval Court. The font was of carved stone, and surmounted by a lofty pinnacled Gothic canopy of carved oak.

Some of the foreign exhibitors showed specimens of ecclesiastical art. Messrs. Poussielgue and Rusand had sent over from France many splendid chalices, chan-

deliers, lamps, monstrances and shrines. They proved that there was more external magnificence in the forms and ceremonies of continental Catholic worship than in that of the Established Church of England. By way of contrast was the solid and sober communion plate exhibited by Messrs. Elkington of Birmingham. Several of the ornate Gothic sideboards and cabinets shown by continental crafts-men would have looked far better if transformed into side-altars in Catholic churches than if given a place of honour in any typical Early Victorian mansion.

This early photograph of the chancel of S. Peter's, Bournemouth (G. E. Street, 1855–79), shows the passion for rich and overcrowded *décor* which marked the eighteen-seventies

5. The high altar at S. Michael's, Tenbury, Worcestershire, as designed by Henry Woodyer in 1856, is a characteristic example of his efforts to break away from conventional Gothic Revival

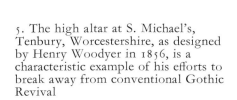

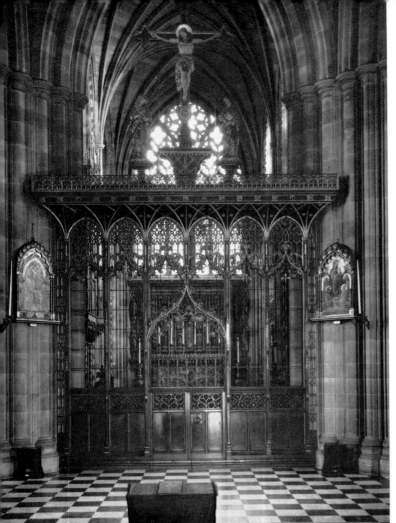

6. Nowhere in England can G. F. Bodley's furnishings and decorations be found in such rich profusion as in the church of the Holy Angels, Hoar Cross, Staffordshire (begun in 1872). The rood-screen would have delighted A. W. Pugin. The font cover is shown on plate 13

This same architect in his later years designed many reredoses like that above the high altar in S. Stephen's, Gloucester Road, Kensington (1901)

When compared with the wild exuberance of the debased baroque or Roccoco furniture, lamps, metal works, statuary, etc., which it is almost impossible to describe in words, the ecclesiastical exhibits at the Great Exhibition of 1851 could hardly hold their own, so most visitors ignored them and passed on.

When one turns over the 328 pages of the folio size *Art Journal Illustrated Catalogue* of the Great Exhibition, dedicated to His Royal Highness Prince Albert, it becomes clear that there can have been no period of history when the externals of Christian worship were so divorced from those of everyday life, no matter whether it was the life of the rich or of the poor. Granting that almost all the domestic furniture and ornaments shown in the engravings are imitations of this or that variant of the Renaissance, mostly florid baroque or Roccoco, it cannot be denied that many of the designs are brilliantly clever. It needed skilled craftsmen to carry them out. How lively and interesting the churches of the early Victorian period would have been if the designers of some of those wonderful sideboards, tables,

CRUETS OR FLAGONS (approved by the Ecclesiological Society)

armchairs, bedsteads, sofas, pianos (grand and upright), fireplaces, chandeliers and much else had been given a free hand. However, there it was: as the result of the rigid principles of Mr. Pugin and the Cambridge Camden Society, by 1851 persons who prided themselves on their 'good taste' were convinced that nothing but Gothic in one form or another was permissible in churches. Heaven could be reached only by passing through a pointed arch, no matter whether it was a Catholic or Protestant one. Of course there were a few heretics prowling around, trying to pervert the simple and ignorant, but they did not carry much weight. The 'Goths' were gaining ground rapidly, and the 'pagans' were soon to be vanquished.

Looking at the Gothic altars, pulpits, fonts, lecterns, screens, church plate, vestments, etc., illustrated in the catalogue of the 1851 Great Exhibition, one would never guess that great and far-reaching changes were taking place in the structure of society and in the distribution of wealth. These medieval-looking church furnishings and ornaments do not look as if they belonged to the age of coal and iron, still less of the railway age. Yet between 1844 and 1848 more than 5,000 miles of railways had been opened in England. Strange to say the influence of medieval architecture is observable in the railways. Some of the new stations, e.g. Temple Meads, Bristol (1846), could have been turned into spacious cathedrals or churches

81

F

without much difficulty. Many of the entrances to tunnels were either Norman or Gothic. Some would have made stately chancel arches. In a curious way medieval romanticism had a bearing on the start of the Industrial Revolution. Those little locomotives of the 'forties, with their tall chimneys and polished brass domes were the contemporaries of some of Pugin's finest Gothic Revival churches, and of those restored by the ecclesiologists. The parallel is irresistible.

By 1851 half the population of Britain had become urban; hence the need for building so many new churches in towns, especially those in the coal and iron producing areas. Though the Corn Laws had been repealed in 1846, the prosperity of the countryside took time to decline. The landlords and their usually comfortably off tenant farmers, most of whom were members of the Established Church, unlike the middle class inhabitants of the industrial towns, who were largely Nonconformists, had enough money to restore and refurnish village churches. While so many of them were being taken in hand by the ecclesiologists during the 'forties, their congregations were still producing food for the population of England.

Both in the country and in the towns the housing of the working class left much to be desired. The cheapest and dreariest of the strongholds of Evangelicalism in the Midland and North of England centres of industry were palatial compared with the slums which often surrounded them. Because there was so much dullness and drabness in the average urban environment, middle class families tried to introduce a note of gaiety into their homes, even if the furniture and ornaments were cheap. But there would be no colour on Sunday. The typical places of worship of the Established Church, even if they pretended to be Gothic in detail, were solemn and awe-inspiring. Black or grey was correct for sabbatical clothes. Dark brown and dull ochre provided a perfect background for them in nearly every church, although there might be a few garish stained glass windows by way of contrast. The favourite and 'correct' colour for the covering of baize or cloth hung over most communion tables was a dark crimson. Vases of flowers had not yet become popular. A cross on or above the communion table was still almost an unknown ornament in an Anglican place of worship. The black gown was still worn by the preacher, except in a few churches of Tractarian leaning.

A safe generalization would be that it was only Mr. Pugin and his disciples who by 1851 had dared to introduce gilding and rich colours into the interiors of churches. Even Roman Catholic congregations did not always approve of such novelties. Yet how different were the interiors of the homes of the upper and middle classes—in them colour abounded, and the furnishings were often rich and stately. Even in the drawing-rooms and humbler sitting-rooms a Gothic tone sometimes prevailed. It might be a table designed in the medieval manner, and on it would be resting the two volumes of Mr. Tennyson's poems, published in 1842, with their bowdlerized Victorian version of the tales of the *Morte d'Arthur*. There was colour too, though dark and sombre, in the average dining-room, enlivened perhaps by one or two of Mr. Landseer's large oil paintings of dogs, stags at bay, or mist-wrapped Highland scenery; may be with examples of the late Mr. Etty's voluptuous yet discreetly draped female nudes. All these things derived from the same fashions as the church furnishings and decorations of both Anglican and Roman Catholic churches in the eighteen-forties and -fifties.

CHAPTER V

PUSEYITE CHURCH FURNISHINGS

THROUGHOUT the eighteen-forties and -fifties it was very difficult for the incumbents of Anglican places of worship to know what new types of furnishings could be inserted without offending either the bishops or the congregations. Most of the episcopate were terrified of novelties, against which they warned the clergy in their Charges. For instance, Bishop Blomfield of London laid down in 1842 that it was wrong to go beyond the decrees of rubrics, but he did not seem to have a clear conception of what was allowed or what was forbidden, except that the surplice could be worn only at the communion table and never in the pulpit. Dr. Howley, the Archbishop of Canterbury, warned his clergy against indulging in any novel customs. He spoke for the majority of the bishops.

One of the boldest of the Tractarian pioneers was the Rev. J. W. E. Bennett, who became vicar of S. Paul's, Knightsbridge, London, in 1840. He began cautiously to raise the tone of the services in this fashionable church; preaching in a surplice, intoning the prayers, dressing his choristers in cassocks and surplices, and making them chant the psalms. Then he assumed the eastward position at the communion table (which he called the altar), bowed to it, and even went so far as to add a cross, candlesticks, flower vases and frontals. This sort of thing shocked Bishop Blomfield, and he condemned such 'histrionic practices.'

By 1850 fashions in church furnishings were regarded as of sufficient news-value for jokes in the pages of *Punch,* a sure guarantee that the subject was now a permanent topic of conversation. Volume XIX (1850) contains a cynically worded article entitled 'Convent of the Belgravians,' which is an obvious indirect dig at S. Barnabas', Pimlico and S. Paul's, Knightsbridge. The writer says, 'Everybody who has a proper veneration for the reredos and who, without holding extreme opinions on the subject of the dalmatic, feels correctly on that of the alb, who has a soul that can appreciate medieval art, and who would revive their ecclesiastical practices and institutions to an extent just tastefully Romanesque, will be "Ryghte gladde" to hear that it is proposed to found a Convent of Anglican principles, under the above title. The vulgar, who think that a minority is necessarily a sect, will of course call it a Puseyite Nunnery; that cannot be helped.' The reactions of the *Punch* artist to the decorations and furnishings of the then two notorious churches in Belgravia are expressed in the drawing, which depicts two crinolined young ladies putting on nuns' wimples. The walls of their boudoir are adorned with mock-medieval devices, including a goose-rampant.

The violent antagonism which had been aroused by even the very mild ritualism in a few Anglican churches by 1850 is proved by other drawings on pages 226 and 227 of this same volume of *Punch*. We are confronted by two ladies in crinolines, wearing nuns' veils, accompanied by a child dressed up in a monkish hood, followed by a footman disguised as a friar. The previous article hinted that the nuns of the Belgravian convent would spend 'their leisure in illuminating books of devotion, practising ecclesiastical tones, and working slippers for the younger clergy.' The costume of the sisterhood will consist in a judicious admixture of the conventual style with the fashion of the day.' [1]

Punch had every reason to amuse its readers with comic drawings and funny articles about all this new game which had become so fashionable in Belgravia and Mayfair. But the players took themselves very seriously. In drawing-rooms and boudoirs ladies and gentlemen argued heatedly over details of ceremonial—the design of a dalmatic, the cut of a chasuble, the shape of a stole. The use of incense provided endless discussion.

It was about 1850 that Lady Mildred Beresford Hope, who, like her distinguished husband, usually worshipped at Margaret Chapel, informed him one Sunday that she was convinced she had seen 'in an obscure part of the altar a small flame flickering in a little saucer, as if waiting to be brought forward.' Mr. Upton Richards, the incumbent, and his curate flatly denied this. They suggested that Lady Mildred, who may have been short-sighted, had mistaken the reflection from the gold embroidery on the chalice veil for a flame. Her husband inclined to think it was merely a domestic night-light. Lady Mildred refused to accept this explanation. She bought a small glass vessel and experimented with spirits of wine, to find out if it produced an effect similar to that which she swore she had seen on that dark winter morning.

We are not told if she was satisfied, but on February 24th, 1850, returning to breakfast after the Communion service at Margaret Chapel, she told her husband that she was certain she had smelt incense. This was confirmed at luncheon by her children's governess, who had been to a later service, but who had not heard of Lady Mildred's discovery. The former announced that she had 'perceived a whiff of a sweet smell, like violets or orris-root.' Mr. Beresford Hope felt that this was convincing proof that Mr. Upton Richards and his curate were surreptitiously burning incense.

Four days later Baron and Lady Alderson showed the Hopes an old thurible they had bought in Germany. Lady Mildred identified it at once with the sort of thing she had seen in Margaret Chapel, although it is not easy to understand how an ordinary censer with a lid could have resembled the 'little saucer' which she maintained she had seen that Sunday morning! Beresford Hope then proceeded to explain that 'the little flame would be that of the charcoal, which has a transparent

[1] Cf. P. F. Anson, *The Call of the Cloister* (1955), pp. 298-9.

bodiless flame of a blueish hue, like spirits, and which would show against the lilac super-altar.' Knowing that Mr. Richards inclined to be careless in many ways, he was quite prepared to believe that the Minister of Margaret Chapel 'did not know that glowing charcoal emits a visible flame, and looking down on it while celebrating, did not see it, which would explain his equivocations.'

Beresford Hope, as befitted his status as the Nestor of Ecclesiology, was doing everything possible to improve the tone of the ritual and ceremonial in his then favourite place of worship, but there were limits to what even he could tolerate. He had presented Mr. Richards with a triptych of the Crucifixion and some medieval ivories, which Mr. Butterfield made into covers of an altar book. Then Mr. Richards wanted a vessel for the rite of unction, explaining that Bishop Forbes of Brechin was willing to bless the oil. At this point Beresford Hope told Richards that he must toe the line. He wrote angrily to a friend that the clergy at Margaret Chapel 'had got up all the little minutiae of Deacon's work' at the celebration of the Holy Communion—'shifting the book and shutting it after the blessing, before Richards had risen from his knees.'. All this silly business was gone through 'in the spirit of a footman and without any real reverence.' [2]

So great was the interest in church furnishings and decorations in the eighteen-forties that people published novels about them.[3] One of the most prolific writers of Tractarian fiction was the Revd. William Gresley, vicar of Boyne Hill, Maidenhead. His stories abound with descriptions of restored churches and their correct or incorrect fittings. *Bernard Leslie,* the first part of which appeared in 1842, advocates 'Catholic worship.' When Part II was published in 1859 Mr. Gresley distinguished carefully between Roman and Anglican ritual and ceremonial. He warned his readers against the 'gaiety and glitter of the Roman ceremonial,' and pleaded for the 'happy mean of the English ritual . . . with its penitential tone, which, if duly carried out, needs very little to commend it to the most fastidious taste.' Then there was the Evangelical novelist, the Revd. Charles Taylor, who in *Margaret, or the Pearl* (1844) revealed the dangers innocent young ladies were exposed to by learning to embroider altar frontals 'adorned with such symbols as the Virgin's head and the papal banner.' It will be remembered that Charlotte Brontë's Eliza Reed in *Jane Eyre* (1847) was a 'rigid formalist,' and found her way over to Rome by way of church embroidery.

As early as 1841 the Revd. Francis Paget, vicar of Elford and chaplain to the Bishop of Oxford, had published a pious story, entitled *S. Antholin's,* which is brimful of ecclesiology. We find fascinating details of an unrestored church, with galleries, box-like pews, a 'low hunting communion table' and a damp, mouldy smell. When Dr. Sharpe, the archdeacon, who is taking a Visitation, comes to Mrs. Clutterbuck's pew, he remarks: 'Pew! I thought it was her bed. Why, it is

[2] Cf. T. W. Law and Irene Law, *The Book of the Beresford Hopes* (1925), pp. 169–71.
[3] Cf. Joseph Ellis Baker, *The Novel and the Oxford Movement* (Princeton, 1932); A. L. Drummond, *The Churches in English Fiction* (Leicester, 1950).

all curtains and pillows.' When the young rector, Mr. Sanderson, decides to call in Mr. Compo to restore and refurnish S. Antholin's, Miss Clutterbuck wants to know what the style would be. The rector, gazing at the drawings, replies, 'Why, ma'am, from its elegant vegetative appearance, I might call it floric Gothic improved.' ('Or Gothic run to seed,' murmurs Mr. Sanderson quietly.)

Mr. Compo's furnishings would certainly have shocked the ecclesiological experts. Among other things he wanted two pulpits of equal height on either side of the aisle. He had ingenious ideas of taking up the smoke from the patent stove in the central aisle through one of the cast-iron columns and planned five-foot high pews to ensure comfort and privacy. A portable font of Wedgwood ware could be placed on the communion table when required. Mrs. Clutterbuck, the squire's wife, presented green and yellow hangings for the communion table and the pulpit, thus 'putting them into the Clutterbuck livery.' Mr. Paget explains that he had found similar instances of this being done. Luckily for everybody concerned, Mr. Compo's new furnishings were burned to the ground, and the rector called in a more experienced architect, who reproduced a cruciform medieval church; furnishing it with a canopied font, stained glass and a stone altar.

The following year Mr. Paget brought out another story, called *Milford Malvoisin,* with the sub-title 'Pews and Pewholders.' This was a sort of apologia for the principles of the Cambridge Camden Society. In 1845 Mr. F. A. Paley, the honorary secretary of the Society, published *The Church Restorers: a Tale Treating of Ancient and Modern Architecture and Church Decoration.* Newman's Tractarian novel, *Loss and Gain,* published three years after his reconciliation with the Roman Church, has much to say about Anglican church furnishings and decorations. In Mr. Paget's story *Warden of Berkingholt* (1843) he ridiculed the eccentricities of the more extreme Puseyites. References to removing pox-pews, scraping walls of whitewash, and more correct furnishings can be found in Anne Howard's novel *Brampton Rectory* (1849). Benjamin Disraeli refers to Irvingite ceremonial in his noved *Tancred* (1847). Perhaps the most widely read of any Tractarian novel, dealing indirectly with the dangers of extreme ritualism and Romanism, was Dr. Sewell's *Hawkstone* (1845). His sister, Elizabeth Sewell, was a famous writer of Tractarian fiction. *Amy Herbert* (1843), *Gertrude* (1845) and *Margaret Percival* (1847) all help us to visualize the atmosphere, if not so much the actual details, of Puseyite places of worship.

But in *Margaret Percival* there occurs an exquisite little vignette of a typical Tractarian restored church: 'Perhaps the first effect was almost too sombre, from the thickness of the dark rafters, and the deep hues of the stained glass windows in the chancel; but the mellowed light softened the brilliance of the colouring about the altar, and of the scrolls, bearing texts from Scripture, which were painted upon different parts of the edifice. That which might have been a loss in actual utility, was a gain in the effect which external causes insensibly inspire.' [4]

The behaviour of the worshippers in such a church is illuminated in the second

[4] Vol. II, p. 433.

part of Mr. Gresley's *Bernard Leslie*. 'For myself,' the author says, 'I think that bowing to the altar is rather a foolish custom, and one not at all necessary to be followed in our churches. . . . The Romanists do not bow to the altar, but to that which is on the altar, the Blessed Sacrament which is left there' (p. 57). The more extreme Puseyites are told that 'crossing oneself in a solemn manner appears a very proper custom, but I should not use it openly, on account of the prejudice which exists against it' (p. 58). Mr. Gresley felt that 'bowing at the Gloria Patri is a reverential custom which I like to see, and it is a useful one.' On the other hand he felt obliged to say: 'Prostration before the Holy Sacrament I cannot approve of, however well intended, because it offends excellent people, and causes a feeling of displeasure at a very solemn moment.'

It was behaviour of this sort in such churches as S. Paul's, Knightsbridge, S. Barnabas', Pimlico, or S. Mary Magdalene, Munster Square, rather than the ritualistic furnishings, that roused the ridicule of *Punch*.

The early Victorian age of church planning, furnishing and decoration has been summed up as 'the period of self-consciousness.' [5] The self-styled ecclesiologists, who were romantic medievalists, 'dreamt of converting England by repeating the architectural triumphs of the Middle Ages and by placing the Prayer Book services in a setting of medieval ceremonial. . . . To a keen young clergyman, fresh from reading the tracts of the ecclesiologists with their over-stressed medievalism, the typical church of the period with a marble font on a pedestal, the panelled pulpit and desk painted white, the crimson and yellow pulpit hangings, the altar frontal of crimson, fringed with black, seemed hardly worthy of the name of a church, in fact definitely pagan.' [6]

It will now be clear enough how self-conscious and pedantic were most of the pioneers of the Ecclesiological Movement in the eighteen-forties and -fifties. Largely indifferent as to whether the furnishings and ornaments of a church were useful or practical, they only minded its symbolic value, and close resemblance to some medieval object. More often than not, the achievement was nothing more than an interesting early Victorian museum-piece; a souvenir of an outlook on life which is now almost as unreal to us as that of the Middle Ages.

[5] G. W. O. Addleshaw and Frederick Etchells, *The Architectural Setting of Anglican Worship* (1958), p. 203.
[6] ibid., p. 204.

CHAPTER VI

'MUMMERIES OF SUPERSTITION'

A LTHOUGH—to paraphrase William Blake—the fields from Islington to Marylebone, from Primrose Hill to St. John's Wood, were being built over with pillars of gold; and the sky of Kentish Town and St. Pancras shone with golden arches here and there; the ecclesiologists realized that their holy war must still continue. They dared not cease from mental fight. They knew that it would be a long time before they succeeded in building their particular new Jerusalem in England's green and pleasant land.

In the February 1851 number of their magazine they reported that S. Jude's, Bristol, had fallen, 'not to violence, not to insolence combined with insidiousness, but to sheer insidiousness—fair promises unblushingly made'—then the choir stripped and banished from the chancel—the candlesticks sent off—the 'holy doors' converted into a reading desk in the nave—the offertory discontinued—daily worship abandoned.

'Farther north, where there was no colourable fear of ministerial influence, no hope of distinguished patronage to justify the motives, a church, raised by the offerings of Englishmen, to build a bulwark of Catholic worship in a vast city where Calvin reigned supreme—a church, voluntarily served by the gratuitous labours of a priest, who had sacrificed health, almost life, to his exertions, that modicum of Catholic ritualism—for it was a modicum—in which he indulged himself, and which was the ground for his support in this land, has been rudely forbidden by one, from whom on all accounts a different treatment might have been expected.

'The Prime Minister has pronounced the ritualism of the Anglo-Catholic Church to be "mummeries of superstition." Lord Ashley would rather worship by the banks of the river side (where he would *not* find S. Paul to join him), than in a church whose chancel "remains as in times past." He and his party are raising an agitation to call upon Her Majesty, Tudor-like, to issue an injunction prohibiting our Clergy from carrying out the Rubric. The Prayer Book is menaced.' [1]

S. Barnabas', Pimlico is the next target; 'a church, of which in our last volume, we said that it was "the most complete, and with completeness, the most sumptuous church which has been dedicated to the use of the Anglican Communion since the revival." This church has been desecrated by the dregs of the populace, the

[1] Vol. XII, New Series IX, pp. 1, 2.

ringleader in the profanation the First Minister of the Crown, and, their brutal sacrilege appeased, its high-minded priest driven from the altars he has himself at his own expense raised.' [2]

No church in England seemed to be safe from profanation by Protestant gangsters. The ecclesiologist gave directions on how to prevent petty sacrilege, which was becoming rife. Aumbries were not safe enough. Altar crosses and candlesticks of valuable metal should be used only on the greater festivals. Strong bars should

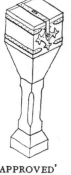

be placed across windows. Every sacristy or parsonage ought to have an iron safe. Altar decoration should not be too costly. Alms boxes should be kept empty.

This state of open warfare against ritualism had the immediate effect of simplifying the fashions in church furnishings throughout the 'fifties.

The state of affairs was different in Scotland, where the Episcopal Church was in the happier position of being a small nonconformist sect. Mr. Butterfield's new cathedral at Perth, the chancel and transepts of which were completed in 1850, and consecrated by Bishop Forbes of Brechin, acting for the aged Bishop Torry of Dunkeld,

'APPROVED' ALMS CHEST received high praise in *The Ecclesiologist*.[3] Special reference was made to the large stone altar with its jewelled cross. The east end of the choir was hung with silk, 'rich and good, but rather dingy.' The bishop's throne, on the north side, was described as 'a pretty piece of woodwork.' The open choir screen, with its doors of wrought iron ('Mr. Butterfield's *forte*') was quite correct. There were some striking brass Gothic gas standards—'very prettily floriated'— to illumine the nave. A gas pipe laid along the back of the rood-screen 'created beads of light, invisible from the nave, lighting up the whole choir with an effect almost magical.'

Few of the English hierarchy were so Catholic minded as those of the Scottish Episcopal Church, and their constant interference, suspicion and ignorance held back the progress of correct taste in ecclesiastical fashions. For instance, the Bishop of Manchester, Dr. James Prince Lee, had taken a very strong line about the furnishings of S. John's, Higher Broughton. He objected to the three sedilia, piscina, credence table and supposed Easter Sepulchre, the 'almerie' and, above all, the figure of the Virgin Mary (with a crown) in the east window. Actually the Easter Sepulchre was nothing more than the tomb of a benefactor, while the mysterious 'almerie' was a safe for church plate.[4]

But there was really no excuse for this ignorance. Plenty of books on the subject had been published by 1850 and more followed thereafter. If the bishops had time to look round the ecclesiastical court at the Great Exhibition in Hyde Park during

---

[2] ibid., p. 2. Mr. Bennett (the 'high-minded priest' mentioned) was forced to resign his incumbency in 1852.
[3] ibid., p. 24.
[4] ibid., p. 45.

the summer of 1851 they would have seen much to surprise or shock them. Nevertheless most of the episcopate went on objecting to what they insisted were 'innovations' in church furnishings—not only vested altars, crosses and candlesticks, but even surplices when they were worn for preaching. The contemporary idea that bishops are behind the times could be more than echoed in the last century.

As might be expected, some of the Cambridge college chapels began to set a higher tone, due to the influence of the Camden Society. The chapel of S. John's by 1852 had been given a dossal of rich woven stuff. The two altar candlesticks were painted in patterns. On the sanctuary floor stood two brass standard candlesticks. A green frontal was embroidered with a cross and the symbols of the four Evangelists.[5]

At Oxford in 1852 Mr. Chamberlain, the vicar of S. Thomas's, already a stronghold of Tractarian worship, published an article on the principles to be observed in ornamenting churches. He laid down that every altar ought to have frontals and a dossal, adorned with the 'proper symbolism.' A single cross was declared to be 'hardly sufficient.'

Mr. Chamberlain was against putting flower vases *on* the altar; better to stand them over or behind it, or in 'naked niches.' He recommended a 'large plate of zinc, diapered, set in a square frame' for holding bouquets of flowers. One could have too many glazed tiles in a church. He himself fancied plain black or red Stafford tiles. By 1847 the incumbent of this medieval church near the newly opened railway station had gathered round him a group of pious ladies, eager to devote themselves to good works among the poor. Some of them wanted to become Sisters of Mercy. Perhaps Mr. Chamberlain was thinking of Miss Felicia Skene and Miss Marian Hughes when he wrote that well meaning ladies ought to refrain from being too symbolical, carrying their notions even to the carpets and hassocks they embroidered. Miss Hughes had already made a chasuble for Mr. Chamberlain—composed of two Oxford M.A. hoods sewn together. This striking red silk vestment is believed to have been the first chasuble worn in an Anglican church for three hundred years. Neither Miss Hughes nor her rector could have dreamed that this odd garment would set such a significant precedent.

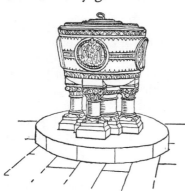

'NORMAN' FONT
Designed specially for Anglican Cathedral, Bombay in 1864 by James Forsyth. 'Significant union of the flowers of the Indian lotus with the roses of England' (*Builder*, 14 Jan. 1865)

[5] ibid., p. 324.

CHAPTER VII

ECCLESIOLOGY ADVANCES

THE fashions of church furnishings in some of the British Colonies a hundred years ago were both original and Protestant. Some fascinating examples of Anglican good taste could be found in Tasmania, which most people still called Van Diemen's Land. In the bishop's parish church at Newtown all the congregation had their backs to the altar, and faced the perched-up pulpit and reading desk at the west end. The style seems to have been splendidly eclectic. Faintly 'Gothick' tracery and plaster niches were mixed up with Louis Quatorze pendentives. The Archdeacon conducted services within a horseshoe shaped enclosure, containing reading desk, pulpit, clerk's desk, communion table and font. Just in front of this liturgical sanctuary were two huge pews for the notabilities, each with fireplaces. The archdeacon, who came from England with Tractarian leanings, was shocked at the furnishings of his church, but he could only provide a 'correct and pretty font.' In the cathedral at Hobart, described by a member of the Ecclesiological Society as 'Government Grecian' there was 'a mountainous pile of woodwork' hiding the so-called altar, composed of a pulpit and reading desk. Still, here and there in Van Diemen's Land there were signs of better times ahead. At Prosser's Plains a small church in the most correct flowing Middle-Pointed style had been erected, though a visitor complained that Mr. O'Connor's stained glass in the east window was 'too pre-Raphaelite' for his taste. The altar front—'not very good'—and the encaustic tiles were gifts from the Mother Country. A simple but neat Gothic font on a stem of clustered shafts, and an alms-box, adorned with beautiful iron-work, aroused fear of Popery just as did the small stone credence cut into the sill of the chancel window. Two panels of the wooden pulpit were hung with purple velvet. The texts embroidered on these pulpit-falls were regarded as a 'novel but effective idea.' The first settlers in Tasmania had some very original conceptions of church planning and furnishing. One new church, regarded by most people as a *chef d'oeuvre* of colonial ecclesiastical architecture, even had a false door in one of its four walls to create a feeling of symmetry. In another place, where it was proposed to add a chancel to the east end of the building, strong objections were raised, on the grounds that sooner or later another 'chancel' would need to be erected at the west end to make the church look uniform.

While British and French troops were fighting the Russians in the Crimea, and

Paxton's great conservatory was being taken down in Hyde Park and re-erected at Sydenham, where it became known as the Crystal Palace, many new churches were being built in England and a greater number of old ones restored and refurnished to bring them into line with the latest fashions. Persons of good taste agreed that, taken all round, the fittings showed a definite improvement. Stone fonts were now the rule, althought not all of them were provided with drains. Open benches were being inserted everywhere. The old-fashioned type of square pew with doors was almost extinct by 1855, except in country churches, as yet unrestored. Stone reredoses, most of them with marble columns, were much in demand. The prejudice against movable crosses could be obviated by painting a decorative cross in the centre of the reredos, or fixing a plain marble one into it. In some churches the Ten Commandments were preferred, either illuminated on the reredos itself or displayed on the sides of the altar. *'Festina lente'* was the order of the day, so as not to offend Protestant prejudices by too much ritualism in furnishings.

It was an encouraging sign of the times that in his new church, S. John's, Limehouse, London, opened in 1853, Mr. Clutton had provided an altar and super-altar, both correctly vested. Moreover he had adorned the whole of the interior with polychrome decoration up to the window levels—diapers on a pink ground. Over the altar a large gilt cross within the centre panel, set off with a pretty floriated border, added to the devotional atmosphere of the sanctuary. Flanking the altar were the Ten Commandments, the Creed and the Lord's Prayer. The chancel was illuminated by two iron gas standards, painted blue. The 'general *coup d'oeil'*— as one visitor remarked—was 'very striking as well as original, not a little foreign in spirit,' quite suitable in a town church.

A young architect, Mr. George Frederick Bodley, showed signs of having the right ecclesiological views. His furnishings at Wedhampton in Wiltshire were pronounced very satisfactory. They included four choir stalls with subsellae, a low panelled screen with metal gates, a properly vested altar, two sedilia of wood, and the east wall draped with rich hangings. The red marble cross inlaid between the two lower foliated circles of the east window, with a long stem of the same material extending down the walls-space between the two couplets of lights which formed the windows, was described by a critical visitor as a 'needless eccentricity.' At Llangarron in Herefordshire Mr. Bodley had designed a new Early Middle-Pointed church which was full of promise. Here was a floriated cross in alabaster on the wall above the chancel arch, and a circle of coloured marbles inlaid in patterns on either side of the stone chancel screen. In S. Michael's, Oxford, there was a striking new reredos designed by Mr. Street, consisting of five stone arches, inlaid with alabaster, flanked with detached shafts of Devonshire marble, with a much pinnacled canopy. Above it the east window displayed good stained glass by Mr. Hardman.

Mr. Benjamin Ferrey's furnishings at Christ Church, Esher, Surrey, were quite up to the standard of S. Stephen's, Westminster. He had provided this First-Pointed building with an altar vested in red velvet, chairs placed sedile-wise against the south wall of the sanctuary, which was paved with encaustic tiles, a simple but effective oak lectern and a stone pulpit of a massive design. The south chancel aisle, arranged in two stories, was allotted to the royal inmates of Claremont and their followers. The arcaded reredos, with black marble shafts, had its panels embellished with polychrome paintings.

It is difficult for us to realize what heat generated a hundred years ago on the subject of altar-chairs and sedilia. The more medieval-minded ecclesiologists of 1854 were terribly shocked to find that Mr. Edward Cutts advocated the former in his *Essay on Church Furniture and Decoration*. Considering that he went so far as to plead for the use of the proper eucharistic vestments, it was most incorrect for him to talk of the 'communion-table' instead of the altar. On the other hand, Mr. Cutts wrote 'very sensibly' on the necessity of reviving polychrome, and his views on textile fabrics and encaustic tiles were quite sound, taken as a whole.[1]

A distinct improvement was being made meanwhile in the furnishings of the Protestant Episcopal Church in America. Mr. Upjohn had shown an example of 'ritualism in the right direction' with the furniture and decorations inserted in Trinity Chapel, New York, though the services were not choral, and gallantry ran to the extreme of placing ladies in the highest chancel stalls. This First-Pointed Gothic church, so it was said, was remarkable for its polychrome. Painted glass was to be found in all the windows. An ecclesiological visitor was sorry to observe the 'uncanonical position of the font, at the east end of the nave.' He also regretted the perpetuation of pew rents. Still, the altar was of stone, immovable and detached, standing at the chord of the apse. Both the altar and pulpit were richly coloured.

From what could be gathered, Mr. Upjohn had not been so successful with S. Paul's, Brooklyn, which Bishop Eastburn had consecrated at a service consisting of Morning Prayer and the ante communion on December 23rd, 1852. This 'beautiful edifice, in the style of the thirteenth century,' had its chancel roof painted blue, but the furnishings consisted merely of a plain communion table, an episcopal chair, and a second ornamental chair to correspond with it.

Far better was the new church of S. Paul, Detroit—a stone building in the Early English style. Most of the windows were filled with painted glass. Below the east window was a panelled reredos, adorned with the Creed, the Lord's Prayer and a few sentences of Holy Scripture, with a few sacred symbols, beautifully illuminated in gold on a blue ground, creating a very chaste effect. On either side of the altar stood two large and beautiful chairs. The woodwork throughout was grained imitation of oak, including the pulpit raised on an elegant stem, with an open stair. The panels of the roof were coloured blue. To add to the comfort of the worshippers the church was entirely carpeted, and well lighted with gas standards.[2]

As to the Colonies, it looked as if it would be a long time before their churches presented anything like a truly Catholic appearance. Things were particularly bad in Newfoundland, where the Anglican Church was reported to be two centuries

[1] Cf. *Ecclesiologist*, Vol. XV, New Series XII, p. 341.
[2] ibid., Vol. XIV, New Series XI, pp. 50–1.

or so behind the mother country—in all respects, at least a quarter of a century, judging from a letter from Mr. William Grey, who was Corresponding Secretary of the Oxford Architectural Society. The state of 'the largish Romish chapel (so-called cathedral) in S. John's,' was bad enough, but the Anglican places of worship were far worse. Nearly all of them were built of wood. As to church furnishings: stale English devices were being palmed off as new fashions. People had hardly heard of the Gothic Revival, although well enough informed in other matters.[3]

The opening of the Oxford Diocesan Training College for Schoolmasters at Culham in 1853 was a hopeful sign of the times. The furnishings of the stately Middle-Pointed chapel, designed by Mr. Joseph Clarke (1819–88) would inculcate correct and Catholic taste among young laymen. The Chapel was paved throughout with Minton's tiles, with a richer pattern in the sanctuary. The carved oak altar was decently vested with a frontal, also the super-altar. The wall behind was boarded and decorated with gold symbols on an emerald green ground—quatrefoils and the sacred monogram. Two years later Bishop Samuel Wilberforce of Oxford wrote to Mother Harriet Monsell, the Superioress of the Clewer Sisterhood, that she must make sure that the religious prints, etc., placed in the rooms, were 'thoroughly Church of England.' He warned her to be on her guard against young women who 'would probably desire to wear or see crucifixes and the like.' [4] No doubt young men at Culham as well as young women at Clewer would have liked a proper brass cross standing on the altar of their chapel; but Mr. Clarke, to be on the safe side of the local ordinary, felt that it was wiser to compromise with a gold floriated cross, surrounded by a powdering of conventionally-shaped flowers. Apparently Bishop Wilberforce did not regard a triple sedilia, a stone credence or an aumbry fitted with an oak door and scroll hinges as suggestive of Romanism. In 1853 it would never have occurred to anybody to use this aumbry in the north wall for the reservation of the consecrated elements. The solid oak choir stalls, some of which were returned against the rood-screen, with a high canopied one for the use of the bishop, were all fitted with subsellae. A low stool, placed in the centre of the choir, was used for chanting the Litany. There were metal gates, painted chocolate and gold, in the central opening of the rood screen.

'We know of few things more gratifying than to be present at the celebration of Divine Service in this chapel,' said the author of *The Ecclesiologist* article.[5] 'Not only is the marked devotional behaviour of the students highly edifying in itself, but the full choral service, at present rendered entirely by men's voices in four parts—the tenor taking the melody—struck us as peculiarly solemn.' On Sundays and holy days Mattins was sung at 8.45 a.m.; Litany and Holy Communion at 11 a.m.; and Evensong at 4 p.m. Three wooden hoops with candles, suspended from the roof, cast a dim religious glow over the choir at Evensong on a winter after-

[3] ibid., p. 156.
[4] R. G. Wilberforce, *Life of Bishop Samuel Wilberforce* (1881), Vol. III, p. 327.
[5] June 1853, p. 151.

noon. The establishment of Culham College was regarded as 'a cheering Ecclesiological fact,' affording 'every reason to trust that good seed is being sown which will bear fruit for generations to come, and bind the hearts of many humble sons of the Church of England more closely to the bosom of their Holy Mother.' Yet much remained to be done to 'give grace and final charm to this House of God.' Every window deserved to be filled with rich stained glass. No 'lettern' graced the floor, no candlesticks the sanctuary or altar. It was to be hoped that many churchpeople would come forward to 'offer the gifts towards a chapel where the services are so constant, so primitive and so Catholic.' [6]

Taken all round, Tractarians could well believe that the winter was past and the spring had come: they could feel it in the air, certainly in the Thames Valley. At Oxford, as we have seen, there was much talk of the ritualism which Mr. Chamberlain had introduced at S. Thomas's, where the services were vigorously and efficiently performed. The music was mainly Gregorian, and rendered by a large voluntary choir. Mr. Butterfield had designed some new altar rails, while Mr. Street had provided desks for the choir boys. Mr. O'Connor was responsible for the medieval-looking stained glass in the east window. The most original gas corona of metal with glass balls had been made by Mr. Skidmore. The old world atmosphere of this little church was increased by the presence of a few black-robed nuns, members of the Sisterhood formally established in 1851 at Rewley House by Mr. Chamberlain. The sisters took charge of the floral decorations in the church, washed and ironed the surplices and albs, and added to the vicar's collection of vestments by their needlework. Among the young men who sang in the choir, two undergraduates, William Morris and Edward Burne-Jones, dreamed of founding a religious Brotherhood, whose patron would be Sir Galahad. It was their experiences at S. Thomas's, perhaps more than anything else, which led these two young men to larger enthusiasms. Both in after years would play a leading part as leaders of fashions in church furnishing and decoration.

There was another church in Oxford which attracted considerable attention at this time, although its pagan style of architecture was frowned upon by the Gothic-minded ecclesiologists. Mr. Bruton had added an apsidal sanctuary to S. Paul's, and given it new open pews, with doors in the side sittings. Within the chancel were benches on either side, with subsellae and desks, resting on uprights of metal work, painted blue and gold. The pavement was composed of black and white marble. There was a stone credence, but the altar frontal was 'not of the right form'—embroidered with a lamb lying on a cross and book. The super-altar bore wooden candlesticks which *The Ecclesiologist* tactfully noted, were not standing in the correct manner. No doubt fear of offending Bishop Wilberforce led to a large plain cross of stone with a crown of thorns around it, the latter being gilt, being fixed to the east wall, instead of a cross being placed on the super-altar. The blue tint on the roof was unpleasing and the emblems of the pelican and the Agnus Dei, shaded in gold, were 'very ill executed.' Mr. Wille-

---

[6] ibid., p. 152.

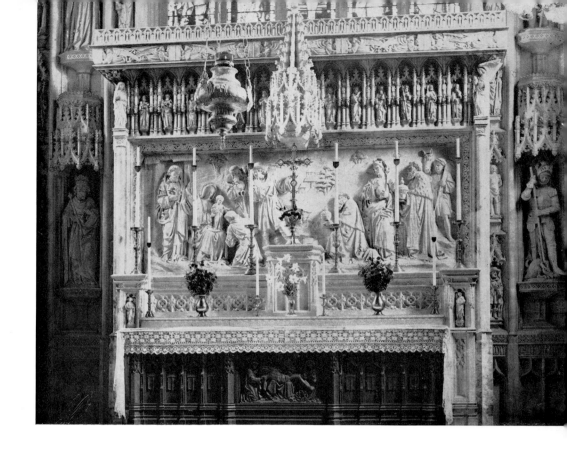

7. J. D. Sedding's amazing versatility is seen in these two photographs depicting the Gothic high altar and reredos in S. Clement's, Bournemouth, Hampshire (1873), and Italian Renaissance baldachin in the Holy Redeemer, Clerkenwell, London (1887)

8. The altar in the chapel of the Franciscan Convent, Bocking, Essex (1898), and the Chapel of S. Gregory and S. Augustine, Westminster Cathedral (1903), show how J. F. Bentley adapted his favourite mosaic decorations to both Gothic and Byzantine styles

ment's Romanesque glass in the round headed windows of the apse was dismissed and came in for ecclesiological censure as well. Readers were told that at S. Paul's 'it was intended to produce the effect of a stately Italian choir.' 'In spite of defects,' the writer conceded, 'this has been to some degree attained.' [7]

Far better were the now completed furnishings in the restored chapel at Merton College, designed by Mr. Butterfield (see p. 137). The Cathedral had a long way to go before it could be regarded as ecclesiologically 'okay,' although a start had been made with Mr. Gerente's rich stained glass in the new east window. The furnishings of S. Mary's still remained in 'their old most unecclesiastical condition.' Mr. Street has done his best to improve the fittings in the chancels of S. Aldate's and S. Michael's. He was also trying to bring the furnishings at S. Giles' up to the mark. In the new church of S. George a 'tame Flamboyant building,' Mr. Harrison deserved to be commended for his tiled reredos behind the altar; though the design as a whole was 'very cold and unattractive.' Three new cemetery chapels proved that there was a desire to pay greater respect to the departed. S. Sepulchre's contained a rather undersized altar in the apse, and a 'lettern' of heavy and coarse workmanship, from which prayers were read daily. In S. Mary's cemetery chapel, near S. Thomas's, could be found an altar, a wooden screen marking a sanctuary; a bier in the middle of the nave, and a desk for reading the prayers.

The third chapel, dedicated to S. Cross, near Holywell church, was furnished in much the same manner. Behind the small altar was a painted reredos of a cross upon a diaper. There was a movable 'lettern,' and some seats with poppy heads, 'of a most ugly design.' These three cemetery chapels were far from being perfect, but they helped to remind churchpeople of those whose course on earth is o'er; a body of people largely forgotten by the Fellows of All Souls, whose college (it must not be forgotten) had been originally founded for the object of praying for the dead.

Another ecclesiologist reported that the state of church furnishings in Liverpool showed very little sign of improvement, in spite of 'great ecclesiastical energy of a certain kind' in the Second City of the Kingdom. At S. Jude's 'the infamy of its arrangement' was almost beyond description. The visitor found a railed-in octagonal enclosure towards the east end of the interior. Within it stood the pulpit, reading-desk and altar (so-called). Three new churches, designed by Mr. Raffles Brown, showed 'such an attachment to a false type, so crotchety a theory of eclecticism, so utterly careless about progress in art, and fresh infusion of ideas,' that it was very doubtful if anything would be developed 'better than the strange edifices already produced' in Liverpool for Anglican worship.

At S. Chrysostom's, Everton, consecrated in 1853, Mr. Brown had furnished the chancel with 'a kind of baby-house stalls.' There was a very odd open reading desk, spangled with quatre-foils. The seats were open, but only children could kneel in them. Underneath each of the gallery stairs, with lancet windows, set in a slope, after the fashion of the famous staircase in Wells Cathedral, was a W.C.,

[7] ibid., pp. 505–6.

G

lighted by a bodiless trefoiled lancet. To make public lavatories part of the body of a church was very bad indeed.

More oddities were discovered at S. John the Divine, Fairfield, then a very fashionable suburb of Liverpool. Here the furnishings were more ornate. The five-light east window was filled with rich stained glass by Mr. Gibbs. There were bronze altar-rails, hangings on the east wall and encaustic tiles in the sanctuary—all very commendable. Unfortunately the wooden eagle 'lettern' looked like a cross between that bird and a solan goose. The roof of the chancel, painted the fashionable shade of blue, was powdered liberally and unpleasantly with stars in various sizes. The ecclesiological visitor was told that the stone pulpit was 'considered an extraordinary work of art,' and he had to admit that, 'though bearing an affectation of oddness,' it had something to commend it. What gratified him far more was learning that in at least one church in Liverpool prayers were said in the chancel.

Perhaps the most extraordinary new church in Liverpool was S. Paul's, Prince's Park, designed by Mr. Samuel Holmes, the late Mayor of Manchester, whose incumbent was the famous divine, Dr. McNeile. The furnishings of this immensely broad building appear to have been in the wildest and most bizarre kind of churchwarden's Gothic. The so-called altar stood at some distance from the east wall, behind a mighty mountain composed of pulpit and reading-desk.

'Observing a mat at the east side of this altar, we inquired its use. "Why, sir," was the reply, "Dr. McNeile reads the *Communion* at the north side of the table; but at the *Sacrament* he stands fronting the congregation." So we have the old Basilican arrangement restored! The pulpit is unique. A kind of iron crane, padded at the end, is attached to the back: when the preacher has mounted his elevation, an official pushes this instrument forward, the divine bestride it, and is ready for his task. In fact, he must present a very tolerable representation of a martyr on the *equuleus:* with the one exception, that in former ages the actor on that instrument was tortured for the amusement of the spectators; here the spectators must be tortured for the amusement of the actor. The pulpitolatry of another arrangement is almost incredible. Suspended in the air, at some distance in front of, and higher than, the preacher's head, is a gas reflector with seven burners. On a Sunday morning the gas is lighted, but kept low. Should the day be foggy, it is turned on in full power; and thus, while the rest of the church is in mist and obscurity, the preacher's head is encircled with a nimbus of glory. We doubt whether ecclesiology can present a more ludicrous spectacle than that of a man preaching on a padded horse, and with the effulgence of seven lamps streaming, at mid-day, on his face. Were the Pope, instead of Dr. McNeile, concerned, would not the arrangement be called, by all good Protestants, a vile parody of Moses on the Mount, and of a still more solemn passage in the Apocalypse?' [8]

Mr. Alfred Holmes, the brother of the architect of S. Paul's, had designed some almost equally original furnishings at All Saints', Great Nelson Street. The pulpit and reading-desk were mounted on four legs before the altar. The great galleries

[8] ibid., p. 409.

were supported on voluted cast-iron piers, with caps which were 'about an equal mixture of Corinthian and a cabbage-head.' In the sham Romanesque church of S. Aidan, Birkenhead, there were heavy galleries; cast-iron piers painted to imitate stone; a pulpit in front of the altar—'dirt, darkness and squalor everywhere.' It must have been a relief to arrive at S. Peter's, Everton, where at least there was a proper chancel, seated stall-wise.

Many more churches were visited by this tireless ecclesiologist in 1853, but the only one which pleased him was S. Martin's, described as 'a very successful example of the way in which the worst church may be fitted for ritual requirements. The *chorus cantorum* here is excellent; and the heartiness of the service above all praise. Unfortunately Anglicized Gregorians are still used. A true Gregorian service, with the same zeal and power, would make S. Martin's an example for that part of England.' [9]

Almost every other town in the north of England, not Liverpool alone, was in a bad way ecclesiologically. Secessions to Rome were encouraged thereby because most of the new chapels erected by this sectarian body were at least furnished correctly. Nevertheless, some points seemed to have been won, even at Liverpool. Open seats, a more or less developed chancel and Middle-Pointed style were generally recognized requirements. It was hoped that greater use would be made of Irish marble for interior work. There was a definite improvement in gas arrangements. But gas pipes taken along piers ought to be coloured and gilded.

In the eighteen-fifties there seem to have been many ladies who, remembering the words of the Catechism which they had been forced to memorize as little girls, really wanted to do their duty in that state of life unto which it had pleased God to call them, and to keep their tongues from evil speaking, lying and slandering. Most of them were fairly comfortably off, and there was no need for them to labour truly to get their own livings; in fact, to do so would have been out of keeping with their status as gentlewomen. Very often they were bored to death as they sat in their drawing-rooms, wondering how on earth to fill up the endless leisure hours. Even in the average country vicarage there were plenty of maids to do the housework. Their mistresses' thoughts were expressed in the words of Dr. Isaac Watts' hymn:

> 'In works of labour, or of skill,
> I would be busy too;
> For Satan finds some mischief still
> For idle hands to do.'

Realizing this, a certain Miss Blencowe got Mr. Masters of New Bond Street to publish a helpful little book on church embroidery. Moreover she was prepared to assist any ladies who wanted advice before undertaking this then still rather novel type of needlework. Attention was drawn to this book by a Revd. Mr. James at the annual meeting of the Architectural Society of the Archdeaconry of Northampton in 1855. He had much to say about the ways in which ladies could

[9] ibid., p. 414.

be usefully employed in work for the improvement and decoration of churches, above all in ecclesiastical embroidery. He remarked: 'If even the time bestowed in working elaborate bands and embroidering cambric handkerchiefs and showy slippers for popular preachers, were bestowed on works not for the man, but for the house—on the church, not on the curate—it would be in better principle as well as better taste.' What Mr. James wanted to do was to direct the attention of well-bred ladies of sound churchmanship, not only to the proper subjects for their church work, but also to the appropriate style in which to execute them. He had to admit that modern church embroidery, with its more regular and rigid forms, did not give such play to fancy as worsted work, as shown in all the fresh colours of a pillow or a screen. But what was the pleasure derived from these adornments for a drawing-room when compared with the spiritual satisfaction of adding to the glory of God's House?

So many things were waiting to be made by idle hands—fair linen cloths for the communion table, pulpit hangings, covers for Bible desks, napkins for alms-dishes and markers for the Bible and Prayer Book. Mr. James suggested that 'a correct and handsome pall for the poor, who are often obliged to pay largely for the use of one, would be a true work of mercy, if supplied gratuitously to all who need it.' Then there were 'commoner and plainer works for those who do not feel equal to the more artistic embroidery'—hassocks, carpets and kneeling cushions. All of these were simple and easy enough and yet, being voluntary offerings, would be doubly valuable in churches.

Mr. James, however, did not want to restrict ladies' church work to the needle. He suggested that some of them might be able to make water-colour or pencil sketches of architectural features in churches, which could be preserved in portfolios. The newly invented art of photography was quite within the compass of woman's hand.' The more talented ladies could find useful employment in the illumination of Bibles and service books, or painting texts to be placed over alms-boxes; in fact there was much scope for the delicate work of the female hand, and exquisite models in the old illuminated manuscripts to follow and study. Ladies with stronger arms and hands might feel inclined to take up wood-carving for church purposes.

What was needed was guidance in every direction, for, as this Northamptonshire clergyman pointed out, 'there are still other more humble spheres in which ladies may be useful in church work and in aiding architectural and ecclesiological societies. Rubbings of brasses, which require nothing but careful and patient manual labour, are most useful in many ways to the antiquarian and architect; and the more graceful adornment of our churches, at the great festivals, is well worth more attention than is generally bestowed upon it, and admits of and, indeed, demands, the exercise of much taste and artistic feeling.'

These were some of the ways that Mr. James indicated by which Anglican churchwomen of a hundred years ago could 'take a greater and more enlightened interest in the architecture and furniture of our churches than they have hitherto done.' He was sure they possessed the willing mind and the skilful hand. Feminine talents deserved to be turned to the best advantage, and what better way could be found than improving the beauty of the House of God?

It was not only Miss Blencowe who was engaged in assisting ladies with church embroidery. Young Mr. Street had brought out a book on the same subject in 1853, with tracings adapted from natural botanical forms. It was felt that these patterns would be very helpful, not only to the wives and daughters of clergymen, but also to the members of Sisterhoods whose health prevented them from engaging in works of charity among the poor, and who had a talent for needlework. There was no doubt that Mr. Street had managed to extract new and beautiful designs from the inexhaustible resources of nature. Great hopes were felt for the progress of church embroidery, once the good ladies had acquired the knack of decorating frontals, stoles, bookmarkers, cushions and hassocks with the life-like flowers and leaves reproduced in *Church Needlework*.

Most, if not all, of the elaborately embroidered cambric handkerchiefs and showy slippers made for popular preachers and pale young curates by the ladies who, rather later, began to read Miss Charlotte Yonge's novels and the stories in *The Monthly Packet,* have long since been thrown away. But in rural parish churches all over England there can still be found specimens of the frontals, pulpit-falls, book-markers, alms-bags—even hassocks—which are now becoming priceless period pieces. Handling them one is transported into the remote and unreal world of the pre-Raphaelites and the *Idyls of the King*. The flavour of lavender and pot-pourri in cloisonné vases is about these specimens of amateur early Victorian church furnishings.

GOTHIC ALMS DISHES (J. Wippell of Exeter), Great Exhibition, 1851

CHAPTER VIII

EPISCOPALIAN AND CATHOLIC CHURCH FURNISHINGS IN SCOTLAND

MOST of the Episcopalian clergy in the north-east of Scotland were sound, if old-fashioned, High Churchmen, but their places of worship had hardly been affected by the ecclesiological movement, even as late as 1845. Old traditions were hard to dislodge, especially in the Buchan District of Aberdeenshire. There still remained chapels where the pulpit stood against the middle of the south wall, with a window on each side; the precentor's desk in front of it, and in some cases, a reading desk between it and the pulpit. These two or three solid wooden structures were railed round, forming a square enclosure. The altar—generally a small wooden table, sometimes covered with a green baize or red frontal enveloping top, front and ends—stood beneath the pulpit and desks. In some places the holy table, as the altar was called, appeared outside the enclosure on its north side. During the not very frequent celebrations of the Eucharist the holy table was usually enveloped with a large linen cloth. Sometimes it was pinned close to the frame-work at both ends.[1]

There was no uniformity in the size of holy tables, or their frontals. At Ellon and Fraserburgh there were loose red cloth covers; at Peterhead a more ornate crimson velvet frontal; at Turriff a blue one with a cross embroidered on it, presented to a member of a congregation by a Nonjuror bishop in London, who felt that it would be treated with greater respect in Scotland. The traditional usages of the Episcopal Church were the result of long years of persecution; and it was safer to plan the chapels on the same lines as the Presbyterian kirks. The first attempt at a chancel was risked at Woodhead, Fyvie, about 1810. Four years later a neo-Gothic chapel was erected at Peterhead, with a gallery round three sides of it. The pulpit, reading desk and precentor's desk, flanked on either side by a winding stair, were placed right in front of the altar rails. The holy table stood away from the east wall of the apse. The same arrangement was adopted at Ellon in 1816. Very few Episcopal chapels contained fonts. Baptisms were performed in basins. However, when Mr. Alexander Simpson designed S. Andrew's Chapel (now the Episcopal Cathedral) in Aberdeen in 1816, using the English Perpendicular style of architecture, he provided both a narrow recess for the holy table and a font.

---

[1] Cf. F. C. Eeles, *Traditional Ceremonial and Customs connected with the Scottish Liturgy* (Alcuin Club Collections XVII, 1910), pp. 23–4; *Ecclesiologist*, Vol. XV, New Series XII, pp. 8–9.

This place of worship was a distinct advance. The furnishings of Mr. Simpson's chapel at Banff, dedicated in 1833, were held to be very promising specimens of ecclesiastical art.

In 1840 new chapels were built at Fraserburgh and Portsoy, Banffshire. Both of them were furnished according to the traditional plan, and as was remarked by a contemporary critic, 'did but little towards raising the ecclesiastical character of the Diocese.'

It was not until 1843 that we find an example of what the Cambridge Camden Society could call 'correct' furnishings in an Episcopal church in the north-east of Scotland, when a young architect, Mr. Hay, designed a very plain First-Pointed Gothic chapel for Cruden, Aberdeenshire, which was definitely in advance of all that preceded it. At the entrance to the small chancel were a prayer-stall and pulpit. The holy table was raised on three steps at the east end of the chancel and backed by a simple reredos. An ecclesiological tourist was greatly edified to find both a 'prothesis' and three sedilia in the sanctuary. The conservative congregation wanted galleries in their new church, but both clergyman and architect objected. They compromised by placing two rows of seats along the north and south walls like the stalls in the choir of a cathedral—those next the wall being raised two steps, and those in front one step above the level of the pews in the middle area of the nave, which were provided with doors. Moreover, there was a fine font of polished granite. From now onwards every clergyman in the north-east wanted to emulate Cruden when his own opportunity for building occurred.

The first sign of real progress was in 1849 when Mr. John Henderson of Edinburgh designed a new First-Pointed church for Woodhead, Fyvie. The interior arrangements of this rural church in Aberdeenshire were excellent. A thoroughly correct granite font stood at the west end of the building. The chancel was paved with encaustic tiles. Prayer desk and pulpit stood on the north and south sides of the chancel arch. The only criticism was the 'jack-in-the-box contrivance of getting into the pulpit through a hole in the wall.' About the same time the Episcopalian congregation at Meiklefolla got Mr. Alexander Ross of Inverness to advise them about pulling down their pulpit, reading desk and precentor's desk which filled up an enclosure against the south wall of their chapel. They wanted to remove the narrow pens, or to convert them into open seats.

By 1850 the ecclesiological movement had made its impact in other parts of the north-east. Messrs. McKenzie and Matthews designed the Middle-Pointed church of S. John the Evangelist, Aberdeen, which was furnished with a Tractarian correctness not surpassed by S. Barnabas', Pimlico, or S. Paul's, Brighton. The noble east window of five lights was filled with rich stained glass. The seats were low and open. Both the altar and pulpit were of stone. The latter—like the one at Woodhead—was entered from the chancel through an opening in the wall. The walls of the chancel were decorated with rich polychrome paintings, and the sanctuary was paved with encaustic tiles. Almost as correct were the furnishings at

S. Drostan's, Deer (1851), and S. Ternan's, Banchory (1851), both churches designed in the First-Pointed style.

It was with the opening of S. John the Evangelist, Longside, Aberdeenshire, in 1854, that the 'Second Spring' really arrived. Here Mr. William Hay of Peterhead had erected a First-Pointed church with a Scottish flavour, and furnished it with low and open seats, a font near the west door, a decent pulpit and a chancel approached by steps—even a sedilia in the south wall of the sanctuary. The eastern windows were to be filled with richly-stained glass, containing appropriate and symbolic designs.

A writer in *The Ecclesiologist* [2] said that in tracing the progress of ecclesiastical architecture in the Episcopalian Diocese of Aberdeen in the first half of the nineteenth century, he would have had 'comparatively no real satisfaction' had he 'not been able to state, in conclusion, that the *material* sign of improvement recorded are the indications of a corresponding progress in the degree of order and regularity which characterize the performance of the services of the Church, accompanied by a higher tone of religious principle among the members. Indeed, the improvement in the style and arrangement of the material temples, and the increased order and zeal among the worshippers have apparently proceeded *pari passu*. The strange anomalies in the performance of the services which were common some thirty years ago, were not less remarkable than those of the barn-like edifices which were called churches. The cold formality of the former found its true symbol in the hideous deformity of the latter. Holy days and saints' days went by unobserved in almost every congregation of the diocese. A single service on Sunday was the rule rather than the exception. The music was *drawling* rather than *singing*. Proper chanting was unknown. *Now,* in every church in the diocese—with perhaps one exception—there are two full services every Sunday throughout the greater part of the year. The bishop in his charges to the clergy has enjoined a strict observance of every saint's and holy day, and a due regard to rubrical requirement. In several churches there is daily service; in almost every congregation the music is of an ecclesiastical character, and in S. John's, Aberdeen, the service is wholly choral. In short, a decent order and uniformity is now the characteristic of the diocese. A great change has taken place. Now the chief evil to be guarded against was attaching more value to outward form and beauty to the neglect of inward truth and sincerity. The material sanctuary should still be the symbol of that other Church which assembles within its walls. A correct and beautiful temple is no fit place for a cold and formal congregation, and a highly wrought ritual is worse than mockery if other than the outward evidence of the burning zeal which exists in the hearts of the worshippers.'

Until about 1811 the black gown had been used for all ministrations by the clergy of the Scottish Episcopal Church. A long time was to elapse before surplices found their way into Scotland, though in some places they were being worn for Morning and Evening Prayer and the administration of the Holy Communion by 1828. The

[2] ibid., p. 18.

black gown still remained the correct vesture for Baptisms, Marriage and Funeral Services for some time afterwards. Just as in England, a black gown was *de rigueur* in the pulpit. The black scarf, otherwise the tippet, was worn by all clergy, until some of the more advanced adopted first a black stole and then coloured ones.

The custom of communicating the sick from the reserved elements was fairly common in some Episcopal chapels, especially in the north-east. The celebrations of the Holy Communion, until about 1840, were usually only four in the year, after which they gradually became more frequent. On the greater festivals a portion of the consecrated elements was set aside; the churchwardens consuming the rest after the service. The former were placed in a cupboard in the vestry, or some other convenient place, until the minister took them with him on his rounds, so that he could give communion to the aged or infirm in their own homes. It was not until about 1850, so it seems, that the traditional Scottish custom of keeping the reserved sacrament in the vestry was abandoned, when a few aumbries in the walls of chancels began to be built for this purpose. Reservation, involving a treatment of the aumbry or tabernacle as a centre of eucharistic *cultus,* was rare in Scotland before the eighteen-seventies. It is doubtful if there were as many as a dozen places where Episcopalians would have bowed or genuflected before the reserved elements of Holy Communion. In this respect they conformed to the custom of the Eastern Churches.

The furnishings and decorations of the Roman Catholic places of worship in Scotland, with but few exceptions, would have provided little to interest the ecclesiologists until after 1850. With the passing of the Catholic Emancipation Act in 1829, there was a spate of church building all over the country, but there was no money to spare for beautifying these chapels—as they were still called. Some were designed in a simple sort of Gothic, others in classical style. Their altars fulfilled the functional purposes for which they were erected. Sometimes they were quite stately, elsewhere as cheap as possible. One of the most original furnishings was the wooden baldachino—evocative of the Moorish details of the Brighton Pavilion—erected over the altar at S. Mary's, Dufftown, Banffshire, sometime after 1825. In the so-called Gothic chapels there was usually an altar, standing in a very narrow enclosure, backed by a much crocketted and pinnacled wooden reredos, sometimes with a painted altar-piece in the centre. The candlesticks, more often than not, were imported from France or Italy, as were the vestments. The tabernacles were often large and ornately decorated with either Gothic or Classical carving. The crucifix generally stood on the tabernacle. Fear of arousing Presbyterian prejudice restrained priests from adorning their chapels with statues. Unlike English Catholics those in Scotland were hardly influenced by the ecclesiological movement of the 'forties and 'fifties.

Augustus Welby Pugin never built a church north of the border. Unlike the Episcopalians, the Catholic body in Scotland which, owing to Irish immigration, was increasing rapidly, did not feel any urge to improve the tone of its services or to introduce a more correct ritual. It was sufficient to provide enough chapels for the laity to fulfil their spiritual obligations, and thus assist them in not falling into mortal sin by missing Mass on Sundays and holy days of obligation. Thus the majority of the chapels erected before 1850 were purely utilitarian. In most parts of the industrial Lowlands there was more than enough zeal in the hearts of the worshippers to make them comparatively indifferent to outward form and beauty. There was no danger in the squalid mining villages that Romanists would start attaching undue value to the material sanctuary. Except in the Northern Vicariate, where Jansenist traditions still lingered, every Roman Catholic chapel in Scotland had one or more 'daily services.' In Glasgow and the surrounding district the poor packed into the chapels three or four times every Sunday morning. There was a completely different ethos between the Papists and the 'Piskies, and this had its effect upon the furnishings and decorations of their places of worship.

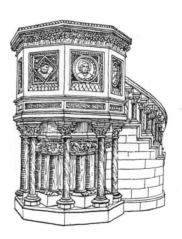

CHAPTER IX

FURNISHINGS OF THE CATHOLIC APOSTOLIC CHURCH

SINCE about 1837 a sort of underground liturgical movement had been going on in England which had no connection with either Rome or Canterbury, but which by the early 'fifties was proving very profitable to church furnishing firms. Little did Edward Irving (1792–1834) suspect that some of his more ardent disciples who attended the Caledonian Church in Hatton Garden, London, where the modes of worship corresponded to those of the average Presbyterian kirk, would form themselves into a new religious body, modelled on what they believed to be the primitive Apostolic Church, governed by a 'college of apostles,' and with a fourfold ministry of prophets, evangelists, pastors and teachers.[1] Irving himself would have been shocked at the elaborate ritual and ceremonial which was later devised by one or two more ecclesiological-minded apostles, and made obligatory in all the so-called 'Catholic Apostolic' churches.

It was in the year of Queen Victoria's accession that eleven of the twelve 'apostles' started on their journeys around Europe to deliver to the chief civil and ecclesiastical authorities (including Pope Gregory XVI and the Emperor of Austria) what were known as the 'Shorter' and 'Greater Testimonies.' For the first time in their lives these devout gentlemen, some of whom had been Presbyterians, some Anglicans, had the opportunity of attending Catholic worship. The story is told that one of the apostles—probably Mr. J. B. Cardale—accompanied by a prophet, found themselves assisting at Mass in Rouen Cathedral. The priest was vested in a chasuble of medieval shape. Suddenly the prophet exclaimed in the spirit: 'Those are the vestments in which the Lord would have His priests serve before Him.' On their return to England this stimulating revelation received in Rouen Cathedral was imparted to the other apostles.

Meanwhile Mr. Henry Drummond, who combined the duties of an apostle with those of director of a London bank, had erected on his estates at Albury, Surrey, a picturesque little church, complete with chapter house, in the most correct Third-Pointed style of Gothic. A new liturgy was compiled, based on Roman and Eastern models, and first used in 1842; the celebrant wore eucharistic vestments.

---

[1] Very few Irvingite churches are left in Britain, or more correctly, the buildings have passed into the hands of other denominations. Since the death of the last of the 'twelve apostles' in 1902 there have been no ordinations, so congregations have dwindled and eventually disbanded.

The Irvingite liturgists must have made a careful study of the numerous publications of the Cambridge Camden Society, also the illustrated books by A. W. Pugin, which came out during the eighteen-forties. All was grist to their mill. By 1845 the Catholic Apostolic Church was observing the traditional Christian seasons, and making use of blessed oil at ordinations and for anointing the sick. Two years

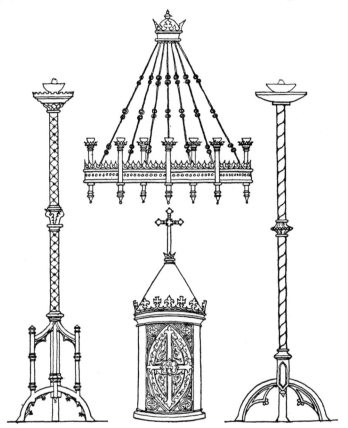

CATHOLIC APOSTOLIC FURNISHINGS (from *Principles of Ecclesiastical Buildings and Ornaments*, by Henry Drummond, 1851)
Seven lamps before the altar; two lamps, standing on either side of the altar; tabernacle

later the apostles decided to introduce a mysterious rite known as 'Sealing,' corresponding to Confirmation. By 1850 every Irvingite church was equipped with a thurible for burning incense as well as at least two lamps in which oil took the place of candles, and a tabernacle for the reservation of the consecrated elements.

During the following year, 1851, Mr. Henry Drummond of Albury published his *Principles of Ecclesiastical Buildings and Ornaments,* which revealed for the first time the symbolism of Irvingite ceremonial. This curious book of forty-three pages is illustrated by engravings, mostly adapted or copied from drawings by A. W. Pugin, including five tabernacles, two round and three square-shaped. There are detailed descriptions of their symbolism; also that of lamps, of which two kinds are allowed: a single lamp always kept burning, and a *corona lucis,* which was 'administered by the local angel and the six elders.' Seven is the proper number. Incense must be used in worship, but never for ceremonial purposes. The thurible must either stand on the table of prothesis, or be swung by an acolyte.[2] Every other use of incense is dismissed by Mr. Drummond as a 'flagrant abuse.' He permits stoles of several colours: purple for the elders, blue for the prophets, scarlet for the evangelists and white for the pastors. The colours must be 'sober, such as are not used in ordinary dyes,' but like those in old stained glass. The eucharistic vestments must be plain, though they can be ornamented with gold ('the emblem of truth'), or silver ('the emblem of love'), no other colours are allowed. Apparels on albs are strictly forbidden. Only the pænula-shaped chasuble is allowed, but it may have an embroidered cross on the back. 'Simple deacons' should wear dalmatics of 'stout white linen'; the 'seven deacons of a Church' must be distinguished by stoles. Confessionals ought to be planned so that the access of the penitents is different from that of the confessors. Mr. Drummond informs us that 'rood screens form no part of Catholic rites, but are Popish rites—the inventions, signs and outward manifestations of priestly arrogance and schism.' He accepts or discards Pugin's opinions according to his fancy. His book ends as follows: 'True taste is the expression of true feeling, and where there is no principle at the bottom, there is no feeling to express. Hence the "histrionic mummeries" and mockeries of Popish rites, almost as much destructive of Christian worship as the baldness of the conventicle.'

There can be no doubt that the wealthy squire of Albury Park was widely read. Some of his knowledge of the 'histrionic mummeries and mockeries of Popish rites' may possibly have been derived from Pierce Connelly, the convert American Episcopalian clergyman who, enchanted with his new faith, more or less forced his wife into a convent so that he could be ordained priest. By 1848 he was Drummond's guest at Albury, and the latter was advising him how to sue his wife for restitution of conjugal rights. It is recalled that Drummond used to 'listen with approval' to what the apostate priest told him about 'the curious ceremonies he had seen in Rome.'[3]

The Roman Catholic body in England was much too preoccupied with the restoration of its hierarchy to bother about this ritualism in a new nonconformist sect, but the rapid increase of Irvingism alarmed the authorities of the Church of England, particularly the Tractarian party. A large number of converts were being made, and 'meeting-houses' opened in quick succession in all the larger towns of Britain.

---

[2] The standing thurible may have been imitated from the rite of the primatial Church of Lyons.
[3] Cf. Juliana Wadham, *The Case of Cornelia Connelly* (1956), pp. 152–3, 157–9. His wife took to convent life so vigorously, in spite of Connelly's repeated attempts to change her mind, that she founded a famous teaching order and is now a candidate for canonization.

The ecclesiologists were really worried when they heard that the Irvingites had commissioned Mr. Raphael Brandon to design a church of cathedral size in Gordon Square, London—far bigger and more ornate than any new Anglican place of worship. The opening function, presided over by the twelve 'apostles,' took place at Christmas 1853. The newspapers gave full reports to the affair, and described the splendour of this First-Pointed Gothic building. The ecclesiologists now were able to obtain a first-hand impression of the furnishings of an Irvingite church in which the worship was performed in all its magnificence. They seem to have been much interested, but puzzled, at the exotic ritualism. The April 1854 issue of their magazine contained a five page article on the subject.[4]

The writer explained that 'the paraphernalia of worship' in 'this complex edifice,' the architectural beauties of which were highly praised, were 'mostly of a temporary character, being the fittings of the old meeting house in Newman Street, which they had somewhat unexpectedly to vacate.' The unfinished nave was filled with open seats, and contained the pulpit. Beneath the lantern of the lofty cruciform church, just westward of the first choir-steps, were returned stalls for the deacons. The choir extended eastwards, rising with three levels, the lowest of which was allotted to the performance of the less important services. It contained the various 'letterns' which Irvingite ceremonial involved. On the second level were the stalls for the elders, and eastward the seat of the 'angel,' suggestive of an episcopal throne. Opposite it was the 'Table of Prothesis,' or credence. The altar, standing most correctly on a footpace, was on the highest of the three levels. It was built of alabaster, richly carved, gilded and coloured. A large brass tabernacle of a most Romish shape was fixed to the altar. There were no movable furnishings; neither a cross nor flower vases. Two brass standard candlesticks stood close to each side of the altar, but instead of wax tapers they were fitted with glasses for holding olive oil. The twelve apostles did not permit lighted candles in the worship of the Catholic Apostolic Church; oil lamps were said to be more scriptural. The consecrated oils were kept in the tabernacle as well as the reserved elements. A richly bound Gospel book lay on the altar. Another lamp was suspended above the sanctuary, and seven more hung over the chancel, all said to have symbolic meanings. The wooden screen behind the altar was merely temporary, and would soon be replaced by an open reredos of alabaster. The purpose of the six stalls on either side of the sanctuary puzzled the visitors. They were intended for the use of the 'apostles' when any of the twelve attended divine service in Gordon Square. Another unusual piece of furniture was a faldstool in the midst of the sanctuary, which was used by the 'angel' when offering 'Intercessions,' with incense burning at his right hand in a standing censer.

Behind the chancel, but with no direct access from the main building, was an eastern chapel, suggestive of a chapter house, surrounded by arcaded stone walls with marble shafts. An altar stood on a dais at the east end. The windows were filled with painted glass by Mr. Ward and Mr. Gibbs. In these windows the judicious Hooker and Jeremy Taylor appeared in company with S. Anselm and

[4] Vol. XV, New Series XII, pp. 83–8: 'The Irvingite Development.'

CATHOLIC APOSTOLIC FURNISHINGS
Angel's Throne, Intercessional Faldstool. Seven lamps and
choir stalls (*c.* 1851)

Bishop Grosteste, as well as several Saxon saints. The purpose of this chapel, so the visitors were told, was for the solemn assembly of the twelve apostles. What astonished the ecclesiologists were the little rooms for the elders along the north side of the nave—'confessionals in fact, though their owners do not admit the name.'

Nobody knew what to make of all this nonconformist ritualism, whether to praise or to denounce it. *The Ecclesiologist* described the whole business as a 'novel delusion,' adding darkly: 'If we permit ourselves to be led away by the outward splendour and skin-deep conformities of the subtle antagonist, we shall become accomplices in all the mischief which it plans against the genuine Catholic Apostolic Church.'

It was indeed a strange phenomenon. There must have been something that appealed to the men and women of the eighteen-fifties that they were prepared to rise from their beds to attend the daily office of morning prayer at 6 a.m., and to return to church at 5 p.m. for Evening Prayer. On Sundays there were more services in addition to the choir offices, at which the psalms were chanted to the Gregorian tones. In every church at 10 a.m. a solemn choral Holy Eucharist was celebrated by the 'angel,' with an administration of the Communion. Then there were shorter forenoon and afternoon services—even a curious rite which corresponded to Exposition and Benediction with the ciborium, at which communion was given on the afternoon of the Lord's Day to those who were not present at the consecration.

Irvingite worship provided Anglicans who craved for elaborate ceremonial with what was lacking in even the most advanced churches. In 1854 there were no Anglican churches in London where eucharistic vestments were worn publicly, and it was not until 1859 that incense was first used (non-ceremonially) in a procession. It would be half a century before any Anglican churches in the metropolis started reservation. The Irvingite short cut to advanced ritual was enthusiastically trodden by a growing number of devotees.

The Irvingite churches were not only richly furnished—to carry out their full services a very large staff was necessary. It is doubtful if even the 'cathedral' in Gordon Square ever mustered the required total of sixty-four—one angel, six elders, six prophets, six evangelists, six pastors and seven deacons—each with one or more 'helps' or acolytes; not forgetting under-deacons, deaconnesses and lay-assistants.

The ritual and ceremonial became more and more ornate; the rubrics more intricate. Holy water stoups were introduced in the eighteen-sixties. The firms which supplied ecclesiastical vestments must have welcomed the Irvingites with a cheer. Doorkeepers, choristers, deacons, under-deacons and angels all wore cassocks of different colours. There was soon a subtle difference in the shape and colour of mozettas. Copes could be either purple or white. Their ornamentation differed according to the rank of the wearer. Albs had to be plain, and no lace trimming was allowed. Dalmatics must be long and ample. The assistant clergy wore long linen maniples, with which they wiped the chalice after each communicant. On Sundays and festivals the fringes of the vestments might be of gold thread, on other days white. It was difficult to remember when stoles must be worn at this or that function, or when one donned a rochet instead of an alb, or when a rochet was worn under a mozetta. Preachers were vested in long full surplices. No Irvingite sacristy was complete without a supply of special slippers or buskins. For some esoteric reason the Catholic Apostolic Church never introduced a sequence of liturgical colours. The eucharistic vestments were always white, except on Good Friday and days of humiliation, when black or violet was ordered by the rubricians. They even laid down that amber or gold glass must be used for all lamps, and that red glass must be avoided. They tolerated a gradine or super-altar, but it was not to be encouraged.

CATHOLIC APOSTOLIC SANCTUARY
Note the oil lamps : the 'Irvingites' disapproved of candles

At one of their assemblies in Gordon Square the Sacred Congregation of Rites issued an instruction that 'a sufficient number of chairs or seats must be provided where priests may receive such as desire to confer with them,' also stools at which their penitents could kneel. The various forms of ordination were almost as elaborate as those of the Roman rite. Quite as much incense and holy oils were used in the 'Order for the Consecration of a Church' as in any medieval *pontificale*.

113

H

Such, in brief, were the strange new fashions introduced by the Irvingites. The makers of vestments, the suppliers of wood and stone furnishings, and the stained glass painters found a new and unexpected market for their goods during and after the eighteen-fifties, because it was not long before almost every large town in England and Scotland had its Catholic Apostolic Church, although none surpassed Mr. Brandon's Gothic building in Gordon Square.

The complicated nature of Irvingite ceremonial involved making provision for the most comprehensive sacristies in all the larger churches, the furnishings of which are unique. In the church at Dundee, for instance, now an Episcopalian place of worship, many rooms open off a long corridor, each having the name of the particular branch of the hierarchy painted on the door. At the lower end, near the main entrance, is a cosy little sitting-room for the deaconnesses and other women workers. Other rooms of varying size are arranged for the acolytes, elders, choristers, and so on. The angel's room, nearest the sanctuary, is like a private study, and has a letter-box in the door. The main sacristy is what one would expect to find in a cathedral or abbey church, with cupboards and vesting tables arranged around the walls. There is a spacious 'Council Room,' with a platform and lecterns, besides two or three smaller offices. It is only after a prolonged inspection of some of the larger Catholic Apostolic churches, many of which have now been closed or handed over to Anglicans or Catholics, that one can appreciate the extraordinary nature of their ritual and ceremonial, which necessitated the erection and furnishing of vestries on a scale found in no other religious body.[5]

[5] On October 6, 1963, the Gordon Square church became the University Church of Christ the King, and began its new life as the main centre for Anglican Student work in London. The original Catholic Apostolic furnishings have been treated with respect. The only noticeable change is that the altars now have candlesticks on their gradines.

CHAPTER X

THE PARIS EXHIBITION, 1855

IT was the Paris Exhibition of 1855 that first made English church furnishers and decorators aware of the goods being produced in Europe, and enabled them to compare foreign articles with their own. Queen Victoria and the Prince Albert went to Paris in August that year, and stayed with Napoleon III and the Empress Eugénie. Many other people followed the royal example and visited the Exhibition at the Palais de l'Industrie in the Champs Elysées. Like the Great Exhibition in Hyde Park in 1851 it included an ecclesiastical section.

The October issue of *The Ecclesiologist* devoted a thirty page anonymous article to the church furnishings and decorations which were on view in Paris. The summing up is interesting. In stone work the palm must be given to the French. This was due largely to the abundance and beauty of material across the Channel. The current French practice gave the workman a free and unconstrained use of his chisel, and enabled him to obtain effects of light and shade, and to study the perspective of ornament with a success entirely unknown in Britain at that date. 'The very best of our stone carving looks tame and like machine work, as compared with French art; and this we attribute entirely to our vicious practice of carving ornaments in a builder's yard instead of on the building itself.'

In woodwork, however, England was, as it had always been, vastly superior to France. 'The revival does not seem to have touched oak carvings across the channel; and artists, such as Viollet le Duc, or the architects of Ste. Clotilde, do not seem to have acquired either a discrimination of style, or to have grasped the fundamental notion of wood. But in panelling, moulding and foliage we have not observed any wood carving which surpasses, if it equals, what is, or was, so well known as "carpenters' Gothic" among ourselves.' [1] As to glass painting, 'the fairest thing to say is that the art is in a condition equally hopeless both in France and England. In many mechanical imitations, or facsimiles, of archaic glass perhaps France has a more pronounced—it certainly has a larger—success. In the attempts to combine purity and correctness of design with the normal requisites of vitreous painting, either country sustains a rivalry in failure.'

In regard to silversmiths' work, the two countries might profitably learn from

[1] p. 297.

each other. England excelled in purity of design, but France distanced it in elegance of execution. 'In delicacy and refinement of chasing, in piercing and twisted work, in jewelling, and above all, in enamels, our ecclesiastical artists have done little which can be compared to the metal altar and its decorations by MM. le Père Martin and Questel . . . Poussielgue Rusand, and the bronzists and enamelists of Paris remind us that we have very much to learn before we can sustain a rivalry in the goldsmith's art.'

In tiles and floor decorations, Mr. Minton's work easily surpassed that of France. The French did not seem to appreciate pavement tiles. No cathedral was much better paved than an English stable, but in its parquet floors, marquetry, the composition of metal and wood in inlaid work, and incised metal generally, France could supply hints which English church decorators could study with advantage.

Before the writer went to Paris he had fancied that in embroidery and needle-work England had attained an unapproachable excellence. At the Exhibition his anticipations were dispelled. The French knew quite as much about this subject as the English.

As to metal work, English products were, generally speaking, heavy and very costly. The French work was nearly as good, and cost less than half the English price. 'The foreign brass is as good as our own; the iron is decidedly inferior.'

Being familiar with the wall paintings and polychrome decorations in English churches by Mr. Pugin and his disciples, which were characterized by extreme delicacy and refinement of technique, it is not surprising to read that 'the French use the brush more freely, and we must fain add more coarsely and with less attention to ancient precedent than has been the rule in England. In the largest polychromatic restoration, that at S. Denis, we have our doubts whether many, if any, of the diapers can be supported by precedent.'

Some of the exhibits shocked the refined taste of English churchmen and churchwomen, accustomed by now to the sober dignity of Tractarian worship, and churches where almost every piece of furniture was 'correct.' The turbulent and anarchical nature of some of the continental ecclesiastical furnishings and decorations were beyond description. A gigantic pulpit of oak, designed by the Abbé Choyer, was summed up as the 'wildest absurdity.' In fact 'nothing could be much more objectionable in a church than this well-meant but preposterous extravagance, in which, nevertheless, the execution is by no means without merit.' Most of the French wood-carving was described as commonplace or cheap. High praise, however, was given to the exhibits from Holland and Belgium, which were less extravagant and more correct according to Camdenian standards than those designed and made in France.

But it was the carved stone altars which puzzled the English visitors brought up on Mr. Pugin. None of them had ever dreamed of anything like the marble altar designed for the new church at Vaugirard in the suburbs of Paris. Here a vast superstructure of two wide stages had the tabernacle resembling a Norman castle, which being rather heavy, was 'playfully relieved at the angle turrets by a huge daisy, which supposing the relative proportions between castle and vegetable to have been preserved, must represent an herbaceous monster at least seventy feet high.' The battlemented tabernacles, which appeared to be 'the normal conception of the French altar,' seemed as bombastic as many of the feminine fashions they noticed on the boulevards. Great exception was taken to the Mariolatry displayed in the symbolic decoration of a marble altar designed by the Abbé Choyer, entitled *'Hommage de tous les siècles à la Sainte Vierge.'* This priest was 'the ecclesiastical hero of the exhibition.' His marble altar for a church at Bordeaux showed 'wonderful spirit and absurdity.' The Abbé's playful genius had found full scope in the carving, which constituted 'a perfect *bestiarium,* as they would have said in old times.' It was alive with snails, caterpillars, butterflies, blind worms, newts, robins, wrens, and there was even a mouse gnawing at the branches. Such naturalistic humour was frowned on by the English ecclesiologists.

In the field of ceramic manufacture France was a long way ahead of England, though Messrs. Minton and Co. had no competitors in encaustic tiles. The reproductions of Majolica, Faenza and Palissy ware were much admired but there seemed no reason why the walls of English churches should not be lined with works equal to those of Della Robbia and the best Sèvres. 'We shall not be content with the uses of English pottery, certainly one of our specialities, until Etruria and Worcester cover our church walls and decorate our sanctuaries. We cannot understand how it is that our artists do not more freely avail themselves of the capabilities of porcelain. . . . Now what decoration is so chaste, so permanent in colour, so easily cleaned, so capable of correct design as a panel of mosaic porcelain for a retable, or chapel, or sanctuary lining? What admirable cornices, what sumptuous panelling, what delicate ceilings could we imagine! Why do we restrict Mr. Minton to our floors?' Nevertheless it was to be hoped that no Tractarian church across the Channel would ever be furnished with the gigantic porcelain font, without a base, but with all manner of emblems, legends, diapers, symbols, cherubs and flowers in the most frightful confusion, which was another monstrosity on view.

The vast metal altar, designed by M. Viollet le Duc for the Cathedral at Clermont, in a mixture of styles from Byzantine to Flamboyant Gothic, seemed positively barbaric, although it represented the sort of furniture that the modern French practice demanded. 'The use of Benediction is creating a revolution in the *Instrumenta altaris.* We now have an altar supporting a closed tabernacle, surmounted by an open baldachin, canopying over the monstrance, which again soars up into pinnacles and turrets. In short, the present French altar affects to combine the movable monstrance, and ciborium, the Spanish metallic *custodia,* the German *Sakrament Haus* and the Italian baldachin; in other words, the handicraft of the goldsmith, stone carver and textilist in one. The attempt is generally a failure.'

There were some exceptions, particularly the metal altar in pure Byzantine style, intended for the church of S. Martin at Lyons, designed by Questel and executed by the famous firm of Poussielgue Rusand. This altar was 'certainly the most beautiful work of Christian art executed in our times.' It was described in detail. Every portion 'of this lovely work' was carried out 'in the purest and most delicate style.' The 'charming group of angels who hang a rosary about the baldachin and the monstrance' was in keeping with the emotional spirituality of the French. The whole thing was of 'the most correct shape and admirable work,' the details of which were supplied by Père Martin. Once again high praise was given to the church metal work shown by craftsmen from Belgium and Holland. The brass eagle-lecterns, candlesticks and the *coronae lucis* were more like those made by Mr. Hardman in Birmingham—less bizarre and exotic than the French metal work, and consequently more congenial to sober English taste.

As to precious metals, the opinion expressed was that English goldsmiths ought to study 'the superior and delicate execution of the French artists.' 'English enamels have yet to be executed; that dead gold and silver are yet scarcely used, and that diapering and demascening of metal on metal are as carefully avoided by English artists as by heraldry itself. We want the material and skill, while France too often lacks the archeological knowledge of detail in the reproduction of *moyen age* metal work.' Some of the French and German exhibits were 'coarsely cast and ignorantly designed,' others as 'very ugly.'

Textile fabrics and embroidery showed a widespread improvement. A knowledge of the 'truer principles' seemed to be making its way. Many firms at Lyons were producing lovely silks suitable for vestments. Even lace work showed a definite advance. Shawl work seemed 'susceptible under the plastic influence of French taste, to be capable of any and every use'—even in banners and canopies. In all textile fabrics the Continent was advancing by leaps and bounds—silk, wool, cotton, velvet and every sort of printed and woven fabrics.

The English ecclesiologists looked a little wistfully at the copes, mitres, stoles and chasubles—'the latter of ancient cut, very beautifully wrought and jewelled, and very pure in design and harmonious in colour,' designed and made by M. André Kriechgauer of Paris, or those which were the work of M. Hubert Ménage. At home nobody like Père Martin, the editor of the *Album de Broderie Religieuse* could design beautiful patterns of ecclesiastical stuffs, or embroideries taken from the paintings by Fra. Angelico. There were no Anglican bishops in 1855 who would have had the courage to wear the pontifical vestments exhibited at the Palais de l'Industrie on the Champs Elysées. However, some of the Belgian copes and chasubles were dismissed as 'very vulgar and in the worst possible style.'

It was obvious that many of the French, Belgian and German designers of vestments had never studied Mr. Pugin's *Glossary of Ecclesiastical Ornament and*

Costume, or even the writings of M. Viollet le Duc, which also advocated the right principles, otherwise they would not have produced such horrible examples of the 'most pronounced rococo kind,' some of which were 'a disgrace to the Exhibition.'

The names of many now almost forgotten French stained glass artists are mentioned; including Didron, Bruin, Bouvières, Gerente, Lusson, Veissière, and Barzelous-Veyrat—all of which conjure up memories of early efforts of mock medieval windows in French cathedrals and parish churches; some full of charming *naïveté,* others vulgar and crude. The ecclesiologists clearly felt that no continental stained glass was better than that produced by their own Mr. Hardman. They thought nothing of the Belgian glass, and do not seem to have been impressed with the exhibits of the famous Munich school.

'We cannot but think that our church decorators would do well to import their finer materials.' Such was the general opinion of the writer of the article. He admitted that both England and Ireland have 'some very precious and admirable marbles,' but after this visit to Paris, and the sight of 'the sumptuous masses of magnificent building stone which every train conveys to Paris, when compared with the miles of paltry brick and stones which are glaring round the British metropolis,' convinced the writer that 'from mere lack of materials, London must be as a capital, the ugliest in the world.' More English churches would have to be adorned with materials from abroad. Within a few years this fashion would be started, due to the influence of Mr. Ruskin.

The long survey of the Paris Exhibition ends with some remarks on funeral monuments. The toy chapels with miniature altars and sham tabernacles playing at sacrifice and sacrament which abounded in the great cemetery of Père la Chaise were held up to derision, although some of them had prettily painted glass and furniture.

One thing is certain : the ecclesiastical furnishings and decorations which were on view in Paris in 1855 had a lasting even if subconscious influence on fashion for many years to come. A 'New Look' had been discovered. English 'good taste' never became so exciting and amusing as across the Channel. The products were not so rich, or so highly flavoured. On the other hand those English church furnishings of the 'fifties and 'sixties now seem less dated than the French equivalents. The former have withstood time better. They may lack brilliance, but they have undeniable quality.

CHAPTER XI

ECCLESIASTICAL FASHIONS OF THE EIGHTEEN-FIFTIES

A<small>N</small> occasional new church proved that Gothic had not triumphed over other styles, even by 1849, when Mr. Vulliamy's neo-Byzantine All Saints', Ennismore Gardens, London, was opened. Here was a spacious sanctuary, arranged correctly; the nave divided from the chancel by a low marble screen, with metal gates. Mr. Owen Jones had decorated the apse with polychrome paintings.[1]

Five years later the ecclesiologists decided that no church could be considered as really correctly furnished unless the sexes were separated. The right place for the men was on the south, and the women on the north. This rule applied to both rich and poor. It was laid down also that the proper place for the *parochus* was the western stall on the south or '*decani*' side of the chancel—'borrowed *mutatis mutandis* from the cathedral model.' Then there must be a 'kneeling hassock' for the altar—'small and striped, with the upper side embroidered.' Little velvet bags were recommended for the collection of alms. They should conform to the correct liturgical colours, and it was appropriate that they should be embroidered with symbolic emblems. This self-appointed Anglican Congregation of Rites decreed

Gothic gas brackets.
1854

BRASS GOTHIC GAS STANDARD BRACKETS, AND CORONA (Skidmore of Coventry, 1854) Surmounted by a crown, adorned with metal foliage

[1] All Saints' has now been turned into a Russian Orthodox church.

that it was expedient to have churchwardens or officials near the door of a church 'to keep order, where lads are wont to congregate.' Zinc plates for taking up the offertory were frowned upon, even if decorated with texts. If the sanctuary had a pavement of encaustic tiles, there was no need for a carpet.

In America, although the 'Greek Revival' in architecture remained a force until the Civil War of 1861–5, the Gothic Revival was fast ousting it. Mr. Upjohn had set an example with Trinity Church, New York, between 1839 and 1846. Mr. Renwick had designed Grace Church for the Episcopalians in 1845, and by 1850 had begun work on S. Patrick's Catholic Cathedral in the same city.

One detail which affected the correct furnishing of Episcopalian churches was the lack of any rubric concerning the position of the font, which in most new places of worship stood by the chancel, not at the west end of the building. By the middle of the eighteen-fifties several more new churches gave evidence of a distinct improvement in ecclesiastical good taste, as then understood. At Holy Innocents', New York, there was an octagonal font of Caen stone; a raised chancel, with a low screen and gates; and six choir stalls on either side of the chancel. Within the sanctuary two sedilia, a credence, piscina and aumbry had been inserted. The windows blazed with stained glass. People said that Zion Church, New York, was probably more richly decorated than any Episcopal place of worship yet consecrated in the United States.

Mr. Upjohn's First and Second Pointed church of S. Mary, Burlington, New Jersey, contained some interesting furnishings. There was a west gallery for the students of the college; and another gallery in the south transept for the pupils of S. Mary's Hall. The nave had open benches. The font stood just outside the chancel arch. The choir was raised on three steps and paved with Minton's tiles, imported from England. The stalls were correctly arranged, and the bishop's chair was said to be the handsomest in the country. Beside it rested his pastoral staff, made of old oak from S. Augustine's College, Canterbury. Three sedilia were provided for the clergy administering the Holy Communion, and near them was a neat bracket credence. Around the altar the open arcade of detached shafts and cusped arches had its upper surfaces inlaid with five crosses of holly wood. Most of the other woodwork was black walnut. The windows were filled with stained glass, and polychrome decorations by Mr. Akeroyd added colour to the walls and ceilings. Over the altar there was an illuminated I H S, with a very elaborate floriated cross on either side. The front of the altar was painted red and picked out with gold, relieved by a few texts in Gothic lettering. A critical visitor wrote: 'Such truly beautiful specimens of ecclesiastical art as this—richly solemn yet with nothing gaudy or tawdry in effect—will speedily render wall decoration as universal in our new churches, as stained glass.' [2]

By 1856 the church tourist in England would have noticed that the furnishings and decorations of Anglican places of worship were becoming more standardized; a good deal of monotony was observable, and there was very little variety in

[2] ibid. (1854), p. 388.

detail. New churches were still being built all over the country, and many more being restored. Certain leading architects, such as Mr. Street and Mr. Gilbert Scott, set the fashions, and a host of less talented imitators followed where these led the way.

But here and there exciting novelties could be discovered, including some of the London churches which were opened in 1856. At S. Andrew's, Stamford Street, Lambeth, Mr. Teulon, evidently influenced by Mr. Butterfield, had combined brick with rare stones in the reredos, which consisted of seven trefoiled arches, serpentine shafts, and circles of the same marble in the spandrils. There was a bold projecting cornice, and a band of encaustic tiles. *The Ecclesiologist* felt that Mr. Teulon deserved credit for his boldness, and hoped that far more use would be made of serpentine, now that it could be steam polished. There was the already popular type of framed communion table of carved oak, and a sanctuary rail of stone. Altogether this church near Waterloo Bridge must have been very colourful and gay before London smoke dimmed the red and white brick in the nave, and the chequered diaper of red brick on a white ground in the chancel.

By way of contrast S. Saviour's, Eton Road, Hampstead, was a conventional type of Gothic Revival church, designed by Mr. E. M. Barry, a son of the more famous Sir Charles Barry, the architect of the Houses of Parliament. Here the incumbent had introduced a very seemly type of mild ritualism. The furnishings were correct. The altar was raised seven steps above the nave floor, and properly vested. The elaborate reredos was adorned with a riot of painted symbols. The side walls were prettily diapered. The blue painted chancel roof was encrusted with gold stars. There was an elaborately carved stone pulpit with marble shafts, and angels in the arcades. The sanctuary rail was of iron, coloured blue, and there were stalls on either side of the chancel, but no screen.

Mr. Ewan Christian, a sound churchman of the Evangelical school of thought, who since 1850 had been architect to the Ecclesiastical Commissioners, had just completed a very different type of church in Nutford Place, Marylebone. Here the visitor found a sort of open bema, projecting into the nave, with the pulpit and reading desk at either end. There was a wooden sanctuary rail of flamboyant design. Around the communion table of carved open wood were painted trefoil patterns. Below the east window, forming a reredos, the wall was diapered in salmon pink.

At Mr. Little's newly opened S. Saviour's, Warwick Avenue, Paddington, below the east window in the Middle-Pointed style, filled with stained glass by Mr. Gibbs, was a stone reredos, composed of canopied panels, divided by serpentine shafts. Each panel was filled with gay painted imitation encaustic tiles—a sham which the purists felt deserving of the highest reprobation. There was the usual sort of Gothic Revival pulpit on a stone base. The whole interior was 'a sight curious enough, but truth forbad calling it beautiful.' Mr. Pugin's ideas of colour decoration in churches had long since been taken over and adapted even to the most moderate of Anglican modes of worship.

Some striking new churches outside London were also completed in 1856; the most remarkable of all being the chancel of S. Mary's, Marychurch, Torquay, designed by an architect named Hugall.[3] It was described as rising above the old nave like 'a miniature Cologne Cathedral, or S. Peter's, Leyden.' There was a spacious sanctuary, raised on two steps. Below the five-light east window an extremely ornate reredos framed a carved stone relief of Leonardo da Vinci's 'Last Supper.' The side panels, which reached to the ground, depicted the Ten Commandments in Gothic illumination. Highly commended were the credence table, the sacrarium and the four spacious sedilia. The five choir stalls on either side of the chancel had 'subsellae.' Behind the stalls were brass gas standards, ingeniously tied together by horizontal bands of brass work, forming graceful parcloses. The organ pipes were blue painted, powdered with gold fleur-de-lis. The low chancel screen was formed of stone panels with Devonshire marble shafts and carved capitals reproducing flowers and fruit. Mr. Hardman had provided rich iron and brass cresting and gates for the screen, set off with many crosses. The stone pulpit had its panels filled with embossed gilt metal, with a cross on the central panel. To add to the devotional aspect of this interior there were multi-coloured encaustic tiles. Most of the windows were already filled with stained glass from the studio of Mr. Wailes.

Another outstanding interior was to be found at Ilam in Staffordshire, where Mr. Scott had been at work on the church. Here an open metal chancel screen had been wrought by Mr. Skidmore, with elaborate cresting and colour. The choir stalls had 'subsellae,' and there were brass standards for lighting on either side of the chancel gates. The east wall of the chancel must have looked very gay, composed of a diaper of coloured tiles, which set off the alabaster reredos, marble shafts and rich arcading. The panels were tiled, with a large gold cross in the centre one. The stained glass by Mr. Clayton in the east window completed the decorative ensemble. Unlike so many churches erected a hundred years ago, the interior of Ilam is more or less unaltered.

Remembering how Dr. Longley, Bishop of Ripon, had objected to an inscription within S. Saviour's, Leeds, pointing out that it would imply prayer for a sinner *after* his death as well as during his lifetime—the sinner in question being Dr. Pusey, who had contributed most of the money for this new church—it was strange to find round the chancel arch of S. John the Evangelist, Cradley, the words: 'Blessed are the dead which die in the Lord.' This new Early Middle-Pointed church was situated on one of the spurs of the Malvern Hills, and was designed by Mr. Preedy of Worcester. It had been built as a memorial to a son of the late Dean of St. Asaph, Dr. Luxmore, the sometime rector of Cradley. The architect had depicted angels with golden censers in one of the many stained glass windows. Moreover, the oak altar had a slab of Painswick stone, and was raised on a footpace. The chancel and sanctuary were paved with Minton's tiles. A low stone screen divided the holy places from the nave. The symbolism of the steps of the Caen stone font forming a cross was interesting: 'the Sacraments have their due and prominent prominence; and indeed all the ritual arrangements and general

[3] Mostly destroyed in the Second World War.

tone and teaching of this church are excellent, forming no small contrast with the miserable barn-like look of the mother church, with its cast iron east window . . . its west gallery, high pews, great "three decker," and poor, unseen altar.' [4]

While British troops were fighting the Chinese and the Persians, and the Crimea was being finally evacuated by the allied armies—a peace treaty having been signed at Paris on March 30th, 1856—more and more men were being employed at home on the restoration of churches. Thanks to the railway systems which were spreading over the country, it was much easier to visit them.

Some very good restoration work had been carried out in Warwickshire, for instance at Southam. Superior stained glass by Mr. Wailes filled the four-light east window. The new altar, consisting of a large slab of oak, marked with five crosses, supported on an oak frame had a frontal and super-frontal of crimson Utrecht velvet; but Glastonbury chairs were used instead of a correct sedilia. Mr. Skidmore's two or three gas standards were worthy of notice, but Mr. Scott, the architect employed, ought to have known better than to allow the rector to use that abominable 'Gothic box' for a prayer desk, which stood by the old pulpit, and blocked up the new desk which was a continuation of the stalls.

At Worm-Leighton, near Leamington, the medieval rood-loft had been preserved, but prayers were not said within the enclosed chancel, where the ancient seats still remained. Here, as in most other churches which had been restored, the seats had been cut down and well arranged.

As to the large parish church at Leamington, its furnishings were most faulty—in fact, it was better not to attempt to describe them. Not so very long ago the ritual was properly carried out here, but the vicar feeling that he ought to 'move with the times,' gave all up and moved to London, where he conducted the services in a proprietary chapel of an extremely Evangelical character.

Quite a number of the restored churches could boast of encaustic tiles and painted glass by Holland of Warwick or Hardman of Birmingham. The Third-Pointed chancel of the otherwise pagan-like S. Mary's, Warwick, had a correctly vested altar standing on a footpace, and the sanctuary was covered with a rich carpet. Highly commended was the needlework hanging used as a reredos, and so were Mr. Skidmore's two brass gas standards on either side of the sanctuary.

But of all the many restored churches in Warwickshire, none surpassed S. John the Baptist's, Wasperton, where Mr. Scott had been allowed full scope for his genius. A visitor remarked that *'Nil desperandum* should have been engraved on its walls, as an encouragement to all who despair of restoring ugly churches.' [5] The rich rood screen was surmounted by a large cross. On the beam itself, in gilt letters, were the words: *Non nobis, Domine, non nobis.* The space between the choir stalls was carpeted. The front and sides of the altar were adorned with Minton's tiles. Standing on the altar were the Book of the Gospels, alms-dish, and two candlesticks. Below the footpace stood two splendid brass standard

[4] ibid., pp. 456–7.
[5] ibid. (1856), p. 131.

candlesticks. The choir stalls were illumined by wax candles on simpler standards. Costly crimson curtains hung down on the east wall. Below the Middle-Pointed east window of three lights, the verse 'Except ye eat the Flesh of the Son of Man, and drink His Blood, ye have no life in you' was engraved on brass. Both piscina and sedilia were used by the vicar. The stone figure of S. Cecilia was appropriately placed on the key-stone of the arch over the organ recess. Two immense wax-candles provided light for reading the lessons at the large brazen eagle. The Hardman glass in the east window was said to be Pugin's last design. Wasperton was indeed a model of what every country parish church ought to be. According to a recent report it still retains its original character.

CHAPTER XII

LEGAL AND ILLEGAL CHURCH ORNAMENTS

Anglican bishops during the eighteen-forties and -fifties were terrified of altar crosses and regarded crucifixes as nothing more than emblems of idolatry. Other furnishings and ornaments, recommended by the Camden Society and ecclesiologists in general, were equally disapproved of. By 1850 church furnishers were wondering what ecclesiastical goods it was safe to make and put on the market, so great was the terror in episcopal circles that the services of the reformed Church of England were being assimilated to those of the Church of Rome.

Matters reached a crisis in 1854 when Mr. Charles Westerton, one of the church-wardens at S. Paul's, Knightsbridge, London, brought a suit against the vicar, the Hon. and Revd. Robert Liddell, in the hope that the Consistory Court of the Diocese of London would order the removal of certain illegal ornaments from S. Paul's, and its daughter church, S. Barnabas', Pimlico.

A great blow was struck to the improvement of the furnishings of Anglican places of worship when late in 1856 judgment was given in the Court of Arches that a movable altar cross was illegal, since it could be regarded only as one of those 'images' which the Injunctions of Edward VI ordered to be destroyed, having been used for superstitious purposes. The Westerton case was indeed a Protestant victory over the ecclesiologists. During the course of this long and vexatious suit, little progress could be made towards correcter ritualism, since neither architects nor clergymen dared buy either crosses or candlesticks. Hence the numerous churches which had been built or restored in which there was merely a painted or fixed stone cross in the reredos. The legal position had become very complicated. Nobody could be sure what ornaments were permitted. The opinion of the more advanced Tractarians was thus expressed: 'As the strict law is at this moment interpreted, we are not certain that we should not be greatly the gainers, in compounding for a movable altar cross and a change of altar frontals, by the universal enforcement, even in Islington and Brighton, of lighted candles, vestments and copes.' [1]

'Speaking from a wide knowledge of facts, we assert further that our ritualists have, as a rule, rigidly confined themselves not merely to what they honestly

[1] ibid., Vol. XVIII, New Series XIV (1857), p. 32.

believed to be sanctioned by the rubrics and proper construction of our formularies, but to a still lower standard. It is the ignorance, perhaps, as much as the malice, of our opponents that has confused—in matters of ritual as of doctrine—what is Catholic with what is "Popish." A deeper knowledge would show them that the Roman Catholic Communion has, in its Oratorian party and their antagonists, a kind of parallel to our own rival schools in the matter of external worship.' [2] It looked as if the ban on movable altar crosses was going to be disastrous to such firms as Messrs. Hardman, which meantime could only find a Roman Catholic market for their goods.

By April 1857 the position had clarified to the extent that the designers and suppliers of church furnishings had a clearer idea of the goods which were lawful and those which were forbidden. A final judgment of the Privy Council had been given on Mr. Liddell's two appeals concerning the decisions made previously in regard to S. Paul's and S. Barnabas's. The things complained of were:

1. An altar, or holy table of stone.
2. A credence table.
3. An altar cross.
4. A cross upon a chancel screen.
5. Altar lights.
6. Frontals of various colours.
7. Linen cloths edged with lace.
8. A chancel-screen with gates.
9. The Decalogue not inscribed on the east wall.

When, after endless discussion, the case emerged from the dark recesses of Doctors' Commons, the Anglican clergy, their architects and craftsmen were told that altar lights and a chancel-screen with gates were not *ultra vires*. The ecclesiologists were thankful that other ornaments could now be added to the original list— the credence table; the cross on the chancel-screen, and the unrestricted use of the cross as a *symbol;* frontals of various colours; and the altar cross *so it be not fixed.* What they lost were—the stone altar, the lace and the permission to omit the inscription of the Ten Commandments in the chancel.

They felt that they had counter-attacked effectively on the Protestant stronghold and could afford to make light of the petty defects in this final judgment of the Privy Council, acting as if it had the authority of the Roman Congregation of Rites. All this fuss about the altar cross was just ridiculous. What was condemned was a fixed stone or metal cross, not *as* a cross, but as part of the structure of an altar. What was *not* condemned was, e.g., a cross of metal or stone standing on the super altar.

What the ritualists gained were:

1. In the chancel and screen, the principle of choral worship, and the separation of orders in the congregation.
2. In the credence, the doctrine of an Oblation in the Eucharist.

[2] ibid., p. 31.

3. In the cross on the chancel-screen the affirmation of the principle of symbolic allusion, and the adherence of the Church of England to historical antiquity.

4. In the permission given to the use of frontals of various colours, they had wrested from the enemy the sacredness of the Christian year, and the ritual commemoration of saints and martyrs.

5. In the altar lights, not only was preserved a symbolic allusion of especial propriety, but what was far greater, a relative dignity as due to the place and time of the celebration of the especial Christian mysteries.

As was pointed out by a writer in *The Ecclesiologist*: 'With an altar or holy table, be it of wood or stone, vested according to the Christian season, surmounted with a cross and reredos on the east wall, furnished with super-altar and altar lights, flanked by a credence table, with a chancel separated by a high screen and gates, and the chancel itself furnished with stalls, and above all, this altar served by priest and deacon in their distinctive vestments, it will be very difficult indeed to persuade, be it friends or foes of the Church of England, that with all this pomp and dignity of ritual permitted and enjoined, our Church does not hold the very highest doctrine, even though the Christian sacrifice be celebrated on a wooden altar, and even though the east wall be decorated with the Decalogue in unintelligible black letter, or though there be a judgment prohibiting—without defining—the additional splendour of two yards of "bone lace." If Puritanism considers this decision a victory, we can only wish its advocates a few more such triumphs. Dr. Lushington's wicked and senseless talk about "meretricious ornaments" and the "servile imitators of a corrupt ritual," we are not likely to meet with in quarters more respectable than that of the *Morning Advertiser*.' [3]

[3] ibid., pp. 116–18.

CHAPTER XIII

WILLIAM BUTTERFIELD

THE next figure of note is William Butterfield (1814–1906), whose influence on the fashions of church furnishings and interior decoration during the second half of the nineteenth century was far reaching. 'This stern Anglican in steel rimmed spectacles' was, we are reminded, the contemporary of Dickens, Thackeray, the Brontës, George Eliot, Anthony Trollope and Robert Browning. Ruskin was five years his junior. We know very little of his early life, before he became the friend of the leading members of the Cambridge Camden Society. By 1847 Butterfield had contributed largely to *Instrumenta Ecclesiastica*—a book of approved designs for church furnishings of all kinds.

Butterfield, throughout his whole life adhered to the most rigid form of High Church Anglicanism. 'Church building and worship were the whole content of his life. He built nearly one hundred churches, restored many others, and his secular work (apart from vicarages) was confined to certain collegiate works in Oxford, two large houses, a hospital and a few other things of small importance.' [1]

In Butterfield's work there is 'none of Pugin's romantic glory, of Scott's paterfamilias geniality, of Street's high enthusiasm. Butterfield stood separate from those contemporaries of his, hardly knew them, and mixed only with the High Church clergy in the constricted social life he allowed himself in his afternoon visits to the Atheneum.' [2] There was always something curiously remote from the humdrum realities in the furnishings and decorations of the places of worship designed by this fierce Victorian architect. His influence was hardly felt outside the Anglican fold. Few Roman Catholic churches built between 1850 and 1900 owe anything to Butterfield. Had he been invited to design one, it is probable that his religious convictions would have made him refuse.

Formerly there were three churches in Scotland in which one could study Butterfield's earlier mannerisms, but very few of his furnishings are left in S. Ninian's Cathedral, Perth, the chancel and transepts of which were consecrated in 1850. The original fittings were described as 'homely' (see p. 90).

The chapel of Trinity College, Glenalmond, begun in 1846, was not consecrated until 1851. Ecclesiologists were greatly shocked at a series of closed box-like pews

[1] John Summerson, *Heavenly Mansions* (1949), Chapter VII, 'William Butterfield, or the glory of ugliness.'
[2] ibid., p. 162.

I

for the parochial congregation, which stood in the ante-chapel. Within the choir, behind an open screen, the boys' stalls were arranged antiphonally, 'but the rows are too numerous to give the effect of stalls,' so we are told. A brass eagle and a litany-stool took up space in the gangway. A critical visitor wrote: 'The sanctuary, which is well raised, is panelled with wood work of a very poor design, unsatisfactorily relieved with gilding. The altar is covered with a velvet carpet, somewhat richly embroidered.' [3]

The same writer maintained that 'the college and collegiate church of the Holy Spirit, in the island of Greater Cumbrae . . . is a work upon which Mr. Butterfield may safely rely for the earnest of a permanent and solid fame.' The church was dedicated on Whitsunday 1851. It is of small dimensions, but very richly furnished and decorated—typical of all that is best of Butterfield in his earlier manner; in fact it is the germ from which much of his later work evolved.

The nave was furnished with chairs for the use of the lay congregation—a great novelty in the early eighteen-fifties. The lofty stone screen of three divisions has two columns of polished Aberdeen granite. Bold and simple tracery fills up the chancel arch, in the middle of which was an elaborately carved stone cross. The chancel ceiling, with polygonal rafters, is painted with dog roses and ferns. There are twelve choir stalls on either side. The sanctuary is spacious and well raised, with simple recessed niches as sedilia. A visitor in the late 'fifties remarked that 'the altar is somewhat short, a very uncommon fault with Mr. Butterfield.' Hangings added to the colour, and the side walls were 'enriched with constructional mosaics in lozenges of coloured files, counterchanged with white slabs of the same form.' We are told, 'in this decoration we begin to see traces of that style which has subsequently acquired far too strong a hold of Mr. Butterfield's affections.' [4] The two windows in the chancel were filled with Hardman's stained glass. All the instruments were sumptuous, complete and correct. No mention is made of an altar cross and candlesticks, they were possibly not introduced until later. A novel feature, certainly in such an out of the way part of Scotland, was the lighting by gas. The nave was lit by a row of several hundred jets at the string-course line. The effect was said to be most successful; 'the only drawback being that the smoke had considerably darkened the wall behind.'

Here on this island in the Firth of Clyde the Episcopal Church in Scotland had established a Collegiate Church, served by a body of resident canons under a provost. Provision was made in the picturesque Gothic Revival building for other clergy residing for the purpose of retirement and study, or as guests; as also young men who were preparing for holy orders. Nowhere in Britain was there anything quite like it. The daily services were fully choral, thanks to the generosity of the founder, the Hon. George Frederick Boyle, who in 1869 became Sixth Earl of Glasgow. There were six resident boy choristers, who lived with the organist, and were taught by him. But we are told that the ritual of the Collegiate Church was

[3] *Ecclesiologist* (1859), Vol. XX, New Series XVII, p. 384. The interior of the chapel has been much altered in recent years.
[4] ibid., p. 381.

'modest,' and that the provost and canons strictly adhered to the set of regulations drawn up for them by Dr. Ewing, the far from High Church Bishop of Argyll and the Isles. Even after more than a century the College of the Holy Spirit, now served by its provost alone, because the dream of the founder was long since abandoned, still preserves its Tractarian atmosphere.

The interior of S. Mary Magdalene's, West Lavington, Sussex, still retains its characteristic early Butterfield feeling, and displays almost none of his later mannerisms. Yet there is already something hard and defiant in its furnishings, that differentiates them from similar work by any of his contemporaries. This church, situated at the extreme west end of Archdeacon Manning's large parish, had been built by his curate Laprimaudaye, and was consecrated on November 26th, 1850. Within three weeks the curate went over to the Roman Church. His former rector followed him in April 1851. One cannot help wondering if Butterfield's rigid Anglican principles had anything to do with this.

There were a few people who criticized the design of S. Matthias's, Stoke Newington, opened in 1850, which was Butterfield's first London church. Amongst them were the ecclesiologists who took great exception to some of the furnishings and decorations of the interior. First of all, there was no chancel screen. Seldom had anything more heavy or positively ugly been seen than the woodwork. The greatest blemish was the reredos, which had exactly the effect of Tunbridge-ware when seen from a distance; the tiles were too highly glazed. The recessed stone sedilia, with wooden seats, were praised and the Gothic gas standards, elegantly designed and wrought, formed beautiful pyramids of flame which lighted for Evensong. There was daily choral service. Mr. Helmore's *Psalter Noted* and *Hymnal Noted* were used, and helped to familiarize the upper middle-class inhabitants of north London with a ponderous type of Gregorian chant. When the church was consecrated there was no stained glass, except that by Wailes in the east window. Soon after this Butterfield designed a *corona lucis* which was suspended over the chancel. It was a thankoffering from the parishioners; Bishop Blomfield having nominated as successor to the Revd. T. A. Pope, who duly seceded to the Roman Church, a clergyman who was prepared to continue the same type of mild Tractarian ritualism.

By 1858 Butterfield's ideas had got as far as New Zealand, where his designs for the Early Middle-Pointed church of S. Matthew's, Auckland, were greatly admired for their bold and then most unusual interior furnishings and decorations. The reredos was intended to be composed of a sculptured band under the three-light east window, against which were apposed four pilasters. The walls were patterned in local stone of a rather deep blue and greenish colour.

The interior of the new chapel of Balliol College, Oxford, showed Butterfield's austerity of taste, or what some people called his craze for sheer ugliness. The stalls were massive. The sanctuary pavements were of mixed marble and tile. the side walls were lined with alabaster, combined with incised lines, richly cross-hatched and filled in with mastic. His favourite wooden sedilia stood under a recessed arch. The reredos consisted of a traceried arcade. Garish colour contrasts hit the eye everywhere. A visitor remarked that 'the decoration of party-coloured bands, after the manner of curtain poles, does not cure the defect of the continual mutation of outline.' It was impossible to praise 'the feeble greenish blue' of the sanctuary roof.[5]

It is difficult for us to recapture the enthusiasm which went with the building of All Saints', Margaret Street. As Beresford Hope pointed out to Benjamin Webb in a letter dated November 1845: 'we must really make our church a model Church: it should have, like S. Saviour's, Leeds, the spiritual advantage of being planted on a site which very much wants one, combined with great artistic perfection.' Eventually a site was obtained in the parish of All Souls', Langham Place. We are told that the dedication was chosen on the ground that it would be easier to adorn the church with the figures of various saints than with illustrations of the history of one particular saint. This would give occasion to offend Protestant prejudices.

Beresford Hope and his friends needed to be circumspect, remembering how strong was the fear of Romanism as the result of Newman's recent secession from 'the Church of his Baptism.'

Margaret Chapel had been closed after its minister, the Revd. Frederic Oakeley, went over to Rome in 1845. It was reopened two years later when the Revd. Upton Richards was appointed. The last service took place on Easter Monday, 1850. The building was then pulled down. The first stone of the new church was laid on All Saints' Day that same year by Dr. Pusey.

Both Dr. Blomfield, Bishop of London, and Beresford Hope found William Butterfield a difficult architect to deal with during the nine years that the walls of All Saints' were rising. The letters that were exchanged show how confused were the ideas then held by all parties on the planning and furnishing of Anglican churches. Butterfield wanted chairs or low benches; Beresford Hope favoured pews. The latter pointed out in a letter written from Belgium, 'The people (here) live in a lodging and dine at a café, whereas English people live in their own houses and dine at their own tables. Also as All Saints' is a parish church, I must as Church Warden, when I am so, allot places to those parishioners who require them. . . . If John Bull will live up to chairs, I shall be astonished. . . . If chairs were introduced in part of the Church it would create a new distinction of castes, the aristos taking the chairs as more exclusive, each man the master of his own seat, of the legs of it, potent to lift it and turn it, while the benches would be left to the poor.' [6]

The size of the crinoline was probably mainly responsible for the substitution of open benches or chairs instead of narrow box-like pews in new churches. On

---

[5] The interior of the Chapel has been much changed in recent years, with the new Renaissance altar and panelling designed by Sir Walter Tapper.
[6] H. W. Law and Irene Law, *The Book of the Beresford Hopes* (1925), p. 175.

July 9th, 1859 there was a drawing in *Punch,* depicting a chair-proprietor in a London park, saying to a lady in a vast crinoline, 'Well, Mum—How many might you be a sittin' on?' On June 23rd, 1860, a notice appeared in *The Times*: 'Ladies persist in attending Divine worship in Crinoline. Pews hired out to accommodate four persons will, therefore, now barely contain two.' *Punch* felt it worth while to print the following letter. 'I myself rent a couple of seats in our parish church, which I attend regularly with my little daughter. The two others are rented to some neighbours of mine—handsome, well dressed good natured women, against whom I have nothing to say, save that they attire their persons from the waist downwards in a sort of steel-ribbed apparatus, like a carriage umbrella inverted, over which acres of silks and muslins and ribbons are festooned. If they arrive before us they quite fill the pew, and my little girl and myself are obliged humbly to creep in under their petticoats; it being as much as we can do to keep our heads above Crinoline during service. If we happen to come before them to church they sit down upon us in the most remorseless way, swaggering and hoisting about their gig umbrellas.'

The comment of 'Mr. Punch' was: 'Magistrates should render Crinoline an element in female convict and workhouse uniform. This might bring into a degree of discredit which it has not as yet contracted from the quality of a class of its wearers who are more numerous than respectable.' On July 27th, 1861, *Punch* had an amusing drawing showing how architects ought to design entrances to churches with wide splayed Gothic openings at the bottom to facilitate the admission of crinolines.

In the end Butterfield won the battle over the seating, and it was finally agreed to instal chairs.

The planning and furnishing of the chancel raised more problems. Bishop Blomfield objected to the gates in the low screen, and refused to give way. It had been taken for granted that there would be a choir school attached to All Saints', but after a while Beresford Hope became sceptical about boy choristers. There was 'all the difference in the world between a chorister brought up on the medieval system and one who after he has been petted and coddled and dressed up at Tichfield Street [Margaret Chapel] or S. Andrew's [Wells Street] becomes at 18 or 19 a tallow chandler. Choristers, mostly unconfirmed, are admitted within the chancel rails, while confirmed laymen are kept out. The Anglo-Puseyite chorister system is out of joint. The remedy is to institute parochial choirs under some sort of guild regulations, irrespective of the quality of their performance.' [7]

By 1853 Beresford Hope was fighting Butterfield about more details of the planning and furnishing. He objected to the frescoes above the altar, the German plan of a choir raised above the nave, and 'the fixed super-altar,' adding: 'Butterfield will, I fear, get more and more wild, and will not stop till he finds himself Butterfield against the world, not as Athanasius; I have often imagined he might be tending to Irvingism.' [8]

[7] ibid., p. 172.   [8] ibid., p. 176.

Bishop Blomfield died in 1856, and Dr. Tait succeeded him as Bishop of London; proving even more difficult to deal with than his predecessor. He insisted that work at All Saints' must be stopped until he had approved the plans. The opening of the new church might have been postponed even longer had it not been that the Prince Consort was taken to inspect it by Bishop Tait. Beresford Hope wrote in a letter that the Prince 'admired all things and showed considerable *nous* upon artistic matters.' Royal approval was enough to make the bishop feel that he could dedicate the church without fear of Protestant protests.

May 28th, 1859, was fixed as the date. Mr. Upton Richards made it as imposing a function as he dared. The Revd. Thomas Helmore intoned the service, using his own *Manual of Plain Song*. When the bishop mounted into the heavy and stately marble pulpit, adorned with mosaics, he took good care to remind the congregation that 'no Church allows such diversity of doctrine as the Church of England.' He begged them 'not to be carried away by the dedication of All Saints',' and expressed the wish that 'every one has his own taste for a simple ritual.'

Then came a hitch in the proceedings. Dr. Tait flatly refused to proceed with the service of dedication until the altar frontal had been removed. Beresford Hope tells us what happened next. 'Richards, for whom I did feel, quite lost his head, and rushed out of Church, not knowing what to do. I went with him, and made him get a tablecloth from the house. An edifying sight, he and another man pulling that on over the frontal in face of the congregation.' [9]

Even the most evangelical Anglican of to-day would not object to the 'ritual' that offended Bishop Tait in 1859. The wooden communion table at All Saints' had no cross standing on it, granted that William Dyce had inserted a crucifix in the centre of the upper row of paintings which filled up most of the east wall. There was also a symbolic cross high up in the polychromatic decorations above the chancel arch. A third cross hardly visible from the nave in this dim dark church, formed part of the carving behind the communion table. Nevertheless loyal Protestants had sufficient reason to fear that Mariolatry would flourish at All Saints'. The lowest middle panel of the reredos had for its subject the Virgin and Child with three angels in adoration. 'Some have accused Dyce of a tendency to sentimentalism in this group, but it is impossible to share the objection. A more lovely and tenderly imagined group was never painted by the artist.' [10]

As a matter of fact it was neither the ceremonial nor the furnishings that disturbed people at All Saints'; it was the overwhelming effect of the interior as a whole. Nothing like it had ever been seen before in England. Mr. Beresford Hope wrote that it was 'the first decided experiment in London of building in poly-chromatic material; and the numerous brood of imitations which has followed its path attests to the vitality of the attempt.' [11]

[9] ibid., p. 167.
[10] T. F. Bumpus, *London Churches Ancient and Modern*, second series, p. 250.
[11] *English Cathedral of the Nineteenth Century* (1861), p. 234.

A century ago, when all the materials were new and not smoke grimed, the effect of the interior of All Saints', Margaret Street, must have been startling. In addition to coloured brick, there was a riot of Devonshire marble, Cornish serpentine, polished Peterhead granite and alabaster. Nowhere could there be found rest for the eye. It was dazzled and distracted. From the diagonal patterns on the stone pavement, right up into the intricate timber roof above the nave. The chancel walls were clothed with more alabaster. Tiles were used for the band of Mosaic picture which covers the entire length of the north aisle wall. Coloured brick in various patterns was used for the shorter wall of the south aisle.

To complete the kaleidoscopic colour scheme there were the stained glass windows, Henri Gerente, a French artist, designed the great west window. Most of the smaller windows had stained glass by O'Connor.

Although the interior of this most unusual church was gorgeous—it is even richer to-day—nevertheless many people criticized it. One was Mr. W. J. Cockburn Muir, who wrote: 'The mind, through the eye, is distracted by a whirling maze of variegated colouring and gilded pictures; and led wandering from this side to that, and to the other, until fixity of meditation becomes impossible. There is everything to make you look *around,* but very little to direct you heavenward. The Object of worship is forgotten, in the gaudy luxuriousness of the scene of worship.' [12] The stern critic finally warns: 'Beware of Colour. Let the Pagan-Art-harlot paint her bold cheek. But do not encumber Christian architecture, and sink her to the dust, with the buffooneries of unmeaning pageantry.' [13]

Mr. Beresford Hope, who dreamed that All Saints' would be *the* perfect church, lost all interest in it after the dedication. It made him very sad, he said. 'Butterfield has so paricidically spoilt his own creation with the clown's dress, so spotty and spidery and flimsy as it looks in a mass now it is all done, and worst of all the church looks so much smaller than it used to do with nothing but the solemn columns to give scale. Butterfield on his side is honestly fanatical in his colour doctrine, and completely believes that I have marred the world's greatest work. . . . *Pour moi,* it is all much the same, as I very likely may never go there again.' [14]

This small church in the heart of the west end of London had a far-reaching influence on fashions in church furnishing and decoration for years to come. As Mr. John Summerson truly remarks, 'from the hardness and ruthlessness of All Saints' emerges that noble elegance which makes it, in some ways, the most moving building of the century.' He also reminds us that 'the first glory of Butterfield is his utter ruthlessness. How he hated "taste." And how right he was. . . . To him hardness and coarseness were a deeply sincere protest against what was wiry, soft and genteel.' [15]

Mr. Summerson also praises the ingenious inventiveness of Butterfield. 'He was, I repeat, an innocent. His sense of composition was perfectly naïve . . . in decoration too, he was often a real primitive, with his zigzags and curls and crudely

[12] *Pagan or Christian?* p. 221.
[13] ibid., p. 276.
[14] *The Book of the Beresford Hopes,* p. 177.
[15] *Heavenly Mansions* (1949), p. 173.

coloured geometry. His painted roofs are like huge ingenious toys from a giant's nursery. . . . To-day, we have an age of taste or, at least, an age eager to become such. Butterfield frowns upon us from the 1850s. Taste is the smiling surface of a lake whose depths are great, impenetrable and cold. At unpredictable moments the waters divide, the smooth surface vanishes and the depths are revealed. But only for a moment and the storm leaves nothing but ripples on the fresh icy surface. Butterfield reminds us of this as we go along Margaret Street or Queen's Gate or the Gray's Inn Road or stand in the red umbrage of Keble.' [16]

Another writer remarks that, 'Five minutes, or even five seconds, in [All Saints'] should be enough to demolish the belief that the Victorian High Church was all facile, sanctimonious, honeyed, self-deceiving. The brutal, exalted, hunched, jarring sincerity of the forms, the violent and homespun chauvinism in the choice of materials, the insistent clamour of symbolic decoration on every flat inch, are all on the same wavelength as the Donne of 'Batter my soul.' [17]

It is not hard to-day to understand the sensation aroused by All Saints' a hundred years ago. The man in the street had never seen anything like it. Some people said that it reminded them of the Pre-Raphaelite paintings; an opinion which was shared by *The Ecclesiologist,* who maintained: 'Here is to be observed the germ of the same dread of beauty, not to say the same deliberate preference for ugliness, which so characterizes in fuller development the latter paintings of Mr. Millais and his followers.' [18] The same writer had nothing but praise for 'the overwhelming flood of gorgeous green and gold light of the west window,' and had to admit that there is 'no church in our Communion that can approach All Saints' in dignity and beauty of the adornment of its most sacred part.' Nevertheless the plain alabaster wall beneath Mr. Dyce's paintings, with a metal cross affixed to it, was 'more conspicuous than graceful.' The brass lettern as 'grandiose,' and the font-cover of wood and brass showed 'too great heaviness.' The very low choir stalls were dismissed as 'not very effective.' However in spite of many defects of detail, 'We have never had occasion to notice a more suitable and dignified adaptation to the Anglican ritual than this magnificent church presents. . . . We do not say that All Saints', Margaret Street, is a perfect "model-church." We have not scrupled here, as always, to criticize freely. But we assert, without fear of contradiction, that our generation has seen no greater or more memorable work, or one more pregnant with important consequences to the future of art in England.' [19]

Many of Butterfield's favourite fashions appeared in his earlier church, S. Thomas's, Leeds (1851), which *The Ecclesiologist* pronounced to be 'quite worthy of All Saints', Margaret Street.' Much of the interior brick work was red, black and white. Above the chancel arch was 'a very elegant pattern, composed of a cross in a circle.' The font was made of Devonshire marbles. The gas standards, with fleur-de-lis heads, were 'very commendable.' [20]

[16] ibid., pp. 175–6.
[17] E. and W. Young, *Old London Churches* (1956), p. 248.
[18] op. cit., Vol. XX, New Series XVII, p. 185.
[19] ibid., pp. 188–9.
[20] This church has been destroyed.

Of the same date were the furnishings of S. Luke's, Sheen, Staffordshire. Here Butterfield inserted a plain alabaster reredos; in the centre of which was a cross of red Devonshire marble, set off with four spots of black marble. The effect was said to be 'very striking.' There were brass altar rails, and 'very elegant candlesticks, enriched with crystals on the knops, and *niello* quatre-foils on the bases.' Most of the choir fittings came from Margaret Chapel, after it had been pulled down.

The new furnishings in the restored church of S. Michael, Hathersage, also belonging to the early 'fifties, roused *The Ecclesiologist* to say that Mr. Butterfield's 'reprobation of frippery, becomes heavy and stiff.' Strong criticisms were made of the pulpit, lectern, stalls, altar rails and font cover, because of their lack of graceful beauty. On either side of the altar, up to the level of the window-sill, were two panels, superimposed, filled with green tiles forming a S. Andrew's cross, and buff centre crosses in each—all alike. The whole effect was heavy and monotonous. 'Mr. Butterfield's talent in floors crosses his way when he designs wall patterns.'

He certainly showed far more restraint in the restoration of the interior of Merton College Chapel at Oxford (1864), where he refrained from the bathroom effect. He provided a correctly vested altar with candlesticks. The reredos was an oak-framed painting of the Crucifixion by Tintoretto. Mr. Hungerford Pollen adorned the roof with decorative painting.

While All Saints', Margaret Street, was being completed, Butterfield was busy fitting noisy and garish furnishings and decorations into other churches. In 1857 he restored S. Peter, Sudbury, Suffolk, where he inserted a wooden altar and super-altar; the latter of novel design, pierced with four circular openings. He filled up the lower part of the east window to make a reredos, covering it with a chain of quatre-foils, each encircling a large flower in gold. In the central panel was a large cross under a canopy. A critical visitor remarked that 'both are somewhat lacking in refinement, and the cross in particular, is so broad in its upright stem as not to leave sufficient room for the arms.' [21]

S. John's, Hammersmith, consecrated in 1859, showed all his favourite mannerisms. On the boarded-in sanctuary roof he powdered wheels and stars on a cold and ineffective grey-blue ground; inserted his favourite wooden seats into the stone sedilia, and erected a reredos composed of many coloured marble tiles and mosaics. S. Mary's, Wavendon, Buckinghamshire, was one of Butterfield's restorations in the late eighteen-fifties. Here he splashed much colour on the roofs and low chancel-screen, 'applied without any delicacy of harmony,' so a visitor remarked. Still, the altar was 'sumptuously vested,' and had a cross and candlesticks.

At S. Mary's, Ashwell, Rutlandshire, about 1856, Butterfield did the same as at Sudbury, blocking up the lower half of the east window to make one of his favourite reredoses of inlaid marble and alabaster. He provided a low chancel screen, a pulpit and a new font with a lofty canopy. What a villager said of the very red brick model cottages for this village, could well be applied to the furnishings of the church: 'They are very convenient, but look so hot-like.' On

[21] ref. to *Ecclesiologist*.

the other hand, Butterfield was equally prolific in interiors as chilly-looking as tiled bathrooms or public lavatories, no matter how garish are the colours.

How utterly ruthless Butterfield could be on occasions was proved in 1876 when he did his best to transform the interior of S. Mary Woolnoth in the City of London, designed by Nicholas Hawksmore between 1719 and 1727. Down came the side galleries. Their richly carved fronts were stuck up on the walls, being too good to throw away or use for kindling fires. Butterfield never liked high pulpits, so he lowered Hawksmore's one by several feet, but for some inexplicable reason the sounding board was left in its original position. He played tricks with the huge black baldachino with its two twisted columns. He must have longed to get rid of it altogether. He covered the ceiling with stars, decorated the walls with polychrome squares, paved the chancel with encaustic tiles, removed the organ to a corner, and by the time he had finished purging the church, Hawksmore would hardly have recognized his own interior, except for the fluted Corinthian columns.

Even more violent was his iconoclastic restoration of S. Clement Eastcheap in 1872. 'He tore out the pews, he lowered the pulpit, he destroyed the gallery, he plonked the old organ down in the side aisle so nobody could sit there. But this was common form; iconoclasts were destroying like this all over England. He went on : he built up high steps to the east of the church and covered them with staring black and white paving, and then with both hands he tore apart the lovely triple altar-piece, flinging the two wings of the triptych on to side walls and leaving the centre mean and pointless where it was. And last of all, his rage collapsed, he put stained glass in the windows so dark that nobody could see what he had done.' [22] Mr. Butterfield had little respect for Sir Christopher Wren.

He was allowed to play about with the interior of S. Michael Paternoster Royal in 1866, but here he did not treat Wren's furnishings in quite such a brutal manner. In 1872 he purged S. Paul's, Covent Garden of Thomas Hardwick the Younger's late eighteenth century galleries, and refurnished it according to his rigid principles. He behaved in a less iconoclastic manner at S. Mary Rotherhithe in 1867, but must have been far happier that same year when furnishing the little polychromed red brick Gothic chapel, which Dr. Tait, the then Bishop of London, got him to design for Fulham Palace.

It is difficult, if not impossible, to form an impression of the interior of most of Butterfield's numerous churches as he himself wanted us to see them. In most of them the polychrome decorations on the walls with their restless stripes and zigzags still distract the worshipper with their complicated patterns. But subsequent generations have either removed the original furnishings, or modified them in one way or another. However in the bound volumes of *The Builder* will be found wood-engravings of the interior of many Butterfield churches.

Those of us who can recall S. Alban's, Holborn, before it was bombed to bits in the last war, will be astonished how different it looked when it was opened

---

[22] E. and W. Young, *Old London Churches* (1956), p. 78.

S. CROSS, WINCHESTER (Typical decorations by William Butterfield, 1865)

in 1863. Instead of Garner's carved wooden reredos above the high altar, the whole of the east wall was filled up by a series of painted glass panels by Styleman Le Strange, the lower part by characteristic Butterfield polychromatic patterns. The engraving shows a carved wooden communion table, with three panels formed of Gothic arches. There appears to be a stone or marble low gradine. The small reredos, dwarfed below the four rows of paintings, carries five circles with symbolic crosses in them, and a large plain white cross in the middle. Above the chancel arch the polychrome decoration is even more riotous than at All Saints', Margaret

Street—lozenge-shaped patterns, broken up with a dozen circles, ranged around and leading up to a larger circle with a symbolic cross in its midst. The chancel is divided from the nave by a low iron screen with gates. The pulpit is massive but unimpressive.

When S. Alban's was completed, its furnishings and decorations were criticized more fiercely even than those of All Saints'. 'The gaudily-striped rafters of the sanctuary recall the corrupt adornment of our Perpendicular churches, and are ill balanced by the strongly contrasted tone of the nave roof in which pale blue and feeble grey predominate. The alabaster-coated lower half of the east wall with its somewhat large, though shallow, arcading and the lozenge-shaped hatching incised on the plain surface above the arcading, recalls similar work in Brasenose chapel. Alabaster is in itself so essentially polychromatic, so delicately tinted a material, that when it is used in large masses we are inclined to think it ought to be left to itself, to serve as a "peacemaker" to other colours and to artificial forms elsewhere, whether of sculpture, of painting, or of incising.' [23] But Butterfield never felt called to make peace with his decorations; he preferred war. Here he differed from most of his contemporaries. The chancel parcloses of iron was much disliked for their 'needless heaviness and solidity—destructive of the very idea of metal work, which is ductility.'

The engraving of the interior of S. Clement's, City Road, shows a typical Butterfield church erected a few years later.[24] The furnishings as drawn by the artist are very different from those which caused such horror to the witnesses called upon to give evidence before the Royal Commissioners on Ecclesiastical Discipline in 1906. There is a very Protestant-looking communion table, reminiscent of that at S. Alban's, Holborn. Immediately above it is a carved stone reredos, with a large marble cross as the central feature. The rest of the east wall is broken up with a jumble of bits and pieces which have no relation to each other; the eye is diverted in every direction. Beneath a five-light window there is an upper reredos with three panels divided by marble columns. There is no chancel arch, but an odd-looking rood-beam at the level of the top of the walls has a large plain cross standing on it. The lower parts of the north and south walls are covered with the usual polychromatic decorations, as is the pavement of the nave and the chancel. The latter has no screen.

Until it was abandoned during the Second World War, S. Michael's, Portsmouth, gave a good idea of a typical Butterfield church, because no drastic alterations had been made in the furnishings. The chapels at Keble College, Oxford, and at Rugby School, completed about 1868 and 1872, are the best places in which to study his 'constructional polychromy,' as he used to call it. As to the chancel of All Saints', Babbacombe (Torquay), erected between 1868 and 1874, described by Mr. Goodhart-Rendel as 'beyond all praise in its inspired strangeness';

[23] *Ecclesiologist*, Vol. XXII, New Series XIX, p. 324.
[24] Destroyed in the Second World War.

Mr. John Summerson feels that it is 'one of the architect's most alarming and ferocious adventures. Nowhere else does his favourite stridency—criss-cross *versus* segment—strike such a terrible note.' [25]

This church at Babbacombe is a veritable museum of Butterfield *bric-à-bac*. The pulpit is built up of black, white and red marble columns and arches—impossible to describe. Two splendid brass standard candlesticks, which must have been designed by the architect, stand beside the equally original font. The low chancel screen of contrasting marbles has some typical Butterfield brass gates. There are all his favourite marble patterns in the reredos. Some of the stained glass adds to the period atmosphere, and helps us to visualize the costumes of the congregation in the eighteen-seventies. The low-backed benches are as uncomfortable as most of those designed by Butterfield.

It is impossible to understand the attitude of High Church Anglicans of the last four decades of the nineteenth century towards church furnishings unless one has made a study of those designed by William Butterfield. Mr. Goodhart Rendel writes: 'An Anglo-Catholic Puritan; a lifelong celibate; a thorn in the side of his dazed but obedient employers; a man scornful of his detractors, and suspicious of his adulators; was there ever anybody less like Mr. Gilbert Scott? That a church could be warm seemed to him an invitation to drowsiness in devotion. For some years, therefore, he refused to tolerate any form of artificial heating, except by braziers of charcoal unpleasant enough to be no more used than necessary. The benches in his churches seem expressly designed to make sitting considerably more of a strain to the worshipper than kneeling.' [26]

Mr. Goodhart-Rendel goes on, 'Butterfield's practice in internal decoration, his tailoring of the "clown's coat" was ruled less by his choice than by the conclusions to which his theories led him. Everything must be as enduring as possible, mere painting being eschewed as transitory. To say that he disapproved of plaster would not be true, since alone among the Puginists he used occasionally on external walls rough plaster very much like what most of them were so busily stripping from churches of earlier centuries. As a general rule, however, he set such store upon permanence in internal decoration that wherever possible he lined his buildings with materials to which time would bring no shabbiness. Decorative painting he therefore held to be less desirable than mosaic or than paintings burnt into the surface of earthenware tiles. For such mosaics and paintings, as for his stained glass, he did not make the cartoons himself, although he sometimes insisted upon modifying and angularizing the work of the artists he employed, probably to their dismay. In wrought ironwork and in marble inlay he especially delighted, taking a great deal of pains in devising their details.

'Surfaces not intended as fields for pictorial subjects he almost invariably patterned with alabaster, marble and tiles; with stonework inlaid with coloured mosaics; or with bricks. Everything small that he designed is apt to seem oddly imperfect and

[25] op. cit., p. 170.
[26] *English Architecture since the Regency* (1953), p. 130.

awkward in itself, but perfect and proper in relation with its surroundings. Had he been an even greater architect than he was, he might, no doubt, have combined particular grace with general harmony and grandeur, but, with that grace lacking, he nevertheless has left to us monuments with which no spectator capable of large appreciation can be seriously dissatisfied.' [27]

To the student of fashions in church furnishings, Butterfield's work is of the utmost importance. The pity is that so much of his movable furniture has disappeared in the past half century as the result of a change in what constitutes 'good taste.' Bits and pieces can still be discovered in some of his lesser known churches, and the searcher will always be rewarded.

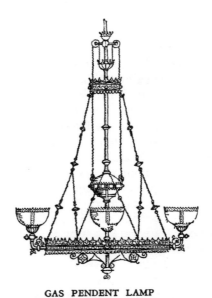

GAS PENDENT LAMP
(Messrs. Hart & Co.)

[27] ibid., pp. 133–4.

CHAPTER XIV

SIR GEORGE GILBERT SCOTT

THIS versatile and prolific architect deserves a place to himself, because of his enormous influence on the fashions of church furnishings and decorations between 1844 and 1878. He might well be called the Bishop Samuel Wilberforce of Victorian church architects because of his safe-treading of a *via media* between two extremes, since 'the degree to which the Oxford Movement took hold of the English Church is very largely due to Bishop Wilberforce. The Church has accepted it in the same modified sense as that in which he accepted it himself.'[1] Shortly after the death of Sir Gilbert Scott, Mr. Edward Middleton Barry addressed the members of the Royal Academy, and said: 'The Tractarian Movement and the Gothic Revival went, indeed, hand in hand; but [Sir Gilbert Scott] was too earnest a champion to wish his cause to be identified with any single party. Like many High Churchmen he desired to tread the *"via media,"* very much as did the late Dean of Chichester; so that Sir Gilbert Scott may almost be termed the Dean Hook of the Gothic Revival.'[2]

This is how Scott explained his position. He wrote, 'amongst Anglican architects, Carpenter and Butterfield were the apostles of the High-Church school, I, of the multitude. . . . They were chiefly employed by men of advanced views, who placed no difficulties in their way, but the reverse; while I, doomed to deal with the promiscuous herd, had to battle over and over again the first prejudices, and to be content with such success as I could get.'[3]

It is interesting to speculate how far heredity may have played a part in this penchant for the *via media*. Scott's paternal grandfather was a famous Evangelical commentator on the Bible, while his father was an Anglican parson of very moderate opinions. It was in 1838 that he designed his first church at Lincoln, followed by others in quick succession at Birmingham, Shaftesbury, Hanwell, Turnham Green, Bridlington Quay and Norbiton, Surrey. In his latter years Scott looked back on them with disgust, saying, 'I had not then awakened to the viciousness of shams, I was unconscious of the abyss into which I had fallen. These days of abject degradation only lasted about two years or a little more, but alas! what a mass of horrors was perpetrated during that short period!' None of his

---

[1] S. C. Carpenter, *Church and People*, p. 261.
[2] Cf. Appendix to *Personal and Professional Recollections of Sir G. G. Scott*, edited by his son (1879).
[3] ibid., p. 112.

earlier churches had proper chancels, and Scott had not begun to think of what the Camdenians called 'ritual propriety.' Then, quite suddenly, he fell under the influence of Pugin, and at the same time began to study the Cambridge Camden Society venture of church planning and furnishing. Though Scott was converted he never became a wholehearted ecclesiologist so far as ceremonial was concerned. In fact, the Camdenians were very shocked when in 1844 he won the prize in the competition for the rebuilding of the Lutheran Church of S. Nicholas at Hamburg, and attacked him in *The Ecclesiologist* for consorting with heretics. A proof of the architect's theological opinions is to be found in his defence, where he explained that there was much in common between Anglicanism and Lutheranism. His opponents were not convinced, and wrote, 'We are sure that the temporal gains of such a contract are a miserable substitute for its unrealness, and—we must say it—its sin.'

But Mr. Scott was still a comparatively poor man, and had to support a wife and growing family. He had shown his business sense when, after the death of his father, he sent a circular letter to all the latter's friends, stating that he had started practice on his own, and sought their patronage. He could not bother himself about the theological views of his clients: he had to make money. He saw nothing illogical in designing the Protestant Martyrs' Memorial at Oxford, and borrowing from Mr. Pugin's books. He must have smiled when Mr. Pugin wrote furiously that the subscribers to this Memorial were 'foul revilers, tyrants, usurpers, extortioners and liars.' His first really big job was the restoration of Ely Cathedral. In 1849 he found himself the official architect of Westminster Abbey. Two years later he accompanied Benjamin Ferrey on an extensive tour of Italy. This resulted in another conversion. Scott returned home 'convinced that Italian Gothic, as such, must not be used in England, but equally convinced . . . that a study of it is necessary to the perfecting of our revival.' In almost all his subsequent work there is a faint trace of foreign Gothic.

Typical of Scott's earlier churches is S. Giles', Camberwell, which he designed in collaboration with Moffatt in 1844, a stately cruciform building in Decorated Gothic. Eventually he managed to persuade a very difficult committee to allow the spacious chancel of three bays, but had to compromise with galleries on iron columns in the nave. There would have been too much Protestant opposition had he dared to make use of the sedilia and piscina from the old church burned down in 1841, so he inserted them into a summerhouse in the vicarage garden. He got away with jewel-like stained glass in the great five-light east window, due to the influence of Mr. Ruskin, but for a reredos all he could risk was an empty row of Gothic niches above the communion table.

By 1855, when Scott was invited to design S. Mary's, Stoke Newington, the French influence in his work had become very marked. The stone carvings exhibited realistic reproductions of natural foliage, flowers and fruit, e.g. oak, bryony, rose, vine, mandrake, currant and mulberry.

Against the east wall of the apsidal-ended chancel stood a reredos which would

9. Two typical examples of Sir Ninian Comper's work

S. Cyprian, Marylebone, London (1903)
—'Beauty by Exclusion'

Wimborne S. Giles, Dorset (1910)
—'Beauty by Inclusion'

10. Two startling contemporary contrasts in 'decent Communion tables' as ordered in the *Constitutions and Canons Ecclesiastical 1604*

Parish Church, Tring, Hertfordshire (F. E. Howard) (*above*)

S. Mary, Bourne Street, London (Martin Travers) (*below*)

The former expresses the ideals of the Alcuin Club, the latter those of the Society of SS. Peter and Paul

have been regarded as rank Popery ten years earlier, for it displayed beneath five richly canopied niches a carving of the Last Supper. The octagonal pulpit was a riot of marbles; and the round-shaped font was adorned with figures of angels in Carrara marble, carved by the younger Westmacott. The stained glass in the windows of the apse was supplied by Messrs. Clayton and Bell, and based upon the best thirteenth century French and German models. Except for the stained glass, which was destroyed during the Second World War, all the original furnishings of this church are still in existence.

It was about the same date as that of S. Mary's, Stoke Newington, that Scott designed the apsidal-ended church of S. Andrew, Westminster. The foundation stone of the Cathedral Church of S. Paul, Dundee, was laid in 1853. Here again he provided an apse. The furnishings were very similar to those in all the churches he was building in the 'fifties.

For lack of space, it is impossible to deal properly with the furnishings and decorations supplied to the many English cathedrals which were restored and replanned by Sir Gilbert Scott.[4] Nobody better than himself realized that these medieval cathedrals had been designed for a type of worship which had little in common with that of the Church of England a hundred years ago. The numerous side-chapels were not wanted any more for the celebration of Mass; all that could be done was to tidy them up, and make them available as mortuary chapels, where recumbent tombs could be placed. Again, Scott was realistic enough to see that solid screens between the nave and choir served no useful purpose. Wherever possible he either pulled them down or opened them up. He accepted the situation as it was, and tried to make the best of it. And how marvellously successful he was in almost every instance. There was no then living architect who could have dealt with the promiscuous herd of mid-Victorian bishops, deans and canons more tactfully and diplomatically than Gilbert Scott did. His replanning and refurnishing of cathedrals was a veritable triumph of *via media* genius.

It was in 1846 that the Earl of Ellesmere commissioned Mr. Scott to design a new parish church at Worsley, near Manchester. Money was no object, and it has been described as 'an opulent church, which bespeaks a pious aristocracy lavishing its new found wealth in the worship of God and enlisting the services of a skilled medievalist to work with unlimited resources to that end. . . . The Ellesmere chapel ironwork is surely as impressive an example of Victorian craftsmanship of that character as could be found elsewhere.'[5] Here can be studied the ecclesiastical fashions of the eighteen-forties in all their glory. There are arches of clustered columns, richly decorated mouldings, carved heads, flowing tracery, rich heavy stained glass and elaborate woodwork. All combine to create religious atmosphere which remains definitely Protestant, in spite of the medieval details.

Scott's extensive restorations at Ely Cathedral started in 1847. He designed new desk fronts for the fourteenth century choir stalls. Here too was his first introduc-

[4] He was knighted in 1872.
[5] J. Stanley Leatherbarrow, *Victorian Period Piece* (1954), p. 154.

K

tion of an open screen, to the designing of which he devoted infinite pains, as he relates in his *Recollections*. The then bishop wanted his stall to be in the usual place, but Scott persuaded him to occupy the stall in choir, used by the medieval abbots, and that the Dean should sit in what had been the prior's stall. Part of the organ went into the triforium and the rest above the choir stalls. The architect tells us that he designed it on the lines of certain medieval organs such as Strasbourg.

At Westminster Abbey, from 1849 onwards, Scott made many changes in the furnishings. He restored the reredos in alabaster and marble, inserted two pulpits, three grilles, and even ventured to provide an extra communion table in Henry VII's Chapel.

There was much more to be done at Hereford Cathedral. He tells us that at the time there was 'a violent agitation, first, for opening out the choirs of our cathedrals; and secondly, for making, where practicable, the choirs more proportioned to present uses, so as to give no excuse for using them for congregational purposes.' Scott adds, 'I was so far influenced by this fancy as regards screens (be it right or wrong), as to have laid down a rule for myself to open out choirs in cases where no ancient screens existed, but not otherwise. I also yielded so far to the argument for choirs, proportioned to practical needs, as to think that, as in this case the old dimensions and landmarks had been lost for twenty years, I was at liberty to adopt what seemed to be a more convenient arrangement. The old choir had extended through the crossing into the nave, the east arm forming only the sanctuary.

'My rearrangement made the east arm the choir, giving up the transepts as well as the nave to the congregation, Practically, for ordinary purposes, this was a gain; for the great diocesan uses it was a loss. From the antiquarian point of view it was an error. I leave it to others to judge of it. I confess I do not think I should now do the same.' [6]

In the early 'sixties Mr. Skidmore made the metal choir screen, which was shown at the Exhibition of 1862. Scott relates that it was offered to him at a very low price, and writes, 'I designed it on a somewhat massive scale, thinking it would harmonize better with the heavy architecture of the choir. Skidmore followed my design, but somewhat aberrantly. It is a fine work, but too loud and self-asserting for an English church. The reredos had already been erected by Mr. Cottingham jun.' [7]

The furnishings in Lichfield Cathedral show Scott at his very best. Here he opened out and rearranged the choir. At a much earlier period, Wyatt had removed the old reredos and extended the choir to the far end of the Lady Chapel. Scott determined to restore the medieval planning. He erected a new reredos on the site of the old one, and designed a metal screen to mark the division between the nave and choir. New stalls, very ornate and adorned with much Gothic woodcarving, were provided. Mr. Skidmore had the chance of his lifetime with the

[6] op. cit., p. 290.
[7] ibid., p. 291.

CHOIR SCREEN, DURHAM CATHEDRAL (G. G. Scott, 1875)
One of several open screens designed by this architect for
English cathedrals

iron parcloses behind the choir stalls and the ultra-Gothic Revival screen, the
intricate details of which baffle description. The gas lighting of the cathedral was
also entrusted to him; including a chandelier in the lantern 'in the form of a horizontal cross' Its many jets provided 'a blaze of lights, at the end of each arm,
casting a radiance down each arm of the cross.'

When Bishop Lonsdale pontificated, he sat on a stately throne, hidden by a
canopy and side screens of typical Skidmore metal-work. The throne was enriched
by statuettes of saints and several angels. Canopied stone sedilia were provided for
the sacred ministers at the Holy Communion. The long high altar, the front of

which was made up of seven Gothic niches, cried out for a High Mass to be celebrated at it. The reredos, completed in 1855, consisted of five niches, with intricate carved decoration, and much symbolic ornament. Above the central panel rose up a much crocketted slender canopy, ending with a cross—almost suggesting that exposition of the consecrated elements has been started by the Dean and Chapter. What with all this, and the new font, corbelled by four angelic faces and figures of saints, there was no doubt (from the point of view of the ecclesiologists) that the restoration of Lichfield was a model one.

Between 1859 and 1870 Scott was busily employed on extensive restorations at Salisbury Cathedral. He provided new choir stalls with canopies, a new reredos, and called in Messrs. Clayton and Bell to adorn the arches of the choir and sanctuary with polychrome decorations. A lesser amount of Scott's furnishings can be found in the cathedrals of Bangor, St. Asaph, Chester, St. Davids, Peterborough, Chichester and Gloucester. He cleared away the galleries from the choir of Ripon Cathedral, but left the stone screen. At Worcester he designed new choir stalls and desks, parclose screens, a reredos, a metal choir-screen, altar rails, and supervised the decoration of the vaulting. He wanted to erect a double open-screen, but this was rejected, and the organ placed, as he says, in 'the usual awkward position.' He admits responsibility for removing the Jacobean and Elizabethan canopies, and the choir screen; and in latter years seems to have been ashamed that he got rid of the 'elegant sounding board from the choir pulpit.'

The restoration of Exeter Cathedral involved endless fights with the Dean and Chapter. Scott insisted on retaining the stone choir screen, but architectural societies and two local architects were furious about it. 'At length,' he said, 'we so far yielded as to pierce the backs of the altar recesses on either side of the screen, which, without sacrifice of any architectural feature, has in some degree opened out the choir to the nave.' [8] He adds that he 'made the reredos too inconsiderable, though not so much as to disarm opposition.' The vaults of the choir and Lady Chapel were decorated, and the bishop's throne restored. 'In all this work I was greatly thwarted by the Dean, but I think the result is good.' [9]

In Durham Cathedral a seventeenth century screen, taken down by Salvin several years before, was replaced by a typical Scott product. New pavements were laid down, and a new lectern and pulpit designed. A needlework dossal was hung over the Purbeck marble slab in the lower part of the existing reredos. The hand of Scott can be detected in many of the furnishings of Rochester Cathedral, where he put back the high altar to its original position, and added screens behind the choir stalls. He also improved the levels of the choir and sanctuary. At Winchester Cathedral, the medieval choir screen was opened out.

This is far from being anything like a complete catalogue of the furnishings and decorations designed by Scott for English cathedrals. All is very good of its kind. Nobody seems to have compiled a comprehensive list of all the churches built or restored by this tireless architect, but it is believed that they number close

[8] ibid., p. 345.
[9] ibid., p. 348.

REREDOS, WORCESTER CATHEDRAL (G. G. Scott, 1868)
One of many similar reredoses designed by this architect
of English cathedrals.

on eight hundred! It was said of him after his death that he 'was not strong enough to resist the pressure and temptations which his lucrative professional engagements brought upon him, for he was of an irresolute and vacillating disposition.' The evidence available, though it does not wholly support this view, does suggest that the problems of home and family made Scott accept more jobs than he could con-

149

veniently handle; but the high quality of his work shows that he never allowed financial considerations to vitiate his standards.

It is worth while studying the altars designed by Sir George Gilbert Scott, especially those he inserted into English cathedrals, because they influenced the church furnishings of other architects for more than thirty years.

The most elaborate high altar reredos in Ely Cathedral was one of the first. It was begun in 1850, but not completed until 1868. The lower part is composed of eleven niches, divided by twisted alabaster columns, and each filled with alto-relievo sculpture. The upper part of the reredos has five 'gables,' the centre one being larger and higher than the others. J. B. Philip did most of the sculpture, and the touches of gold and colour were added by Mr. Hudson of South Kensington Museum. The mosaics were carried out by a Mr. Field. The rich Ely reredos has a curious affinity with some of those designed by A. W. Pugin. Young Gilbert Scott may well have been emulating the master!

Reference has been made already to the alabaster reredos with inlaid marbles that Scott designed for Lichfield Cathedral in 1855. In S. George's Chapel, Windsor Castle, the alabaster reredos (1863) extends the whole length of the east wall. The three centre panels contain white marble carving. The canopy has a row of small statues and many pinnacles and crockets. The Westminster Abbey high altar reredos (1867) has a central panel done in mosaic by Salviati, representing the Last Supper.

The carved stone reredos in S. John the Baptist's, Cirencester, Gloucestershire, was also erected in 1867. After it had been coloured and gilded in 1889 it resembled A. W. Pugin's work even more closely, and it can be regarded as the prototype of the earlier reredoses designed by Sir Ninian Comper.

The reredoses in Gloucester and Rochester cathedrals were put up in 1873. The former contains realistic groups of figures carved by Mr. Redfern. The three upper turrets, suggestive of iced wedding cakes, have statues of angels in the niches. Later on this sumptuous structure was gilded in places. In comparison with Gloucester, the Rochester reredos, built of Caen stone, is a more modest affair, with its realistic centre panel of a sculptured Last Supper. The Salisbury Cathedral reredos has much in common with the alabaster, marble and malachite reredos at Worcester, erected in 1875, but the former is less ornate. In each case the stone carving was done by Farmer and Brindley. At Worcester the seated figure of Christ the King occupies the central niche; at Salisbury the centre panel, enclosed in a Gothic arch, with four angels on top of it, contains a large crucifix, with figures of our Lady and S. John.

The Exeter Cathedral high altar and reredos (1876) were an astounding mixture of marble, alabaster, malachite, amethyst, cornelian, jasper, onyx, garnet, blood-stone and lapis lazuli. The whole structure was profusely inlaid and gemmed, and the three sculptured compartments contained realistic low-relief carvings. Objections were made that this reredos would encourage 'ritualism.' The architect was told that he must avoid making the Virgin Mary too prominent in the panels representing the Ascension and Pentecost. The reredos disappeared during the restoration of the cathedral after the Second World War, and was re-erected in Heavitree Church. In conformity with contemporary fashions, the high altar now stands out isolated and alone—simple and dignified. Far less ornate are the wooden altar and reredos in Chester Cathedral erected in the same year. Here, as at Westminster Abbey, the reredos was given a centre panel of the Last Supper, done in mosaics by Salviati of Venice. Farmer and Brindley carved the woodwork.

Holy Trinity Church, Watermoor, Gloucestershire, contains a characteristic example of a late Gilbert Scott carved stone reredos with marble columns. Erected in 1881, this and many similar reredoses designed by this great Victorian architect, were copied or adapted by many lesser masters right on into the twentieth century.

Gilbert Scott's later restorations and furnishings of cathedrals were more or less contemporary with the more famous novels of Anthony Trollope, and belong to the same world. *Barchester Towers,* published in 1857, gave the English Cathedral of the middle 1850s a permanent niche in fiction. Most of Scott's earlier clients among the Deans and Chapters were like the clergy of Barchester, who were 'High and Dry' rather than Evangelical or Puseyite. 'They all preached in their black gowns, as their fathers had done before them; they had no candles on their altars, either lighted or unlighted; they made no private genuflexions and were contented with such ceremonial observances as had been in vogue for the last hundred years.' But by the time that Scott had restored the last of the cathedrals the situation was very different. What, a few years before, was regarded as scandalous ritualism was becoming, due to the spread of the ethos embodied in Scott's work, the accepted accompaniments of Anglican worship.

A few of the clergy who employed Mr. Scott tended to share the views of the Revd. Caleb Oriel, B.D., in *Dr. Thorne* (1858), who 'delighted in lecterns and credence tables, in services at dark hours of winter when no one would attend . . . and in all the paraphernalia of Anglican formalities which have given such offence to those of his own brethren who live in daily fear of the scarlet lady.' [10] Yet the majority of these Tractarian incumbents emulated Dr. Arabin, who had scorned matrimony for many years and ended up by marrying Miss Gresham, with the result that her rival, Miss Gushing, joined the Independent Methodists. She cut up the cover she had embroidered for a credence table, and made it into slippers for her favourite preacher.

By the time that Scott had finished his cathedral refurnishings, there survived few bishops' wives like Mrs. Proudie, who regarded 'services on saints' days as rank popery, and who had been known to accuse a clergyman's wife to her face of idolatry because the poor lady had dated a letter, S. John's Eve,' so Trollope writes in the *Last Chronicles of Barset* (1867). Even if few of the fittings and decorations designed by Mr. Scott had anything Popish about them, by the middle 'sixties, it would have been rare to find any of their clergy, prepared to agree with that militant Tractarian, Dr. Arabin, who 'professed himself a confirmed Protestant.' [10a]

[10] Chap. XXXII.
[10a] *Barchester Towers,* Chap. XX.

Scott's restored and replanned cathedrals remind us of Archdeacon Grantly in *Barchester Towers*. They are not unfriendly to Tractarian fashions, but when we look at their furnishings and decorations, we feel that the clergy at the time when the splendid work was completed, would have thought twice about crossing themselves, or preaching too strongly about the Real Presence. Very often the *tout ensemble* is a brilliant and showy veneer.

It is not surprising that there is a sameness about the Scott furnishings in the countless churches he designed or restored. He and his large staff of assistants were kept so busy that they had no time to think out anything new. He left his mark all over Britain during the 'fifties and 'sixties.

Scott always maintained that All Souls', Haley Hill, Halifax, Yorkshire, was his best church. The foundation stone was laid in 1856, and the building was opened four years later. The total cost was defrayed by Mr. Edward Akroyd, a wealthy mill-owner, and one hardly dare think what it would be to-day. The style of architecture is what was then called 'Second-Pointed,' now known as Decorated Gothic. And All Souls' was decorated from floor to ceiling! It is doubtful if any other Anglican church in England gives such a perfect idea of what the man in the street a hundred years ago felt to be the ultimate in ecclesiastical good taste.

The High Church ecclesiologists, who were not too well disposed towards Scott because of his frequent pandering to Protestant prejudices, were 'happy to say that in this case, was the best and highest embodiment of the principles of our ritual we have yet seen in any church of Mr. Scott's design. Here is no compromise; no subordination of ecclesiology to architecture; no sacrifice of the kernel to the shell. The choir and the altar form the proper climax of the design; they are the cynosure by which the artist has steered his course. The same harmony is to be observed in the decoration considered as a whole. And it is a most curious proof of the degree to which this unity of thought and design has subdued individual caprice and eccentricity, that the stone carvings of the foliage, etc., throughout the church are more moderate and unexaggerated than we have seen for many a year in Mr. Scott's churches, and that Mr. Skidmore in his screens and parcloses has restrained the exuberance of his vigorous fancy.' [11]

In the February 1860 number of *The Ecclesiologist* this church was described in great detail. Pleasure was expressed that the wainscotted nave seats were open, and moulded with carved ends. The fronts of the seats facing the chancel had elaborate carving of rich geometrical tracery. The chancel stalls and clergy seats were carved with even greater elaboration. The whole church was laid with tiles, which increased in richness as one approached the altar. The pulpit was characteristic of the architect—Caen stone and coloured marbles. The stately circular font was carved in serpentine. A low alabaster wall surmounted by a screen of hammered iron, divided the nave from the chancel. The gates were composed of rich scrolls of wrought iron, the work of Mr. Skidmore. He had provided more metal screens between the chancel and the side aisles, which were elaborately wrought and

[11] ibid., Vol. XXI, New Series XVIII, p. 148.

banded to the marble shafts of the columns. Highly commended were the two massive brass gas standards with numerous jets which, when lit, cast a rich glow over the sanctuary. Other gas-lights, rising out of lobes of crystals, were fixed to the metal parclose screens. The conventional foliage of the brass standards for gas in the nave showed a true appreciation for Gothic art. Their taste and high finish were remarkable.

The stone carving in the decorations aroused the utmost enthusiasm among the disciples of Mr. Ruskin. Natural forms had been copied. It was easy to recognize the maple, ivy, thorn, columbine, marsh mallow and other leaves found in Yorkshire. The fine tint of the stone used helped to bring out the minute details of the carving. There was a superb alabaster reredos in two stages. The lower stage, against which the holy table rested, had a geometrical diapering of coloured marbles, surmounted by a richly carved cornice, supported by octagonal shafts with carved caps. The upper part was formed of recessed panels. In the centre one was an inlaid cross of coloured marbles. On either side were three recesses filled with alabaster figures of the three Maries, S. John, Nicodemus and Joseph of Arimathea —all scriptural saints. The communion table was of oak, and covered by a rich frontal of crimson velvet, very beautifully embroidered by two ladies. There were diapers of stars of various shapes. In the centre the ladies had worked the sacred monogram surrounded by conventional foliage, all in gold coloured silk. Two brass candlesticks of very ornamental design stood on the altar, as well as a brass-gospel desk. The sacred vessels were copied from ancient models, and made of silvergilt. The lectern, just outside the chancel gates, took the form of a brass eagle standing on a globe; its circular-moulded pedestal had brass lions for feet. Few Anglican churches in Yorkshire could boast so many statues and medallions of Old and New Testament saints.

Painted decorations, supervised by Messrs. Clayton and Bell, covered the walls and ceilings. Over the chancel arch was a large mural representing the Adoration of the Lamb, evocative of the work of Fra Angelico. Many well-known artists had been called in for the stained glass in the windows—including Mr. Hardman, Mr. Wailes and Messrs. Clayton and Bell. This stately church was described as an almost unique specimen 'of the triumph of ecclesiology, at once so magnificent and so independent,' and a lasting memorial to its noble-hearted founder. All Souls', Haley Hill, played the same part in influencing fashions of church furnishing in the north of England as did All Saints', Margaret Street, in the south. Both arose within the same years, and each expressed the mentality of its architect. To-day both strike us as terribly dated, but a hundred years ago they spoke to the younger generation with the authentic tongues of prophecy.

Another and even larger church was built by Mr. Scott in Yorkshire at the same time as All Souls', Halifax—S. George's, Doncaster. He chose a very elaborate form of Decorated Gothic, and a lofty tower rose over the central crossing. After this cruciform church had been opened in 1860 it was subjected to some very severe criticisms. The ecclesiologists maintained that it was improperly and incon-

ALL SOULS', HALEY HILL, HALIFAX (George Gilbert Scott, 1860)

veniently arranged for Anglican services. The chancel levels were 'not very satis-
factorily managed,' and the altar was low and undignified. The eye rested, not
on the sanctuary, but on the great east window as the central object of the building.
Beneath the window was 'a rather mean arcading, and an insignificant reredos, with
six small sculptured heads in relief in the spandrels of the niches, and coloured
marble shafts.' There was a credence table on the north side of the sanctuary,

154

suggesting that the Doncaster Use involved the celebrant at the Holy Communion standing at the north end of the holy table. The absence of sedilia confirmed this. The cramped sanctuary was marked off by rails of weak design. In the nave was 'a cumbrous reading-desk for two persons, elaborated with marbles, standing against the north-western face of the south-western lantern pier.' Opposite the reading-desk was a temporary pulpit. The seats throughout were of oak, and open, but placed on deal platforms. The numerous gas standards were of a 'rather inelegant design.' The south chancel aisle, known as the Forman Chapel, was 'the gem of the church,' and was paved throughout with encaustic tiles. Unfortunately, instead of containing an altar it served as the baptistery. The serpentine marble font was described as 'noble,' even if it lacked a cover. There were good windows by Mr. Wailes. The church also contained 'a fair window by Mr. Hardman.' [12] At S. George's, Doncaster, the architect had spent vast sums of money on the structure and very little on the furnishings. It is doubtful if Scott would have lingered long over these ecclesiological strictures.

Scott was prepared to please any client, especially if by so doing it would involve adding more ornamental detail to a building. Employed by Edward White Benson, the headmaster of Wellington College and the future Archbishop of Canterbury, he raised no objections to sculptured symbolic foliage, thus described by Benson. 'In the Antechapel are none but such plants as grow in wild and desert places, out of the Church—thorns, brambles, also the Fig and the Apple which are emblems of our Fall. Over the Archway is a Maple spray with the Joy of Loves therein. Within are rich and glorious plants—and in every window may be seen the significance of the plant in symbol of the subject of the window according to my list. In the Apse every capital has special relation to the window: i.e. to the Ascension, Evergreens, Water-lily (Baptism), Pomegranate (Heaven's Treasure), Maple (Power of Keys).' [13] It is to be hoped that the boys of this public school, opened by Queen Victoria in 1856 as a memorial to 'the Iron Duke,' derived spiritual benefit from this costly and elaborate vegetable symbolism selected by their revered headmaster.

Fully to appreciate a typical Gilbert Scott church, designed at the peak of his middle period, one must visualize it filled with well-to-do ladies dressed in enormous crinolines. By 1860 a fashionable skirt was ten yards round. As much as 100 yards of material were needed for tulle dresses worn in summer, because they were trimmed with so many ruches. The crinoline which was contemporary with Gilbert Scott Gothic Revival was a frame work of bamboo, whale-bone or metal hoops, suspended from tapes, increasing in width towards the hem. It did away with the many petticoats of the eighteen-forties, which went with the 'First' and 'Second Pointed' churches of that decade. We must think of the cathedrals restored by Mr. Scott with ladies squeezing themselves into vacant choir-stalls at Mattins

[12] Cf. ibid. (1860), pp. 145–9.
[13] A. C. Benson, *The Life of Edward White Benson* (1899), Vol. I, p. 172.

or Evensong, looking forward to hearing a boy soprano's solo in a pretty anthem. Most of them are wearing tiny poke bonnets or saucy little capote hats, tied under the chin with silk ribbons, like the bonnets. Over their shoulders are draped large square-shaped shawls, folded in a triangle, with the point hanging down the back. The lower part of the dress affected by most of these upper class ladies is divided by horizontal lines, frills or flounces, which may range from fifteen to even twenty-five rows. The sleeves of the wasp-waisted bodices are tunnel-shaped; some with undersleeves of white tulle, attached to the elbow with elastic.

As to the wealthier male worshippers on a Sunday morning at All Souls', Halifax; S. George's, Doncaster; or in any of the cathedrals restored by Mr. Scott, most of them as they walk up the nave or aisles to their seats are carrying immense silk hats. They wear short loose fitting overcoats, generally brown or dark blue, if not black. Some display checked waistcoats. The older men still sport standing collars and cravats, but the younger ones prefer neckties. A few more dashing gentlemen may sport a cloak instead of a coat. Rather tight striped trousers are regarded as suitable wear with 'Second Pointed' ecclesiastical architecture.

Then these gentlemen and ladies return home for their Sunday midday meal; some on foot, others driving in their barouches, landaus or 'sociables.' The typical Victorian dining-room to which they returned was nothing if not stately. The table, sideboard and chairs were invariably of mahogany. The table itself had to be of a sufficiently massive construction to support the respective weights of the decanters and side dishes, and the monumental silver *épergne* which was the centre piece. Against a background of patterned dark crimson wallpaper, 'that colour being considered quite rightly, as stimulating to the appetite,' the worshippers at any of Mr. Scott's churches discussed the sermon and exchanged the latest gossip; their buttoned boots resting on footstools or a fine Turkey carpet. If they glanced up at the walls they would be confronted by gold framed steel engravings of religious subjects, or family portraits or oil-painted landscapes by reputed old masters.

Few of these upper-class ladies and gentlemen, unless they happened to be 'High Church' or Roman Catholics, were in the habit of going out before breakfast to attend an early service. Osbert Lancaster reminds us that 'the dining room of the period had taken over the function of a private chapel in that it was invariably the scene of family prayers. . . . So lasting were these traditions that the childhood memories of many still comparatively young retain their ineffaceable impress. Thus the sight of a Van de Velde seascape still brings the taste of mulligatawny soup whistling up from the author's subconscious, while the flavour of Bordeaux pigeon summons with all the completeness of Proust's tea-soaked madeleine an unforgettable cloud of Monsieur Doré's angels hovering over the Colosseum.' [14]

Whenever Mr. Scott found himself with limited funds for building or restoring

[14] *Homes Sweet Homes,* p. 42.

a church, he invariably sacrificed the kernel for the husk, and saved money on the furnishings. It probably never struck him that one reason for erecting a church is to protect the objects used in Christian worship·and the worshippers. Take S. John the Evangelist, Sandbach, Cheshire—a fairly typical 'Early Middle-Pointed' design of the late 'fifties. He certainly gave his clients a showy church, both externally and internally, never sparing his decoration, but a contemporary visitor could not say much in praise of the ritual arrangements. The sanctuary was 'lean and bare'; the altar, 'unworthy of its place'; and there was 'no reredos at all.' The seats in the nave were of varnished deal, and all that could be said of the pulpit was that it had a 'polypodal stone base.' The square-shaped font was dismissed as 'rather ugly.' But the very much enriched porch had a door with 'exaggerated floriated iron-work.' Mr. Scott did not bother to provide a chancel screen, but he inserted the most wonderful Venetian Gothic tracery in a two-plane screen between the choir benches and the vestry, which took up the north choir-aisle. The architect's love of opulent effects came out with the black and white marble paving in the chancel. He economized with plain white paving in the nave and transepts.

It was in 1859 that Scott was let loose on Wren's church of S. Michael, Cornhill, and apparently allowed to do anything he liked with its Classic interior. When every trace of paganism had been swept away, the Prince Consort was invited to inspect the Christian transformation scene, and give it his blessing. The original pews and solid wainscot had been replaced by open benches, and Wren's altar-piece hauled down. As substitute, an ornate stone, marble and mosaic reredos consisted of three niches with round-headed arches, surmounted by a highly decorated cornice. Two almost life-size statues filled the two side niches; the centre was painted with Gothic diapering, in the middle of which a circle contained an alpha and omega. The neat little altar was vested with a close-fitting embroidered frontal and super-frontal. Iron altar rails of Gothic design added to the tasteful appearance of the sanctuary. The floor of the chancel was paved with black and white marble. Among the new furnishings were a pulpit and choir stalls, decorated with much symbolic and naturalistic carving. On the first bench-end south of the chancel was a chalice and olive branches—the latter 'copied from a branch gathered, by permission, in the Garden of Gethsemane.' One of the bench-ends displayed a Scape-Goat wandering in the wilderness, with the mark of the High Priest on its forehead. Cleverly done forked lightning indicated Divine vengeance. Scott cast out all Wren's furnishings except a gilt wooden Pelican of Piety.

But he dethroned the poor bird from over the altar piece and banished her to the tower vestibule. The seventeenth century architect would not have recognized his windows after Mr. Scott had filled them with what he called 'Italian transitional' tracery. The walls and ceilings were covered with elaborate polychrome decoration, and the columns given neo-Norman caps. *The Ecclesiologist* said that Mr. Scott had 'fused the vaulting into something transitional between Pointed and Italian,' and maintained that 'the great ugly stable-like circles of the clerestory became roses under his plastic hand.' Fashions change, and a hundred years later

Scott's costly polychrome decorations disappeared under a new coat of white and gold paint.

During the eighteen-sixties he designed three more churches in or near London, which contained his favourite type of furnishings—S. Matthias, Richmond; S. Stephen, Lewisham; and S. Clement, Barnsbury. Even more richly furnished and decorated was S. Mary Abbot, Kensington, completed in 1879, where as Mr. Bumpus points out, 'we perceive that spirit of academicism, that fearfulness of overstepping the limits of conventionalism, from which the architect could never free himself.' [15] S. Mary's Episcopal Cathedral, Edinburgh, begun in 1874, and consecrated five years later, has much in common with S. Mary Abbot, though on a far larger scale.

The new chapel at Exeter College, Oxford, completed by 1861, was regarded by contemporaries as a very successful specimen of Mr. Scott's more ornate style, but one critic remarked that 'it is scarcely a merit that it strikes every observer as a close copy of the Sainte Chapelle.' It was pointed out that the ornament was 'purely architectural.' The woodwork fittings were dismissed as 'wanting in dignity.' The same writer said that the ritual arrangements did not correspond with the grandeur of the apse; that the altar was mean, and had no candlesticks. Even worse there was 'a kind of recessed pew for the rector's family on the north side of the sanctuary; treated somewhat like a low chantry.' Provision was made also for the college servants in the somewhat cramped antechapel. The writer remarked, 'What they want, and what the rector's family also want, is *parochial* worship. The services of the college chapel are suitable only for the special use of the members of the college.' Having criticized the furnishings of the chapel very freely, the visitor added, 'but nothing we have said is meant to abate our great admiration of the chapel as a whole.' The altar may have been mean, but the organ, placed at the west end of the antechapel, had a most elaborate case.

Mr. Scott's churches, in some respects, seem to express the character of *Hymns, Ancient and Modern*, the first edition of which was published in 1861. It was intended as a comprehensive hymnary—unlike the *Hymnal Noted*, which was High Church, or Bickersteth's *Nine Hundred Hymns*, which was Low Church. As one of the compilers wrote; *Hymns, Ancient and Modern* was 'as good a book as the Church generally, in its present temper, would accept.' The ecclesiologists regretted the needless tampering with the plainchant melodies. Other people felt that they savoured of Romanism, even in their expurgated versions. No matter, this new hymnary soon found its way into churches of all but the two extremes of Anglicanism. Like Mr. Scott's churches, it had what we should now call an ecumenical result. And like mid-Victorian church embellishment, so long out of fashion but slowly creeping back into its own, *Hymns, Ancient and Modern*, unrevised, revised or edited for schools, is proving its lasting worth.

S. Barnabas', Ranmore, Surrey, which Scott built in 1860, still retains an almost

---

[15] *London Churches, Ancient and Modern* (Second Series), p. 303.

unchanged interior. There is a barbaric crudity about the rich furnishings which is reminiscent of Butterfield. The whole effect is very foreign, and shows how the architect had been influenced by his travels abroad in France, Italy and Germany. At this exotic little building on the North Downs, near Dorking, we find a very different Mr. Scott to the man who furnished and decorated cathedrals and churches in the 'seventies. It is difficult to remember that Ranmore was designed by the same architect as, for instance, All Saints', Ryde, Isle of Wight, consecrated by Bishop Samuel Wilberfore in 1872. Here the guide-book informs us 'the interior is beautifully finished.' A typical Scott pulpit of variegated alabaster is held by a base composed of fluted columns of white marble. The marble font is elaborately carved and the reredos is quite as rich as that at All Souls', Halifax, designed nearly fifteen years earlier. Most of the Decorated Gothic windows are filled with Clayton and Bell stained glass.[16] Here—as in so many of his churches—Scott managed to produce a gorgeous interior which, in some indefinable and elusive manner, expresses the safe *via media* preferred by the majority of Victorian Church people.

In his own sphere, Sir Gilbert Scott was a really great architect and designer of church furnishings. Mr. T. F. Bumpus, writing nearly half a century ago, said of him, 'When a man of real ability, diligence, knowledge and technical skill finds that the public holds him to be the best in his calling and confides to him the most important works it desires to be executed, he is not to blame for accepting its estimate as the true one; for diffidence, in any department of activity, except pure literature, is not the road to fortunate achievement.' Mr. Bumpus felt that Scott 'takes his place rather with those skilled Italian workmen who hew from the marble block, with consummate dexterity, than the sculptor whose brain devised and whose fingers shaped the model.' Writing from the point of view of a High Churchman in the first decade of this century, Mr. Bumpus maintained that 'Scott rarely, if ever, succeeded in realizing the liturgical ideal and uses of a church, the more sacred parts of too many of his churches being disappointing; for while they abound in much beautiful and appropriate detail, they lack dignity and religiosity, and evidently not in his mind the dominant feature of the building, up to which all other parts should grow.' [17]

But the whole point is that almost every interior furnished and decorated by Sir Gilbert Scott does express the particular 'religiosity' which his clients demanded, and knew they would get from him. They were certain that they would have full value for their money, and that there would be nothing in the way of furnishings or decorations which would be in the least offensive to sound moderate Church folk who, at the same time wanted God's House to be as sumptuous as their own mansions. Mr. Scott could supply both. Kelham Hall, near Newark (1858), and Walton Hall, near Warwick, erected the same year, show us that he was quite as capable of designing magnificent Gothic Revival mansions as churches in the same style. Kelham had its ornate private chapel. The Albert Memorial in Hyde Park (1862–72), St. Pancras Station and its Hotel, the Broad Sanctuary Buildings,

[16] Some now destroyed.
[17] ibid., pp. 236, 237.

Westminster, and Glasgow University—each in their own way help us to understand his ecclesiastical work, for there was little or no difference between his secular and religious architecture.

His contemporaries often accused him of greed and avarice, because he grasped every opportunity which came his way. But those who were his friends judged him as a man of most lovable character. This quality is reflected in his work: he always tried to give people what they wanted, even if he charged highly for services rendered. We of the present generation are just beginning to appreciate his value.

To understand what Sir Gilbert Scott felt about church furnishings the best thing to do is to walk round the Albert Memorial, erected between 1863 and 1872, and study its decorations. Dr. Nikolaus Pevsner describes this 'memorial to our Blameless Prince' [18] as 'the epitome in many ways of High Victorian ideals, and High Victorian style, rich, solid, a little pompous, a little vulgar, but full of faith and self-confidence.' [19] What the architect felt about it is best given in his own words, 'My idea in designing it was, to erect a kind of ciborium to protect a statue of the Prince; and its special characteristic was that the ciborium was designed in some degree on the principles of the ancient shrines. These shrines were models of imaginary buildings, such as had never in reality been erected, and my idea was to realize one of these imaginary structures with its precious metals, its inlaying, its enamels, etc. . . . This was an idea so new as to provoke much opposition.' Mr. Layard, who supervised the sculptures after the death of Sir Charles Eastlake, said, 'I am convinced that if so great and splendid a monument had been erected in Italy or in Germany, our countrymen would have gone many thousands of miles to see it, and would have pronounced it an example of the superiority of foreign over English taste. I am equally convinced that such a monument could not have been erected out of England.'

As we gaze in wonder at this stupendous mock-medieval ciborium, with its pink columns of Ross of Mull granite; the gorgeous Salviati mosaics; the white marble frieze round the base, carved with figures of painters, poets, composers, architects and sculptors; the various marble groups, and countless smaller bronze statues; it is easier to understand the mentality of their creator. Beneath the canopy of the ciborium is the seated bronze statue of 'Albert the Good'—canonized by Queen Victoria, if not by the Roman Congregation of Rites. Had such a shrine been erected in any Anglican cathedral eighty or ninety years ago, Protestants would have been roused to furious indignation, especially if the bones of a saint had been laid to rest beneath it, instead of a statue of a German prince. It is in this respect that the Albert Memorial resembles the furnishings of Sir Gilbert Scott's cathedrals and churches: no matter how splendid they are, they never suggest anything Tridentine. They stress the husk rather than the kernel of liturgical worship.

[18] *The Builder* (1863), p. 361.
[19] *London, except the Cities of London and Westminster* (Penguin, Buildings of England series) (1952), p. 254.

S. Cuthbert, Kensington
(W. Bainbridge Reynolds, 1887)

S. Andrew, Roker, Co. Durham
(Ernest Gimson, 1906)

11. Contrasts in lecterns of different periods

S. Mary, Great Warley, Essex
(Sir William Reynolds-Stephens, 1904)

S. Paul, Brighton (J. Hardman and Co.,
c. 1850)

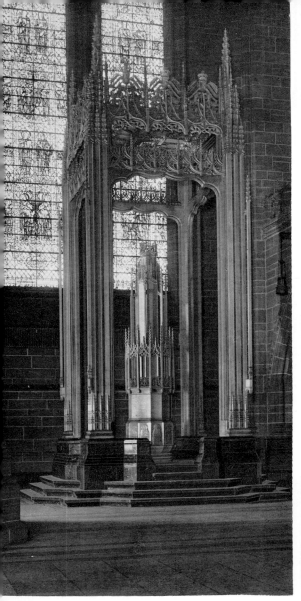

All Saints, Babbacombe, Devon (W. Butterfield, 1868)

Liverpool Cathedral (Sir Giles Gilbert Scott, 1940)

12. Three different fashions in fonts

S. Mary, Great Warley, Essex (Sir William Reynolds-Stephens, 1904)

CHAPTER XV

THE RISE OF RITUALISM

NEVER had so many new churches been built in England or old ones restored as in the year 1857. But they attracted only limited interest, the general public being more concerned with the Indian Mutiny which broke out in March of that year. People were too preoccupied throughout that year with warfare in India to have time for church furnishings and decorations, although considerable attention was drawn to them at the Fine Arts Exhibition, opened at Manchester in May 1857.

In ecclesiological circles strong protests were raised against the new Gothic reredos in Llandaff Cathedral, which Mr. Seddon had imitated from a tomb in Westminster Abbey, and placed across a Norman arch immediately behind the altar. Many other cathedrals were in process of restoration and being refurnished. Mr. Christian was busily employed at Carlisle; Mr. Scott and his numerous assistants were supervising work at Peterborough, Lichfield, Canterbury, Chichester and Worcester; not to mention countless medieval parish churches up and down the country. Other architects, including Woodyer, Butterfield, Christian, Norton, Preedy and Street, found they could hardly keep pace with commissions. Some of Mr. Teulon's furnishings and decorations were eccentric but novel, particularly those at Holy Trinity, Hastings; S. Giles, Utley, Glocestershire; Oare, Wiltshire; S. Peter, Angmering, Sussex; and Bottesford, Lincolnshire.

The furnishings of several more college chapels at Oxford and Cambridge had been brought into line with what was regarded as correct taste.

Overseas, and in the far distant colonies, altars, pulpits, fonts, choir-stalls and many other *instrumenta ecclesiastica,* which would have horrified worshippers twenty years earlier, were being inserted into Anglican churches and cathedrals, although it had to be admitted that progress was slower than at home. On the Continent the same zeal for the beauty of God's House was noticeable. Several new churches, gorgeously furnished in the Gothic style, had been erected in France. The new furniture and decorations in Cologne Cathedral were on view. There were many interesting fittings to be seen at Worms, Treves, Munich and in other churches throughout Germany. The wood and stone carvers, and the metal workers in Belgium were kept busy all the time. Their productions were exported to England, and found their way into many Roman Catholic churches. In every country of

L

Europe the stained glass painters had orders pouring in. Every firm was trying hard to imitate the glories of medieval glass painting, not always with the happiest results. There were an increasing number of people whose tastes made them prefer the more realistic and gaudy glass turned out at Munich. English churchmen and women were becoming more familiar with Plainchant and Gregorian music. The traditional Anglican psalmody was frowned on by the ecclesiologists. Surpliced choirs of men and boys had become common by the end of the eighteen-fifties, although in Romanist places of worship in England mixed choirs in west galleries were still the rule, and seemed likely to remain so.

The church tourist in England found much that was encouraging, no matter what county he investigated. Take Warwickshire as an example—its restored churches contained a fair number of correct furnishings. At Holy Trinity, Coventry, Mr. Skidmore had supplied a nice font-cover of polychromed iron, adorned with water lilies designed from nature. Here the old Jacobean altar had been retained, with a slab of white marble. On it stood two large candlesticks, presented by Dr. Hook, a former rector. The churchwardens at S. Michael's in this same town had strongly objected to an altar cross and two wax candles. The chapel, dedicated to S. Osburg, designed by Mr. Hansom for the Latin rite and consecrated in 1845, contained some good Gothic furnishings in the style of those advocated by Pugin, and a splendid set of Mass cruets of medieval design. The crucifixes and candlesticks in Mr. Pugin's little church at Kenilworth, begun in 1841 but not completed until 1852, were all well designed. But here, as in almost all other Roman Catholic churches, so any tourist of correct taste inclined to feel, there was something lacking in the manner of arranging pictures, hangings, flowers, etc. The stately Gothic church of S. Thomas of Canterbury, Erdington (1850), was marred by incongruous pictures and statues. On the whole, Anglicans might be thankful for the recent judgments of the Privy Council which prevented their churches being disfigured with vulgar ornaments which, even if they appealed to the simple piety of the increasing number of poor Irish Papists in England, were offensive to the more refined tastes of cultured English Church people.

Mr. Wardell's Second-Pointed churches at Clapham and at Greenwich, both completed in 1851, were admirable specimens of the purest Gothic, but, like so many other Roman places of worship in England, their movable furnishings left much to be desired. The new Jesuit church in Mayfair, where the high altar had been designed by Mr. Pugin shortly before his death, and the great east window copied by Mr. Scoles from the one in Carlisle Cathedral, was an exception to the general rule. In 1857 the double *jubé* or rood-screen still stood in its original position at the entrance to the choir of S. George's Cathedral, Southwark. What the ecclesiologists would have said if they had known that it would be pulled down and re-erected as a choir gallery at the liturgical 'west end' of the church is better left to the imagination! They would have been equally shocked if they had lived to see the gorgeous brass lectern shoved out of the choir, and hidden away in a corner of the far end of the north aisle. 'Whilst we, of the Church of England, are waging war'—so wrote an Anglican one hundred years ago—'and a successful war too—against pews, galleries, whitewash, I wish, for the sake of Christian art common to us both, the Roman Catholics would lend a hand and wage war with plaster statuary, paper flowers, and execrable pictures.' [1]

There were few Roman churches in England which could show such correct furnishings as those found in Mr. Woodyer's new church of S. Michael and All Angels, Tenbury, Worcestershire, which had just been completed by 1857. Here the interior of this early Middle-Pointed building, erected chiefly at the expense of the famous musician, the Revd. Sir Frederick A. Gore Ouseley, Bart., contained an oak altar, placed in the chord of the apse, with a reredos of the same material, surmounted with a canopy, and adorned with polychrome. Above the altar was a tall and slender metal cross, terminating in white flowers. A pair of handsome candlesticks stood on the super-altar, which itself was correctly vested. A tourist noticed a very pleasing frontal of rich crimson velvet, embroidered with passion-flowers. The sanctuary had a tesselated pavement, and the rest of the chancel was paved with encaustic tiles. The stalls were placed in the crossing of the transept. Although they were not returned, they were provided with subsellae. The iron rood-screen, standing on a stone base, lacked a cross, but there was the compensation of a row of seven candlesticks.

The sacramental nature of the worship in this most correctly furnished new church, was emphasized by the magnificent font of Caen stone, with green marble panels. Its cover was lofty, and raised by means of a windlass. An original feature was the well in the north-east corner which supplied water for the font and for cleaning the church. The mighty organ—one of the largest in England—filled up the south transept. The front pipes were all polychromed, the upright ones being painted with figures and mottoes relating to the dedication of the church to the angels. Perhaps this church was a little too glaring, due to the colours of the tiles and the painted decorations. The writer of the report stated, 'We should be still more glad if the noble organ were used to accompany the simple but sublime chants for the Psalms which western Christendom has known and honoured for more than a thousand years; but it is something that the choral service of S. Michael's will not suffer by comparison, with respect to chasteness and decorum, with that of any cathedral in the United Kingdom.' [2]

It was early in 1857 that a young architect, Mr. William Burges, was awarded the first prize in a competition for an Anglican Memorial Church at Constantinople. His 'ritual arrangements' aroused much comment, for the choir was placed at the crossing of the central lantern; the eastern limb serving as the sanctuary. The novel feature was a ciborium over the altar, which, as the ecclesiologists pointed out, was 'a distinctly *primitive,* and not Roman arrangement'; one which 'might

[1] ibid., Vol. XVIII, New Series XV (1857), p. 216.
[2] ibid., p. 222.

be well treated, so as to suit our ritual.' Mr. Street's design was more suggestive of that 'austere and rugged architecture of the North,' and looked somewhat exotic for the shores of the Bosphorus. Even the furnishings conveyed the idea that this was an 'English memorial church,' because of the elaborate Gothic reredos with side screens of iron; the richly decorated Gothic pulpit, and the two rows of choir stalls. Mr. Bodley intended to clothe the walls of his church with mosaics of an Italian or Sicilian character. A study of nearly fifty designs submitted proved conclusively that fashions in church furnishings were becoming far more eclectic, even if the majority of the competitors could only think in terms of First or Second Pointed Gothic.

From time to time in the later 'fifties there were faint whispers of protest against the stripping of plaster and whitewash from the walls of medieval churches. Many were thus transformed into stone caverns, for there was little or no colour added to create the illusion of warmth. This reversal to the Stone Age in churches, curiously enough, was coexistent with over-furnished houses; hence the feminine urge to drape bare church walls with horticultural decorations at the greater festivals. When almost every room in a rectory was carpeted, and probably provided with Nottingham lace curtains as well as heavier curtains, and pelmets around and over windows, as well as velvet or plush valances along mantelpieces—the latter adorned with little bobbins—the contrastingly chilly effect of God's House must have been remarkable.

Architects and church restorers were warned to work more cautiously—they had destroyed enough already, not knowing what they destroyed—and in some cases, from a want of art-feeling or art knowledge, or insensibility to the beauty, poetry and religion of church symbolism—not caring if they destroyed it. 'T.G.P.' wrote an indignant letter to *The Ecclesiologist* on February 8th, 1858, craving 'to *sound the note of caution*—to beg those who love their sacred buildings, who revere the spirit of devotion which first inspired the arts of the Middle Ages, to go to work with *tenderer hands.*' The writer maintained that 'if church architecture is to be restored in its fullness, its decorative colour *must* be studied. If churches are to be decorated, they must be done *properly* or *not at all.*' [3]

Another new phenomenon beginning to make itself felt was to have a curious influence on the furnishing of churches. This was the presence of non-communicants at the Holy Communion. Even the most advanced Puseyite clergyman had not yet dared tell their flock to 'hear Mass' on Sundays and holy days; but in some churches people remained behind after Mattins for a later celebration of the Communion, although the worshippers had already received the Sacrament at an earlier hour. The church newspapers were full of this controversial subject.

The rector of Wantage, although the founder of the Community of S. Mary the Virgin, didn't approve of midday choral Eucharists, and doubted the value of non-communicating attendance at them. He never introduced a Sunday 'High Mass' at the parish church of SS. Peter and Paul, Wantage, which was restored and

[3] ibid., p. 114.

refurnished by Mr. Street in the late eighteen-fifties. Here were to be found new stalls for the surpliced choristers. The older stalls were reserved for the clergy on more solemn occasions. Mr. Street had designed an original pulpit of alabaster with marble shafts. The sides were pierced and filled with richly wrought iron tracery. The stem was a central shaft clustered round eight smaller columns. To Mr. Butler it was compatible with honest loyalty to the Church of England to erect a very rich reredos of Painswick stone, adorned with alabaster and marbles of various colours. At his request Mr. Street inserted a beautiful cross inlaid in the central pedimented space. To complete the glory of this ancient House of God there were some gorgeous polychromatic decorations on the east wall of the nave, and on the spandril-spaces of the nave arch.

Miss Elizabeth Lockhart, the first Mother Superior of the Wantage Sisterhood,[4] would possibly have been in less of a hurry to follow her brother over to Rome had she waited to see the Catholic appearance of the restored parish church. All she could do in 1850 was to make the little chapel of the Home for Penitents look more solemn and bright when it was opened. She wrote to a friend, 'I should like you to have been with us. . . . The altar, with its pure white frontal, ornamented with five gold crosses, candlesticks and altar-plate really befitting an altar, and between the candlesticks and a three-branches light in the centre four vases, very beautiful in themselves, filled with white camellias and a wreath of flowers resting upon the window-sill above.' [5]

The fittings and decorations of the private oratories of some of the first Anglican Sisterhoods do not seem to have influenced the ecclesiastical fashions of parish churches. Some of them were highly original and eclectic. S. Dunstan's Abbey, Plymouth, where Mother Lydia Sellon was dreaming of becoming the 'Abbess-General' of all religious communities in the Church of England at home and overseas, had a remarkable temporary chapel in what was intended to be the refectory. The dais at the east end, where the Lady Superior would have sat at meals, was carpeted with needlework. Beneath Mr. Butterfield's large east window was an oak table, vested with a frontal of the finest white cashmere. It was not long before a cloth-of-gold frontal was added, embroidered with the Sacred Name in Hebrew. In the late eighteen-fifties a white marble cross, candlesticks, flower-vases, a Hebrew Bible and the 'Chapter Service Book' stood on the improvised altar. Beside it was an ewer and basin, used when the Lady Abbess washed the Sisters' feet. For some esoteric reason, a massive oak chest of medieval pattern stood in front of the altar, suggestive of the Ark of the Covenant. It contained the Rules of the Sisterhood, and was secured by heavy padlocks, each of which had its own key. The Lady Abbess had a permanent throne on the epistle side of the sanctuary. About 1859 a crozier was fixed to the throne to indicate the exalted status of the 'Mother of the Three Rules.' Within this oratory the Sisters recited an expurgated translation of the Sarum Breviary, with bits from other breviaries inserted; some hand-printed, others in manuscript.[6]

4 Founded in 1848.
5 A. J. Butler, *Life and Letters of W. J. Butler* (1897), p. 136.
6 Cf. T. J. Williams, *Priscilla Lydia Sellon* (1950), pp. 206–7.

At East Grinstead, Dr. Neale's Sisters of S. Margaret had to be content at first with a tiny oratory, originally built as a workshop. Mr. Bodley was called in to give it a more devotional atmosphere before the opening function in 1856. Dr. Neale bought a small tabernacle in London, placed it on the altar, and started continuous reservation of the consecrated elements. By 1858 he had acquired a monstrance, and familiarized his growing community with the extra-liturgical Roman rites of Exposition and Benediction.[7]

Nothing like this would have been tolerated in the chapel of the medieval-looking House of Mercy at Clewer, designed by Mr. Woodyer, and opened in 1855. Bishop Wilberforce had told Mr. Carter, the Warden of the Sisterhood of S. John the Baptist, that there must be no crucifixes or any religious symbols that were not 'thoroughly Church of England.' [8] Neither the Sisters' oratory, nor the temporary chapel used by the penitents called for particular notice, although the altars were properly vested with frontals.

If some of those early Anglican Sisters went to stay with their families during their occasional holidays, they must have been unpleasantly surprised as they contemplated the strange diversity in church furnishings. If, by any chance, one of Dr. Neale's Sisters from East Grinstead had found herself in Mr. Truefitt's new church of S. George, in Tuffnell Park, Holloway, which was opened in 1857, she would have had to make the best of a large 'preaching house,' arranged like an amphitheatre. The 'stage' was occupied by a communion table, placed between, but in front of, a vast reading desk and pulpit. No provision was made for Exposition and Benediction. As a contemporary visitor remarked, 'we should not deny to the architect the credit of having contrived a singular and picturesque structure, which would be thoroughly suitable for Cushing's American Circus.' There were no windows, but the top of the conical roof was of thick glass.

Contemporary with Mr. Truefitt's circus-like church in Holloway was Mr. Street's admirable combination of Pointed architecture and ritual correctness at All Saints', Boyne Hill, Maidenhead, not far from Clewer, and where the presentation of Anglican modes of worship was similar. The first impression of the gorgeous interior was rather startling from the overpowering redness of the walls. A low stone chancel screen, with upper iron work, carried prickets wrought by Mr. Skidmore. The stone pulpit was embellished with marble mosaics. The wooden lettern took the form of an overfed eagle. The choir stalls were finished off with poppy heads. Behind them metal screen-work, copied from that round the tomb of one of the Scaligers at Verona, had been clamped into the walls, where the stalls themselves made the division. The sanctuary was the *chef d'oeuvre*. 'Well raised up,' a visitor remarked, 'it terminates in an elaborate reredos, decorated with diaper-work, incised and filled up with mastic, of a reticulated pattern, admirably uniting dignity and grace. In the panel over the altar itself is a raised cross of alabaster,

[7] Cf. F. L. Cross, *Darwell Stone* (1943), pp. 310–11.
[8] R. G. Wilberforce, *Life of Bishop Samuel Wilberforce* (1881), Vol. III, pp. 326–7.

which, from being of the natural colour of that material, while the panel in which
it is placed is darkened with diaper, stands out admirably.' Two pairs of brackets
in the reredos for the candlesticks and flower vases were an original feature,
designed to make the furnishings of this church comply with the judgment of
1857.

The architect's sister had embroidered the rich frontal, and her needlework was
displayed also on the velvet backing of the triple sedilia. Over the chancel arch
Mr. Street had painted a 'Majesty,' as symbolical of the Doom in a modified form.
The windows were all filled with painted glass or grisaille, the designs having been
made by the architect.[9]

Movable altar crosses, despite the final judgment of the Privy Council in 1857,
were not often to be found in new or recently restored churches. Mr. Teulon, in
particular, would make no provision for them, and invariably inserted a plain
marble cross into his reredoses usually composed of brightly coloured tiles. He
could not resist polychromatic decorations, a weakness shared by Mr. Bassett
Keeling, most of whose furnishings embodied everything that was worst in the
latest craze for foreign Gothic. Wherever they still remain, nearly all Mr. Street's
many reredoses of the late eighteen-fifties have a plain marble or alabaster cross
set into the central panel.

Many of the Anglican bishops were even scared of built-in altar crosses. When
the new chancel of S. Bartholomew's, Sydenham, was consecrated in 1858 the
Bishop of London refused to conduct the ceremony until a simple cross, formed
of coloured tiles, had been removed from the central panel of the arcaded reredos.
But Dr. Tait was nothing if not inconsistent, for a few months later he unprotest-
ingly consecrated S. Paul's, Bow Common, Stepney, where Mr. Rhode Hawkins
had added a fixed cross behind the communion table.

It was still very difficult for architects and church furnishers to know what fittings
to insert into Anglican churches. Between August 1859 and July 1860, Hawks-
moor's majestic church of S. George in the East, Stepney, now a desolate ruin as
the result of enemy action in the Second World War, was the scene of constant
riots because its rector, the Revd. Bryan King, had introduced a surpliced choir,
lights on the altar and the use of the chasuble in the celebration of the Holy
Communion. Matters reached a pitch on Sunday evening, January 29th, 1860,
when the scene became, in the words of *The Times,* 'devilish.' The Gregorian
chanting was disturbed by cat-calls and blasphemous shouts by a mob brought into
the church by the brothel-keepers and publicans in the Ratcliff Highway. At the
close of the service some of the crowd made a rush at the altar, hurled down its
cross and candlesticks, while others threw hassocks at the gas chandelier suspended
over the apsidal chancel. The rioters were finally driven out by the police. On
other Sundays orange-peel and other more objectionable missiles were thrown at

[9] The interior of this church remains more or less as designed by Street, except for the obliteration
of the reredos.

S. MARY'S, ITCHENSTOKE (H. Conybeare, 1868)

the rector as he stood in the reading desk in his white surplice. New fashions in church furnishings and vesture were not appreciated in the East End of London, or in many towns of the north of England, where riots against ritualism took place about the same time.

Punch repeatedly drew attention to the latest clerical fashions, and never tired of jokes about the Puseyite churches. In mid-September 1859 it was suggested that 'perhaps the effeminate parsons whose heads are turned with the love of dress, will ultimately take to wearing *"Le Follet"* (the Crinoline) under their ecclesiastical petticoats.' A fortnight later, 'a parson, to be popular, should try to copy the late

168

Charles Matthews at one of his "At Homes," and in the performance of the service, should act up to the pattern of those popular entertainers, who represent at least a score of characters per night, and the merit of whose acting is the marvellous rapidity with which they change their dress.' *'Disturbances in the Eastern Church'* is the title of another article (which appeared in the same month) about the riots in S. George's-in-the-East. 'The Clergymen who officiate in the Eastern Church are attired in the very height of Puseyite fashions, wearing vestments of gay and gaudy colours, green for example, and, for aught we know, *mauve*. They also give themselves the same airs and graces as their brethren, we might almost say their sisters, in the Churches of the West. As in the West, so in the East, these innovators have excited great tumults among the laity, attended with manifestations of an iconoclastic spirit, which reverend gents who think fit to make images, figures, or Guys of themselves had better beware of.'

Punch reflected all too faithfully the prejudices of the average middle classes who disapproved violently of ecclesiastical innovation. An attack on Puseyite parsons typified by Mr. Bryan King, who is reported to have said that he 'could never again put on those beautiful robes,' proceeded thus:

'Poor Mr. King! "Oh dear! I shall never put on my beautiful robes again." Thus we imagine the reverend gentleman's lament—or might we not say the lament of the reverend lady? "Oh, my beautiful robes! Oh, my handsome stole! Oh, my splendid cope! Oh, my pretty alb! Oh, my love of a chasuble! Oh, my duck of a dalmatic. Boohoo!" However Mr. King despairs a little too wildly in his excess of grief. He may still put on his beautiful robes in private, and, thus attired, admire himself in the looking glass. Will none of his disciples get up a testimonial for him? Say, a pair of ear-rings to match his beautiful robes, and to set them off in proper style, a variety of Crinoline?' [10]

Dr. James Price Lee, Bishop of Manchester from 1848 to 1870, was strongly opposed to any innovations in church furnishings that had even the faintest suggestion of Popery. A visitor in 1857 reported that his Cathedral was 'sordidly kept and miserably abused.' A new glazed stone reredos did little to improve the look of the altar, though the candlesticks and the ancient credence, 'relics of the better times of Manchester Churchmanship,' had been suffered to remain. At Holy Trinity, Hulme, designed by Mr. Scott in 1843, the sanctuary was properly furnished, and the altar, though far too small, had candlesticks. This church, with all its faults, had an historical value in the ecclesiological revival. S. Margaret's, Whalley Range, built in 1848 by Mr. J. P. Harrison, had been well furnished, but as in many other Manchester churches it had been tampered with. The very small altar was correctly vested, and there was a tiled reredos. The stalls were no longer used by the choir. The wooden eagle lectern had been banished to the vestry. The architectural features of a number of other churches were quite good, but little or nothing could be found in praise of their furnishings or decorations. Manchester was definitely not a happy hunting ground for the ecclesiologists a hundred

[10] ibid., November 19th, 1859.

169

years ago, except for some of the Roman Catholic churches. Our friend seems to have been glad to rest in Pugin's S. Wilfrid's, Hulme, Papist church though it was, for here 'the inside was simple and solemn.' The chancel and its aisles were screened and parclosed; and all the colour and decoration reserved for them and their altars. But there were no stalls in the chancel—'very unlike the old churches of England.' Worse, the whole area of the nave and aisles was 'occupied with mean open fixed seats, divided by fixed barriers into various divisions.' [11] Ecclesiological development was not the most conspicuous feature of Mancurian progress.

Far more cheering were the signs of improvement along the south coast of Sussex, where many churches had been restored and decently furnished by 1857. Reredoses with painted crosses in their central panels seemed to be fashionable, but at S. Andrew, West Tarring, a double triangle had been used as a more appropriate eucharistic symbol. 'We wish,' a tourist wrote, 'we could have given a more cheering report of the internal condition of the magnificent collegiate church at Arundel. At least the structure of the choir and chapels has been made good, and the windows all glazed; but the squalor and desolation of the interior is still very sad; and although it could not be expected that the Duke of Norfolk, whose seignorial rights over the eastern portion we are not lawyers enough to define, should contribute to bringing it into a condition suited for Anglican worship; yet we trust that the claims to his ancestors' tombs will not be overlooked. . . . The once rich stalls both of the choir itself and of the lady chapel are a hideous collection of *débris;* and the series of high tombs of the Fitzalan Earls calls for the most extensive yet delicate repair. In the meantime the ecclesiologist can study the spectacle of a church in England which has retained *in situ* four stone altars, three of them still bearing their *mensae,* the reredos of the high altar still standing, and a contemporaneous grille filling up the entire chancel-arch.' [12] Much needed to be done at Arundel. The eastern part of the nave aisles was choked up by galleries. There was an imposing central rostrum; composed of a pulpit, 'flanked by matching tubs for the reader and the clerk.' To complete the *décor,* the original stone pulpit had been 'neatly cushioned up as a private box . . . for a single individual.' It would be sixteen years before this church could be compared with the great French Gothic edifice (in communion with Rome) that the Duke of Norfolk had arranged to build across the road.

The Church of England in Canada had set a good example to the numerous Roman Catholics in Montreal with the furnishings in the new Middle-Pointed Cathedral. It was designed by Mr. Wills of New York, and fortunately the bishop was sound ecclesiologically. It was the largest cathedral of the Anglican Communion in North America, and worthy to be compared with the new Roman Catholic cathedral which was to be designed in the pagan style. The altar stood on a footpace. On the south of it was a triple sedilia, and on the north the episcopal

[11] ibid. (1857), p. 310.
[12] ibid., p. 340.

seat. There were two rows of stalls in the choir. For some odd reason another seat or throne was being provided for the bishop at the nave end of the stalls.

Even in Ireland better things might be expected in the no distant future, considering the excellently devised ritual arrangements in Mr. Slater's new cathedral at Kilmore, where the Protestant bishop was allowed plenty of space for pontificating at confirmations and consecrations. There were correct choir stalls with subsellae and even sedilia in the sanctuary, which was raised two steps above the choir. A fully choral service had been introduced. Here was a better cathedral than many of the grandest in England.

Fashions in church furnishings continued to provide material for plenty of arguments in 1858, an exciting year in many respects. In January the newspapers were concerned with the attempted assassination of Napoleon III. A fortnight later the mighty *Great Eastern* was launched. In India began the long siege and final relief of Lucknow. The first Atlantic cable was laid in August. In September excitement rose to fever pitch over the public meetings in London protesting against the practice of 'auricular confession' in Puseyite churches. When one contemplates the implacable public hostility to all Tractarian worship one is filled with admiration for the perseverance not least of the architects and church furnishers of the time, who remained loyal, in spite of intense opposition to ideals which only seem slightly ludicrous in a new historical concept.

Many new places of worship were being built for the Protestant Episcopal Church in America, some of which in their furnishing showed real Catholic feeling. There was talk of erecting a cruciform cathedral in New York—large enough to hold eight or ten thousand worshippers, besides a choir of five hundred. Pews and pewrents would be eschewed. 'The vast area should be for ever free from the pollutions of bargain and sale. Its lofty walls should never re-echo to the sound of the auctioneer's hammer.' Of course there would have to be choral services twice daily, and still more often on Sundays and festivals; 'a staff of from twelve to twenty-four clergy—all *mediocriter docti in plano cantu*,' forming a body of city missionaries, living under a dean, precentor, treasurer and chancellor; these four having sufficient income for the maintenance of a wife and family, but the canons living in a brotherhood. Round this centre there were to be choristers' schools, seminaries for the priesthood, a church-hospital, a sisterhood-house, a dispensary, an infirmary, an asylum for aged clergy, and a library. But this spectacular dream of a medieval cathedral establishment in the heart of Manhattan, costing millions of dollars, got no farther than the handsome quarto volume of the *Transactions of the New York Ecclesiological Society* for 1855.[13]

Some of the American ecclesiologists of the late eighteen-fifties favoured apsidal chancels, maintaining that square ones proved the Popish origin of the Church of England. Transatlantic Protestant feeling tended towards a Celtic succession for their branch of the Anglican Communion. The Revd. John H. Hopkins Jnr.

[13] Cf. *The Ecclesiologist* (1858), Vol. XIV, New Series XVI, pp. 30–1.

argued strongly for the apsidal east end, especially because it would allow the celebrant to stand, facing the people, at the east side of the altar. He even drew up a 'Standard of the Protestant Episcopal Church' in defence of religious aesthetics, and ended with a long argument on the expediency of the use of art in church decoration, showing with numerous examples that great progress had been already made. The altar windows of Trinity Church, New York, glowed with stained glass. The windows of Holy Trinity, Brooklyn 'formed in themselves a pictorial Bible.' The interior of Grace Church, New York, was 'adorned with multitudes of canopied saints in the aisles and transepts, besides having a fine altar window representing our Lord in glory, and several other corresponding pictures of saints.' Oil paintings suspended over their altars were to be found in the churches of the Holy Apostles, and that of S. Clement, New York; Holy Cross, Troy; S. Paul, Boston; and Christ Church, Hartford. An altar piece by a well-known American sculptor added to the beauty of the Church of the Annunciation, New York. These, and other churches mentioned by Mr. Hopkins, were 'enough to show that the Church mind in the United States is already far above the dead level of puritanical prejudice, and to encourage us to hope for the best results in the future from an increasing breadth of views among the clergy and people.' [14]

The official style of the Anglican Church in the United States might be Protestant, but the rich altar-plate of Trinity Chapel, New York, could hardly be more Catholic than that used in the places of worship of the Roman Communion in that city. The two chalices, two patens, a large paten on a foot, and an alms dish were of parcel-gilt, chased and enamelled very richly, with symbols, groups, figures and inscriptions.

If there were more churches provided with altar plate like that of Trinity Chapel, Episcopal churchmen could indeed 'rejoice to see that the service of God's Altar is, in our day and in our land, at length found to be worthy both of the cost and the thoughtful care and labour which have been freely and lovingly bestowed, in this work, upon the holy vessels of His sanctuary.' [15]

Ecclesiology, as we have seen, took a long time to take root in North America, for it was stony ground. In places, even as far back as the late 'thirties, High Church doctrines were preached from the pulpits, but the ceremonial remained austere and puritanical. In the little wooden chapel of the Nashotah Community in the forests on the shores of Lake Michigan, the only evidences of ritualism in the eighteen-forties were a cross surmounting the altar, with a vase of flowers on either side of it, and a chalice in front. It was rumoured that Bishop Ives of South Carolina, about 1849, had given permission for the reservation of 'the consecrated elements after Communion; a practice used in the Roman Church,' in the chapel of the Society of the Holy Cross, at Valle Crucis. Strange things went on elsewhere, especially in Dr. Muhlenberg's church of the Holy Communion, New York, which after 1845 was the first in the city to administer the Sacrament weekly. Dr. Muhlenberg fancied 'bright lights and fragrant flowers' and styled himself an 'Evangelical

[14] ibid., p. 33.
[15] ibid., p. 33.

Catholic.' It was not until early in the eighteen-sixties that even linen vestments were introduced into a few Episcopal churches in America. Lighted candles were the first step on the road to Rome.

It was not only in Anglican circles that the services of leisured ladies were used for the adornment of churches. In Germany the cause of Christian art was being

TYPICAL FESTAL 'GARNISHINGS' OF THE EIGHTEEN-SEVENTIES

encouraged in a similar direction. Hardly anything could be more advantageous for this cause than that the female world (*Frauenwelt*) should be again associated with it, as it was in past centuries. A magazine published at Stuttgart had the title '*Kirchenschmuck, ein Archiv für weibliche Handarbeit*' ('Church Ornament, a Magazine for Female Handy-work'). Here was much entertaining and instructive information, including patterns for embroidery and needlework, chiefly after ancient originals. New hangings for Cologne Cathedral, with a surface of about 950 square feet had been made by some German ladies. They created the effect of mosaic, and were executed by means of pieces of silk fastened upon linen. The contours and shadows were done in needle-embroidery.

The English 'Ladies' Embroidery Society,' founded in 1854, had been kept busy making frontals and altar cloths. The members gave their labour gratuitously. Mr. Bodley had supplied the design for an altar cloth for Peterborough Cathedral. More than a dozen parish churches had been enriched with frontals of admirable workmanship in 1856.

The fashion for adorning churches, in season and out, which advanced during

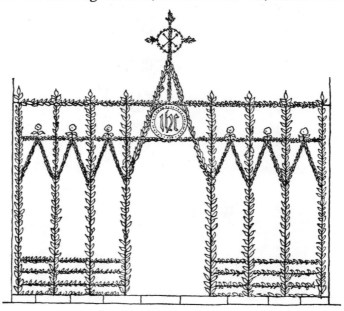

TEMPORARY ROOD SCREEN

the 'fifties, included floral decorations. The riot of horticultural displays led to strong criticism. The real architectural features of a church were often disguised and marred by sham reredoses formed out of laths and evergreens. 'J.C.J.,' wrote in *The Ecclesiologist*: 'To my mind nothing seems so unreal and wretched than this vegetable construction, a few bits of holly seeming to support the masonry above. It reminds one of the twaddling derivations of Pointed architecture from interlacing boughs, or the frontispieces to German songs and almanacs.' [16]

There were even worse abuses in many Anglican parish churches—'texts and other devices carved, as it were, out of box, etc., after the fashion of the trees in the shape of fat lions or poodles in *Mr. Punch's* garden; or the mustard and cress Johns and Maries in our own, when we were babies. If we want texts, or legends,

[16] ibid., Vol. XIX, New Series XIV, p. 38.

at all, they should be honestly written or emblazoned. The wreath also, that most obvious, and, if well and variously made, prettiest of all floral decorations, is used the worst.' All this feminine frippery was getting out of hand.

War was still being waged against pews. A new and hopeful agitation against this abominable plague had been inaugurated in 1858. Both Low and High Church-men were now united in denouncing the pew system. The time had come to gut at least one of the London churches, and throw open its whole area. It was proposed to petition Parliament to forbid the erection of any new church where the seats were not wholly free and unappropriated. No distinction of rich and poor would be tolerated in the House of God. Every seat should be 'Free and Open.'

The refurnishing of several cathedrals went on throughout 1858. Some splendid work had been completed at Ely. The east window had been filled with stained glass by Mr. Wailes, which for brilliancy and clever contrasts was felt to approach the best French glass of the thirteenth century. There was a new and gorgeous reredos, gilt and coloured, with a carved figure of Christ in its central panel.[17] Stone screens had been placed behind the stalls, which themselves were to have their panels and niches filled with sculptures. Soon the north transept would glow with colour, and more stained glass windows and frescoes were visualized. Mr. L'Estrange had been commissioned to decorate the new boarded-in roof of the nave with paintings similar to those in the church of S. Mary Magdalene at Hildesheim. Countless gifts had been made to the dean and chapter.

Furnishings of a very different character, but equally rich, had been designed by Mr. Teulon for the stately chapel at Blenheim Palace. This versatile architect showed great skill and ingenuity in giving a more correct ecclesiastical tone to Sir John Vanburgh's original design. The reredos consisted of a most elaborate arcade of seven arches, cinque-foiled, round-headed, rising from marble shafts. Each arch contained a scene from the Passion in high relief. Above were foliated arches, each containing the bust of an apostle and a rich crest, flanked by angels blowing trumpets. There were ornate metal altar rails; stalls for the ducal family of great richness, with screen work at the back, blazing with colour, gilding and legends. The elaborately carved font was furnished with a rich cover and a crane of metal work. The pulpit was a riot of marble and alabaster.[18] The double lectern, with a pelican on the crest, angels seated at the base, and the Five Wounds on the book boards, had nothing comparable to it in England. The windows were waiting to be filled with glowing stained glass by Mr. Clayton. 'We have seldom had to chronicle a more remarkable, or more sumptuous undertaking,' remarked the egregious reporter.[19]

Ecclesiastical good taste was slowly broadening. A proof of this was found in

[17] See p. 150.
[18] The pulpit is now in Waddesdon Church, Bucks.
[19] ibid., p. 72.

the ecclesiologists' welcome to Mr. Wigley's English version of *St. Charles Borromeo's Instructions on Ecclesiastical Buildings*.[20] Unlike Mr. Pugin, St. Charles was no medievalist. The basilica, pure and simple, was his dominant ideal, though he does not seem to have objected to a rood or a screen. This book, dedicated to Cardinal Wiseman, had, of course, a definite polemical object. The purpose of the editor was 'to construct a new ecclesiological party in his own communion, which shall marry the Gothic of Pugin and his school to the ultramontanism of the "Oratory," and recommended medieval forms by the contemptuous rejection of that indigenous tradition which has sanctified to England their old English development.' [21] Mr. Wigley wrote in his preface : 'In the notes and illustrations, we have endeavoured to show the practical worth of the Instructions, by pointing out how they have been, and may be still carried out; and in the truly Catholic spirit of our author, we have chosen in preference examples taken from the Basilicas of the Christian Metropolis, to which he so frequently refers. We hope thus to assist in removing from our English Catholic Architecture, the Anglican tendency with which it is threatened; as we should ever endeavour to impress upon ourselves the great fact that we are but a branch (and almost a *new* shoot) from the ever prolific Roman stem.' [22]

Although most of Mr. Wigley's illustrations of church furnishings are Gothic in style, they belong to a different world to Pugin's. The high altar standing beneath a Gothic baldachin is utterly Roman in feeling, as are the baptisteries, in spite of all their medieval-looking pinnacles and crockets. Mr. Wigley has disguised a typical Italian confessional in Gothic garments and even his paschal candlestick, combined with two ambones, is Gothic—in its Italian form.

In 1860 many copies of this book were bound up with *The Sacristan's Manual*, compiled by the Revd. J. D. Hilarius Dale, which soon became an almost official manual of church furniture, ornament, etc., among Catholics of the Latin rite in England. It found its way into many ritualistic rectories, where the directions given to Roman priests and sacristans were diligently followed by their Anglican opposite numbers. Some clergymen wondered how to interpret the words of the preface to the Book of Common Prayer, 'And the chancels shall remain as they have done in times past.' Why moreover should chancels be furnished in precisely the same manner as in the fifteen-fifties. So, for lack of any Anglican Congregation of Rites, when in doubt they fell back on Fr. Hilarius Dale's *Sacristan's Manual*. This useful little book told them how to take care of church furniture; the manner of cleaning it; and even how to grow flowers in room windows, to save money in buying them from florists.

Anglican ecclesiologists, except those blinded. by anti-Popery, welcomed Mr. Wigley's book as an important contribution to popular ecclesiastical literature, which deserved study even by those who differed widely from the conclusions

[20] Published by Dolman in 1857.
[21] ibid., p. 101.
[22] op. cit., pp. vii–viii.

either of the writer or translator. 'How far the English Romanists claiming to be the real and sole representatives of that medieval Church which built those cathedrals, those abbeys and those parish churches which are in their decay of this kingdom, may relish to be rebuked by an architect—himself of the Gothic school—for "Anglican tendency," and to be told that they are "almost a new shoot" from Rome, is a matter of taste which we leave them to settle'—such were the words of one reviewer.[23] 'In our judgment nothing was ever said at the most rabid country meeting during the frenzy of the Papal Aggression so truly severe as this dictum of its admirer and advocate.'

But it was not only Mr. Wigley who was helping to bring about a change of taste in church planning and furnishing; the Revd. J. H. Pollen was hinting at a revival of the basilica, and had written a learned article on the subject in a magazine published by the Catholic University of Ireland. Mr. Pugin had ceased to be regarded as infallible even in the best circles. Mr. Pollen's new church in Dublin, designed under the direction of Dr. J. H. Newman, the rector of the Catholic University, had furnishings and decorations more suggestive of those in churches of some of the Oriental rites.

HOLY TRINITY, PRIVETT (A. W. Blomfield, 1882)

[23] *Ecclesiologist* (1858), p. 102.

M

CHAPTER XVI

RITUALISM POPULARIZED

THE publication of the *Directorium Anglicanum* by the Revd. John Purchas in 1859 drew the attention of the public to the latest fashions of public worship found in 'Puseyite' churches. This encyclopedic volume was the first attempt to provide practical directions for the 'decent and orderly performance of all rites, functions, Offices and Ceremonies of the Church, according to the ancient Usages of the Church of England.' *The Ecclesiologist* felt that Mr. Purchas had been unwise to reveal so much to 'a scoffing and irreligious public.' It regretted the policy of this publication; it was wrong for Anglicans to borrow from modern Roman usage where ancient practice is obscure and doubtful. 'We inherit the old English traditions, and none other. We know that this rite has its perplexities, and that the unreformed Use of Sarum is sometimes less convenient as a precedent than the reformed Roman. But if we are to choose our models it becomes a mere question of individual taste. The practical lesson to be drawn from the difficulties of the subject is one of cautious moderation which, in matters of ritual, most of us would do well to learn.' [1]

Mr. Purchas, at that date a curate at S. Paul's, Brighton, informs us in his preface that the rubrics of the Book of Common Prayer were never intended as a complete 'Directorium,' neither were those of the ancient English or the modern Roman Missal. His book 'puts the priest of the nineteenth century on a par with the priest of the sixteenth century as to ritual knowledge.' Eucharistic vestments, Mr. Purchas averred, as well as altar lights and an altar cross 'of statutable authority' ought to be included in every church.

When the second edition of the *Directorium* appeared in 1865, Mr. Purchas was seen to have moved onwards and upwards. He was now much more specific in his ceremonial regulations. Cassocks and surplices must be bought for the choirmen and boys, also books with plainsong, from which they would sing in their proper place in the chancel. Every church must be provided with at least one thurible and incense; candlesticks; crosses, both on the altar and on the rood-screen; flower vases and banners. Processions with the chanting of 'ancient hymns,' eucharistic and other 'ancient vestments,' much bowing to the altar, signs of the cross, and other reverences are ordered. We read that 'the Church of England is still substantially one with the Church of England of the ninth century, and

[1] op. cit., Vol. XX, New Series XVII, p. 33.

consequently—in the face of modern Latin customs—national peculiarities have been consistently and properly respected' by the author.

That this extraordinary and expensive volume must have found a market is proved by the publication of a third edition in 1866, which was edited by Dr. Frederick George Lee. He hopes that the revised version of the book may 'render practical help to the extension and consolidation of the great Catholic Revival—a most necessary work of preparation on the part of our National Church, for the still greater and more important work, in which many believe she will take a leading part in promoting the future Corporate Reunion of the Christian family.' A comparison of the illustrations with the first and second editions show how far ritualism has advanced by this time.

The altars are shown with at least two gradines, and six or more candlesticks, besides many more brass flower vases. Some have riddel curtains. The embroidery on the frontals and vestments is typical of the period, with much use of natural forms of flowers and branches. It is hard to believe that these ornately furnished chancels were inspired by any known 'Ancient Use of the Church of England.' They derived straight from Pugin's *Glossary,* with a faint flavour of Ruskin and the Pre-Raphaelites. They share that overcrowded feeling with some of the early Burne-Jones paintings and Morris stained-glass windows.

Popular taste in church furnishings was directed on the same lines by Mr. Charles Walker's *The Ritual Reason Why.*[2] This little book soon became the vade-mecum for all Anglican ritualistic layfolk. For the next sixty years the furnishings of most Anglo-Catholic places of worship would be influenced by those clergy and pious laymen who were either 'Roman' or 'Sarum' in their liturgical tastes. Each party was violently opposed to the other, and much literature was devoted to propaganda either on behalf of the 'modern Western Use' or of the 'Illustrious Church of Sarum.'

In spite of the persecution of ritualistic clergymen which began in earnest towards the end of the eighteen-sixties, and ended with the Public Worship Regulation Act of 1874, church furnishers found an increasing market for their goods. A fourth edition of the *Directorium Anglicanum* appeared in 1879. Dr. F. G. Lee, now vicar of All Saints', Lambeth, wrote in his new preface: 'The Catholic type of service, at the restoration of which his lamented friend, the late Mr. Purchas, and himself first aimed twenty years ago, is now quite common and current in the Established Church. The high standard of previous centuries, before negations became popular and potent, has been actually reached; so that, in every diocese of England and Wales, changes for the better have been practically and generally effected, which at length Church authorities (now that the battle of decency and order has been fought and won) tacitly approve. . . . Improved taste in matters artistic has now condemned ugliness, disorder and Puritanic baldness; and so serves the Catholic cause well.'

By 1879 the instructions for the furnishing and adornment of altars are based

[2] First published in 1866.

mostly on the current rules of the Roman Church. The gradines have now reached a height of anything between six and twelve inches. Most of the altars illustrated have either a cloth dossal or a reredos of triptych form. But there is still no reference to a tabernacle or even an aumbry for the reservation of the consecrated elements. It was only in a few chapels of Sisterhoods that reservation had been started, although, of course, every Catholic Apostolic church had its tabernacle.

Mr. Street was one of the few architects who supported the Pre-Raphaelites wholeheartedly. At the twenty-first anniversary meeting of the Ecclesiological Society, held on June 11th, 1860, 'The Tendencies of Praeraffaelittism, and its connection with the Gothic movement,' was the subject chosen for a debate. The President, Mr. Beresford-Hope, gave a brief history of the movement since the publication of the first issue of the periodical named the *Germ* in 1850. He explained that 'Praeraffaelittism,' from its first starting, had two distinct principles at work: one was a sort of mysticism, half-hieratic and half-theological, but the other was a strong realism—'a determination to paint nature absolutely, as naturally, or more naturally, than nature itself.' He inclined to think that 'Praeraffaelittism' had done good, though it was not itself the highest aim of art, certainly not the highest aim of that religious art whose handmaid was Gothic architecture. The very essence of Gothic architecture was the imaginative scale it created—the production of the idea of infinity within limited space: while in Classical architecture finite and measured dimensions were the artist's aim.

One after another, those Anglican churchmen who were interested in architecture, church furnishings and decoration, jumped to their feet in an attacking or defence of the Pre-Raphaelites. Mr. Burges said the Pre-Raphaelites had tried to do in painting what the Cambridge Camden Society did in architecture: they went back to the first elements just in the same manner that architects were referred to the old churches; they kept to nature as the chairman wished architects to keep to old churches. He hoped that the Pre-Raphaelites 'would break the facial line of Greek face which the president so much admired, and thought that if the Venus were turned into flesh and blood, she would not be such a creature as any one here would admire.' Mr. Seddon then tried to clarify the basic principles of this new movement. He was followed by Mr. Gambier Parry and Lord Alwyn Compton, both of whom talked vaguely about Art.

Mr. Street, after this long discussion, said that most of the speakers had misrepresented both the ideals and the results of Pre-Raphaelite art. The very fact that all these painters had 'a most enthusiastic love of Gothic architecture, surely ought to be a consideration in their favour.' He even claimed that 'the Ecclesiological Society would be devoting itself to the principles with which it had started, if it secured for their artists the walls of some churches, on which to develop their art.' Mr. George Williams thought that the ecclesiologists 'owed [the Pre-Raphaelites] a very large debt of gratitude,' and said that 'there was a great deal which they might do in the decoration of works of eminent architects, now engaged in the production of structures, not only in this country, but even at the antipodes.'

After yet more debating, Mr. Seddon mentioned that certain Pre-Raphaelite artists had been already commissioned to execute works for Anglican churches. A reredos for S. Paul's, Brighton, had been painted by Mr. Burne-Jones; and Mr. Rossetti had done an altar-piece for Llandaff Cathedral.[3]

It seemed to have been a narrow victory on points to the defenders of Pre-Raphaelitism. What Rossetti and his colleagues thought of the cumbersome ecclesiological debate on their activities is not known; but it can be guessed.

An ecclesiological tourist reported in 1860, after a visit to Stamford and Leicester, that 'magnificent restorations have been carried out; but with a bold disregard to proper ritual arrangements. In almost every restored church I have visited, a decent altar is never to be seen. In many places, in the midst of carved stalls and stained glass, a small, rickety, worm-eaten table is thought good enough for the celebration of the highest act of Christian worship. The vestry-tables are always better, and an exchange might often be effected with advantage.' [4]

Many strange discoveries were made in other parts of Britain. For instance, in a new church at Ebbw Vale in Monmouthshire, Mr. Norton had been asked to design a large baptistery, sunk in the floor, for adult immersion; it being found that many persons in the South Wales mining districts insisted upon this manner of receiving the sacrament. Here and there in Wales some good churches had been built and others restored. An outstanding example was S. Margaret's, Bodelwyddan, Flintshire, designed by Mr. Gibson, erected and endowed at the sole expense of the Dowager Lady Willoughby de Broke, who appeared to be a very sound churchwoman, with fairly correct ideas on ritual arrangements. There was a most ornate chancel, the walls of which were clothed with rich marbles and much carving. The elaborate range of stall-work along both sides of the chancel was continued as a reredos along the east wall, backed with delicate and beautiful marble work of a chaste salmon colour. A critical visitor felt that there was, however, 'a want of reality in this beautiful work, which becomes mere ornamentation, as the actual seats are mere long benches of oak; and—though with desks in front, having panelling and poppy heads—not occupied by the clergy or the choir.' [5] Mr. O'Connor had filled several of the well moulded windows with some of his best stained glass.

Mr. Edward Pugin's Roman Catholic church at Wrexham, opened in 1857, aroused the wrath of *The Ecclesiologist*: 'At the east end of the Lady Chapel is a paltry coloured statue of the Blessed Virgin Mary on a pedestal, without any altar below. The chancel has neither stalls nor screen: the choir occupies a western gallery! The nave is filled with open seats, the places being assigned to particular holders by cards, as in some of our own modern churches. . . . The altar is without merit; and the canopy over it seemed to us inelegant. Two large figures of angels,

[3] Cf. *Ecclesiologist*. Vol. XXI, New Series XVIII, pp. 246–51.
[4] ibid., Vol. XXI, New Series XVIII, p. 293.
[5] ibid., p. 350.

of a very sentimental sort, stand in the chancel. The church is disappointing, both architecturally and ritually. . . . Some very poor pictures are placed against the walls.' [6] Many new churches of the Roman Communion up and down England showed a lack of taste in their furnishings; nearly all of them had western galleries for a mixed choir of men and women, and very few had been provided with decent chancels or rood screens.

Anglican churches in London showed some startling contrasts in their furnishings and ritual arrangements in the early eighteen-sixties. Setting an example of correctness in ecclesiastical fashions were, of course, S. Barnabas, Pimlico; All Saints', Margaret Street; and S. Mary Magdalene, Munster Square; but at Berkeley Chapel, Mayfair, could still be found a fashionable place of worship, coloured a warm drab inside, upholstered throughout with pink velvet and draped with curtains on brass rods. The most conspicuous feature was a handsome and highly polished stove, which completely dwarfed a tiny communion table. The preacher at Berkeley Chapel, where the atmosphere was fragrant, not with incense but expensive perfumes or smelling salts, was clad in starched white bands, and a black gown of rich ribbed silk. If the preacher condescended to arrive in the chapel before the sermon, 'he sat in state near the communion table, cross-legged in a bulbously-stuffed armchair, facing the congregation, for he thought himself too weak to kneel; waiting for the special feature of the day—his own academical and graceful discourse.' [7]

In most rural parishes it was still felt to be dangerous to introduce even the mildest of new fashions for fear of arousing protests, if not riots. Typical of not a few country churches was Sunningwell, a village four miles from Oxford, where the vicar had the courage to insert a temporary reredos with a cross on it, and even lighted tapers during the celebration of the Holy Communion. He allowed his curate, Mr. Lee, to procure cassocks and surplices for the choristers in the chapelry of Kennington; and, when the weather was fine, they processed thus vested from the schoolroom to the church. Moreover, it was Sir George Bowyer, a local Roman Catholic landlord, who presented the *red* cassocks to Kennington. This was probably the first instance of such garments being worn in the Church of England outside royal foundations, and they soon became the *dernier cri* for choir boys. It needed a good deal of courage, even in the late 'fifties, to wear a surplice and stole in the pulpit of a country church, where it had always been the custom for the preacher to remove his surplice before he mounted the pulpit; the black gown being regarded as the correct garment for preaching.

Few took kindly to the new fashions in church furnishings, as the pages of *Punch* still testify. 'Seeing that the Puseyites do all they can to make their services theatrical, we should fancy that an extra "effect" might be produced if their

[6] ibid., pp. 400–1.
[7] H. R. T. Brandreth, *Dr. Lee of Lambeth* (1951), pp. 15–16.

"yellowish white cloaks" were fashioned *à la* opera cloak, and if a crush hat were used as headgear. The "broad gold lace embroidery" which is worn by way of "trimmings" smacks somewhat of the footman rather than the clergyman; but perhaps this is used to indicate humility, and to be a badge to mark the servants of the Church.' [8]

'*Fashions for Festivals*' is another gossip paragraph of the same character. 'Fancy a lot of young parsons collected together and staring in at Messrs. Faldoral and Sons' window, or being taken by their female friends to the establishment of that enterprising concern, shopping. Imagine the assistants behind the counter saying, "Any other article today, Sir?, allow me to tempt you with an alb—sweet things in stoles, Sir? Neat dalmatics, very chaste. Pretty patterns for chasubles, Sir; charming copes; last Spring fashions from Paris, and novelties from Rome." ' [9]

For nearly twenty years the ecclesiologists had looked upon Scotland as the most fertile ground for their principles to take root. It was a great shock to them in 1857 when a controversy started around the doctrine of the Holy Eucharist, by reason of sermons preached by Bishop Forbes of Brechin, and the Revd. Patrick Cheyne, rector of S. John's, Aberdeen. As has been stated, this Episcopalian church had been opened for worship in 1851. The architects, Messrs. McKenzie and Matthews, had provided furnishings which were regarded as most correct. There was a simple sung Eucharist on alternate Sundays, at which eucharistic vestments were worn and two candles lit on the altar. This was very daring, and aroused much comment. Mr. Cheyne felt obliged to resign, and in 1859 Mr. F. G. Lee agreed to be his successor. By 1864 he had managed to erect a new church, S. Mary's, Carden Place, designed—largely by himself, though with the collaboration of Mr. Alexander Ellis—for the correct performance of Anglican ceremonial. But Dr. Suther, the Bishop of Aberdeen and Orkney, refused to consecrate the building until the crucifix and other figures and inscription had been removed from the rood-beam. Objection was raised also to the lamp suspended before the altar; the use of vestments; and an altar in the crypt or mortuary chapel. The Bishop seems to have had a particular dislike of copes and white stoles.

The only vesture he allowed was a surplice and a black stole. He demanded a written promise from Mr. Lee that he would never burn incense on any occasion. The young rector pointed out to his bishop that the Canons of the Episcopal Church nowhere define whether lamps, chandeliers, gas brackets or candlesticks are, or are not, to be erected in a church or chancel; nor do they specify anything as to their shape, number, material or position. He reminded him that a lamp hung before the communion table in his own cathedral church of S. Andrew, and produced countless reasons in favour of retaining the furnishings to which the bishop objected. The situation became impossible by 1866, when Mr. Lee saw no alternative but to resign the incumbency. Such were the sort of difficulties which arose in Scotland in the early eighteen-sixties, and which must have affected the market for

[8] January 7th, 1860. A paragraph entitled 'Clerical Old Clo'men.'
[9] March 30th, 1861.

church furnishers and decorators. An even more extraordinary state of affairs existed at Perth, where Dr. Charles Wordsworth, Bishop of S. Andrew's, Dunkeld, and Dunblane, refused to worship in his own cathedral because he objected to the very mild ceremonial which had been introduced by Provost Fortescue and the Precentor, Mr. Henry Humble.

Two important Architectural Exhibitions held in London in 1860 showed how many Roman Catholic churches were being built in Britain and Ireland. The comparison of their planning and furnishing showed that Anglican ecclesiologists differed widely from their Papist opposite numbers. This was made clear by the drawings and photographs of Mr. Edward Pugin's new churches at Cork, Northampton, Dublin, Liverpool and Nenagh. S. Mary's, Lanark, designed by Messrs. Hadfield and Goldie could have been planned for nothing but Roman forms of worship. This was obvious by the high altar, raised on four steps, surmounted by a massive tabernacle and throne for exposition. The same features were shown in their large Middle-Pointed church at Phipsborough, near Dublin. Mr. Wigley had designed an Italian-Pointed church for Cork, where an apse and a baldachin gave the whole interior 'a somewhat Basilican effect.' A critic remarked, 'As far as we can judge by the specimens shown, Pointed appears to be in the ascendent among the Anglo-Hibernian Romanists, but high screens have quite vanished, and with them the peculiarly English ecclesiology of Welby Pugin.' [10]

To a large extent the influence of the ecclesiological movement had been confined to certain areas of England. Even by 1860 there were still large districts quite untouched by Tractarian teaching, at least so far as the externals of worship were concerned. A typical backwater was the Isle of Wight. Several new Gothic churches had been erected in the 'forties and 'fifties, but their fittings were still Protestant. In Mr. Hellyer's Holy Trinity, Ryde, the congregation were so conservative that they preferred to have doors to their pews. At the west end of this Early-Pointed building, there were galleries for the children, with little bridges connecting them across the tower arch. Candle-lamps of a most domestic pattern helped the preacher to read his sermon at Evening Prayer. A visitor noted that this otherwise dull church provided a daily service and a weekly communion, both of which were most unusual in the Isle of Wight. He looked in at S. James's Proprietary Chapel (see p. 48), and was horrified to find in the centre of the building a towering pulpit in front of the communion table, flanked on either side by a reading desk and a clerk's desk. The box-like pews had doors. The east window opened into a room, so that an overflow congregation could hear the sermon preached by a popular Evangelical divine.[11]

The same church tourist visited S. Mary's, Ryde. This Roman Catholic church, designed by Mr. Hansom, had been opened in 1849. Here our ecclesiologist felt

---

[10] *Ecclesiologist* (1860), pp. 175–6.
[11] S. James's still remains almost unaltered, and is a priceless period piece of early nineteenth century Anglican church arrangement and furnishing. Very few specimens of this type of church have survived.

more at home, as he found a graded triple sedilia and a double piscina. He admired the elaborate stone reredos, with the fine painting of the Crucifixion, said to have been copied from the Sistine Chapel at Rome. It was a treat to come across a church with chairs instead of pews.

There was in fact only one Anglican church in the Isle of Wight to which anything like a 'correct ritual' obtained. This was the little First-Pointed church at Haven Street, designed by Mr. Hellyer. It had a properly vested altar standing on a footpace, a low pulpit and chancel stalls. Unfortunately these were occupied on Sundays by young ladies, and not by surpliced choristers.

It is a pity that our tourist did not give his impressions of the furnishings in Whippingham Church, designed by Albert, Prince Consort, and rebuilt by Queen Victoria in conjunction with him in 1851.[12] Had his visit to the Isle of Wight been a year or two later, he would have found all the furnishings of the newly opened Holy Trinity, Ventnor, absolutely 'correct.' The reredos of alabaster and marble; the pelican feeding her young; the borders of vine, wheat, passion flowers and lilies were most devotional. The richly carved Caen stone pulpit, and the pure alabaster font with its clustered columns were of refined taste, only to be expected in 'The Queen of Watering Places,' otherwise 'The English Madeira.'

In the early eighteen-sixties Mr. Teulon was still inserting some remarkable furnishings into churches both old and new. At S. Mark's, Staplefield, Sussex, people gazed in amazement at the panelled east wall, and the exceedingly rich reredos of stone, marbles and mosaics. When they knelt to receive Holy Communion they looked up at the words: 'Lord, evermore give us this bread.' As they moved up through the low stone chancel screen, richly carved, they were met by two figures of angels, where the gates ought to have hung. Another imposing reredos designed by the same architect was in S. John the Baptist's, Netherfield, Sussex—an elaborate composition of stone, enriched with Devonshire marble and mosaic tesselation. In the five panels there were pretty decorations of symbolical flowers—roses, lilies and vines—with appropriate texts. The incumbent had felt he could risk the holy monogram with a cross in the centre panel, besides adding angels bearing labels on the sides and crest of this reredos. Mr. Teulon fancied five niches and carved angels for his reredoses: he designed another at S. Leonard's, Misterton, Leicestershire, and indulged in a riot of naturalistic carving on the new choir stalls in S. Mary's, Sandringham, Norfolk; introducing the olive, the ranunculus and the convolvulus. Carved archangels guarded the stall-ends, Uriel being the fourth. Evidently the Prince and Princess of Wales were less opposed to ritualistic symbolism than the redoubtable Queen Victoria.

An interesting indication of a change in fashions is observable by 1861, when persons of taste were discussing the proposed replanning and refurnishing of S. Paul's Cathedral, London. Wren's solid choir screen already had been pulled

[12] With but few exceptions most of the present fittings are of subsequent date, including the marble reredos, which is a memorial to Queen Victoria, and the Battenburg Chapel, with gunmetal screens, a sarcophagus, etc., designed by Sir Alfred Gilbert.

down, so that there was an unbroken view of the whole interior. *The Ecclesiologist* wanted to see a low screen consisting of 'a plinth of black marble, from which should rise polished columns of serpentine and porphyry with gilt capitals, supporting a rich entablature of alabaster profusely gilt and inlaid with mosaic in the style of that opus Alexandrinum which has proved itself so effective and so durable in some of the Roman churches, as for instance in the Lateran, with a pediment over the central arch, as richly decorated as the architect chooses. Between the columns we would place rich iron railings gilded, *made to open for the service,* about 6 ft. high, with massive brass gates to admit to the choir; and at intervals along the top of the entablature standards for gas of brass or iron gilt—a mode of lighting which, at Ely, has been found very effective, and to enhance greatly the general effect of a rich screen.' [13] Unfortunately this proposal was not adopted. Such a screen of such a type would have considerably enhanced Wren's cathedral.

Even more astonishing was the suggestion that a 'grand baldachin' should be erected over the altar—'which we should like to see placed on the chord of the apse at once. S. Paul's seems to us to be the very place for one of those gorgeous erections, which the taste of the last century lavished out on Gothic churches, where no one wishes to see them.'

Twenty years earlier nobody would have dared to write in this magazine advocating furnishings in the Renaissance style—it would have been regarded as heresy! Ecclesiastical good taste was becoming less rigid. The writer explained that Wren himself visualized such a baldachin. In Dugdale's *S. Paul's* (Ed. Ellis, p. 189, note) it was stated that the architect intended to place over the communion table a hemispherical canopy, supported by four wreathed pillars of the richest Greek marbles, with proper decorations of architecture and sculpture. It was not until May 1958 that this mid-Victorian dream of a 'grand baldachin placed at the chord of the apse' was realized when the new high altar, with its magnificent baroque canopy, designed by Mr. Stephen Dykes Bower and Mr. Godfrey Allen, was consecrated by the Bishop of London, in the presence of the Queen and the Duke of Edinburgh. One fears that Queen Victoria would not have approved of the rich ceremonial at this service of historic importance, above all when the Bishop of London traced five crosses upon the marble altar with holy oil. No matter: Sir Christopher Wren, had he been alive, might well have felt that at long last his conception of the east end of the cathedral had been achieved by these costly new furnishings.

Another and equally urgent matter was colour—the 'one uniform brown' which 'overspread the church.' On entering the building the senses were 'deadened by the horror of great darkness,' and the general feeling of coldness. It was hoped that it would not be long before the walls would glow and glint with marbles and mosaics. The windows should be filled with the richest stained glass. 'Let us only imagine the wondrously beautiful effect that the dome would present, if all its windows were filled with glass, and its walls and mouldings so enriched with colour as to harmonize with them; and its nave, transepts and choir were each to open out

[13] Vol. XXII, p. 104.

from the central space with as brilliant a vista of gold and colour. The style of glass should, we think, be the richest used at the Renaissance; clear, brilliant, and calculated to transmit as much light as possible in a flood of colour into the church.' [14]

People continued to argue over the right and wrong use of colour in church decorations, just as they had been doing for the past twenty years, and had not come to any definite conclusion how or where it should be applied. Some clergymen and architects felt they must strip walls of plaster and leave the stone bare. But most of the arguments in the early eighteen-sixties dealt with the use of paint or coloured tiles or marbles. Permanent materials were fast becoming more fashionable.

It is curious but significant that the fashions in church furnishings of this period show little influence of the type of goods which were being produced by the firm of Messrs. Morris, Marshall, Faulkner & Co., which opened premises at 8 Red Lion Square, London, in 1861. They styled themselves 'Fine Art Workmen in Painting, Carving, Furniture and the Metals.' Although both Street and Bodley employed them on several jobs, they did not for some reason establish a big ecclesiastical connection.[15] But how splendid if more churches of the eighteen-sixties and -seventies had stained glass windows designed by Burne-Jones or Maddox-Brown, if their furniture had been like that which Morris put into the Red House, built for him by Philip Webb at Upton, Bexley, Kent, in 1859. What delightful screens would have resulted if designed like the staircase at the Red House. The sideboards and settles provide ideas for many altar-pieces, reredoses and pulpits. Most of the furniture was hand-made, coloured and decorated. If only some of the churches of this decade could have had their walls hung with tapestries or printed cottons, instead of being made to resemble public lavatories with garish glazed tiles. Morris tried to turn his house into something akin to a typical medieval church, which was a riot of rich colour. Those who can recall the Green Dining-Room at the Victoria and Albert Museum, which was destroyed in the Second World War, and which was decorated by Morris's firm in 1867, will regret that he was not allowed to supervise the furnishings of churches. But there remained an unbridgable gap between the ecclesiastical and the secular in art as in so much of the rest of life.

In 1861 Mr. Beresford Hope published his *English Cathedral of the Nineteenth Century;* a book largely concerned with planning, furnishing and decoration. *The Ecclesiologist* pointed out the great difference in the planning of Catholic and Anglican cathedrals: 'Our own Reformed use, requiring but one altar, would find its highest embodiment in such a plan as that of Milan cathedral, which was designed for the single altar of the Ambrosian rite. But in practice we have been forced to content ourselves with something much simpler. Such for instance are the plans of Mr. Butterfield's cathedral for our own communion built

[14] ibid., p. 107.
[15] See p. 228.

at Perth, and the more elaborate one designed by Mr. Slater for Inverness, in the diocese of Moray and Ross.'[16] Neither of these cathedrals, although designed for Tractarian modes of worship, included even one side chapel.

Mr. Hope was in favour of a revival of the basilican plan, but in this, as in much else, 'the *mauvaise honte* of the English character had hitherto been an obstacle in the way of improved ritual.' Mr. Hope gave 'a very humorous description of the feelings of an ordinary Englishman when he sees a surpliced choir-man, gratuitously attributing to the latter a shyness which, under similar circumstances, he would himself feel. No doubt he is right, too, in arguing that the volunteer movement, which has already broken down much of the exclusiveness of the national temperament, will soon tell in its effects in this direction among others.' Uniforms worn by the Volunteers aroused almost as much excitement in 1861 as did ecclesiastical vestments.

The writer took Mr. Hope to task for reasons why the chancels must remain as in times past, although he was prepared to adopt his conclusions. He felt that Mr. Hope was 'carrying his conservatism too far when he assumes the appropriateness of our traditional church arrangements for our present services, forgetting, as it seems, how suitable the ambons of a *chorus cantorum* such as that of S. Clemente would be for the Lessons and Exhortations of the English Prayer Book?' A hundred or so years ago most High Church Anglicans still preferred brass eagles to ambons, and if any one had dared to remove the birds and rearrange chancels on the basilican plan, it would have been regarded as vandalism, except by some of the *avant garde*.

One pities the architects of the eighteen-sixties and -seventies when faced with the solution of the problems of refurnishing a medieval English cathedral in such a way as not to suggest that it had been planned for any other worship than that of the Book of Common Prayer. A Gothic cathedral made provision for many chapels and chantries, but as Mr. Beresford Hope pointed out, 'all these are features belonging to the ancient ritual, in which we of the Reformed Church, so far as they have not been otherwise turned to use, are only called upon to feel an antiquarian and artistic interest.' [17] All that could be done with the now redundant and desecrated chapels was to use them for the reception of monuments or memorial windows. Cenotaphs, designed in the medieval manner, could fill up empty corners, where altars had once stood. But stately processions, with lights and incense, such as were part of the Use of Sarum and other diocesan variants of the Roman rite in England previous to the Reformation, had not been revived in cathedrals, so aisles and ambulatories could not be put to any liturgical purpose.

Although Mr. Beresford Hope may have been correct in maintaining that the 'Reformed use' of the Church of England required no more than one altar, never-

16 ibid., p. 166.
17 ibid., p. 75.

theless as weekday celebrations of the Holy Communion began in cathedrals, it became obvious that the handful of worshippers were lost in the choir stalls, even more so in the nave. So the dean and chapter of one cathedral, then another,

REREDOS, LADY CHAPEL, CHICHESTER CATHEDRAL
(Carpenter and Ingelow, 1882)

decided that there were practical reasons, which had nothing to do with a desire to encourage ritualism, for placing a second holy table covered with 'a carpet of silk or other decent stuff,' and 'a fair linen cloth at the time of the ministration' [18] in some other convenient part of the cathedral, usually in the medieval Lady Chapel behind the choir.

[18] *Canons of 1603*, no. 82.

This was how the chapels and chantries of English cathedrals gradually resumed something of their pre-Reformation appearance. The many new altars were not needed for the celebration of private Masses, but they certainly added to the æsthetic value of the building as an ancient monument. Nearly a hundred years have passed since Mr. Beresford Hope published his *English Cathedral of the Nineteenth Century*. He would get a shock if he could see how most of them have been refurnished in the twentieth century. No country in Europe can now claim better kept ancient cathedrals.

In the eighteen-sixties there was a move to revive the basilican planning and furnishing of Anglican cathedrals and churches, but as Mr. Beresford Hope pointed out, in the far off times when people were accustomed to seeing the celebrant standing behind the altar there was 'no irreverence connected with it.' He added, 'but what would now be the first idea which its revival would awaken? I fear, the familiar and unseemly one of a public lecturer standing behind his baize-covered table. But if the officiator did not assume this position, again I say the basilican revival would be a counterfeit. Besides, the Torcello apse filled with the choir would have a very unfortunate resemblance to a concert at S. James's Hall.' [19]

Cathedral and church restoration and refurnishing was proceeding apace in France as in England, but tourists of refined taste took a low view of the æsthetics of French clergy and laity. Mr. Parker of Oxford, whose knowledge of ecclesiology nobody could question, took the same line but admitted there were many exceptions. Mr. Ruskin, with a flow of eloquence, inclined to defend the French, despite all the damage which had been done to many churches. As might be expected Mr. Street tried to be kind to everybody. Finally, Mr. Beresford Hope, in his usual pontifical manner, as President of the Ecclesiological Society, 'still believed that the seminary education of France had not so developed the spirit of historical inquiry as to make the priest what it made of the English clergyman, a good ecclesiologist.' At the same time he reminded his hearers that those who live in glass houses should not throw stones, and that a few stones accurately thrown might destroy much of the Englishman's usual self-esteem. These worthy gentlemen plainly had no wish to encourage French fashions among Anglicans.

A second Great Exhibition was held in London between May and November 1862, this time at South Kensington. Most of the furniture and interior ornaments showed the same Baroque or Rococo feeling as those of the 1851 Exhibition, except that they were even more extravagant and opulent. They expressed the spirit of the Second Empire in France rather than that of the court of Queen Victoria, and were a perfect background for vast crinolines.

The Medieval Court enabled visitors to study what progress had been made in ecclesiastical good taste in the past decade. A good number of stained glass firms exhibited windows; among them being Heaton, Butler and Bayne, whose style

[19] ibid., p. 187.

was sentimentally Gothic. The work of Lavers and Barraud also had a nice devotional feeling, and Ballantyne and Son of Edinburgh clearly knew how to appeal to the popular taste; whereas the windows shown by Messrs. O'Connor, and Messrs. Clayton and Bell were somewhat archaic. Heaton, Butler and Bayne were out to spread stained glass in houses as well as churches, and anybody could enjoy and understand the imitation sixteenth century window of 'The Last Shot of Robin Hood,' designed by Mr. Sebastian Evans. Critics felt that there was much excellence in the realistic glass painting shown by Messrs. Claude and Hampton of London.

In metal work Messrs. Hart and Son showed some good Gothic gas fittings, lamps and tabernacles. Skidmore's Art Manufacturing Company displayed the new screen for Hereford Cathedral, produced at Coventry from designs by Mr. Gilbert Scott. It was made of iron, brass and copper; with much intricate natural foliage. Rudolphi of Paris had sent over a great Gothic reliquary, intended for Roman Catholic ceremonial. The Royal Prussian Iron Foundry showed a cast iron Gothic font. Hardman remained faithful to the traditions of the fourteenth and fifteenth centuries with the brass eagle lectern, gas standards and candlesticks. Their splendid display of sacramental plate showed the most refined taste. More ecclesiastical plate in the medieval manner, by Messrs. Keith, had designs which had been approved by the Ecclesiological Society. Elkington and Son's stand included two Gothic croziers. Mr. Norman Shaw's Gothic writing-table combined with bookcase, made of wood and stone, looked extraordinarily like a side altar and reredos.

The Art Journal published a magnificent illustrated catalogue of this exhibition, similar to that produced for the exhibition of 1851. A long article by the Revd. Charles Boutell devoted to the Medieval Court shows us the average cultured visitor's views of church furnishings of the early eighteen-sixties. Mr. Boutell was highly critical. Having dealt with all the chief exhibits, he dismissed them as a failure—'*failure* even in perfect copying.'

'Even the very best things are mere parodies of something which refuses to be parodied successfully. They belong neither to one period nor to another.' But he maintained that the Medieval Court is well worth studying and that its Gothic revivers have not existed in vain. He ended, 'If any lingering doubts until now have obscured the clearness of [the revivers'] vision, this Court can scarcely have failed to have dispersed and dissolved them. They must renounce medievalism at once and for ever, unless they are prepared to encounter the alternative of renouncing all pretension to the reputation of true artists—unless they are willing to leave the revived Gothic to sink through their enfeebled grasp into a hopeless inanition. There is abundance of life in Gothic Art—witness the Hereford screen. It is quite possible, also, that its healthy vitality should be exhausted—witness the Medieval Court of the International Exhibition.' [20]

In the eighteen-sixties all sorts of novelties began to appear in the church furnishings which would not have been tolerated by the Cambridge Camdenians

[20] ibid., p. 208.

of the 'forties and 'fifties. There were, for instance, the eight 'roof elephants' inserted into Benjamin Ferrey's 1845 church at Wickham in Berkshire. Brought from the Paris Exhibition of 1863, four of them had been intended for the rectory, but they were too big, so went into the church. Four more were made of *papier maché,* painted and gilded.[21]

Henry Woodyer, who had come a long way since his earlier churches, had developed a Gothic style of his own by 1863, when S. Paul's, Wokingham, Berkshire, was opened. Here the fittings were rich and very original. His 1862 rectangulated tracery filling the tympanum of the chancel arch of Christ Church, Reading (suggestive of a rood screen, and said to symbolize the lifting of the veil of the temple) was another novelty to be found in Berkshire. Woodyer's love of ornate decoration can be found in the paintings on the chancel walls and roof of Greenham Church, Berkshire (1874–88). They are in marked contrast to the restrained simplicity of Street's carved stone reredos in the apsidal chancel at Fawley, on the Berkshire Downs (1866), or the garish colours in Teulon's church at Leckhampstead, erected about ten years earlier. Then at Cold Ash, near Newbury, could be found in C. N. Beazley's new glazed brick interior a 'huge barrel of a pulpit inlaid with marble rose buds, a marble lectern, and originally designed font.' [22]

GASFITTINGS (Kidbrooke, 1868)

[21] Cf. Murray's *Berkshire,* edited by John Betjeman and John Piper, 1949, p. 92.

[22] ibid., p. 121. Berkshire, the home of that devotee of Victorian church architecture, Mr. John Betjeman, has been dealt with adequately in his *Collins' Guide to English Parish Churches* (1958), pp. 90–5.

CHAPTER XVII

RESTORATION RUNS RIOT

B Y the eighteen-sixties Victorian architects—good, bad and indifferent—had left their indelible mark on an enormous number of old churches in England.[1] A certain standardization was the final result.

But there are exceptions to the general mediocrity of restorations. Here and there churches contain interesting collections of furniture and decorations of almost all styles from the eighteen-fifties until the present time; one of the best is S. John the Baptist, Frome Selwood, Somerset. After the Revd. W. J. E. Bennett resigned the living at S. Barnabas', Pimlico, in 1852 (see p. 84) he became vicar of Frome where he continued to beautify the medieval parish church for the next thirty-four years. He died in 1886, and his successors have gone on adding to the *décor*. It needed some courage in the late 'sixties to erect a stone-carved outdoor Gothic Revival 'Via Crucis,' even if there are only seven 'Stations' besides the last scene of the Passion at the north porch. The sculpture is typical High Anglican of the period—very realistic and devotional.

Most of the aisle windows are filled with Kempe stained glass. Within the chapel of S. Nicholas, gorgeously decorated with marbles, is the font. The steeple-like cover was designed by J. L. Pearson, and added in 1884. Elaborate iron screens divide the chapel from the church. The Lady Chapel was restored and refurnished in 1864. Both the reredos and stained glass were designed by C. E. Kempe. S. Andrew's Chapel contains a memorial window to Bishop Ken, the work of O'Connor. The Caen stone altar, with its brass tabernacle, date from 1892, and were designed by Harry Hems of Exeter. The latest chapel—again typical of the change of fashion—is that dedicated to S. Francis of Assisi. The altar was designed by W. H. Randoll Blacking, with a painted reredos by Christopher Webb.

The splendid rood-screen and loft displays carved figures from Ober-Ammergau. Within the chancel much inlaid marble and alabaster paving is intermixed with encaustic tiles. Above a characteristic late Anglican Gothic Revival reredos of

[1] The following are some of the architects who were the leading restorers up to about 1865: W. Butterfield, R. C. Carpenter, E. Christian, J. Clarke, B. Ferrey, J. E. Giles, P. C. Hardwick, G. M. Hills, J. Norton, J. Hayward, A. Salvin, G. G. Scott, G. E. Street, J. P. Seddon, J. P. St. Aubyn, W. White, H. Woodyer, R. J. Withers, S. S. Teulon and E. G. Paley. But there were other and lesser known architects who refurnished medieval churches.

N

Carara marble, carved by Forsyth, is a five-light east window by Clayton and Bell. Seven magnificent lamps of Italian workmanship complete the furnishings of the sanctuary. No attempt has been made to bring the interior of this ancient parish church into line with the latest phase of ecclesiastical good taste. Its walls have not been whitewashed to resemble those of a scullery. This museum of Victoriana at S. John's, possesses a character seldom found in similar large English parish churches. For some strange reason there is no reference to Frome Selwood in *Collins' Guide to English Parish Churches*.

The brief descriptions which have been given of other restored churches and their furnishings are enough to show how many conform to the imaginary interior visualized by Mr. Basil F. L. Clarke, who sums it up as symbolizing 'spiritual pride, self-sufficiency, clericalism, complacency, Philistinism and patronage of the poor.' [2] Such was the far from happy result of a quarter of a century's ecclesiological zeal.

The interiors of the churches of the Latin rite which had been built in the same period, especially the smaller ones in towns or villages of the north of England industrial areas, convey an utterly different impression. Most of them were designed in the Early English or Decorated style of Gothic. An apse was more popular than a square east end. More often than not a large inside porch bore a gallery for a mixed choir. Standing in the porch were usually one or two tables, beside which on a Sunday morning stood men who gave change for the money which in many places had to be paid for a seat. At each door often hung a china hóly-water stoup. The seating generally consisted of low benches. Where there was no central aisle, iron rods usually divided the benches in their midst. The font was commonly placed at the west end of one of the aisles. Not infrequently there was a railing around the font, to give the idea of a baptistery. Around the walls of the nave or aisles hung framed oleographs or prints representing the fourteen Stations of the Cross, seldom marked by any artistic quality, though capable of stimulating devotion among the unsophisticated. Brightly coloured plaster statues of our Lady, S. Joseph and the Sacred Heart would be in evidence, standing on wooden pedestals; probably with iron or brass stands beside them for votive candles. Somewhere or other one or two varnished deal confessional boxes added little to the dignity of the interior. Where money was more plentiful they might be built into the walls, with two doors—the one for the priest, the other for the penitent. The pulpit was seldom so ornate as those found in Anglican churches, and neither brass eagle lecterns nor litany desks needed to be provided. Hymn boards were uncommon. Choir stalls were very few and far between. The chief difference in the planning of a Catholic and Anglican sanctuary was that the communion rails of the former were placed at the entrance to the chancel; more correctly there was no chancel, only a much larger sanctuary than that found in a restored Anglican church. Sometimes, but not always, there would be benches for the acolytes on either side of the sanctuary. A standardized type of altar had been evolved by the eighteen-sixties, which was repeated with slight variations all over Britain and Ireland. The front consisted

2 *Church Builders of the Nineteenth Century* (1938), p. 244.

of stone carving with marble columns. Embroidered frontals and super-frontals were almost unknown, despite Mr. Pugin's efforts. However, trimming the altar cloths with lace, which had been forbidden to Anglicans by the Privy Council Judgment of 1857, was permitted. The altar, in most cases, was designed more as a base for an elaborately carved stone reredos, the central feature of which was a tabernacle, its brass door encrusted with jewels, pebbles or enamels; over which was a throne for exposition with the monstance. Standing on one or more gradines —what the ecclesiologists called super-altars—would be six brass candlesticks, several flower vases of the same metal, and at the evening service of Benediction at least two brass branch candlesticks, each with six tapers. Wooden steps, to enable the priest to get at the throne, often stood near the altar. It was rare to find a sedilia. A wooden credence table was preferred to the stone recess with a shelf and a drain recommended by the ecclesiologists. As it was seldom that High Mass took place, the priest only required a single chair on the south side of the sanctuary, and two or three stools for the altar boys. Polychrome decorations on the walls and ceiling were added if money was available. Stained glass, often rather worse than that found in most Anglican churches, filled most of the windows sooner or later. A gong or a hand-bell stood on the right hand side of the altar steps. Lastly, one piece of furniture which always distinguished a Roman from an Anglican place of worship was the ever burning lamp before the altar on which the Blessed Sacrament was reserved; not forgetting the small glass vessel, with a purificator beside it close to the tabernacle.

The typical church of the Latin rite of the eighteen-sixties may have symbolized a priest-ridden congregation, but there was little or no trace of that spiritual pride, self-sufficiency, complacency or the patronage of the poor, with which Anglicans are charged. In fact, the atmosphere tended to be thoroughly vulgar. In many places the churches had been mainly built by the pennies of the poor. They were Mass-houses for the masses. They had been planned and furnished for functional purposes and not for æsthetic effect. A cultured ecclesiological visitor, inspecting any such Roman church, would walk out in disgust, because so few of the furnishings were 'correct.' But what else could be expected? So few priests 'came out of the top drawer,' except those who had abandoned the 'Church of their baptism' for that of Rome.

If one chanced to visit any Romish chapel on a Monday morning the interior would be filled with a faint odour of stale incense, probably mingled with gas; and if in an industrial district, almost certainly the not so agreeable after-smell of unwashed humanity and dirty old clothes. The correctly furnished Anglican churches generally had their own smell of brass-polish, soap and water, and very frequently that of musty hassocks combined with oil lamps or gas. On the greater festivals they were more fragrant with the scent of floral decorations.

Sometimes one comes across a Roman Catholic church, obviously dating from the sixties or seventies of the last century—even in remote parts of the Scottish Highlands—where the furnishings are most *recherché*. A breath of Belgravia or Mayfair

S. FRANCIS', GORTON, MANCHESTER (Edward Pugin, 1863–72)
This high altar, together with those at Leith and Ushaw College, show how
the design of Roman Catholic altars during the second half of the nineteenth
century was influenced by the importance attached to Benediction and
Exposition of the Blessed Sacrament. In each case the altar itself is over-
shadowed by the lofty throne.

drawing-rooms has unaccountably reached the back of beyond. In most cases they
prove to have been built by some of the aristocratic converts that followed Manning
over to Rome after 1851—Lady Lothian, the Duchesses of Buccleugh, Hamilton

and Leeds—the Feildings, Campdens, Norreyses, and so on. Then came a lull, but after 1869, several more extremely rich converts indulged in church building on a grand scale; the Marquis of Bute and Sir David Hunter-Blair being among them. Then there was Lady Herbert of Lea, always giving generously to the building or furnishing of a new Catholic place of worship. The pious Lady Georgiana Fullerton was another member of the Farm Street congregation who assisted to spread Jesuit ideas of ritual and ceremonial in churches up and down the country. Nevertheless most of the altars, statues, Stations of the Cross, and other 'objects of piety' were paid for by the working classes, brought up on the tradition that they must never refuse money for the 'chapel.' It is this proletarian quality of the furnishings of by far the greater number of the churches of the Latin rite in England dating from the 'sixties and 'seventies which makes them so interesting to the student of ecclesiastical taste.

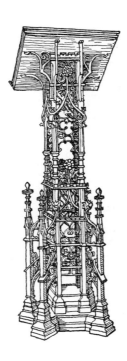

CHAPTER XVIII

'THE ART OF GARNISHING CHURCHES'

IT was about this time that Mrs. Monica Thurgood published a chatty little book entitled *Church Embroidery,* with the object of increasing the business at her shop in Finchley Road, London. A catalogue of goods sold is included. It mentions, among other articles, altar-kneelers, alms-bags and antependiums; bannerettes and book-markers; foot and fender-stools; chalice-veils, cushions and chancel carpets; sachets, sermon-cases, slippers, smoking-caps and stoles. Mrs. Thurgood gave lessons in embroidery in class or singly. Her book, with its most detailed instruc-

'BANNERETTES' (1870)

tions on materials and stitches, evokes a fascinating period atmosphere—even the note that smoking-caps can be supplied with or without tassels. Apparently sermon-cases, made of velvet or silk 'of any church colour' and embroidered with pious emblems, were in great demand. Mrs. Thurgood cannot have been ritualistic in her churchmanship, because she informs her readers that frontals must be of crimson velvet or cloth. She allows them to be draped with 'stoles,' and permits a harmless centre monogram.

A much more important book from the point of view of documentation is *The Art of Garnishing Churches at Christmas and other Festivals* by Edward Young Cox, which first appeared in 1868; by 1871 it had reached a third edition, in which much additional matter was inserted.

A study of this formidable work emphasizes how much more leisure was enjoyed by the devout in the eighteen-seventies than to-day. It must have taken hours to make the wreaths; devices in evergreens, everlasting flowers, berries and moss (real and artificial). As to the illuminated and emblazoned texts and devices—the worked or illuminated banners—they must have kept pious hands busy for months before the greater festivals. Decorations in straw were recommended as 'most effective,' especially if the straw-tissue letters were arranged on a crimson cotton-velvet ground. Where a church did not possess a structural reredos, a 'very pleasing effect' could be obtained by constructing a

EASTER DECORATIONS (Edward L. Cutts)
These two drawings show how temporary ecclesiastical decorations made a perfect background for the fashionable feminine costumes of this period. A fascinating pattern is achieved out of the overwhelming details

temporary reredos, its framework composed of laths and stout wire. Pretty Gothic canopied-shaped arches could be easily crocketed by mounting two or three sprays on wire, and then the crockets so formed could be fixed by twisting the end of the wire round the arches at regular intervals. Wall diapers, formed of evergreens and flowers, could have a very pleasing effect against the east end of a chancel. More elaborate diapers could be cut out of sheets of perforated zinc. The simple lattice pattern could be left open, and covered with evergreens and illuminating, in oil colours or gold, small ornamental crosses and other devices on the white calico groundwork. Four illustrations (in colour) show us what these temporary reredoses looked like.

CHRISTMAS DECORATIONS AND TEMPORARY REREDOS
(S. Matthias, Stoke Newington, *c.* 1870)

These temporary reredoses are extremely elaborate. They are Gothic going mad. Just as awe inspiring are the instructions on how to make chancel screens out of a framework of laths, around which Gothic arches could be formed out of evergreens, flowers and suitable emblems and devices. Nothing in a church must be left without decorations. Every gas standard must be treated with wreaths of evergreens and everlastings. Not a column or a spandril of an arch must be left bare, so as to show forth the words of the *Benedicite*: 'All ye green things upon the earth bless ye the Lord: praise him, and magnify him for ever.'

A sure proof that money could be made out of this kind of thing is the price list at the end of the book, which was published by the firm of Cox and Sons from their 'ecclesiastical warehouse' at 28 Southampton Street, London. More than fifty monograms, crosses, etc., cut out to shape as a groundwork for devices in evergreens, berries or everlasting flowers are catalogued in perforated zinc, cardboard, and in linen carton-paper. One can take one's choice of even more illuminated

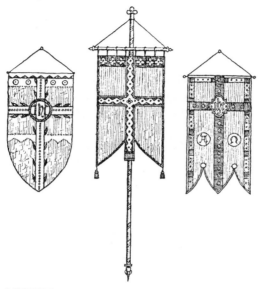

BANNERS
(from *Christmas Decoration of Churches,*
by Edward C. Cutts)

monograms, crosses and devices of several sizes and various materials. There is a selection of some sixty illuminated banners made of prepared calico or cloth; and an equal number of illuminated texts, large and small, according to price. Among the nine temporary reredoses advertised, the most expensive is a twelve feet long item, richly illuminated in colours and gold on a ground of prepared cloth. It costs £5 5s., a lot of money in the eighteen-seventies. Few ecclesiastical repositories to-day could boast of such a splendid display of polished brass flower vases, which muster more than twenty in this catalogue. Nor would you find those charming letters and devices in straw, the everlasting or artificial flowers, or the imitation holly berries, leaves, and dried moss. Sixteen species of everlasting flowers are advertised. The best imitation passion flowers cost half-a-crown each; the most costly roses are 10s. a dozen.

Messrs. Cox and Sons were right up to the minute. Their little book also includes a prospectus of a Society of Decorative Art which was under their direction. They had no intention of manufacturing 'spurious *modern antiques*.' 'The teaching of the old masters,' they announce, 'will be observed in the spirit rather than the letter. Educated people have learned to detest the heavy cumbrous forms and inharmonious colouring which were tolerated in the last and the earlier part of the present century; and it is not necessary that the reform should be conceived in a spirit of slavish adherence to medieval models. . . . We must respect the old models, not for their antiquity, but for their intrinsic excellence.' Not only did the firm supply materials for decorations of churches; it also took over the business of Mr. Keith, the silversmith to the Ecclesiological Society. So it was able to market the church plate designed in the first instance by Mr. Butterfield, Mr. Street and Mr. Burges.

Studying the photographs and engravings (plain and coloured) in Mr. Cox's book one is transported in imagination to a social era almost as remote as the Middle Ages. The world of the eighteen-seventies, just after the Franco-Prussian war, aimed at cosiness in all interior decoration. This was obtained by thick draped curtains, excluding all light and air. Just as churches were cluttered up with decorations by Mr. Cox, so every fashionable housewife filled her rooms with sofas, stools, chairs, little tables and what-nots. She had a passion for tassels, fringes, bobbins, peacock's feathers, and lacquered bullrushes. All her table-cloths touched the floor, and table-legs were regarded as slightly indecent, just as were columns in churches, at least on the greater festivals. This excessive decoration of churches achieved much the same atmosphere as that of rooms crammed with curios, knick-knacks and mass-produced ornaments; not forgetting the heavy curtains and *portières* draped over doors and windows.

The frontispiece of Mr. Cox's book is a faded photograph of the interior of a handsome church. Above the chancel arch a representation of Leonardo da Vinci's Last Supper in mosaic is surrounded by hand-painted art tiles. The temporary decorations include the dossal behind the altar, which is of coloured cloth bordered with lace, bearing an illuminated text, with wreaths of foliage hung in festoons. The columns of the chancel arch are almost hidden with evergreen wreaths, and a riot of foliage surges in the spandrils. There are so many banners, bannerettes, illuminated texts, and devices worked in everlasting flowers, that no wall spaces or columns are left bare. Another faded photograph depicts a Second Pointed Gothic interior with an even more lavish display of decorations, including a wonderful temporary reredos formed on a framework of iron wire, with shields cut out of cardboard and illuminated. These fashions in church furnishings persisted until about 1890.

Banners and 'bannerets' became very fashionable in churches which were far from being ritualistic strongholds. Parish magazines often refer to their 'picturesque effect.' As we have pointed out already, the preparation of long streamers of evergreens, which were often mixed with everlasting flowers, took days and often weeks. On the eve of the festival the ladies and some of the more devout male sex mounted ladders and suspended these wreaths between the columns, or wove them round the mouldings of the arches. How gay churches looked in those far off times, when instead of silent electric bulbs or concealed flood-lighting, gas jets hissed on elegantly designed brass or wrought-iron Gothic standards, forming lovely pyramids of flame.

After Mr. Beresford Hope had deserted All Saints', Margaret Street, for

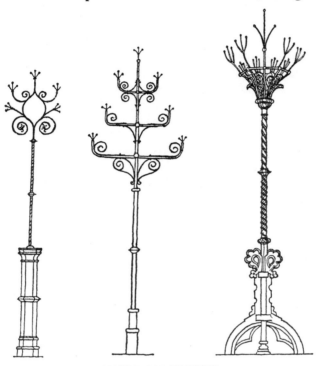

GOTHIC GAS FITTINGS

S. Andrew's, Wells Street, just round the corner, the furnishings of this Perpendicular church, designed by Mr. Samuel Dawkes, and opened in 1847, became increasingly correct ecclesiologically, although already it had obtained a name for itself by the daily choral celebration of Mattins and Evensong, and the surpliced choir of men and boys. In 1862 Mr. Benjamin Webb was appointed vicar, and remained at S. Andrew's for twenty-three years. It is not surprising that this clergyman, one of the two founders of the Cambridge Camden Society, would ensure ritual correctness in conformity with the best traditions of Anglicanism. Mr. Beresford Hope with many other devout men and women of High Church views, came to regard this dark and not very beautiful church as their spiritual home. All was reverent, orderly, dignified. Mr. Webb entrusted Mr. Street with the improvement of the furnishings. He inserted a screen and parcloses to the chancel; supplied a pulpit of a Spanish model, and got Mr. Redfern to carve a gorgeous

203

stone reredos. Mr. William Burges designed a litany desk. The east window had been filled with Hardman stained glass shortly after the opening of the church, but the light became still more dim and religious after Messrs. Lavers and Barraud, and the firm of Clayton and Bell had filled up all the other windows. Embroidered altar frontals and stoles, costly eucharistic plate, and richly bound Office books, were added to the *trésor* of this fashionable place of worship.

There was a certain *cachet* about S. Andrew's, Wells Street, difficult to define, but still remembered by a few old people. This church set a fashion of perfectly conducted Anglican worship which was High Church without being in the least Anglo-Catholic. The music was as ornate as the furnishings. Twice daily, as we have said, the finest Anglican psalmody as well as the most elaborate anthems were rendered by the choir school. On Sundays and every 'Red Letter Day' in the *Book of Common Prayer* there was a solemn celebration of the Holy Communion, sung frequently to English adaptations of the Masses of Beethoven, Cherubini, Schubert, Haydn, Mozart, Hummel, and other continental composers. During the early 'seventies Charles Gounod used to attend the services when he was staying in London. Several of his Passiontide motets, adapted from the Latin, by Mr. Webb, were first sung in this country at S. Andrew's.

The congregation, most of whom arrived in their own carriages, were either members of the nobility or of the opulent upper-middle class. They expected the floral decorations on the greater festivals to be as costly as money could provide. After Mr. Beresford Hope became a churchwarden in 1853, he contributed many of the flowers. He records that he bought four standard pink azaleas for 30s. each in 1863, and expected them to bloom alternate years. By Easter 1866 three had died and the fourth was dying. Hope was very much annoyed. His wife, Lady Mildred, wrote to Mr. Benjamin Webb: 'It was a great waste of money. . . . They have cost us in mere care and forcing for the last two years from 15s. to £1, and they should have lasted for years. You have little idea of the amount of work and expense on our garden, which plants for the church, flowers and fruit for architectural dinners and the carriage of them all imposes on the Bedgebury estate.'

Considering his vast wealth, and the luxurious standard of living of this Kentish squire of the middle of the last century, he seems to have worried unduly about his church flowers. It was at Christmas 1863 that he wrote to the vicar, undertaking 'to bear the sole cost of a spruce which you [Webb] can buy in Covent Garden for 1s. 6d. or so, an arrangement cheaper and easier than sending one up from Bedgebury.' The vicar replied that 15s. was the lowest market price and that he was quite willing to undersell Covent Garden.[1]

Even S. Paul's was affected by contemporary fashions. At Christmas 1868 the choir was decorated for the first time. Some courage was needed to place a cross on the communion table at the Epiphany, although it was worked in silver thread on a red ground. Growing bolder, the dean allowed some ladies to erect a semi-circular background to the altar for Easter. This temporary reredos consisted of

[1] Cf. *The Book of the Beresford Hopes*, p. 192.

crimson curtains. Surmounting it was an embroidered cross, with the text 'He is risen.' Hothouse plants, price £20, were provided by one of the canons to enrich the effect. This seems to have been the first time that there had ever been a cross over the altar in Wren's cathedral.[2] Under Dean Church, of course, S. Paul's became renowned and influential for its standard on Tractarian post-Newman liturgy and theology.

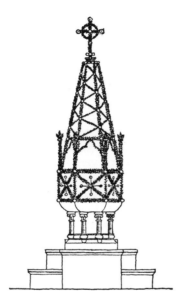

FONT DECORATED WITH
TEMPORARY COVER
(*Christmas Decoration of
Churches,* p. 50)

---

[2] Cf. *The History of S. Paul's Cathedral,* edited by W. R. Matthews (1957), p. 268.

CHAPTER XIX

WAR AGAINST RITUALISM

ONE of the reasons for this craze for inserting temporary decorations in churches was the fear of Romanism and Ritualism. Permanent furnishings seemed to drive the anti-Ritualists mad. Besides it was much cheaper to endure the desecration of temporary decorations. In 1869 there were two cases of this terror of Popery in disguise within a few miles of each other in Lancashire. A certain Captain Schofield, who had already subscribed £4,000 towards the erection of a new church by Street at Milnrow, insisted on the removal of a red Maltese cross on a white ground in the centre of the reredos. Unless this was done, he refused to present bells, pulpit and lectern. Street compromised and substituted, what was apparently innocuous in the eyes of the wealthy benefactor, a bleeding heart!

On October 2nd this same year, the building committee at Swinton decided to remove the marble and alabaster cross which Street had designed as part of the reredos for their new church. Riots were feared at the dedication ceremony, or Dr. Prince Lee, the Bishop of Manchester, might object to the cross. Later on this 'little art treasure' was fitted into the reredos, occupying its rightful place. People had not yet forgotten how this ultra-Protestant prelate had abolished choral services in Ringley chapel in the parish of Prestwich. He maintained that they were 'Romish,' because they allowed 'vicarious worship.' [1]

Punch continued to voice the feelings of the average Englishman on 'Puseyite' ecclesiastical fashions. *Parsons in Petticoats* reads: 'Reverend gentlemen of extreme High Church proclivities are very fond of dressing up like ladies. They are much addicted to wearing vestments diversified with small and gay colours and variously trimmed and embroidered. There is the chasuble, and cope, and stole, and dalmatic, besides the alb in which they are accustomed to deck themselves out *à la Romaine,* and moreover there may be, for aught we know, the casaque, the burnous, and the visite, and the capote, and the fichu, and the pardessus. If they have taken to go about the streets in their petticoats, they have adopted the best possible plan to get a large following. At any rate they will be sure of having no end of a tail of street-boys for acolytes. But let them take heed lest they stumble. If they will wear long dresses, they should loop them up. Hoops are going out; but the sans flectrum crinoline is still advertised in the *Morning Post.* Let them don

---

[1] Cf. J. Stanley Leatherbarrow, *Victorian Period Piece* (1954), pp. 78–9.

the steel cage under the muslin, or alpaca, or tarlatan, or *poult de soie,* or satin, or whatever it is their robes are made of. By this careful and cleanly contrivance, they will be enabled not only to preserve themselves from being tripped up by their own skirts, but also be lift their trains out of the mire, and keep them from sweeping the pavement clear of orange peel and other things. At the same time if they affect the *Ignatius chaussure,*[2] they will enjoy the advantage of showing their sandals, or, in case they prefer the more modern style of embellishment for the foot and ankle in association with crinoline, of making an edifying exhibition of their Balmoral boots.' [3]

In September 1865 *Punch* felt it worth commenting on the report printed in the *Daily News* on the opening of S. Michael's, Shoreditch, designed by James Brooks. The Bishop of London had refused to proceed with the consecration service until 'four handsome bouquets' had been removed from the altar. He then told the assembled clergy that they must take off their richly embroidered stoles; saying 'quietly but sternly: "The Clergy of my diocese must appear in the ceremonial of to-day in the simple dress of Clergymen of the Church of England." ' His Lordship also refused to continue the service until a 'rough sketch of the Crucifixion with figures of S. Mary and S. John behind the communion table' had been taken down. This was impossible at the moment, so the vicar, architect and the two churchwardens were made to sign a paper promising to have the offensive cartoons removed as soon as possible.

From about 1856 until 1882 a continual war was being waged against church furnishings and ornaments by the more erastian and Protestant-minded section of the Church of England. Looking back the whole thing strikes us as a storm in a tea-cup. First of all were the notorious riots at S. George-in-the-East in 1860 and the following year.[4] What chiefly roused the fury of the mob (and which most of the bishops wished to suppress) were *'The Six Points'*—the eastward position at the communion table, eucharistic vestments, altar lights, the mixed-chalice, wafer bread and incense. The greatest of all the lay Protestant crusaders was Lord Shaftesbury, who wanted Parliament to make illegal 'all vestments, albs, tunicles, stoles, censers, copes, and candlesticks.' Bishop Wilberforce of Oxford expressed the opinion of most of the episcopate when in 1866 he declared that the ritualists were trying to reimpose on the Church of England the 'manifold hardness of Roman ritual, from which she was delivered at the Reformation, not the gradual growth of a national worship in a moderate and sober development of ceremonial.' Bishop Tait of London was equally convinced that ritualism was a growing evil which could only be suppressed by legislation, but he was not quite clear what form it could take.

It was the Revd. Alexander Heriot Mackonochie, vicar of S. Alban's, Holborn, who suffered more for his convictions than any other clergyman. The case of

[2] An allusion to Fr. Ignatius, whose Anglican Benedictine community at Norwich had obtained much notoriety.
[3] June 10th, 1865.
[4] See pp. 167–8.

S. MARY'S, WHITECHAPEL, LONDON (Edward C. Lee, 1878)
An early break-away from conventional Gothic Revival

Martin *v.* Mackonochie came before the Court of Arches in December 1867. The final judgment, given the following year, showed how unfavourable to Anglo-Catholicism was the legal interpretation of obsolete formularies.

In 1869 the Revd. John Purchas, the author of *Directorium Anglicanum,* who had been the perpetual curate of S. James's, Brighton, since 1866, was

208

All Saints, Babbacombe, Devon (W. Butterfield, 1868)

S. Mary, Great Warley, Essex
(Sir William Reynolds-Stephens, 1904)

13. More phases in fashions. Two pulpits and a font

Holy Angels, Hoar Cross, Staffordshire
(G. F. Bodley, 1872)

Painted reredos, Lyndhurst parish
church, Hampshire (Sir Frederick
Leighton, *c.* 1860)

Shrine of Our Lady, S. Mary, Bourne
Street, London (Martin Travers, 1930)

Carved stone reredos, Hurstpierpoint
College (Carpenter and Slater, 1875)

charged by a retired colonel in the Court of Arches for having worn or caused other to wear during divine service, cope, chasuble, alb with apparels, and other illegal vestments; that he formed processions with a crucifix, lights, banners and incense; used lighted candles on the holy table during the celebration of the Holy Communion, mixed water with the wine, and elevated the Consecrated Elements. The case was undefended, and not all the presumed illegal actions and ornaments were condemned. But the promoter of the case appealed to the Judicial Committee, and he having died suddenly, the appeal was continued by a retired Indian judge. Eventually a ruling was given that during the Communion service the celebrant must stand at the north end or side of the holy table, so that his 'manual acts' can be seen by the people; that only ordinary leavened bread is legal; that water must not be mixed with wine, either before or during the service; and that the biretta is an unlawful headgear in the Church of England.

Needless to say, *Punch* made merry over all this fuss about birettas in Brighton. Mr. Purchas was honoured with a whole page cartoon, entitled 'The Ritualist Rebuked.' Mr. Charles Walker, the *caeremonarius* of S. James's Church, and author of *The Ritual Reason Why,* was reminded that a zuchetta means a little pumpkin, and that such headgear for acolytes is only suited for those with pumpkin-shaped heads.[5]

Punch had no mercy on clergymen who fancied French or Italian fashions in church furnishings or ornaments: 'An Anglican clergyman wishing to do the thing well should apply to Miss Herbert at the S. James's Theatre (a saint's theatre too!), who has got a properly vested altar, including the two candlesticks, which was used as a property in *Much Ado about Nothing,* and we have no doubt ample use will be found for it in the latest act of the Ecclesiastical Drama, which, by the way, might very appropriately adopt the above mentioned Shakespearian title.'[6]

In 1867 a Royal Commission on Ritual was set up. It issued four reports, the last of which appeared in 1870. On August 31st, 1874, Parliament passed the Public Worship Regulation Bill, which came into force on July 1st, 1875. Then followed a series of once famous trials of ritualistic clergymen for illegal ceremonial; including Thomas Pelham Dale (1876); Arthur Tooth (1876), and Sidney H. Green (1879). The last named spent a year in Lancaster Gaol, as the penalty for wearing vestments and burning incense at S. John's, Miles Platting, Manchester.

'The Six Points' specified already were almost a matter of life and death to the ritualistic clergymen and layfolk of the 'sixties and 'seventies. They affected not only the furnishings of churches, but also the livelihood of artists and craftsmen; even the business done by the shops that sold the articles required for carrying out some of the 'Points.' Ecclesiastical fashions had to conform to rigid regulations of English civil courts or the whims of individual bishops. 'The Six Points' (with the biretta as a seventh 'sacramental' in some cases) were regarded almost as part of the deposit of faith. They could not be given up under pain of mortal sin. Rather

[5] October 24th, 1868, and December 3rd, 1870.
[6] July 21st, 1866.

O

S. ALBAN'S, HOLBORN (*c.* 1875)
The high-water mark of 'ritualist' *décor;* in perfect harmony with
the female fashions of the eighteen-seventies. It is interesting to compare this drawing with the rebuilt church, designed Adrian Gilbert Scott

than do so, Anglo-Catholic incumbents were willing to face persecution, fines,
imprisonment and even martyrdom.

Looking back over nearly a century, it is difficult to understand the mentality
of those utterly sincere and devoted clergymen. After all, what were the 'Six
Points' but an Anglican adaptation of the then current rules of the Sacred Congregation of Rites intended for the liturgy of the Roman Church only? Even from
the Roman point of view the 'Six Points' were not explicitly 'Catholic.'

S. MARTIN'S, BRIGHTON (Somers Clarke, Jnr., 1875)
Gothic Revival *décor* runs riot!

Considering that there appears to have been no uniformity in the position of the celebrant of the Eucharist during the first three centuries of the Christian era, it is curious that the nineteenth century Anglican 'Ritualists' attached so much importance to the 'eastward position' at the prayer of consecration, which involved turning their backs to the people. To-day it seems just as odd that these men were convinced that they could not fully proclaim their priesthood unless they were clothed in certain garments, usually of a rather debased late medieval shape, some of them not worn in any of the Eastern Churches. When the Judicial Committee of the Privy Council and the Court of Arches gave judgment that the chasuble, alb,

S. BARTHOLOMEW'S, BRIGHTON (Edmund E. Scott, 1875)
With its seven lamps, and altar raised on many steps, this lofty
church was considered to be the model of ritualistic 'correctness'

tunicle, dalmatic, stole and maniple were illegal vestments, the ritualistic clergy
could have got round the letter of the law by adopting the oriental phainolion,
sticharion, epitrachelion and epimanika. After the ceremonial use of altar lights
had been forbidden, all that had to be done was to black-out the chancels, and
illuminate them with lamps filled with olive oil, suspended over or before the
holy table.

After both the Court of Arches and the Judicial Committee of the Privy Council
had made the 'mixed chalice' illegal, the Anglican ritualists do not seem to have

consoled themselves with the realization that, in this respect, the ceremonial of the Church of England had been brought into line with that of the venerable Church of Armenia. Again, one wonders why such importance was attached to the use of wafer bread, considering that all the Eastern Churches, including those in communion with Rome, use leavened bread in the celebration of the Holy Eucharist. It is even more difficult for us to understand why these persecuted parsons felt that they could not say Mass without many genuflections and prostrations. After all, these modes of reverence are of comparatively late introduction, and unknown in most Eastern rites. Neither are they uniform in the variants of the Roman rite.

Lastly, even if the ritualistic clergymen were forbidden to burn incense during public worship, the letter of the law did not specifically stop them from doing so in a fumigatory manner before the congregation had arrived. Such a use would have been in keeping with the Post-Reformation practice in the Church of England. Incense was burned in several cathedrals, royal chapels and parish churches during the seventeenth century. When the ritualists of the eighteen-sixties were trying to introduce the Roman ceremonial use of incense, there were still men living who might have seen it burnt in a non-ceremonial manner in Ely Cathedral.

It was hard on the church furnishers when the sale of thuribles, vestments, candlesticks, cruets, and even birettas became confined to churches in England under the jurisdiction of the hierarchy set up by Pope Pius IX in 1850. It is surprising that such shops in London, Birmingham and elsewhere did not emulate Demetrius the silversmith of Antioch who, so we are told in the Acts of the Apostles, 'used to make silver models of Diana's temple, and so gave plentiful employment to the craftsmen.' There is no evidence that any nineteenth century Demetrius called a meeting of the workmen who were in the same trade, by way of protest that their business was being ruined; and, that like the temple of the great goddess Diana, many Anglican places of worship were being shorn of their greatness.[7]

* Legal; ‡ Illegal.

Subject of Decision	Consistory Court	Bishops and Archbishops	Court of Arches	Judicial Committee of Privy Council
I. CEREMONIES				
Incense—ceremonial use		‡1899	‡1868 ‡1870	
Incense—non-ceremonial use		*1899		
Chalice mixed in service time		‡1890	‡1868 ‡1870	
Mixed chalice		*1890	*1870	‡1871
Processions as ceremonies			‡1870 ‡1874	
Distribution of ashes			‡1870	
Use of holy water			‡1870	
Use of sacring bell		‡1909		
Covering of crucifix in Lent and uncovering at Easter			‡1870	
Bowing to Crucifix			‡1879	
Baring table on Good Friday			‡1870	

[7] Chief 'Ritual Decisions' of the Church of England. This table gives an idea of the problems which had to be solved by church furnishers during the second half of the nineteenth century, owing to the confusing nature of ritual and ceremonial legislation.

Fashions in Church Furnishings

Subject of Decision	Consistory Court	Bishops and Archbishops	Court of Arches	Judicial Committee of Privy Council
Making sign of the cross		‡1890	‡1874	
Kissing gospel book			‡1870	
			‡1874	
Eastward position at prayer of consecration		*1890	‡1870	
			‡1874	*1877
Use of wafer bread			*1870	‡1871
			‡1874	‡1877
Ablutions in church		*1890		
Reservation for any purpose		‡1899	‡1907	
II. ORNAMENTS PROPER, i.e. used in services, and so ruled by the rubric				
(a) *Of the Church*				
Credence table	‡1855		‡1845	*1857
Altar lights—ceremonial use	‡1855	*1890	‡1856	‡1868
			*1868	
Altar lights—non-ceremonial use	*1855			
Gospel lights, or ceremonial use of lights over and before table, or Paschal candle			‡1870	
Processional lights		‡1899	‡1870	
Lighting or distributing candles on Candlemas Day			‡1870	
Embroidery and lace on fair linen cloths	‡1855		‡1856	‡1857
Coloured altar cloths	‡1855		‡1856	*1857
Crucifix—ceremonial use			‡1870	
Banners—ceremonial use			‡1870	
			‡1874	
Image of infant Jesus at Christmas			‡1870	
Dove at Whitsuntide			‡1870	
Use of biretta			*1870	
(b) *Of the Ministers*				
Cope at Communion service in parish churches			*1870	
			‡1874	‡1871
Chasuble at communion service			*1870	‡1871
			‡1874	‡1877
White alb plain			*1870	‡1871
			‡1874	‡1877
Surplice at Holy Communion			*1870	
Tunicle at Holy Communion			*1870	‡1871
			‡1874	‡1877
Cope not at Holy Communion			‡1870	
Apparelled albs			‡1870	
Circular tippets			‡1870	
Amice			‡1874	
Stole			‡1870	
Maniple			‡1870	
			‡1874	
Dalmatic			‡1870	
Black gown in pulpit				*1897
III. OTHER ORNAMENTS, not used in services, but ruled by discretionary faculty				
Stone altar	‡1855		‡1845	‡1857
Baldachin	‡1873		‡1856	
Reredos as decoration	‡1880	‡1874	*1874	*1875
Second holy table, if for convenience	*1887			
Stations of the Cross—full series			‡1876	
Chancel gates	‡1877			
	*1885		‡1876	
Flower vases on holy table		‡1847	*1870	
Cross on holy table	‡1855		‡1856	*1857
Cross attached to table				‡1857
Cross on retable			‡1875	‡1876
Cross on screen	*1901		‡1876	‡1877
	*1909			
Tabernacle for reserved sacrament	‡1900			
Curtains behind and at ends of table (if not preventing celebrant taking the north-end position)	*1908			

(This list has been adapted from *The Prayer Book Dictionary* (1913), pp. 715–17.)

Even the really advanced Ritualists were not entirely in agreement about 'The Six Points,' and this must have added to the worries of the church furnishers as well as the architects. For instance, Mr. West, the vicar of S. Mary Magdalene's, Paddington, was determined to adopt altar lights again by March 1870, but said he would not do so without consulting his brethren. At the same time he was not going to change the 'Paddington Use' of celebrating Mass at the north end of the altar. It is curious that he did not think of moving Mr. Street's communion table forward from the wall of the apse and administering the Lord's Supper behind it, which the more 'Roman' of his brethren would have recommended in these times.

All this was evidently discussed over the tea tables by the devout female sex in 1870. We can picture them in their drawing-rooms; the walls covered with pictures, and the overmantel of the fireplace draped with plush. Almost all of them would have a gilt French clock in a glass case as its centre piece, with two large vases on either side, and smaller ones in between. As these ladies went to and from church on Sundays they resembled tropical birds or beetles, with their bustles sticking out behind, and their heads adorned with feathered hats or bonnets. Perhaps some of the mothers taught their children *Mr. Punch's A.B.C. for Youthful Anglicans,* in which they would memorize among other letters:

> C is a Chasuble, hung on a peg,
>   And useful to hide the defects in the leg.
> D's a Dalmatic, for festival use,
>   Embroidered all o'er by an Anglican goose.
> E is an Eagle, which serves as a desk,
>   In part medieval, in part arabesque.
> F is a Frontal, which gracefully fell
>   O'er the altar, affronting the people as well.
> O is the Orphrey, a piece of embroidery
>   Worked o'er the vestments to make them more tawdry.
> T is the Thurible, whose very smell
>   Incenses the people, and makes them rebel.[8]

The problems of rebuilding and refurnishing hundreds of churches during this period when Lord Shaftesbury and others were waging war against 'Ritualism,' is revealed in a series of letters written by Mr. Eden Nesfield to the then rector of S. Mary the Virgin, Radwinter, Essex. The all but rebuilt church was consecrated with much solemnity on May 25th, 1870. The music at the Communion service was the *Missa de Angelis* and the plainchant hymns, etc., in Helmore's *Directory.*

Nesfield designed a mahogany altar, painted all over with cherubims in panels, with a pelican and chalice in the centre panel. He would have liked to put in a stone altar but this was not allowed so he compromised with a marble plinth. The altar was 'movable' in the strict sense, but so heavy that it would have been almost impossible to shift! He hoped 'there would be no fuss about it.' He wanted

[8] April 8th, 1871.

to add a gradine, with a simple brass cross, two candlesticks and flower vases but feared that 'Shaftesbury won't let him.' In one of his letters he sketched a rood-beam with a large plain cross and a row of twenty-six candles. This could be supplied 'for £20, all painted.' The body of the church was lit by paraffin lamps, which as the architect explained could 'easily be made quite pretty, with sconces or reflectors behind.' There were candles on the choir stalls, and 'two big gooseberry bushes' of candles on each side of the altar. The chancel walls and roof were

A 'GARNISHED' CHURCH (1870)

decorated with paintings. Both a sedilia and a wooden credence table were provided.[9]

There were few churches where such rich permanent decorations and ornaments were introduced. In the average Anglican parish the clergy and pious helpers were still content to indulge in an orgy of temporary decorating for the greater festivals (*vide supra*, pp. 198–205). The fashion had become so widespread that in 1871 the Church Building Society had to issue a series of directions to restrain the zeal

[9] The existing chancel screen of metal dates from 1880–5. The new reredos is a sixteenth century structure with small free-standing figures against shallow carved backgrounds. The furnishings of this church are very sumptuous. (Cf. *Essex*. The Buildings of England, Penguin Books, p. 291.)
  Another example of Eden Nesfield's restoration work of the same date can be found at S. Mary's, King's Walden, Hertfordshire.

of the decorators. They are similar to Mr. Cox's advice in his *Art of Garnishing Churches at Christmas and other Festivals.* The first thing is to '*plan* the scheme of decoration, and not to waste power where it will be thrown away. . . . Colour must be added to the berries, flowers, etc., so that it will "tell." ' Church decorators are advised: 'Allow time for the final touches which Royal Academicians give to their pictures after they are hung. These final touches include a wreath to be made a little fuller here by sticking in a few supplementary twigs; a few superfluous leaves to be cut off there to make the outline of a device more distinct; and a bunch of flowers to be put here, to heighten the effect; and then let all the litter be swept out of the church and out of mind—in time for a bright festal Even-Song.'

The fashion for producing this periodical transformation scene in Anglican churches persisted well on into the 'eighties and 'nineties. In 1882 the Revd. Ernest Geldart published *The Art of Garnishing Churches,* which contains even more elaborate instructions.

CHAPTER XX

GEORGE EDMUND STREET AND
JOHN LOUGHBOROUGH PEARSON

REFERENCE has been made already to some of the earlier church furnishings and decorations designed by G. E. Street and J. L. Pearson, who with G. F. Bodley, were the outstanding ecclesiastical architects after the death of Sir Gilbert Scott in 1878.

It is difficult to define the chief characteristics of Street's furnishings. They were usually unpretentious. That is to say, they fade into and form part of the whole interior instead of standing out from it. Street seldom left an altar or reredos alone. He made them less conspicuous by adding stone carved or polychromic decoration around the sanctuary. In most of his larger churches he avoided making a focal point of the altar. In recent years most of Street's chancels have been changed, so it is difficult to find an existing example of his work in this field.

One of these richly decorated chancels in its original state can be seen in the engraving of the interior of S. John's, Torquay (1861–71), facing page 325 of Eastlake's *History of the Gothic Revival* (1872). A brass eagle lectern stands on the tesselated pavement between the rows of rather dull Gothic choir-stalls; those in front having lancet openings through which the cassocks and surplices of the choir boys must have been visible. Wrought iron gas fittings stick out from the walls and columns. Four steps lead to the altar. There is hardly room on the top step for the celebrant to stand, far less to genuflect. It would be interesting to know why so many Victorian architects refused the clergyman a decent footpace. The altar, presumably of carved and varnished oak, is hidden by a richly embroidered frontal, adorned with conventionalized flowers and sacred monograms. There is neither a cross nor candlesticks, but the elaborate carved stone reredos has a low relief panel of the Crucifixion in the centre. This reredos is merely a part of the Decorated Gothic arches and the two rows of vescica shaped openings which are carried round the sanctuary. The stained glass in the great five-light east window was designed by Burne-Jones, and carried out by Morris and Co. It was this same artist who painted the panels on the north and south walls of the chancel. What with the clustered shafts of polished Devon marble with bands of differently coloured Devon marble, and still more colour in the stone vaulted roof, the eye has nothing on which to focus. It must have been Street's intention to make people see his

S. JOHN'S, TORQUAY (G. E. Street, 1870).
A typical example of a richly furnished chancel in an Anglican
church of this period

chancel as a whole, and not to concentrate on the altar, because exactly the same
effect was obtained at All Saints', Boyne Hill, Maidenhead (1855); S. James the
Less, Westminster (1862); and in several other churches he erected in the 'sixties.

By the end of the eighteen-fifties Mr. Street had evolved his own style of church
furnishing; a little dull, but thoroughly conscientious. He had to consider the

particular churchmanship of each client, and could seldom risk anything unusual. 'Correctness' was all. In the 'Geometric-Pointed' church of S. Paul, Herne Hill, London, he inserted choir-stalls, and employed Hardman to fill the five-light east window with stained glass. Contemporary critics said that the alabaster reredos was 'very good,' and admired its angle shafts of green serpentine, the rich cresting, the panels inlaid with variegated circles, and a large centre cross 'pattée, charged with annulets.' There was also a splendid font, and a pulpit enriched with marbles. Mr. Ruskin pronounced S. Paul's to be 'one of the loveliest churches of the kind in the country, and one that makes the fire (that destroyed the original) a matter of rejoicing.'

In 1858 Mr. Street completed a new church at Whitwell, near York, the .furnishings of which were highly commended. Here he inserted a reredos composed of tesserae, with shafts on either side, and an ornate cross in the middle. The stone pulpit displayed circles of alabaster and Devonshire marble. The font was enriched with inlaid disks of alabaster and marbles, and had a wooden pyramid-shaped cover. At the same time this busy architect made a wholesale restoration of Wymering Church, Hampshire, at the request of the wealthy High Church squire-parson, Mr. Nugée. More of Street's furnishings of this date were inserted at S. Mary's, Hanley Castle, Worcestershire; and at Howsham, Yorkshire.

In 1860 he was busy at the restored medieval churches at Stone, Kent; Upton Magna, Shropshire; and Hanbury, Staffordshire. Next we hear of him at Chalvey, Buckinghamshire; Denstone, Staffordshire; Stourbridge, Worcestershire; Lilleshall, Shropshire; and at Edermine in Co. Wexford.

S. Peter's, Bournemouth, which approached completion in 1861, attracted much attention for the richness of its fittings. A novel feature were the gabled chapels eastward of the transepts, intended for the use of children. All the new work was reported 'very beautiful and ornate.' Open metal screen-work divided the choir from the transepts. The sanctuary was lined with marbles in patterns, and the carved stone reredos was of great splendour. Over the choir arches were large circles sculptured in relief with angels.

S. James-the-Less, in Garden Street, off Vauxhall Bridge Road, London, which was consecrated in 1861, showed Mr. Street, both in style and materials, rebelling against insular precedent. Many people felt that this strange looking church was much too 'foreign,' both outside and in. The reredos was typical—a rich mosaic of marble, the cross forming a portion of the latter, and inlaid in red marble and not projecting, with a bold cornice of an Early French type. There was a low alabaster super-altar on which stood two candlesticks.

A cultured visitor wrote that the treatment of the remaining wall space of the sanctuary was 'particularly commendable as the first really artistic adaptation of mastic incising which we have seen on the walls of our churches. On each side are represented under canopies the holy women respectively of the Old and the New Covenant: graceful figures boldly etched in with the heads standing out from the darkness of the backgrounds, not merely lined out like a magnified design of Retsch or Flaxman. The whole effect is very much like that of a Flemish or

German brass of the best kind relieved of the confusing glare of the metallic ground. In this experiment we see the opening to infinite development of constructional iconography.' [1] But the double-round-headed credence, with its off carving in the head, was dismissed as 'an instance of the caprice in which a man of unquestionable powers will occasionally indulge, and we should hardly imagine that the miniature tables of the commandments ranged in close proximity will, in the long run, prove of much utility to the studious members of the congregation.' To add to the richness of this church, the sanctuary pavement was of mixed marble and tiles. The woodwork of the stalls was simple and solid, in spite of the peculiar form of the poppy-heads. The chancel was divided from the nave by a low stone screen, supporting open metal work of mixed iron and brass, the former painted chocolate red. Over the chancel arch was a mural painting by Mr. George Frederick Watts, R.A.; of which the subject was a modified doom, with our Lord on His throne, attendant angels, but no devils casting souls into everlasting fires. The same ecclesiologist wrote, 'We are no advocate for forced antiquarianism; but there is a limit of modern feeling which the painter who works in a Gothic church ought not quite to touch.' Nor did Mr. Street's novel gas-fittings meet with approval. Due to the polychromed dado running round the interior, dark red with occasional tessera of strong buff, S. James's looked very garish. In some of the stained glass windows Messrs. Clayton and Bell had introduced single figures, almost as red as the walls around them. The bright, strong coloration of the roof was also condemned by most of the critics. The furnishings and decorations of this church, as well as its general design, proved how much Street had absorbed by his travels in France, Italy and Germany between 1850 and 1857.

From his youth Street held very strong opinions on the relationship between art and religion. 'This great truth must be grasped,' he wrote, 'that Christian Art is never properly developed except by an essentially Christian intention on the part of the artist, as well as on the part of those who employ his talents. The Church architect must thoroughly believe the doctrines of the Church for which he builds, and must lead a life of—to say the least—fair conformity to her rites and discipline. He must also be fairly acquainted with her ritual and usages.'

Street felt that every detail of a church should assert the supreme control of the master mind in one complete achievement. The result was that most of his churches 'shaped themselves into the ideal shape for rendering the liturgy of the Church of England according to the best Victorian tradition which Street, who had sung in a Church choir, understood so well. Tractarian liturgical formulæ had led public worship into a custom of an elaborate Mattins or Sung Eucharist, sung by a surpliced choir in full view of the congregation at the east end of the church.' [2]

The thirteenth century doctrines of Durandus concerning Christian Symbolism, as introduced to Anglican readers by J. M. Neale and Benjamin Webb in 1843, were still taken very seriously nearly thirty years later. A writer in *The Builder*

[1] ibid., Vol. XXII, New Series XIX, p. 325.
[2] J. Stanley Leatherbarrow, *Victorian Period Piece* (1954), p. 164.

(June 17th, 1871) said: 'We architects should infuse a symbolic spirit into the minutest details of all sanctuary work, even in the dimensions of the altar itself. I recommend my brother-architects in no case to carry out an altar less than 7 ft. 5 in. long (both symbolical numerals), and when possible to exceed this length to let the mystic number 5, so closely associated with altar ritual, determine *in the inches* the exact length of the slab.'

George Edmund Street tried to find symbolic reasons for the details of the furnishings and ornaments he inserted into most of his churches. The feeling that symbolism was the correct thing persisted among Anglican architects for nearly half a century, but when J. T. Micklethwaite published his *Modern Parish Churches* he pleaded for a return to common sense, and wrote: 'As for *symbolism* which some people would have us believe was the ruling influence in the old plans, I do not think it had anything in the world to do with them. Ceremonial was sometimes symbolical, as also were some of the decorations of the churches, but the churches themselves were arranged to suit the practical requirements of those who were to use them.' [3]

In the church of SS. Philip and James, Oxford (1862), Street was content with a plain wall lining for the chancel, which heightened the effect of the rich inlay and Earp's carving on the reredos. When the church was opened people said they had never seen such a devotional interior. The ornaments and decorations were greatly admired, including the Clayton and Bell stained glass, and the altar cross inlaid with olive wood from the Garden of Gethsemane. There was a splendid brass lectern and other striking metal work. The distribution of the gas lights was most effective. At evensong in winter the choir men and boys in their white surplices were brilliantly illuminated by rows of jets running along the north and south parclose screens.

Four years later he designed the village church at Fawley on the Berkshire Downs, where the carved stone reredos, with a panel of the Crucifixion in the centre panel, stands out in the apsidal sanctuary. Eastlake maintains that the oblong altar piece carved by Earp, with mosaics by Salviati, in Brightwalton Church, Berkshire (1862–3) 'exactly realize that combination of quaintness and grace which is so characteristic of medieval work.' [4]

Street was happier when designing small village churches than large town ones. Perhaps the most characteristic of them all is at Holmbury S. Mary, Surrey (1877), one of his last creations and built to please himself. The furnishings are restrained with much of the quality of Keble's *The Christian Year*. They are the perfection of Tractarian Anglicanism.

Bare walls show up the richly carved stone reredos with five panels in the Chapel of S. Margaret's Convent, East Grinstead, Sussex (1865–70) where a dramatic effect is created by the tall columns of black marble on each side of the sanctuary. Street designed some fine stalls for the wide and lofty choir. Each seat was carved on the under side by one of the Sisters. Whether he would have

[3] p. 56.
[4] ibid., p. 323.

approved of the six candlesticks, tabernacle and permanent exposition throne which in recent years have been placed on his altar, is somewhat doubtful.

Two of Street's finest town churches—All Saints', Clifton, Bristol (1868), and S. John the Divine, Kennington, London (1870)—were destroyed by enemy action in the Second World War. At S. Mary Magdalene's, Paddington, London (1867–73), and S. Margaret's, Liverpool (1869), the well-meant zeal of Anglican Papalists has resulted in the removal or hiding of most of the architect's original furnishings, and the substitution of baroque ornaments which have created a different atmosphere. But there still remain churches designed or restored by Street in England and a few in Scotland and Ireland, where the *décor* had been left largely as he intended.

The furnishings, ornaments and decorations in the many churches designed by John Loughborough Pearson, like the buildings themselves, differ considerably from the work of his greater contemporaries. His style was too individualistic to find many imitators. In most of his churches the stone·vaulting is so fascinating that one is not immediately conscious of the fittings; the eye is drawn up to the roof. 'In the design of such vaulting,' Mr. Goodhart-Rendel remarks, 'he had no equal, a statement that even a superficial study of his churches will corroborate.' [5]

The solid brass eagle lectern which Pearson designed for his first London church, Holy Trinity, Vauxhall Bridge Road (now pulled down), was first used at the funeral of the Duke of Wellington on November 18th, 1852. This massive and extremely heavy piece of furniture was lent to the dean and chapter of S. Paul's for the occasion.

The engraving facing page 327 of Eastlake's *History of the Gothic Revival*, depicting the apsidal chancel of S. Peter's, Vauxhall, opened in 1863, helps us to grasp Pearson's earlier conception of the ideal Anglican altar and its surroundings. There is a low plain stone chancel screen, surmounted by elaborate wrought iron grilles; with a square shaped and richly decorated stone pulpit at its north side. The first things to catch the eye are the two tall wrought iron Gothic gas standards on either side of the choir. Eastlake tells us that the stalls were 'severely plain in general form,' and depended 'for their effect on the novel introduction of iron grille-work which rises behind them, and forms a canopy overhead. It is impossible to praise too highly the skill and attention which have been bestowed on the design of these screens, and indeed the whole of the metal-work in this church.' For the rest of his life Pearson would continue to design metal screens of which the same could be said.

The altar, as shown in the engraving, is vested with an embroidered frontal and super-frontal, typical of their period. S. Peter's was planned for ceremonial worship, so there are two candlesticks and two flower vases on the single gradine, but no cross. The rather heavy alabaster reredos, enriched with coloured marble and gold mosaic, has a large floriated cross as its central feature. It can have been seen by few people in the nave. The walls of the apse, immediately above the reredos,

[5] *English Architecture since the Regency,* p. 212.

and around the sides, below the triforium, are decorated with seven fresco paintings by Messrs. Clayton and Bell; arranged so that the Crucifixion comes immediately above the altar. Stained glass fills the single lancet windows. They were designed

S. PETER'S, VAUXHALL (J. L. Pearson, 1865)
Note the carved cross as part of the reredos, the chancel screen,
pulpit and gas-standards

by Westlake and carried out by Lavers and Barraud. Other mural decorations were painted by Clayton and Bell.

S. Augustine's, Kilburn, was started in 1871, but not completed until 1880. It has been described by Dr. Nikolaus Pevsner as 'one of the best churches of its date in the whole of England, a proud, honest, upright achievement, even if suffering

S. Alban, Copnor, Portsmouth (Sir
Charles Nicholson Bt., 1914)—Anglican

Ascension, Chicago, U.S.A. (J. N.
Street, 1893)—Episcopalian

15. Four later variations in Gothic Revival furnishings

S. Gregory, Preshome, Banffshire
(Peter Paul Pugin, 1896)—Roman
Catholic

All Saints, Dorchester, Mass., U.S.A.
(Cram, Goodhue and Ferguson, 1898)
—Episcopalian

16. S. Johannes Church, Basle, Switzerland (Burckhardt and Egender, 1936). 'The uncompromisingly severe interior reflects the philosophy of the [Calvinist] congregation which did not allow any suggestion of a mystical atmosphere, sculpture or paintings' (E. D. Mills, *The Modern Church*, p. 42)

All Saints' Church, Basle (Hermann Baur) shows a fairly characteristic Catholic sanctuary of the same period, also expressive of the 'new look' in ecclesiastical *décor*

(as all High Victorian ecclesiastical architecture must) from a total lack of inspiration in the details.' [6] The stone reredos was carved by Nicholls. There is a striking stone rood-screen, and the favourite Pearson iron grilles within the choir arcades. The walls of the transepts, the south chapel, and the freize above the nave arcades are adorned with paintings by Clayton and Bell. This same firm carried out most of the stained glass in the windows. To add to the richness of the *décor* there are several Italian 'old masters,' presented by Lord Northcliffe, which hang on the walls. This once famous centre of militant Anglo-Catholicism conveys, alas, the impression to-day of being moribund; its magnificent furnishings and decorations, not to mention the ceremonial to which they were the background, have ceased to draw the crowds which filled this great church half a century ago.

Many of Pearson's earlier churches are in the north of England. Several in Yorkshire were built during the 'forties; including those at Ellerker, Elloughton, Wauldby, North Ferriby and Ellerton. He restored and refurnished others between 1850 and 1870. S. James's, Weybridge, Surrey (1846–8), and S. Peter's, Daylesford, Worcestershire (1859), are typical examples of his styles in the south and west counties. The former is Carpenter-like English fourteenth century, the latter French in inspiration.

S. George's, Cullercoats, Northumberland (1865–84), contains a rich variety of his furnishings and decorations. Above the altar the carved text 'How amiable are Thy dwellings, Thou Lord of Hosts ' was surrounded by a border of vine leaves and heads of barley. On each side was an emblem of the Holy Trinity, with many bright hued flowers, with the inscription underneath of 'Alleluia.' The side walls of the chancel were adorned with more texts, with borders of green leaves. Around the capitals of the pillars were carved geraniums, heather, holly, ferns, mosses and furze 'in great profusion, but in admirable taste.' The church, when newly opened must have suggested an exhibition of stone horticulture, because of the floral wreathes in every possible position.

'The most brilliant mass of colour is on the font—a pyramid of flowers of light colours'—so continues the contemporary account. 'The effect of the whole is charming, and affords an idea of what willing heads and hands can do, and will do if rightly directed in the adornment of God's House by the use of what is among the most beautiful of all that He has given us.'

How generous Church people could be in the 'sixties is proved by some of the gifts made to Pearson's church at Cullercoats, whose tall spire serves as a beacon far out at sea. A massive and costly set of communion plate and richly bound service books were presented by the Duchess of Northumberland. Among the other sumptuous accessories were a superb altar cloth of the richest crimson velvet, beautifully embroidered linen cloths, a chalice veil and six alms-bags. The cushions for the altar rails were worked and presented by the ladies of the parish. The fishermen paid for the stained glass windows, and a Captain Soper gave the lectern.

About the same time Pearson designed a small apsidal church at Appleton-le-

---

[6] *London, except the Cities of London and Westminster* (The Buildings of England, Penguin Books, 1952), p. 297.

P

Moors in Yorkshire, which contains some rich and characteristic furnishings of his earlier period. Another Yorkshire church—Wentworth—which dates from between 1872 and 1877, built for Earl Fitzwilliam—has been described as 'a suburban intruder, rather vulgarly showing off.'

S. John's, Red Lion Square, London, and S. Alban's, Birmingham, were built in the last two years of the 'seventies. Their furnishings had much in common. The former was a victim of the Second World War, and what was left of the church, after German bombs had done their worst, was pulled down. Pearson gave each of them an elaborate wrought iron rood screen, but the Birmingham church lacks the striking painted and gilded triptych reredos above the high altar, which was part of the charm of the interior of S. John's, Red Lion Square.

It was in 1878 that Pearson was commissioned to design a cathedral for the newly formed diocese of Truro. The furnishings and decorations of this great Gothic Revival building, mainly in the Early English style, are similar to those in most of the parish churches he designed in the next twenty years. His work from then onwards became both in form and in detail much more standardized. There is little wrong with their quality, but they tend to be cold and hard when compared with the refined creations of Bodley and Garner.

Many of the fittings of the cathedral were added after Pearson's death, but the choir stalls and the bishop's throne are good examples of his taste in woodwork. The great Bath stone reredos, with its confusion of carved groups and single figures, was repeated on a smaller scale in several of his later churches; so were the sanctuary steps of Italian marble, the mosaic pavement, the brass gas standards and the metal communion rails.

The stone reredos in Bristol Cathedral is of the same type as the Truro one; also that in S. Agnes, Liverpool (1883–5)—one of Pearson's most attractive interiors. More or less contemporary were S. John's, Upper Norwood; S. Michael's, Croydon; S. Barnabas, Hove; and S. Michael's, Headingley, Leeds.

He gave the Norwood church a stone rood screen, like the one in S. Augustine's, Kilburn. A light metal screen, resembling those at S. Alban's, Birmingham, and S. John's, Red Lion Square, was added to the Headingley furnishings. S. Stephen's, Bournemouth, begun in 1881, but not completed until 1896, has an almost perfect Pearson interior in which the altars, reredoses, stalls, pulpit and pavements show all the mannerisms of his later period. Everything is very rich, yet the combined effect is curiously cold.

The refurnishing of the choir of Peterborough Cathedral included a new high altar, surmounted by a magnificent Gothic baldachin, with four marble columns, and the arches and spandrils enriched with alabaster and mosaic. Here he paved the choir and sanctuary with marble, creating a very sumptuous effect.

It is difficult to catalogue Pearson among the designers of ecclesiastical *décor*. 'His churches are unmistakably late nineteenth century, in spite of their medieval-isms,' Basil Clarke writes. 'They may remind travelled ecclesiologists of churches in France; but in fact they are not like any others. They are English, in spite of certain features borrowed from abroad. They are churches designed for the carrying out of the services of the English Prayer Book in the manner that became customary in a large number of parishes during the second period of the Catholic revival, and for the accommodation of large Anglican congregations. And they are planned according to the good taste, common sense and deep ecclesiological knowledge of one man.' [7]

Unlike Bodley and Garner, whose churches were being built throughout the same period as those designed by Pearson, and almost invariably for parishes which had been influenced by the Catholic revival, he was never affected by the Pre-Raphaelites. Nor is there anything to suggest that Pearson was influenced in his younger days by Pugin or the Camdenians. The furnishings of his churches, like the buildings themselves, are intensely individual. They may not be all alike, but if one has become familiar with one of his churches it is not difficult to recognize another. It is remarkable that the Tractarian movement in the Church of England produced three such utterly different architects as Butterfield, Bodley and Pearson; each of whom found his own distinct idiom in the design of a suitable background and accessories for carrying out the services of the Book of Common Prayer, as interpreted by the second generation of Tractarians.

Pearson's furnishings and decorations, like those in Truro Cathedral which were designed round about 1879, have very little in common with those of the average upper-class house of the same period. How odd his carved stone reredoses look if one visualizes them as the background for a procession of ladies in long tight skirts, fur cape, muffs and toques—the sort of people whom George du Maurier drew for *Punch*. Even more incongruous against such ecclesiastical scenery are the old ladies of the same period in their cloaks and bonnets. It is not easy to picture the average working man of the late 'seventies garbed in moleskins or corduroys, harmonizing with a Pearson background—even if he were employed as a labourer, laying a marble pavement or fitting together a metal screen. His cold, hard, built-for-eternity church interiors are far removed from the *décor* of the typical drawing-room of the cultured and artistic worshipper, with its spidery furniture, 'art embroidery,' fringed tablecloths, round gilt-framed mirrors, Japanese fans, screens and wicker armchairs. Heavy velvet portières and peacocks' feathers would look very odd in one of his chancels. Pearson never thought of providing 'Children's Corners' for the little girls with their long hair and pinafores. On the other hand it is not so difficult to picture the tight waisted young ladies drawn by Du Maurier playing a gentle game of tennis in long skirts; moving from the rectory garden into the church for Evensong. Their clothes for church and for tennis were identical. Many of Pearson's finest church interiors were contemporary with the 'Æsthetic Movement,' but their æsthetic quality is utterly different from that of Burne-Jones' paintings or what was caricatured in Gilbert and Sullivan's operetta *Patience*. They do not make one think of Walter Pater's *Marius the Epicurian*, although they may evoke memories of the olive-green bound later works of Ruskin. Perhaps this is because both are so chaste and detached from the sordid realities of ordinary life.

[7] *Church Builders of the Nineteenth Century*, p. 197.

CHAPTER XXI

GEORGE FREDERICK BODLEY

NO English architect between 1860 and 1900 did more to direct taste in ecclesiastical *décor* than George Frederick Bodley (1827–1907). During those forty years his highly original style, imitated but never surpassed by his juniors, set the tone especially in the more conservative Anglo-Catholic circles.

He was the son of a prosperous physician, who claimed descent from Sir Thomas Bodley of Oxford. While George was still a small boy his father moved to Brighton, and later on to Harley Street, where his patients numbered many of the nobility. The Bodleys appear to have been a cultured family, with authors, musicians and painters among their circle of friends. It was almost a foregone conclusion in the 'fifties that young George should serve his apprenticeship with Mr. Gilbert Scott, then at the peak of his fame, but he was not influenced by his master.

Bodley's first commission was to add an aisle to the church at Bussage in Gloucestershire in 1857, where the incumbent was a brother of John Keble. In 1861 he began work on S. Michael's, Brighton, and got William Morris to design several windows. In after years he used to refer to it as 'a boyish, antagonistic effort.' The reredos and the decorations of the chancel were greatly influenced by Italian Gothic, similar to what Mr. Street had revived the same year in S. James the Less, Westminster. S. Michael's indicates that young Bodley must have been reading Mr. Ruskin's *Seven Lamps of Architecture* and *The Stones of Venice*. His friendship with Dante Gabriel Rossetti, William Morris, Ford Maddox Brown and Edward Burne-Jones resulted in all of them taking a hand in the decoration of S. Martin's, Scarborough, opened in 1863. They did the paintings on the panels of the pulpit. Philip Webb, the architect of Morris's 'Red House' at Bexley Heath, Kent, decorated the roof. Before long Bodley became the chief patron of the firm of Watts and Co., from whom he obtained most of the rich velvets and other fabrics used for frontals and curtains. He also designed some of the earliest Morris wall papers, and gave advice on tiles and stained glass.

Amongst the Pre-Raphaelites Bodley 'felt especially the dominant influence of Rossetti, for whose painting, but especially for whose poetry, he always retained and expressed the warmest admiration. His own poetic temperament and mystic sense responded readily to Rossetti's.' [1]

[1] Edward Warren, *The Life and Work of G. F. Bodley (Journal of the Royal Institute of British Architects*, 1910, p. 309).

Indeed some of the interiors of the churches designed by Bodley during the 'sixties and 'seventies express the rhythm of Rossetti's sonnets:

> 'This is that Lady Beauty, in whose praise
> Thy voice and hand shake still,—long known to thee
> By flying hair and fluttering hem,—the best
> Following her daily of thy heart and feet,
> How passionately and irretrievably,
> In what fond fight, how many ways and days!'

> (*The House of Life*, lxxvii, *Soul's Beauty*.)

When one looks up at his earlier rood-screens, altars, pulpits or the glass windows painted by Morris or Kempe, one is moved to repeat:

> 'The blessed damozel leaned out
> From the gold bar of Heaven;
> Her eyes were deeper than the depth
> Of waters stilled at even;
> She had three lilies in her hand,
> And the stars in her hair were seven.'

> (*The Blessed Damozel*, i.)

Unlike Butterfield, who loved exposed brickwork, and the natural colouring of all materials, Bodley could seldom resist painting and gilding his roofs, walls and woodwork. As Mr. Warren has pointed out: 'he was never content with a church until he had brought the whole interior into harmony as he conceived it—a harmony which governed the whole design and its furniture down to the minutest detail of glass, metal or needlework. Marble he almost never used in a church, except for floors, or for an occasional font.' [2]

The first two churches in which the real Bodley characteristics appear are All Saints', Cambridge (1864) and S. Salvador's, Dundee (1865). In the former we find Morris stencilling—red, white and dark grey—on the walls; with rather brighter colours on the ceilings. The glass in the east window is by Morris and Co., some of it designed by Burne-Jones, then only about thirty years old. The interior of the Dundee church features a gilded wrought iron screen, dark woodwork, much diapered walls, and a magnificent carved wooden reredos, painted and gilded. The traditional Scottish 'Sacrament House' for reservation, standing against the north wall of the sanctuary, is an uncommon article of furniture. [3]

The interior of S. John the Baptist, Tue Brook, Liverpool (1868–70), has an A. W. Pugin atmosphere, and shows how much Bodley must have been influenced by his predecessor. The walls and ceilings are covered with elaborate painted decorations, now mellowed with age. The massive wooden chancel screen, once bright with gold and colour, is faded to a rich dull brown. The general effect of

[2] ibid., p. 310.
[3] It is in use no longer. A small tabernacle has been placed on the high altar.

this church is that of a much worn Persian carpet. As in most of Bodley's churches, the high altar is raised on many steps. Beneath the five-light east window is a typical example of his favourite painted and gilded reredoses, with a slightly projecting tester. The rich effect of the interior is increased by baroque Aubrey Beardsley-like ornaments on all the three altars, added at a much later period (see p. 323). 'The Blessed Damozel' does not appear to be embarrassed by having to keep company with 'Mademoiselle de Maupin'!

Bodley had now acquired a partner—Thomas Garner (1839–1906). Their close association continued until 1898, when Garner 'went over to Rome,' to the sorrow of Bodley, who remained throughout his life a devout High Anglican.[4]

To deal properly with the furnishings and decorations of the Church of the Holy Angels, Hoar Cross, Staffordshire (begun early in 1872, but not completed until 1906), would need a book on its own. Here can be studied every aspect of Bodley and Garner's work. This warm-red sandstone fourteenth century Gothic church, though not large, is covered in every inch of its interior in rich decorations. The lofty font cover is painted green and gilded with doors that open on either side. Around the aisle walls are Stations of the Cross, painted by De Wint and Boeck of Antwerp. They are enclosed in wooden panels with doors. There is a painted oak rood screen. The wealth of decoration on the high altar reredos, the walls of the chancel and the many ornaments are no more baffling to describe than the countless *objets d'art* which can be found in the four side chapels. The windows, with their elaborate tracery, are filled with stained glass by Messrs. Burlison and Grylls; all of them supervised by the architect.

As Mr. Edward Warren said nearly sixty years ago: 'Internally Hoar Cross is the fervid, almost passionate, realization of an ideal. Seen, as I last saw it, in the deepening twilight of a clear autumn evening, when the details of its interior are softening into gloom, and the chancel, with its stately altar, its sumptuous hangings, and its gleam of gold, is dimly visible beyond the screen, while the rich tones of its painted windows make a soft resplendent glow, it gives an indescribable impression of medieval glamour, of poetry and mystery; a visionary rehabilitation of the ancient glories of the Church.'[5]

Set beside a quiet road in the midst of still unspoilt English Midland countryside, far from any town, Hoar Cross is a veritable museum, containing perhaps the finest examples of late Gothic Revival furnishings and decorations to be found anywhere in Britain; all of them characteristic of ecclesiastical good taste in the 'seventies. The only criticism which can be made of Hoar Cross is that it is almost *too* perfect, refined and exquisite.

The versatility of Bodley and Garner is shown even more strongly in S. Augus-

---

[4] After Garner's reconciliation with the Roman Church in 1898, and the cessation of his long partnership with Bodley, he continued to practice as an architect. A few characteristic examples of his furnishings can be found at Downside Abbey, where he designed the choir, completed in 1905. The altar and reredos in S. Isidore's Chapel should be mentioned.
[5] ibid., pp. 314–15.

tine's, Pendlebury—a lofty red brick church on an exposed spot about five miles west of Manchester—a proletarian background utterly unlike that of the church at Hoar Cross.

Here there are only very narrow processional aisles. The lower part of the walls are panelled and painted in the almost invariable Bodley venetian red. High up in each of the recesses of the shallow nave arches are painted panels of saints. A dark stained wooden screen divides the chancel from the nave. As at Tue Brook, there is no rood. The oak choir stalls, with canopies, are elaborately carved. The altar is raised eight steps above the chancel, and has one gradine, on which stand six very tall candlesticks, fitted with even taller dummy candles—favourite Bodley furnishing. The dull gold and red reredos, with painted figures of saints, could only have been designed by him. Above it a large eight-light window is filled with Kempe glass, as are most of the other windows in the church. The curious screened-in triple wooden sedilia is pure Bodley. Significantly, no provision was made for a side-chapel, although the services at Pendlebury were always conducted on High Church lines. Eighty years ago the Tractarian belief that the post-Reformation Anglican use required only one altar still persisted. Taken as a whole, the furnishings and ornaments in this immensely lofty church, designed in the late Decorated style of Gothic, are splendid period pieces. It is good to find that the interior remains almost as it was planned in the eighteen-seventies, except for a tiny chapel which has been squeezed into the narrow aisle on the south side of the chancel. Every detail combines to achieve a decorative harmony. The factory workers for whom this great church was built were very proud of it, although one wonders how many of them felt really at home in this imitation fourteenth century interior.

Bodley and Garner, never tried to appeal to the masses when furnishing and decorating their churches. They would have been shocked if anybody had suggested that this mock medieval world was not appreciated by Christ's poor and simple, whose needs in the eighteen-sixties and -seventies more than to-day, had to be carefully considered. The typical Bodley and Garner church reflected the sixteenth century prose of the *Book of Common Prayer,* with a reverent ceremonial and Gregorian chanting, but the idiom of the factory or dockside labourer, or for that matter of the bourgeoisie, which had grown up with the Industrial Revolution, was a very different affair.

About the same time as Bodley and Garner were supervising the details of their exquisite ornaments and decorations in S. Augustine's, Pendlebury, in Manchester five miles away, the Jesuits were telling Joseph Hansom that they wanted rich and splendid altars to appeal to the average worshipper in the wide and lofty Church of the Holy Name. Gothic Revival tinsel and glitter were as important as stimulants to popular devotion as florid music at Benediction sung by a mixed choir. Compare these two churches of the same date. One is the expression of rarified and highly cultured Anglicanism; the other of garish but eminently practical Romanism. A comparison of contemporary church furnishings of the 'sixties and 'seventies shows the great gulf between the Anglican and Roman examples.

In the same year appeared Bodley and Garner's altars, reredoses and screens at Hoar Cross, and those by Charles Buckler in the Dominican Church at Haverstock Hill, London; also Joseph Hansom's many-statued reredos in S. Aloysius', Oxford. Another instance of contemporary Anglican and Catholic *décor*, Bodley and Garner's Pre-Raphaelite trimmings in S. Martin's, Scarborough, and George Goldie's altars in S. Wilfrid's, York, were both built in the same year. Buckler was one of the few Catholic architects who still tried to create a quiet English medieval glamour in his interiors, several of which are contemporary with Bodley and Garner's earlier churches, e.g. those at Slindon, Sussex; East Hended, Berkshire; and at Windsor. But the fittings in most cases are merely a poor evocation of A. W. Pugin—pretty, but uninspiring.

The boldness and daring of the churches designed by Bodley and Garner during the eighteen-seventies can better be appreciated after a glance at the domestic furnishing of the period. The Pre-Raphaelites, and latterly the domestic decorations of William Morris and Co., had infiltrated into a few families, but the average house was still characterized by pretentiousness, sombreness and costliness. To-day we can hardly realize how gay and colourful a typical Bodley church must have appeared, and what a contrast it made with the drawing-room or dining-room of its more prosperous worshippers.

It was still the age of gas or oil lighting. Most of the wealthy people who found the money to build Bodley's churches, and wanted his late-medieval furnishings, would have had their drawing-room walls covered with florid English papers, which provided the background for the then fashionable ebony or ebonized wood furniture, standing on Kidderminster carpets. Most of the tables, chairs and sofas (except where the family had not cast out its antique furniture) was hard, bright and machine-made.

It would have been rare to find a fashionable drawing-room without an elaborately carved overmantle—probably in ebony or gean wood. Many were supplied by Messrs. Waring and Gillow. Some would have served admirably for the display of reliquaries in a Catholic church, instead of being used for china or silver ornaments. What with the soft velvets, deep pile carpets, portières, mirrors, gilt frames, curtains (lace and plush), the potted ferns and palms, amid all the dark gleaming furniture, it is puzzling that well-to-do people could accept this divorce between the backgrounds of their religious and secular life. What a contrast there was between a Bodley church and its secular equivalent—a typical dining-room, with its dark crimson papered walls, brown lincrusta dado, deep freize, large oil paintings in heavy gilt frames, enormous mahogany sideboard, massive and highly polished table of the same wood, and rows of upholstered chairs to match it. Above the table hung a great gas chandelier. On the marble mantelpiece, more likely than not stood a large marble clock, with two marble cast iron or papier-mâché 'ornaments' in the form of statuettes on either side of it. The mirrored sideboard would display silver salvers, a polished oak or mahogany tantalus and cut-glass spirit decanters. Few Anglican churches in England were filled with the fumes of incense and most dining-rooms were similarly untainted by tobacco smoke.

One can picture the scene at Hoar Cross, with the Hon. Emily Charlotte Meynell-Ingram, robed in her widow's weeds, accompanying her guests to the church designed by Mr. Bodley in memory of her husband. The fashionably dressed residents and visitors at Brighton and Scarborough wend their way to two more Bodley churches. The prosperous business men living on the outskirts of Liverpool, drive up to the new church at Tue Brook, with their wives, sons and daughters. The congregations who gathered in Camden Town or at Pendlebury for morning or evening service on Sundays are garbed in a more subdued manner, in keeping with their lower status in life.

Most of the upper class ladies wear capote hats. Their silk or velvet gowns are draped with many pleats, with overskirts rather like curtains or portières. They project behind, because all but the elderly have adopted the fashionable bustle, which by the mid-'seventies had developed into a horseshoe of shaped bars, suspended horizontally by tapes. It resembled a bird cage. What with the bustles and the tight corsets the ladies found it almost as difficult to walk as if they were medieval knights encased in armour. The men sported morning or frock coats and glossy top hats.

The service over, they make their way back homewards. After perhaps an hour and a half of Mr. Bodley's imitation medievalism the ladies foregather in their boudoirs before luncheon. What a contrast! For here are thickly draped curtains; sofas and stools with tiny tassels, and more curtains or portières over the doors.

The legs of the many little tables are hidden beneath plush cloths that almost touch the floor. How bare the church must have seemed in comparison with the boudoir, with all its curios, and hundreds of little ornaments, the chief purpose of which is to gather dust. Wherever there is space on tables or shelves are photograph frames, wax flowers and statuettes. Mingled with the water colour paintings and more photographs on the walls are vases of tall bulrushes and peacocks' feathers, and rows of plates on or above the beading below the ceiling.

The furnishings of S. Michael's, Camden Town, London, opened in 1876, shared the exotic quality of Hoar Cross and Pendlebury, and S. German's and S. Saviour's, Roath, Cardiff, which were inserted about 1880. In all these churches the same austere reserve combines with that delicate and refined use of colour which are characteristic of Bodley and Garner. When the Duke of Newcastle asked the partners to design him a sumptuous private chapel, planned on the scale of a parish church, they worked under much the same conditions that they had enjoyed with the Hon. Mrs. Meynell Ingram at Hoar Cross. S. Mary's, Clumber, Nottinghamshire (1886–9), with its magnificent chancel screen and rood beam, richly decorated font, pulpit, altars and Kempe stained glass, has been described by Dr. Pevsner as 'an eerie memorial to the passing of an age.' In 1938 the adjacent ducal mansion was pulled down completely. So the church stands alone, 'poignantly beautiful and inappropriate,' amid clumps of oaks and cedar, close to an artificial lake.[6]

Nearly all the many churches designed between 1886 and 1896 contain the same standardized Bodley and Garner furnishings and decorations. No matter how refined the details, how exquisite and restrained the colours, the *tout ensemble* often seems stale and lifeless. Certain tricks and mannerisms, repeated endlessly with slight variations, become wearisome. The final period of the Bodley and Garner partnership is best seen in the Church of S. John the Evangelist, Oxford, built for the Cowley Fathers, and completed in 1898. The long choir, planned for the use of the community, is divided from the relatively short nave by a carved oak rood screen. The other woodwork—pulpit, lectern and screens, etc., is marked by the same refined austerity. The arched ceiling is delicately diapered, but the colours are so subdued that one is hardly conscious of them. The high altar has the lofty gradine with the sham tabernacle in the middle that Bodley seemed to fancy in his latter years. Originally there was a tall dossal of some brownish neutral tint, against which rose six tall candlesticks and the crucifix. The pale greens and golds of the Kempe windows completed the *décor* of this lovely church, in which no detail could offend the sensitive taste. Brightened up in recent years, it still retains its own atmosphere, expressive of the Anglicanism of the 'naughty nineties.'

Standing in the Cowley Fathers' church at Oxford it is difficult to realize that while it was being decorated in this restrained manner the newspapers were full of the trousseau lingerie of Miss Consuelo Vanderbilt, whose marriage to the Duke of Marlborough took place in November 1895. It is perhaps even harder to think of the furnishings designed by Bodley as being exactly contemporary with Aubrey Beardsley's first drawings in *The Yellow Book;* and even more incredible, the start over in America of the world-wide fame of 'The Gibson Girl.'

The Eton Mission Church (1893) must have been designed to uplift the inhabitants of the Hackney Marshes in East London. The furnishings are almost identical with the mother house of S.S.J.E. at Oxford. S. Mary's, Eccleston, Cheshire (1894), and S. Aldhelm's, Branksome, Bournemouth, which is rather later in date, belong to the same period.

Holy Trinity, Kensington (1904) and S. Edward's, Holbeck, Leeds (1907) are perhaps the best places in which to study Bodley's later ecclesiastical furniture and decoration. The former has an open chancel; the latter a rood screen running right across the nave and aisles. The chancels of both churches are paved with polished black and white marble.

In addition to the many churches designed by Bodley and Garner between 1870 and 1898, there are others up and down England which contain altars, pulpits, fonts, screens, etc., which are equally typical of the two partners. Some are by no means in keeping with their surroundings; others fit in perfectly. It did not matter very much whether they were designing an altar for a small medieval church like that at Hickleton, Yorkshire, or for town churches, such as S. Alban's, Holborn;

[6] Cf. *Nottinghamshire*, Penguin 'Buildings of England' series (1951), p. 53. The chapel is now used by the Military College which has a lease of most of the Abbey.

S. Barnabas', Pimlico; S. Stephen's, South Kensington; or S. Mary's, Nottingham, to mention but a few places—altars and reredoses were basically similar. Almost every reredos consists of two or three rows of carved and canopied wooden statues, surrounded by a deep and richly carved frame; the whole thing coloured (mainly in a dull shade of red) and profusely gilded. Six tall candlesticks usually stand on top of the high gradine; the cross rests on a decorated box-like structure, that conveys the idea of a tabernacle. Projecting from the sides of the altar at an angle of 45° are iron rods, from which hang brocade or stamped velvet curtains of sub-dued colour, supplied by Messrs. Watts and Co. Two brass or silver standard candlesticks on the sides of the footpace, and three or seven brass or silver hanging lamps with ruby glass containers for the oil, complete the Bodley sanctuary.

His work has now acquired the *cachet* of a period piece, but he is not quite old enough to be admired by the present generation. Mr. Goodhart-Rendel feels that 'in the design of ornament Bodley showed greater accomplishment than Pearson, and gained by it as many admirers as by his architecture. As a colourist, also, he had a great reputation, although one difficult now to account for. He delighted in brownish tones, and if compelled to retain existing stained glass by Pugin or Wailes would coat it with umber glaze. His decoration as a whole is hardly as inventive as had been Pugin's, but surpasses it in what Victorians called "refinement"; and what is thought of it will depend upon what is thought of that quality. It certainly has another quality, that of harmony, which it would be wrong to belittle.' [7]

The significance of Bodley's ecclesiastical *décor* in relation to its period is explained by Mr. Goodhart-Rendel: 'The particular style of Bodley . . . was very faithfully mimicked, both by his many pupils and by others with whom he has no personal encounter. It satisfied completely the aspirations of those who believed that the road to national sanctity lay through the older public schools and universities, guarded by Anglican scholarship from the intruding errors of Geneva or of Rome. It was not exactly what the Ecclesiologists had hoped would emerge from their campaign; they had intended something a little more popular, a little more at home in the slums, a little less aloof from the "progressive" temper of the day. But it was they who were responsible for it, and it was they who had long-drawn the aisles, had storied the windows, had segregated the surpliced clergy and choir in screened enclosures, had converted the draped table into the vested altar, and had turned the eyes of architects back to a style that had proved harder to develop than to imitate. Things might not have turned out quite as they expected, but in the result there was much more to rejoice over than there was to deplore.' [8]

[7] *English Architecture since the Regency* (1953), p. 214.
[8] ibid., pp. 214–16.

CHAPTER XXII

FURNISHINGS AND DECORATIONS BY LESSER MASTERS

S O many architects were designing or restoring churches between 1860 and 1880 that it is impossible to describe the characteristics of all their furnishings and decorations. Some of them have been dealt with in previous chapters, or will be referred to later.

JAMES BROOKS

James Brooks (1825–1901) deserves a further tribute, but his ecclesiastical *décor* was seldom up to the standard of those splendid brick churches he designed in London and elsewhere. Contemporary engravings enable us to visualize the contemporary fittings of S. Columba's and S. Chad's, Haggerston, and S. Andrew's, Plaistow. The two Haggerston churches had variations of the same type of low stone chancel screen and pulpit. Each was provided with an altar vested with a frontal, well raised on steps at the east end of the chancel; square at S. Columba's and apsidal at S. Chad's. Above each altar was a reredos of five panels; the centre one being higher than the others. S. Andrew's, Plaistow, also had an apsidal chancel, and the details of its low screen, altar and reredos were almost identical with those in the two Haggerston churches. The engravings show that the three churches had painted panels above and around their reredoses, and below their lancet east windows. It is only at S. Columba's that Brooks dared to put a cross and two candlesticks on the super-altar. In the other two churches he settled for a carved cross in the reredos.

The low side aisles in S. Columba's had their blank walls enriched with carved panels. It is not clear in the engraving whether these were Stations of the Cross.

Mr. Francis Bumpus points out that in these Haggerston churches, 'in no case can it be said that the altar has been gilded at the expense of the roof-tree, for except those absolutely necessary at the outset, the *instrumenta* of worship have been provided from time to time as means allowed. While exceedingly simple and severe, they are of a style quite *sui generis,* the architect having infused into them a spirit of originality which just hits the happy mean between the commonplace and the bizarre.' [1]

[1] *London Churches Ancient and Modern,* Second Series, p. 292.

The *'instrumenta* of worship' supplied by Brooks in 1869 soon ceased to satisfy the Anglo-Catholic clergy of S. Columba's and S. Chad's. In the past eighty years a transformation scene has been carried out in both of them. The architect would hardly recognize their interiors now. The same thing can be said of the brick interiors of S. Michael's, Shoreditch (1865), and S. Saviour's, Hoxton (1866) in which most of the furniture and ornaments are now far more evocative of continental Catholic worship than of the mid-Victorian High Anglicanism for which most of Brooks' churches were planned.[2]

It is not difficult to understand why James Brooks paid so little attention to the designs of his altars and reredoses. No doubt he remembered what had happened at S. Michael's, Shoreditch, in 1865, when the Bishop of London insisted on the removal of flower vases and the cartoons for mural paintings above the altar. By this time he knew that sooner or later the clergy of the new churches in Haggerston and Plaistow would insert furnishings and ornaments on the sly.

'Ritualistic Theatricals at Shoreditch' is the title of an article in *Punch* for September 21st, 1867. It shows the sort of things that were done in many other Anglo-Catholic churches after they had been safely consecrated. We learn that 'the altar was handsomely lighted up with no less than fifty-six wax candles, besides two large candelabra, one north, the other south, in addition to a long row of tapers on the rood screen and a profusion of gas jets into the bargain. It was also tastefully decorated with flowers, exhibiting a scene, at least, fully equal in brilliancy to anything of the kind ever witnessed at the Horticultural Gardens.'

In fact this Solemn Evensong for the Octave of the Dedication of the church must have been a wonderful display of the latest ecclesiastical fashions. There were choristers in gay apparel, clad in scarlet cassocks and cambric cottas. The cross bearer was attired in a bright red robe, with two strips of cambric; the one in front, the other behind.

Indeed it must have been a most colourful and resplendent scene that September night in Shoreditch, with the myriads of flickering tapers and hissing gas jets; the heavy perfume of the flowers; the spectacle of the gorgeous copes, the scarlet cassocks, and the filmy cambric cottas. By way of contrast there were the black monkish robes of Brother Ignatius, complete with tonsured head, a rosary hanging from his girdle. The Bishop of Capetown in his Convocation robes added to the scene.

All this roused *Punch* the year before to publish a cartoon, showing 'Dr. Protestant' saying to the proprietor of a church furnishing shop: 'Take your gewgaws to the old lady at the Cross-Keys opposite, she likes them, and I won't have them.'[3] A month later appeared another drawing entitled 'Incense-ibility,' showing a Puseyite parson as he sniffs samples of incense inquiring, 'You are sure this is something quite new?' The 'Incensor' replies, 'Oh yes, Reverend Father, it has all the Beauties of the "Jockey Club" without its profanity.'

[2] S. Saviour's was damaged during the Second World War, and pulled down afterwards.
[3] November 17th, 1866.

S. COLUMBA'S, HAGGERSTON (James Brooks, 1869)
Like most of the London churches designed by Brooks, S. Columba's
was planned for what was regarded as 'advanced ritual.' Most of the
furnishings depicted here have now disappeared as not being in strict
conformity with the latest decrees of the Sacred Congregation of Rites

WILLIAM BURGES

We can still study characteristic examples of the rich and sumptuous ecclesiastical furnishings designed by William Burges (1827–81) in S. Finbar's Cathedral,
Cork (1865–70); S. Mary's, Studley Royal, Yorkshire (1871); Christ the Consoler,
Skelton, Yorkshire (1871), and elsewhere. Burges was a great Gothic Revival
architect, but even more remarkable as a designer of furniture, plate and jewellery.
The house he designed for himself in Melbury Road, Kensington between 1870
and 1881 was a museum of strange and somewhat barbaric furniture and decora-

238

tions. His work at Cardiff Castle (1865) is characterized by a similar wild Gothic fantasy.

No Catholic cathedral in Ireland has such a perfectly decorated interior as S. Finbar's, Cork. It glows with rich colours, and every detail of its furnishings is original, possessing a quality lacking in the work of most of Burges's contemporaries. It recalls Grimm's Fairy Tales or Wagner's *Lohengrin*. The same Wagnerian opulence (or vulgarity) is even more apparent in the interior of Studley Royal Church, quite his most extravagant effort. The chancel walls are lined with alabaster. Its pavement records the principal buildings of Jerusalem. Looking down on the sanctuary floor one discovers in mosaic the Garden of Eden, and the four rivers, Gihon, Pison, Tigris and Euphrates, flowing from vases in the hands of figures. Professor Lethaby wrote, 'architecture to Burges was play-acting—and yet he was earnest and thorough, a real make-believer, although the idea of being a medieval jester must have occurred to his quick mind.' [5] Unfortunately there were no other medieval jesters among the Gothic Revivalists. Most of them took their job too seriously. Thanks to Burges, we can still prowl around a dozen or so churches erected in the 'sixties and 'seventies and enjoy the possibly unconscious humour of their *décor*. Some are as funny as medieval bestiaries; others are grim and defiant, but never are they dull.

AUSTIN AND PALEY

We find nothing of this kind of humour in the furnishings designed by that prolific architect, Edward Graham Paley (1823–95); most of whose Anglican churches were built in the north of England. They are all honest and conscientious, and whatever may be lacking in their interiors, they express admirably the temperament of the average Lancashire or Yorkshire worshipper. Paley continued turning out churches between 1844 and 1895; at first often in collaboration with Edmund Sharpe, and latterly with H. J. Austin. The pulpits, choir stalls, fonts and communion tables are generally admirably designed for 'moderate' Anglican ceremonial.

SAMUEL S. TEULON

Reference has been made already to some of the churches designed by Samuel Sanders Teulon (1812–73). Their interiors are often garish, but the furnishings and decorations are generally *sui generis*. Teulon had a passion for striped walls, elaborate naturalistic carving, marble and alabaster.

Two of Teulon's most characteristic churches are in Hampstead. S. Paul's, Avenue Road, dates from 1864. It has been described by Dr. Nikolaus Pevsner as displaying all the architect's 'sense of sensational display, crude, heavy, noisy, and impressive.' The original garish interior of polychrome brick has recently been toned down in conformity with contemporary good taste. S. Stephen's, Rosslyn Hill, was completed in 1876. The vaulted chancel and apse, as well as most of

---

[5] *Philip Webb and his Work*, pp. 72-3.

the interior decorations, show Teulon's eccentricities to perfection. One wonders how the upper middle class congregations in the 'seventies liked worshipping in this strident interior. The elaborate foliaged capitals and Mooresque arches supplied an appropriate background for the many flounced dresses, the tight waisted bodices and the saucy little hats or bonnets of the female congregations. The interior of S. Mary's, Ealing (1866–73) shows Teulon in another mood, harsh and domineering, stressed by the tall iron shafts which support the galleries and roof.

ARTHUR BLOMFIELD'S S. BARNABAS', OXFORD

When S. Barnabas', Oxford, was opened in 1869 the ecclesiologists were dumbfounded by Mr. Arthur Blomfield's brick replica of an Early Christian basilica. The architect explained the choice of this unfamiliar style was due to enforced economy, but 'not one single item of the design from first to last was altered or cut down in the slightest degree to reduce the cost.' This new church in the western slums of Oxford had precedents in T. H. Wyatt's basilica at Wilton (1841–5) and J. W. Wild's less ornate Christ Church, Streatham (1842). S. Barnabas', Oxford, was the first Anglican church to be provided with a baldachin over the altar. The apsidal chancel looked far less splendid than it does to-day, because most of the decorations were added later. It soon became the mecca of ritualistically minded undergraduates, because the ceremonial at the 'High Celebration' was much more satisfying than that of either the Cowley Fathers' tin tabernacle on the Iffley Road, or S. Thomas's, near the railway stations, and far more 'Catholic' than the tone of the services at Mr. Street's Gothic Revival church of SS. Philip and James. Not until the Jesuit church of S. Aloysius was opened by Cardinal Manning in 1875 were Oxford Roman Catholics able to compete with the glamour of the Anglo-Catholic ceremonial offered by Mr. Montague Noel, the first vicar of the basilica of S. Barnabas.

G. BASSETT KEELING

Most of the churches designed by G. Bassett Keeling (1836–86), according to Mr. Basil Clarke, 'are a caricature of everything that was worst in the foreign Gothic craze.' [6] Judging from contemporary illustrations, the interior of S. George's, Camden Hill, London, must have been great fun when it was opened in 1864; an indescribable riot of contrasted brickwork, much stone carving, wrought iron grilles, encaustic tiles, and other ornate furnishings which were not meant to encourage 'ritualism.' In recent years the interior of S. George's has been brought into line with another trend of fashion. The theatre-like projecting wooden galleries have been removed, the brick work cream washed, and other interesting period pieces have disappeared. *Plus ça change, plus c'est la même chose.*

WILLIAM WHITE

Perhaps it was William White (1825–1900) who produced the most eclectic and gorgeous backgrounds for *via media* Anglican worship during the 'sixties and

[6] op. cit., p. 258.

'seventies. Think of the interior of that very odd church, All Saints', Notting Hill (1850–61); or rather, as it was seen by worshippers after it was completely furnished by about 1880. They must have been almost blinded with the black, red and buff tiles, which mingled with the brick courses. Then there were gold, red and blue circles and triangles; as frames for decorative flowers. The walls of the sanctuary had been frescoed by Henry Holiday. Clustered columns of various marbles added to the scenery. The alabaster reredos had much carving by Redfern, including a central figure of our Lord, vested in alb, crossed stole and cope, seated above the Angel of the Resurrection. Lower down were standing and sitting figures of Old and New Testament saints.

The parish church at Lyndhurst in the heart of the New Forest is another example of the always colourful Gothic Revival work of William White. It was begun in 1858. Mr. John Betjeman has reminded us: 'Lyndhurst was the home of Victorian romance—wild nature after the smoke of towns, fir trees with a faintly Rhineland look, oak woods which took one back to the Forest of Arden, cultivated people instead of the vulgar throng. Ah! What a paradise it must have been to those rare Victorian souls! They expressed their gratitude in the huge church they built of red and yellow brick. Lyndhurst parish church is in the most fanciful, fantastic Gothic style that ever I have seen, and I have seen a great deal. . . . Inside the brick columns have pipes of Purbeck marble round them and their capitals were carved by Mr. Seale with leaves of New Forest trees. . . . The tracery of the windows is as strange as tropic plants. Some of the stained glass windows are by Morris and Burne-Jones and Rossetti. The prevailing colours inside are red and yellow. But Victorian stained glass and Victorian coloured brick does *not* go with frescoes. Lord Leighton came to stay with Hamilton Aidé, the song writer, and he painted a fresco over the altar of the church free of charge. It shows our Lord in white in the middle with the foolish virgins on one side and the wise ones on the other.

'Lyndhurst church is capital, full of originality and thought and care. It expresses the courage and conviction of the Victorians. It is their lasting monument, towering on its mound above the gables of the Victorian houses and the oaks and beeches and fir trees of the New Forest.' [7]

This versatile architect designed a large number of churches all over England, some of which still contain his original furnishings and decorations. Among those in or around London are: S. Mark, Battersea Rise (1873); S. Michael, Clapham (1881); S. Mary-le-Park, Battersea (1883); and Holy Saviour, Aberdeen Park (1859). One of his earliest churches is at S. Hilary, Cornwall (1854); adorned with paintings in recent years by Ernest Proctor and other artists of the Newlyn School.

EWAN CHRISTIAN

Furnishings more in keeping with Evangelical ceremonial can be found in some of the numerous churches designed by Ewan Christian (1814–95)—often good

[7] *First and Last Loves* (1952), pp. 199–200.

Q

sound workmanship, but seldom very inspiring. Like the majority of his churches, the fittings are mediocre, and have been said to be 'distinguished more for quietness and repose than for architectural effect. . . . His hatred of shams was proverbial.' [8]

Reference should be made to All Souls, Harlesden, Middlesex, which dates from

S. FRANCIS', SHEFFORD, BEDS (S. J. Nicholl, 1884)
Typical congestion of furnishings in a Roman Catholic
church of the eighteen-eighties

1879. It was designed by a now almost forgotten architect, E. J. Tarver. Here his octagonal crossing, inspired no doubt by that of Ely Cathedral, has some fascinating timber construction in the real English Gothic tradition. Some of the furnishings and decorations of this unusual interior are worth study.

Throughout the 'sixties and 'seventies many Roman Catholic churches were

[8] *Ewan Christian* (Anon.) (1896), p. 21.

STANBROOK ABBEY, WORCESTER (Edward Pugin, 1875)
Typical English Benedictine fashions of the eighteen-seventies

being built all over England, besides those which have already been mentioned.
A number still retain their original altars, reredoses, pulpits and decorations.
Matthew Ellison Hadfield (1812–85) designed S. Thomas's, Gainsborough, The
Holy Rood, Market Rasen, and the Sacred Heart, Hoyland, Yorkshire, between
1865 and 1868. All contain good, functional furnishings. Joseph Hansom (1803–
82), in collaboration with his brother Charles, was as busy as ever; with more fine

Gothic Revival churches to his credit; including those at Bath (1863), Devonport (1861), Scorton, Lancashire (1860), Arundel (1875), S. Marychurch, Torquay (1865–9), the Holy Name, Manchester (1871), and the Servite Church, Fulham Road, London (1876). The Hansoms showed very little variety in the designs of their altars and reredoses. Priests expected towering erections with lots of crockets and pinnacles, with the eye focussed on a jewel encrusted brass tabernacle and exposition throne. It was seldom that the Hansoms provided an alternative. Just as the Latin Mass was celebrated in more or less the same manner in every church, so was its background as familiar to those who assisted at it. You knew what to expect in a Roman Catholic church, and you were not surprised, shocked or disappointed.

Other almost forgotten architects went on designing similar sanctuaries, e.g. S. J. Nicholl (1826–1905), Edward Pugin (1834–75), F. Pownall and T. J. Willson (1823–1903).

Few of the churches designed for the celebration of the Latin rite during the 'sixties and 'seventies were original and 'clever' and this may be why they now seem far less dated than many of their Anglican contemporaries. Homely and cheerful, they are sometimes rather vulgar according to present day fashions. The austerity movement between the two wars got rid of much Victorian junk. Yet when one discovers any such church still in its pristine state, there is a feeling of being welcomed into a nice overcrowded sitting room belonging to an elderly spinster; the same sense of warmth and cosiness; qualities which are absent from the majority of modern Catholic churches. The polished or lacquered brass candlesticks and flower vases; the plaster or Carrara marble statues with their votive candles; the marble altars with their red or green coverlets, often embroidered with *'Sanctus, Sanctus, Sanctus,' 'Ave Maria'* or some suitable text; the much worn velvet or woollen kneelers at the communion rails; the ruby glass in the brass sanctuary lamp; the potted palms on the marble-paved sanctuary floor; even the massive varnished pitch-pine confessional-boxes—all these familiar furnishings create the feeling of being in a good, honest, well-to-do middle or working class Victorian family.

Such churches remain a lasting memorial to Victorian Catholicism, especially in the industrial north. For, as Archbishop David Mathew reminds us: 'Catholics had benefited by the general improvement in the condition of the workers which was slowly developing. . . . The strong devotion to the religion of the Irish hearth was manifest. They benefited from the parish churches which their fathers lacked; their social life was vigorous, and there was a deep sense of solidarity. . . . It was this generation which built so many of the schools. They would never refuse money for the "chapel." Housing conditions were now rather better and employment, though badly paid, was constant. As the families sat in the kitchen at the hot Sunday dinner, with the girls in print dresses and the boys talking of the new League Football and the first boxing successes of Jim Driscoll, they would always have the money ready for the collector coming Sunday after Sunday for the school building. This generation among the workers had a profound reverence for the Mass; broad constant humour, vitality; a virile faith.' [9] Many of the churches built for and used by the working class families pictured by Archbishop Mathew have furnishings and decorations which reflect these characteristics.

Probably what distinguishes the furnishings and decorations of Roman Catholic from Anglican places of worship built during the 'sixties and 'seventies is that the majority of the former were inserted to stimulate the devotion of the working classes, whereas the latter were what represented the constantly changing 'good taste' of the employers of labour, or the 'idle rich.' Just because of this there is a subtle and not always suspected affinity between the furnishings of the typical High Victorian nonconformist chapel and the Catholic 'chapel' of the same period. Both were genuine expressions of popular art.

[9] *Catholicism in England* (1936), pp. 234–5.

CHAPTER XXIII

JOHN DANDO SEDDING

B Y the early 'eighties most church furnishings in England had become standardized. It was high time that new fashions were introduced, and the man to do this was John Dando Sedding (1838–91).[1] In 1858 he became a pupil of G. E. Street, in whose office he acquired a sound working knowledge of Gothic Revival architecture. We are told that young Sedding 'soon developed ideas and devoted himself to a study of the later types of our Gothic architecture found in the village churches, the essential Englishness and home-wrought work of which appealed to his regard. He made a close study of ecclesiastical architecture and decorative work connected with churches. With this went a sensibility nervously alive to proportion, mystery, splendour, colour, sheen; in a word, the æsthetic sense. However much was of gift in his genius, it was the genius of hard work; and he was heard to say at this time, 'even the lunch hour was often spent in working at the miniatures in the Manuscript Room of the British Museum.'[2] He left Street's office in 1863, and spent the next two years mainly in designing chalices, patens, embroideries and wall papers. In 1865 he became a partner with his brother Edmund who was practising as an architect at Penzance. When Edmund died three years later John moved to Bristol. Those years spent in the west of England had a great influence on his later work, which always showed a strong affinity especially with the late medieval churches in Somerset, and in a lesser degree with the more rugged buildings in Cornwall. Sedding always thought of churches like plants which had grown up naturally in the soil best suited to them. Botany was one of his lifelong interests. He loved arranging flowers, and they appear again and again in all his decorative work; in metal, wood, stone and embroidery.

By the middle of the 'seventies Sedding, now married, had moved to London, where he continued to make use of his exceptional knowledge of natural forms in almost every kind of decorative work, both of a domestic and ecclesiastical nature. It is recorded that he 'would spend many hours of his summer holidays in making careful studies of a single plant, or spray of foliage, painting them as Mr. Ruskin had taught him, in sienna and white, or in violet-carmine and white.

---

[1] Most of the facts given here are taken from *Holy Trinity Sloane Street* by Francis H. Spicer, a very detailed history of this London church, published with its parish magazine in 1955. Miss Dorothy M. Sedding has also helped with biographical notes on the life of her father.

[2] Spicer, op. cit., p. 107.

Leaves and flowers were, in fact, almost his only source of decorative design.' [3]

S. Alban's, Holborn, became his favourite church, and from 1882 to 1889 he was one of its churchwardens.

S. Clement's, Bournemouth, begun in 1872, contains many interesting examples of Sedding's early ideals of church furnishing and decoration. Both chancel and side chapel have elaborate stone screens; also carved stone reredoses. Emblems of S. Clement are carved on the font, the lamps, pulpit rail, and even on the pavement. The saint's monogram is noticeable in the windows, alternating with roses and crowns. A figure of S. Clement, holding a model of the church, is carved as a bench end. All the furnishings of this stately church, freely treated in a late fourteenth century Gothic, repay careful study. Sedding was fast evolving a style of his own.

While this church was rising Sedding met John Ruskin 'who told him that he must always have pencil or chisel in hand if he were to be more than an employer of men on commission. He took the advice to heart and formed a school of masons and carvers. Scores of small parish churches in the west of England were restored and beautified by Sedding; this was work in which he excelled. It was the beautiful work in the vicarage and church of S. Clement's, Bournemouth, that opened people's eyes to what he could do.' [4]

All Sedding's churches are original and interesting. 'He did not confine himself to one style,' Mr. Basil Clarke points out, 'and did not work for long in any one. He used in his own way the Gothic of the late fourteenth and fifteenth centuries; but he expressed himself in many different ways, using all of them with sympathy and ability. He had a great dislike of trade art, and wanted the best in everything. He was not content to design a church and leave it to the ecclesiastical furnishers to fit it out. He designed screens, reredoses, crosses, plate and decorations. The conventions of ecclesiastical ornament made no appeal to him, and he never descended to the mechanical use of symbolical devices. He did not pepper his work with conventional sacred monograms. As and Ωs and evangelistic symbols. He wanted "fresh air and reality." A church ought to be "a design *by* living men *for* living men," and he pictured a church "wrought and painted over with everything that has life and beauty—in frank and fearless naturalism covered with men and beasts and flowers." ' [5]

The chance of a lifetime came in 1886, when the Anglican authorities bought the Spa Fields Chapel in Exmouth Market, Clerkenwell, which belonged to the Countess of Huntingdon's Connexion, pulled it down, and asked Sedding to design a new church to be built on the site. When a drawing of the interior was published in *The Builder* of May 7th, 1887, readers could hardly believe their eyes—had this Gothic Revival architect gone clean off his head? The design appeared to have been inspired by some of Wren's churches in London. The new Church of the Holy Redeemer was consecrated on October 7th the following year.

[3] ibid., p. 110.
[4] ibid., p. 110.
[5] *Church Builders of the Nineteenth Century* (1938), pp. 195–6.

Revolutionary was the only adjective to be used to describe the interior. The marble high altar, with six candlesticks and a crucifix standing on it, stood beneath a vast baldachin, which as the *intelligentsia* pointed out, was vaguely similar to that designed by Giovanni Caccini in 1599 for Brunelleschi's church of S. Spirito in Florence. The cupola rested on marble columns and pilasters of Corinthian style, with statues of angels at its four corners. On the top of all was what appeared to be a nude figure of the risen Christ. The spacious sanctuary was enclosed by low marble rails of Classic design. Around the base of the Corinthian columns dividing the nave from the aisles was panelling. Their capitals were carved by F. W. Pomeroy. The simple wooden pulpit of wood had a sounding board. Behind the baldachin stood another altar with a Renaissance reredos. The whole effect of the interior reminded people of the nearby Italian Church in Hatton Garden, designed by Brydon in 1863, although not so garishly decorated. Or was the Church of England trying to emulate the Classic splendour of Herbert Gribble's Oratorian church at Brompton, which had been consecrated in 1884? No matter, the Holy Redeemer, Clerkenwell, established Sedding's reputation as a bold and original architect, who had at length cast off the shackles of Gothic Revivalism. The impression was so Italian that Walter Pater is reported to have said that it made him 'think how some of the Renaissance churches at Venice, or Wren's London churches, must have looked when they were fresh and clean.'

Another and even greater opportunity for Sedding to give free rein to his imagination came in 1887, when he was asked to prepare designs for a new church to replace Holy Trinity, Upper Chelsea, a Gothic 'chapel of ease' to S. Luke's, erected in 1830 from the design of James Savage. The new church was consecrated on May 13th, 1890. Since 1930, when the interior was whitewashed on the advice of Mr. F. C. Eden, the effect is very different from the original—dull gold and yellow walls into which his furnishings and decorations merged, instead of contrasting. But tastes had changed after forty years; white interiors had become fashionable, due largely to Dr. Percy Dearmer. He was an honorary curate at Holy Trinity from 1924 to 1929, so his influence may be discernible in what others would now call desecration. The style of the church is a mingling of the Flamboyant Gothic of France with the Perpendicular of England. In this setting Sedding showed his urge to break away from the Gothic revival, because the high altar, pulpit and font, and the baldachin and altar enclosure of the north aisle are all in the Renaissance style. Sedding was determined to give craftsmen the same opportunities which the fabric had given to him as an architect. He invited many well-known artists of the day to collaborate with him—Sir Edward Burne-Jones, William Morris, C. H. Whall, F. W. Pomeroy, Harry Bates, Onslow Ford, Hamo Thornycroft, F. Boucher, H. Starkie Gardner and Alfred Gilbert—all famous in one or other line of decorative work. But as Mr. Basil F. L. Clarke remarks: 'the several artists have hardly worked as a team, and the church as a whole hardly "hangs together." The fittings are mostly very good, though in some cases rather "arty," but they are not very congruous with another. The church as a whole is a brilliant attempt: but it can hardly be called a success. Perhaps, under the circumstances, it could hardly be that.'[6]

The chancel is separated from the nave by a low screen of Devonshire marble, in the centre of which a flight of white marble steps leads up to the chancel. On either side of the head of the stairs green marble pillars support bronze angels, bearing scrolls, the work of F. W. Pomeroy. The added hammered work of the wrought iron gates was designed by Sedding's assistant and successor, Harry Wilson. The choir stalls of dark stained oak incorporate beaten and cast bronze panels, containing angels holding scrolls. All the figures were modelled by F. W. Pomeroy. There are more angels and cherubs at the backs of the boys' seats.

The twelve feet long altar is raised on more steps. Internally it is of oak, but the front is of marble, with a carving of the Entombment of our Lord, the work of Harry Bates. Sedding first had the idea of giving the high altar a baldachin, with four pillars, but for some reason or other it was abandoned in favour of a reredos. After his death, Henry Wilson prepared designs for a colossal reredos, which would have blocked the lower part of the great east window. He felt that this reredos would help to convey a feeling of mystery, and wrote that once this has been achieved 'the spirit of the spectator is kept on the alert and that most delightful of all sensations, the expectation of surprise, is awakened and gratified. More than this, to say, as many do, that because a certain window had been designed, nothing should be placed in front of it, is to assume that the building was made for the window and not the window for the building. It is to forget that in the Christian Church the altar and its surroundings form the feature, the reason of the building's being, and that though the eastern wall be built of precious stones and the window glazed with gems and jewels, yet reredos and tabernacle tower over all.' The present marble reredos would hardly have satisfied Sedding. He designed the brass altar cross, decorated with beaten silver, topazes, amethysts, carbuncles and crystals. The two candlesticks are of similar design to the cross.

Above the choir stalls are carved figures and reliefs of English saints, and certain post-Reformation churchmen who have not been formally canonized.

The striking, but not very original, stone and marble pulpit of Renaissance design is supported on columns of alabaster and red marble. The baptistery is at the west end of the side chapel in the north aisle, with the font of Mexican onyx. Around the shaft is a band of cherubs carved by F. Boucher under the direction of Onslow Ford. The baldachin over the side altar rests on four Ionic columns of red marble. The painting on the front of the altar, based on the theme 'All men seek Thee,' was the work of W. Reynolds-Stephens. It was Harry Wilson who designed the bold yet exquisite metal grille behind the altar, which was wrought by Nelson Dawson.

Most of the other furnishings in this church were added after Sedding's death, and in general they are worthy of his setting. Some, such as the wrought iron electric light fittings, were designed by him. He never lived to see his masterpiece

[6] op. cit., p. 196.

enriched with stained glass, but it is known that he asked Burne-Jones to submit designs for some of the windows. The great twelve-light east window, with its flamboyant tracery contains glass; the forty-eight individual figures of which were drawn by Burne-Jones, and the foliage and surroundings by William Morris. They were translated into stained glass by Messrs. Powell.[7]

There are very marked differences of opinion about Holy Trinity, Upper Chelsea. Mr. T. Francis Bumpus wrote about half a century ago: 'If any one would understand what has been effected for Christian art in England in the last quarter of a century, he should visit in succession, first any church of that date, and then Holy Trinity. I do not say that it is a perfect "model church," but assert, without fear of contradiction, that our generation has seen no greater or more memorable work, or one more fraught in important consequences to the future art of England.'[8] Mr. H. S. Goodhart Rendel, however, describes Holy Trinity as a 'Bric-à-bac church in the sense that the fittings designed for it by its architect are in miscellaneous and entirely unrelated styles'; adding that this 'strange mixing in the furniture of rococo ironwork, of Italian Renaissance marble work, of semi-naturalistic carving, was a peculiarity not shared by many of its architect's contemporary brethren, and never became the characteristic of a school.'[9] This church is 'Sedding's last and most mature work, and the outstanding example of the Arts and Crafts Movement in the ecclesiastical field.' So says Dr. Pevsner.[10]

The furnishings and decorations of this church remind one of this description of its architect: 'He was exactly like a bird hopping from twig to twig, from bough to bough, as he hovered over the many drawings which were his daily work, settling here a detail, there a moulding, as the impulse of the moment seized him, and though at times his staff were puzzled to account for, or to anticipate, his ways, and though the work was often hindered by them, they would not have had it otherwise. Those *"gentilesses d'oiseaux,"* as Hugo says, those little birdy ways, so charming from their unexpectedness, kept them constantly on the alert, for no one ever quite knew what he would do next.'[11] As one wanders around Holy Trinity there is always the feeling at the back of one's mind: 'What *is* Sedding going to do next?' This quality of unexpectedness makes it both an exciting and a restless church. The bird-like architect is always alighting on one bough, and hopping off to the next. It is easy to picture him rushing 'fearlessly across the scaffoldings; his animated gestures as he talked among the workmen; the kindly *bonhomie* of his ways with them; to hear his free and fearless use of their own tongue, one would have thought he had been a workman all his life. . . . He spent many happy moments, hovering about amongst the workmen, criticizing and correcting their carving, making fresh designs upon the wood and having them cut under his

[7] The windows in the Lady Chapel were designed much later by Sir William B. Richmond, and carried out by James Powell and Sons. Other windows came from the workshops of C. W. Whall.
[8] *London Churches*, Second Series, p. 370.
[9] *English Architecture since the Regency*, p. 178.
[10] *London. The Buildings of England* (1952), p. 89.
[11] F. H. Spicer, op. cit., p. 115.

directions, chatting cheerily with the workmen as they laboured, filling them all with enthusiasm for himself and for his work. He taught them to forsake the miserable copyism of pseudo-Gothic art, and to carve from nature, from the living flower, bird or beast upon the bench before them, and their carving grew to be a nearer approach to Browning's high ideal of perfection.' [12]

Sedding gathered round him a loyal and devoted group of young men who worked in his office at one time or another. First and foremost was Henry Wilson, who became his chief assistant, and who, after his death, completed many of his furnishings and decorations. Sir Charles Nicholson was another of his articled pupils. Others included A. H. Powell, H. W. Finch, J. Paul Cooper—all of whom made their mark in the Arts and Crafts Movement of the 'nineties. Sir Charles Nicholson has written: 'Among architects of his day, Sedding had many admirers, a few imitators, and many whose work was influenced by his example—among them perhaps the best known was the late Leonard Stokes. Others less gifted sometimes imitated his eccentricities, without appreciating his merits.'

Unfortunately his influence on fashions in church furnishings did not last. Sedding agreed with the author of *The Stones of Venice* that 'For the professional stylist, the confirmed conventionalist, an hour in his garden, a stroll in the embroidered meadows, a dip into an old herbal, a few carefully-drawn cribs from Curtis's *Botanical Magazine*—or even, for lack of something better, Sutton's last illustrated catalogue—is wholesome exercise, and will do more to revive the original instincts of a true designer than a month of sixpenny days in a stuffy museum. The old masters are dead, but the "flowers," as Victor Hugo says, "the flowers last always." '

Sedding tried to put fresh life and reality into his church furnishings and decorations. In the words of a letter to Professor Lethaby, he says: 'We must clothe modern ideas in modern dress; adorn our design with living fancy. There is no hope in honest error, none in the icy perfections of the mere stylist. . . . Instead of Syon cope angels or stumpy Norfolk screen saints, we shall have designs by living men for living men—something that expresses fresh realizations of sacred facts, personal broodings, skill, joy in nature, in grace of form, and gladness of colour.'

Actually, there are not many churches in which Sedding's back-to-nature ideals of decoration and furnishing can be found. In addition to the three mentioned already, there are S. Elwyn's, Hayle, Cornwall; All Saints', Falmouth (which he regarded as his best work); S. Dyfrig's, Cardiff; S. Edward's, Netley, Hants; S. Peter's, Ealing. He restored about twenty churches, most of them in Cornwall, Devon and Somerset. Very often it is impossible to tell whether the work is by Sedding or by Wilson, because the pupil, and later the chief assistant, so completely absorbed the manner of the master.[13]

---

[12] ibid., p. 116.
[13] J. D. Sedding is sometimes confused with his elder brother Edmund who died in 1868; also with Edmund's son Edmund, most of whose work was in Cornwall and Devonshire.

CHAPTER XXIV

ECCLESIASTICAL AESTHETICS IN THE 'EARNEST 'EIGHTIES'

EXCEPT those designed by Bentley, Bodley, Pearson and Sedding, not many churches erected in the eighteen-eighties contain furnishings and decorations worth mentioning.

S. Cuthbert's, Philbeach Gardens, Earls Court, London, which was designed by Hugh Roumieu Gough (1843–1904) and begun in 1884 is one of the exceptions. Here can be observed the art of William Bainbridge Reynolds (d. 1935), whose work was typical of the Arts and Crafts movement. He designed and made the imposing lectern of wrought iron and repoussé copper; the communion rails, the piscina and sedilia; the altar rails of the Lady Chapel and its screens; the clock and the Royal Arms; the organ case and some of the stained glass windows; and the splendid paschal candlestick. The towering carved wooden and much crocketed reredos was designed by the Revd. Ernest Geldart, a clergyman whose taste was thought highly of in the 'eighties. The bridge-like rood-beam was planned to contain a small altar, on which was a tabernacle for the reservation of the consecrated elements. S. Cuthbert's was one of the first Anglican churches in England to start reservation. Some Italian baroque paintings, and stained glass by Kempe, add to the splendour of this stronghold of Anglo-Catholicism.

Equally magnificent in their own way are the mosaics in the Albert Memorial Chapel at Windsor Castle, the work of the Baron Triquetti, which were completed by about 1880. These mosaics and the other furnishings of the Chapel, including the metal work, are almost as opulent as the dining-room table of 'Sir Gorgios Midas' as drawn by George du Maurier in *Punch* (1876). Actually they reveal the taste of Queen Victoria.

Just as characteristic of this decade, though of lower middle class Anglicanism, were the fittings of churches designed by James Brooks, Somers Clarke, Bassett Smith, J. Newman, J. E. K. and J. P. Cutts, Stephenson Clarke—to mention but a few names. In their time, between 1880 and 1890, people thought them quiet, reverent and devotional; nowadays they would be dismissed as deadly dull.

The 'eighties were nothing if not earnest. The paintings of both Sir William

Orchardson and Sir Edward Burne-Jones reflect this earnest mood from two opposite angles: the former with their mixture of French, Victorian and classic elements; the latter with their minute detail, richness of design ·and colour, and placid melancholy. But it was only in a very few churches, such as S. Cuthbert's, Philbeach Gardens, or those designed by Sedding, that one found any trace of the Æsthetic Movement, or of William Morris's dictum: 'Have nothing in your house but what you know to be useful or believe to be beautiful.' Among the upper classes beauty was being ardently sought for, but for most people this meant the

S. NICHOLAS, GREAT YARMOUTH (1882–5); des. ex. by Buckley & Co.

beauty expressed in the paintings of Sir Frederick Leighton or Sir Lawrence Alma-Tadema. The appeal of the allegorical pictures by Sir Edward Burne-Jones or Mr. George Frederick Watts was more limited. Few of the church furnishings and decorations of this decade were influenced by the Queen Anne revival started by Norman Shaw.

In the homes of the well-to-do, drawing-rooms and dining-rooms remained as congested as they had been in the 'seventies, but some of them now displayed wall papers of William Morris and Co., on which were hung even more peacocks' feathers, blue and white china, and other Japanese knick-nacks. Yet, as Mr. Osbert Lancaster has reminded us, from Tulse Hill to Belsize Park 'room was found for all and the artistic little snuff-box from Yokohama shared a corner of the mantel-piece (now tastefully draped with fringed green plush, with the shell-work light-house from Shanklin).' [1]

The men and women who left these overcrowded rooms on Sunday mornings and evenings to sit under the richly carved stone and marble, or oak pulpits; who turned their eyes to the far from interesting Gothic Revival communion tables, reredoses and choir stalls, were just as stiffly garbed. The male sex showed its

[1] *Homes Sweet Homes*, no. 46, 'Earnest 'Eighties.'

respect for the Sabbath by frock or 'morning' coats, striped trousers and low top-hats. In winter black overcoats hid the suits. Few of the younger men would have dared to sport the popular flat straw 'boater' on a Sunday.

We can picture their women folk shoving their way into the pews; their bustles and tight skirts emphasizing the bust and abdomen. The dresses were often looped up at the back, or caught up at the side. Tight waisted jackets, trimmed with fur in winter, were fashionable. So too were saucy little high bonnets or capote hats. But here and there among the congregation would be detected a lady in flowing garments like those of the wan and weary maidens in *Patience*. She at least could appreciate the artistic background provided by a Morris or Kempe stained glass window.

The furnishings and ornaments for churches of the Latin rite in England and Wales became more or less standardized after 1881, when Bishop Vaughan of Salford, who was translated to Westminster in 1892, and created Cardinal Priest the following year, published for general use the Directions which had been laid down in the Sixth Synod of his Diocese.[2] The object of this booklet was to 'show forth the Roman Rite in all its completeness' in accordance with the Decrees of the Sacred Congregation of Rites, Pope Benedict XIV and the First Council of Westminster. The result was a final blow to most of the principles laid down by Augustus Welby Pugin between 1840 and 1852. The interior of a Catholic church might still *look* Gothic, but that was all: the substructure was Renaissance in spirit. To put it differently, it was a Classic body dressed in mock-medieval clothes.

First of all, Bishop Vaughan disapproved of windows placed at the back of high altars in new churches, because 'they are apt to distract the eye, to interfere with Exposition, etc.' Detailed instructions were given about the planning of altars, including a rule that the sanctuary 'should be covered with a green carpet up to the base of the steps.' On festal occasions the steps or the altar, or at least the top step 'should be covered with a more handsome carpet.' We read that 'the tabernacle should be of moderate proportions; its form either octagonal, hexagonal, square or round, with a roof in the form of a dome or apex, terminating in a small cross, or a figure of our Lord risen, round which the veil should be gathered in so that it should fall over the Tabernacle.' Tabernacles should not be constructed on more than one of the side altars. Although few priests in the eighteen-eighties observed the rule, Bishop Vaughan insisted that 'even if the Tabernacle be rich and costly, the Veil may not be dispensed with.' He condemned the custom (then very common) of not covering tabernacles with veils, and pointed out that 'two pieces of stuff before the door do not satisfy the prescription of the Roman Ritual.'

Antependia (frontals) must conform to the Roman pattern, and be fixed on frames. No longer could sedilia of the medieval pattern, or even a stone credence

---

[2] A second edition, revised by the Rev. George B. Tatum, appeared in 1902. An enlarged edition, prepared by this same priest of the Diocese of Southwark, with the co-operation of Mr. Osmund Bentley, the son of the famous architect, was published in 1912.

built into the wall, be tolerated. The seats of the sacred ministers must be a long bench, covered with cloth, green or violet, according to the season. The glass of the lamps before the Blessed Sacrament must be white, and the lamps must be uneven in number. Bishop Vaughan insisted S. Charles Borromeo's instructions on the planning of baptisteries must be carried out. This meant that the medieval English position of the font, raised on steps, which had been revived by Pugin, was tolerated no longer. Vestments had to conform to the shape worn in Rome, as had been laid down by the First Council of Westminster. From now onwards the Gothic vestments as depicted in Pugin's *Glossary of Ecclesiastical Ornament and Costume* (1844) were frowned upon by most of the Catholic hierarchy of England and Wales. They did not object to new churches being designed in Gothic Revival, but the planning and furnishing had to be post-Tridentine and ultra-montane for preference. From roughly 1880 Catholic churches in Britain took on quite a different 'look' to Anglican places of worship, no matter how 'High' the latter might be. With but few exceptions even the most extreme Anglo-Catholics retained the long medieval chancel (often with a rood-screen), but almost all new Catholic churches were designed with shallow chancels, like Renaissance churches. Because the Church of England had no Sacred Congregation of Rites to draw up rules about church furnishing and ornaments, a far greater diversity of ceremonial details obtained. This remained the case until after Mr. Geoffrey Webb published his *Liturgical Altar* in 1933. A revival of interest resulted in the traditional and national forms of pre-reformation liturgical art in England.

The Gothic Revival furnishings and ornaments in churches designed by Messrs. Dunn and Hansom are a perfect expression of Catholic taste during the 'eighties and early 'nineties. Typical of contemporary fashions is the altar of Blessed Oliver Plunket (originally the high altar) in Downside Abbey Church, which was blessed in 1882. An even more stupendous erection is the high altar in the main chapel of S. Cuthbert's College Chapel at Ushaw, Co. Durham, also of the same period. This mountain of stone crockets, canopies and pinnacles, of which the exposition throne is the central feature, reaches almost to the roof. The Ushaw high altar is a grand and lavish conception. Between 1887 and 1890 the two partners were able to do pretty much what they liked in the Church of Our Lady and the English Martyrs at Cambridge, thanks to the generosity of Mrs. Lyne Stephens. The altars are extremely rich and ornate, with much carving and statuary by Boulton of Cheltenham.

Some of George Goldie's best churches belong to the eighteen-seventies, and they generally contain altars and pulpits, as grand and lavish as those designed by Dunn and Hansom. Characteristic examples can be found in S. Joseph's College Chapel, Mill Hill (1871); the Assumption Convent Chapel, Kensington Square (1875); and S. Mary's Cathedral, Middlesborough (1878). His son, Edward Goldie, had the same love for elaborate altars and reredoses; typical of them being those in the chapel of Hawksyard Priory, Staffordshire (1894).

Ever since the Oratorian Fathers closed their chapel in King William Street in 1853 (see p. 40), and moved to Brompton (then a suburb of London), they had continued to stress the *'Romanità'* of S. Philip Neri, both in the furnishings of their new church, and in the services. This church, little better than a long flat-ceilinged hall, contained seven side chapels, each with an altar, pictures or statues that must have pained Gothic enthusiasts. The decorations of the sanctuary, with its gilt and marble high altar, were rich and splendid. There were red damask hangings, and an inlaid wood floor. Unlike most Catholic churches in England, the circular tabernacle was completely covered with a veil, and above it was suspended a tester or baldachin, in conformity with Roman custom. The Birmingham Oratorians had a somewhat similar church which, like the one at Brompton, was regarded as merely temporary. By 1877 the need for a permanent church in London had become imperative. A prize competition was held, and out of about thirty possible designs, that of Herbert Gribble was chosen. The building was completed in 1883.

For the next ten years the furnishing and decoration of the interior went forward, with the addition of altars, marbles, pictures and statues. The Lady Altar, a magnificent seventeenth century baroque creation, came from a secularized church in Brescia. By the time the marble panels around the sanctuary were completed in 1888, no Renaissance church in Britain could compare to the London Oratory for the splendour of its *décor*. 'Someone has said that a walk round the Oratory consoles a man who wishes to go to Italy but cannot afford it.' [3]

The canopied stalls, altar and decorations of the Chapel of the Little Oratory are equally magnificent specimens of Italian Baroque.

This great church in the heart of the west end of London exercised a persistent influence on ecclesiastical fashions throughout the 'eighties and 'nineties.

We must try to picture the Oratory as designed for the background to the fashionable ladies and gentlemen portrayed by George du Maurier in *Punch*. It is easy to visualize Lady Gorgios Midas, Lady Snobbington, Mrs. Ponsonby Tomkyns and even the Cimabue Brown family, against this baroque *décor*. The less wealthy members of the congregation had drawing-rooms furnished like those in du Maurier's illustrations, with heavily draped fireplaces, wicker armchairs (sometimes disguised with cretonne or chintz covers); almost certainly gilt French clocks in glass cases and countless vases and ornaments on the plush or velvet-draped mantelpieces. The exhibition at the Grosvenor Gallery in 1884 featured among other paintings Sir Edward Burne-Jones' *King Cophetua and the Beggar Maid*, and several provocative 'smudges' by Mr. Whistler. How odd the Oratory, and any of its Anglican neighbours, would look to-day if the feminine worshippers were dressed like those of the middle 'eighties—coy little flower-decked hats or toques, tight waisted bodices, and bunched-out frocks, with a dozen or more flounces up. to the knees, and a shawl-like sash above them.

[3] *The London Oratory 1849–1949* (1949), p. 22.

17. High altar, Atherstone parish church (F. E. Howard)
A splendid example of the so-called 'English altar'

18. Liverpool Cathedral (Sir Giles Gilbert Scott). The enormous reredos becomes the focal point of the interior, completely dwarfing the high altar

Another and equally foreign expression of ecclesiastical good taste in the 'earnest 'eighties' was created in the Imperial Mausoleum at Farnborough, Hampshire; now known as S. Michael's Abbey. This exotic cruciform French Flamboyant Gothic church, with a Renaissance dome above the crossing, was designed by Monsieur Destailleur of Paris, and opened in 1888. Until 1949 the furnishings and ornaments of both the crypt and the upper church remained a mirror of the Second Empire outlook on worship. Around the three vast Aberdeen granite sarcophagi containing the bodies of the Emperor Napoleon III, the Empress Eugénie, and the Prince Imperial, would be found *immortelles* of artificial flowers, some protected by glass. The altars, pulpit, choir-stalls, organ case, crucifixes, candlesticks, candelabra, Stations of the Cross, painted plaster statues, and the copies of two of Rubens' paintings hanging above the two side altars of the upper church, were all typical of the most expensive *bon-dieuserie*. They might have been specially designed as a background for the sugary music of Gounod's masses. Electric light had not been installed, so the faint smell of gas conjured up mental pictures of the overheated salons of the Tuilleries, Chantilly or Fontainebleau: its soft hissing the distant *frou-frou* of crinolines. After High Mass or Benediction, when a film of incense softened the lines of the architecture, it was easy to believe that the whiff of perfume might be parma violet or patchouli, coming from the ghost of some exquisitely dressed lady-in-waiting who had knelt on one of the crimson velvet upholstered ebony prie-dieus—even Eugénie de Montijo herself. But a new generation of monastic caretakers of the Mausoleum came along who regarded the *décor* of the Second Empire with horror. They got rid of most of the movable fittings to ensure 'greater liturgical correctness'—even giving the high altar, from which the stone exposition throne had been sawn off, a dossal and riddel posts in the correct Percy Dearmer fashion! [4]

Neither the furnishing and decoration of churches, nor any externals of public worship in England were affected by new movements on the continent. Neither Catholics nor Anglo-Catholics knew about what would now be called the Liturgical Movement in Germany. This started after the two brothers, Maurus and Placid Wolter, and another monk of the newly restored Benedictine Abbey of Beuron, in the upper Valley of the Danube, visited Solesmes in 1863, and sat at the feet of Abbot Guéranger, the author of the *Liturgical Year*. The *Külterkampf* of 1875 drove monks of Beuron to Erdington in England and to Prague in Bohemia. In 1872 another colony of German monks had founded the Abbey of Maredsous in Belgium. These monasteries became strongholds of a reform movement in the externals of worship; fostered by the publication of vernacular missals, books and pamphlets.

During the eighteen-seventies a School of Art was established at Beuron, under the leadership of Dom Desiderius Lenz (1832–1928) and two other monks, Gabriel Wüger and Lukas Steiner. The first paintings produced were inspired by Overbeck and the Düsseldorf artists, but it was not long before Dom Desiderius

[4] These items have since been abolished.

R

evolved his own theories of religious art, derived from what he believed to be those of ancient Egypt, the shape of human bodies being based on the proportions of numerals. The Beuron monk-artists were far more rigid than the English Pre-Raphaelites had been. Their stiff hieratic art made little appeal to the masses, but by 1890 it was the last word in correctness among the *avant-garde* Catholics on the continent of Europe. Altars, pulpits and fonts were designed in a neo-Egyptian style. They were the prototypes of what another generation would try to evolve in a striving after simplicity. In a curious way there is something quite 'modernistic' about the S. Maurus Kapelle at Beuron, designed by Dom Desiderius Lenz about 1870. Decorative paintings and altar-pieces by the Beuron artists were carried out, among other places, at the Benedictine Abbey of Emmaus, Prague and at Monte Cassino. The last great work undertaken by this school was the marble and mosaic decoration of the crypt at Monte Cassino, opened in 1913.[5]

English church furnishers and decorators of the eighteen-eighties owed little to the ecclesiological researches of Rohault de Fleury, whose seven volume work of reference, entitled *La Messe,* appeared between 1883 and 1889. Nor is it possible to trace any influence from, for instance, the great German Gothic Revival architect, Reichensperger, who owed so much to A. W. Pugin. English church planning at this time does not seem to have been affected by the work of J. Alberdinck and P. Cuypers in Holland, or by that of J. Bethune in Belgium. These three men, each in his own distinctive manner, were carrying on the traditions that Bodley, Pearson, Street, and lesser known masters were developing in England.

There are some, but not many, of the famous strongholds of extreme Anglo-Catholicism which still preserve furnishings and ornaments picked up in Belgium, France or other continental countries, when the vicars or curates were holidaying abroad. Bruges in particular was a happy hunting ground, and the firm of Louis Grossé did an extensive business with the export of vestments, banners, statues, etc. So did the many shops in the Place Saint Sulpice in Paris that specialized in *objets de pieté.* It gave a church a more Catholic look if the ornaments came from a Catholic country. You could not be quite sure if Jones and Willis, Thomas Thomason and Co., Messrs. Burns and Oates, Thomas Pratt and Sons, John Hardman and Co., or any other firm in England at that date supplied church furniture and ecclesiastical goods which possessed the indefinable *cachet* of those bought on the continent. It was safer to obtain the real thing from Rome, Paris or Bruges. This style of church decoration, now a thing of the past, had not a little in common with that super-sophisticated decorating taste which appeared in Paris after the Second World War. Mr. Cecil Beaton tells us 'the aim of those who have acquired this predilection is to assume character rather than an effect that is pleasing to the eye; and the character must be of a stolid nature. Certain objects and colours are given prominence because, while they might seem ugly from one

[5] cf. A. Pöllmann, o.s.b., *Vom Wesen der hieratischen Kunst* (1905); J. Kreitmaier, S. J., *Beuroner Kunst* (1914).

point of view, they have the virtue of being able to evoke the period of security enjoyed from 1860 to 1900.' [6]

Although the Anglo-Catholic clergymen of that period may not have admitted, or even realized, the reasons for dressing up their churches in Belgian or French fashions, the basic motive was certainly to create the illusion of security, and to evoke memories of happy days across the Channel. Thus such a church as we have in mind would be haunted with souvenirs (mostly rather debased Gothic Revival) that meant much to the often lonely and frustrated pioneers in the crusade for the revival of Catholic ceremonial. The result was seldom anything more than a *pastiche,* but even this sometimes managed to recreate the atmosphere of a French or Belgian church, just as the Brompton Oratory helped to make people feel they were in Italy. Like some of the modern *pasticheurs* mentioned by Mr. Beaton, the 'ritualistic' vicars and curates of the 'seventies and 'eighties, more often than not, tried 'to produce character rather than to create loveliness.' [7] This same tendency, with the accent on German, Italian or Spanish baroque, was to reappear even more aggressively among advanced Anglo-Catholics shortly before the First World War. [8]

Far and away the most splendid piece of Anglican ecclesiastical *décor* which possessed character rather than beauty was the vast and very ornate stone and marble Gothic high altar (including a brass tabernacle and exposition throne) which Fr. Ignatius inserted into his never completed church at Llanthony Abbey about 1880. It came from Munich, so had the virtue of being a real Catholic *objet de pieté.* A newspaper reporter who visited the abbey on the feast of the supposed Apparition of our Lady, when throughout the 'eighties crowds of tourists and pilgrims used to wend their way up the narrow valley in the heart of the Black Mountains, wrote, 'stout curtains drawn over the windows completely keep out the daylight, to give effect to the hundreds of tall and short wax tapers lighting up the shrine, and the enthroned statues and images presented a most fairy-like appearance through the thick clouds of incense which filled the lofty edifice.' Moreover there was a 'tremendous clash of cymbals' as the procession entered before High Mass 'to the voluptuous swell of music sweeping through the building,' not forgetting 'a display of gorgeous vestments.'

Strange as it may sound, what Fr. Ignatius, the Anglican Benedictine, was trying to achieve in the Black Mountains with his wonderful high altar, myriads of candles, clouds of incense, sentimental hymn tunes, and soft modulations of the dulciana on the organ swell at Benediction and Exposition, was very similar to what Fr. Faber and his Oratorians had been doing at Brompton since the early 'fifties. The difference was that in the latter case the background was Italian Baroque instead of Gothic Revival. But deeper still lay the fact that the Oratorians were obedient to authority, whereas Fr. Ignatius obeyed nobody but himself.

The church which he tried to build is now a ruin, but the altar and reredos can still be studied as a fine Victorian period-piece. They were taken down and re-erected in S. Julian's, Newport, Monmouthshire. Without all the original

[6] *The Glass of Fashion* (1954), p. 280.   [7] ibid., p. 284.   [8] See pp. 316–28.

accessories, much of the glamour has gone. An almost identical reredos, supplied by the same Bavarian firm, which was the focal point of S. Mary's Catholic Cathedral, Aberdeen, until a few years ago, has been the victim of a recent change

S. MARY'S CATHEDRAL, ABERDEEN
Standardized type of Roman Catholic high altar after 1860. This fine example (imported from Munich) was destroyed in 1959, because of the urge to administer the Lord's Supper facing the people

of mode. After being smashed to bits the 'relics' of the carved angels and saints were taken to Pluscarden Priory. Eventually the monks used most of them to make a rockery. Other pieces of the discarded reredos were fitted into part of an interior wall, where they may puzzle antiquarians of some future generation.

CHAPTER XXV

JOHN FRANCIS BENTLEY

JOHN FRANCIS BENTLEY (1839–1902) was a contemporary of George Frederick Bodley. He was reconciled with the Roman Church in 1861, and is best remembered as the architect of Westminster Cathedral, the commission for which came from Cardinal Vaughan in 1894. Bentley designed four Catholic parish churches, but only two of them were furnished by himself. On the other hand his output of furniture and decorations for other churches was enormous. He specialized in the use of marble, alabaster and mosaics, but was equally at home with wood and metal. He carried on Butterfield's love of lining interior walls with marble, and like Bodley had no scruples about painting woodwork. He designed a large number of stained glass windows; most of the earlier ones being in conjunction with the firm of Lavers, Barraud and Westlake.

Bentley served his apprenticeship with Henry Clutton (1819–93). His first original work was the baptistery of Clutton's church of S. Francis of Assisi, Notting Hill (1860), for which he provided a red granite font, with an oak cover. His altars in this same church are the prototypes of almost all subsequent ones. We find the same love of colour, with rich effects produced by marbles, mosaics and enamels. Bentley got N. H. J. Westlake to do some paintings on gold backgrounds; the first of many works in which they collaborated. The high altar and reredos, completed in 1862, display a gorgeous mixture of marble, glass mosaic and black cement, set in alabaster. The Lady Chapel altar is equally ornate. This church contains other furnishings designed by Bentley; including a monstrance, votive candlesticks, frontals, reliquaries, altar candlesticks, crucifixes and vestments. The painted decorations on the walls were added at a later period.

The Oblates of S. Charles, who served the church in Notting Hill, found him other work during the 'sixties which included a high altar at S. Peter's and S. Edward's, Palace Street, Westminster; and furnishings at S. Mary of the Angels, Bayswater. Priests seem to have found this young convert architect easy to deal with, and he was commissioned to design altars, reredoses and other furniture for S. Mary's, Crook, Co. Durham (1864); S. Oswald's, Old Swan, Liverpool (1867–8); S. Patrick's, Liverpool (1868); S. Peter's, Doncaster (1867), and in other Catholic churches up and down England. It is interesting to compare this work with Bodley's altars, screens and decorations of the same period. Bentley showed little or no trace of Pre-Raphaelite influence. Unlike Bodley's ecclesiastical *décor* which was hardly likely to appeal except to the *cognoscenti,* Bentley's rich and colourful marbles and mosaics could easily be understood by the average middle-class Roman Catholic, as well as the older aristocracy, personified by Fr. Herbert Vaughan, the future Cardinal.

Bentley, unlike Bodley who, so far as is known, never designed any furnishings for Roman Catholic churches, had no scruples about accepting orders from Anglican clients. Among the latter were a font and a drinking fountain for Barbados; a

S. PETER'S, VERE STREET (J. K. Colling, 1882)
Pulpit, lectern and choir stalls

reredos for S. Mary's, Collaton, South Devon; and furnishings for S. Augustine's, Northbourne, Kent—all carried out during the 'sixties.

Neither Our Lady of the Holy Souls, Kensal New Town (1881) nor Corpus Christi Church, Brixton Hill (1886), both of which were designed by Bentley, contain any examples of his furniture and decoration. The new church of S. Mary, Chelsea, which he designed in 1879 is a good place in which to study his favourite style of altar. The striking hanging rood shows a figure of Christ the King robed in a scarlet dalmatic.

CHURCH OF THE HOLY ROOD, WATFORD (1889–1900)
Characteristic example of work of J. F. Bentley; the
architect of Westminster Cathedral. Note rood loft
without screen beneath it

The Church of the Holy Rood, Watford, erected at the cost of Mr. Tapprell
Holland in 1879, and finally consecrated in 1900, is a veritable Bentley museum.
If he had never built another church, this one would have given him a place
among the greatest of Victorian architects. Dr. Pevsner believes it to be 'one of the
noblest examples of the refined, knowledgeable and sensitive Gothic Revival of
that time.' [1]

The most striking feature of the interior is the bridge-like rood beam, with its
tall crucifix and figures of our Lady and S. John, standing on curved branch
supports.

The woodwork is painted a deep crimson, with touches of gold. The painted

[1] *Hertfordshire,* Penguin Buildings of England series (1953), p. 265.

decorations on the ceiling are not unlike those carried out by Bodley and Garner, but the colours are much brighter—Venetian red contrasting with white. The spacious sanctuary—not crowded up with stalls as in almost every Anglican church of the same period—is made glorious with gold and colour. Beneath a seven-light

OUR LADY OF THE ASSUMPTION, WARWICK STREET, LONDON
The former Portuguese and later Bavarian Embassy chapel (1780), with furnishings and marble mural decorations by J. F. Bentley (1877)

east window, filled with rich glass by Burlison and Grylls, rises up a splendid reredos; a riot of carved woodwork, with a fretted canopy, all painted and gilded, bright red being the predominant colour. The four main panels contain painted angels, robed in white on a red ground. The front of the altar is a single slab of red marble, inlaid with two pomegranites of marble and pearl, shading from green to opalescent white. The domed tabernacle, candlesticks and crucifix were specially designed by the architect to harmonize with the reredos. The sanctuary walls are adorned with painted figures of saints on red grounds. The white marble altar steps, and the sanctuary paving are in keeping with the whole *décor*.

The three chapels are filled with similar ornate furniture. Mention must be made of the flamboyant gilded iron grilles. The smaller chapel of the Holy Ghost, erected as a memorial to the donor of the church, is the most magnificent of the three—a blaze of red and gold, and many precious marbles. The exquisite detail of the canopied shrines of our Lady and the Sacred Heart is worth study.

Finally there are the pendant electric light fittings, added in 1899, which show that Bentley was not uninfluenced by the 'Art Nouveau' movement. The wrought iron communion rails erected in 1889 might have been designed by J. D. Sedding at the same date.

The sober Anglican furnishings in S. Luke's, Chiddingstone Causeway, Kent, were designed in 1897 by Bentley who was recommended for the job by the famous portrait painter, John S. Sargent. They are a great contrast to those in the Catholic church at Watford. Bentley is said to have remarked to Mrs. Hill, who paid for the church: 'You notice I have made the leopards in the encaustic tiles all putting out their tongues at you, because you are Protestant!'

The altars, shrines, screens, etc. in the Redemptorist church of Our Lady of Victories, Clapham, the dates of which range from 1883 to 1892, are extremely rich, but do not clash in the least with the earlier parts of the church, designed by William Wardell in the eighteen-fifties. Bentley's new apse at the former embassy chapel, the Church of the Assumption, Warwick Street, was his first effort in the Classic style. It was added in 1875, but the mosaic and marble decorations (reminiscent of those in the chapels at Westminster Cathedral) belong to the period after 1900.

About the same time he was commissioned to furnish Edward Goldie's recently opened church of S. James's, Spanish Place. Here he designed five altars and reredoses, as well as mural decorations and smaller furniture. Early in the 'nineties Fr. Bernard Vaughan, s.j., called in Bentley to furnish and decorate the Chapel of Our Lady of the Wayside in the Church of the Holy Name, Manchester. The Society of Jesus also employed him in the chapel at Beaumont College, Old Windsor, which he refurnished and redecorated. For the Jesuits again he designed the adjacent S. John's School (1888), and provided its chapel with characteristic rich Gothic Revival furniture. The chapel of the Hammersmith Seminary (1884) —now the Convent of the Sacred Heart—is Perpendicular Gothic in style, but the furnishings are not Bentley's work.

It would be impossible to mention all the ecclesiastical furniture designed by him at one time or another. He was equally at home in all metals, needlework, wood-work and stained glass.[2]

[2] They are described and illustrated in *Westminster Cathedral and its Architect* by Winefride de l'Hôpital (2 vols., 1919).

When Cardinal Vaughan in 1894 decided that the time had come to make a start on a cathedral at Westminster, he decided against competition, and chose his own architect. One day His Eminence called at Bentley's office to announce his appointment as architect. When Bentley tried to thank the Cardinal for this great honour, his Eminence replied, 'You are not to thank *me;* it is your fellow architects you have to thank.' Bentley would have preferred to design a Gothic church, but the Cardinal had decided that it must be in the Christian Byzantine style; largely because it would be cheaper in the long run. The whole building could be erected and the decoration of the walls left to future generations. A great Gothic cathedral would have to be built of stone, with much carving, inside and out. A Byzantine one could be constructed mainly of brick. So it was that Bentley, now aged fifty-five, had to acquire a working knowledge of a complete alien style of architecture. The methods of construction too, involving the use of domes, had to be learned.

In November 1894 he left London, bound for the north of Italy, where he examined Romanesque churches. Then followed six weeks in Rome, with shorter periods in Bologna and Ravenna. Having reached Venice he made a minute study of S. Mark's. His plans to sail to Constantinople came to naught: news came of a serious cholera epidemic there. So he was never able to absorb the details of the greatest of all Byzantine churches—the Hagia Sophia—or any of the smaller masterpieces of the same style in Greece. His biographer writes: 'It was a disappointment, but when condoled with, on his return, at not being able to finish the itinerary, he remarked: "San Vitale at Ravenna and Lethaby's book really told me all I wanted." ' [3]

When studying Bentley's chapels in Westminster Cathedral it is important to remember that his actual knowledge of Byzantine art and architecture was extremely limited, and confined to what he had seen at Venice. It was there and at Ravenna that he increased his already wide knowledge of marble and mosaic for interior decoration. He simply substituted round arches for pointed ones, and changed the details of the decoration. The materials used were much the same as he had been employing for over thirty years.

The baptistery and the chapels of SS. Gregory and Augustine, the Blessed Sacrament, S. Thomas of Canterbury, and the Holy Souls, all contain characteristic examples of Bentley's later furnishings and decorations. Many of the details of the marble work in the Lady Chapel and elsewhere were actually designed by him, but the other chapels which have been completed since his death in 1902 were furnished and decorated by other architects.

Bentley's original idea for the baldachin over the high altar was something similar to the type of that of Sant-Ambrogio at Milan, with four columns. He wanted them to be of opaque yellow Veronese marble, but Cardinal Vaughan had set his heart on onyx monoliths. The existing baldachin, with eight golden marble columns and the decorations in mosaic, designed by Mr. J. A. Marshall, were completed in 1908.

[3] ibid., Vol. I, p. 35.

Westminster Cathedral is so well known that there is no need to describe its furnishings and decorations in detail, in so far as they have advanced in the past half century. The introduction of Byzantine architecture into Britain in the eighteen-nineties had far-reaching results. A few churches had been designed in this style previous to 1894, but most architects felt that it was unsuitable to the northern climate and alien to the landscape. Westminster Cathedral changed this point of view. Many other churches have since been designed in the Byzantine style, and Bentley's style of marble and mosaic decoration has been imitated from one end of Britain to the other; a style that has the advantage of being easy to keep clean in the smoke-laden towns of the industrial areas of the North and Midlands. Here there is a lot to be said in favour of sanctuaries that resemble bathrooms.

Without the inspiration supplied by Bentley, it is doubtful if much later architects such as Bower Norris, Mangan or Coia, would have erected neo-Byzantine Catholic churches, and had them furnished with mosaics and marbles. But it is really Cardinal Vaughan, not Bentley, to whom we owe these home-grown evocations of the Near East because it was he who settled on Byzantine for his beloved cathedral. Bentley himself was probably happier designing church furnishings in a style more in keeping with Christian worship in Northern Europe.

CHAPTER XXVI

CHURCH FURNISHINGS IN THE 'NAUGHTY 'NINETIES'

THE better church furniture and decoration of the eighteen-nineties expressed much the same spirit as the costumes of the men and women who worshipped in these buildings. They were also a reflection of the then fashionable domestic furnishings.

By 1897, the year of Queen Victoria's Diamond Jubilee, the average well-to-do drawing-room had become perhaps even more crowded than in the 'eighties. Pseudo-Hepplewhite chairs, tables and sofas in rose-wood or satin-wood were much in demand. 'Overmantels' rose up above sham 'Adam' fireplaces, and some of them were masterpieces of skilled wood-carving. Fortunately there were plenty of maidservants to dust the pretty little china figurines and other 'ornaments' which cluttered up the shelves and brackets of these overmantels. The many 'occasional tables' displayed countless photographs in silver frames, which needed frequent polishing, as did the innumerable silver boxes, with the other knick-knacks and *bijouterie*, picked up in curiosity shops or brought back from abroad. The homes of retired Anglo-Indians generally contained a host of brass trays, candlesticks, bells, gongs, etc. Floral decorations still played an important part in both domestic and ecclesiastical settings. Many a young lady had to spend at least half an hour every morning 'doing the flowers,' which meant refilling the vases. Potted ferns, palms, aspidistras and india-rubber plants also needed watering. Many upper-class houses boasted a conservatory. Even in suburbia a gardener was regarded as essential.

We can picture the more leisured worshippers of the devout female sex in the eighteen-nineties filling up their weekday afternoons leaving cards on their neighbours, or entertaining them to tea in drawing-rooms where on dark winter days a soft light from electric bulbs or gas fittings, draped with frilly silk shades or frosted glass, helped to conceal their ages. No powder or any sort of 'make-up' was recognized in respectable families.

The younger ladies had adopted the new corset, which eliminated the abdomen, giving a protruding bust, and a graceful sway-back like effect when they rose up. Their ground-length skirts were trumpet-shaped. Beneath them were rustling silk petticoats, trimmed with flounces, often threaded with velvet ribbon or silk. When the skirts were raised to cross the street, a *frou-frou* of silk was visible. Sleeves were invariably of the leg-of-mutton shape, widest at the arm-holes. Such was the appearance of the more fashionably dressed feminine worshippers during the eighteen-nineties. The churches they attended might have been, and often were, perfect backgrounds for such costumes.

Greatest of all church architects of this period was George Halford Fellowes Prynne (1853–1927). His churches and their furnishings and ornaments, evoke memories of highly respectable and prosperous households between 1890 and 1900; especially those in the outer suburbs of London, where several of them can be found.[1]

S. Peter's, Staines, Middlesex, which was not fully furnished until about 1897, contained typical Fellowes Prynne fittings and decorations, including his favourite stone rood-screen, derived from those in such medieval churches as Stebbing and Great Bardfield, Essex. A contemporary drawing shows a richly carved wooden altar, with four brass candlesticks placed on a gradine. The brass cross, standing on a sham tabernacle, was backed by a tall brocade dossal, with a slightly projecting and purely ornamental tester. The stone pulpit was draped with an embroidered 'fall.' The walls of the sanctuary (so it was reported) were bright red brick with polychrome insertions. The architect supervised every detail of the furnishings including the mats and kneelers, which he specially designed.

Fellowes Prynne loved tall dossals, sham tabernacles and testers which served no functional purpose. Many of his altars have panels filled with sentimentalized copies of Fra Angelico angels or saints.

Much lacquered or highly polished brass is to be found in his churches, just as it was in so many upper middle class dining and drawing-rooms of the same period. So was produced the same combination of prettiness and stiffness. Brass pots with palms, aspidistras or india-rubber plants were still fashionable in suburbia. Most of this architect's churches though 'high' were not 'extreme.' He provided nearly all of them with cosy little 'Morning Chapels,' generally with apsidal east-ends. A typical Fellowes Prynne 'Morning Chapel' evokes far off memories of one of those Turkish 'cosy corners' in a drawing-room of the eighteen-nineties. In them, so elderly people will recall, there were usually Persian rugs (real or imitation) spread on the highly polished floor; velvet curtains draping an alcove; a divan covered with rich rugs; a mother of pearl inlaid table; and dusty palms in oriental pottery bowls. Within these cosy corners ladies in long swathing skirts and blouses with leg of mutton sleeves and high boned collars took afternoon tea together. The *décor* of a good Fellowes Prynne church invariably included a shining brass eagle-lectern and a richly carved stone pulpit. The stained glass in the windows helped to create an effect both devotional and cheerful.

Not every clergyman was satisfied with this popular architect. At Sunbury-on-

[1] e.g. Holy Trinity, Roehampton (1898); S. Peter, Streatham (West end only, 1887); All Saints', Dulwich (begun 1887); S. Peter, Staines (1893); and S. Saviour, Ealing (1899, now demolished). All Saints', Elland, Yorkshire (1899) is equally expressive of the prosperity of a West Riding mill town at the same time.

TYPICAL G. FELLOWES PRYNNE DÉCOR, 1902

Thames, only five miles from Staines, the Revd. W. J. Scott had filled up the east end of S. Saviour's with an extremely ornate Baroque altar and reredos, complete with vases of artificial flowers on the gradine. His 'Roman' outlook was stressed by the words *'Adoremus in aeternum sanctissimum sacramentum'* embroidered on the altar cover, beneath which hung nearly a foot of lace, hiding the top of the panelled silk Italian frontal. The *décor* of this Middlesex sanctuary has a historic significance, because it pre-dated by more than ten years the first efforts made by the Society of SS. Peter and Paul to transform Anglican churches into a resemblance of Catholic ones in Italy, France or Belgium.[2]

The fittings of the churches designed by J. E. K. and J. P. Cutts between 1890 and 1900 can only be described as dull. Most of these suburban churches were left for adornment in the future; then the wars came, followed by the decline of the suburbs, and nothing was done.

Belonging to the same school were C. Hodgson Fowler, R. J. Johnson and E. P. Warren. Two or three churches were furnished by Basil Champneys during this decade. Austin and Paley were still designing Gothic Revival furniture for their churches, mostly in the north of England. Bodley, James Brooks and a number of lesser men were hard at work, but there was a sameness about much of the work produced. Probably there was no demand for anything original, and it would have been rejected by clients. The furnishings and ornaments of the majority of Anglican churches built or restored in the eighteen-nineties were the outward expression of the religion of their clergy and congregations—insular and conservative.

Much the same spirit characterized the furnishings and ornaments of Roman Catholic churches in Britain, although those designed by Leonard Stokes, J. F. Bentley and F. A. Walters show a striving after something new. Bentley's contribution to ecclesiastical *décor* is dealt with elsewhere. Peter Paul Pugin, Edward Goldie and Fr. A. S. Scoles—to mention some of the most favoured architects—were merely repeating with slight variations the same themes of earlier Gothic Revival men.

Both Anglicans and Catholics wanted their churches to 'look like churches'; and they had fixed ideas as to what this meant. There was no opportunity for making experiments now. Church furnishing firms, as well as architects, had to supply the goods wanted by their customers. The taste of late Victorian clergy and layfolk was known and had to be catered for.

We must try to fit into a mental scrapbook the earlier drawings of Phil May and the later ones by George du Maurier with such churches which were in use by 1894. The 'New Woman' in her mannish costume, as well as the 'New Man' in his 'Norfolk suit' and straw 'boater,' could be found in the congregations. Miss Marie Corelli's latest novel *The Sorrows of Satan* was regarded even in respectable rectories as uplifting and of a good moral tone; but conventional churchpeople in 1894 were not quite sure if they dared go to see Mrs. Patrick Campbell and Mr. Beerbohm Tree in *The Second Mrs. Tanqueray* at the Haymarket Theatre.

Few of the churches built in the eighteen-nineties show in their fittings any trace of the new movement in house furnishing which was being popularized in England by C. F. Annesley Voysey and Ambrose Heal. These two men, with other pioneers, rejected all stylistic features, and strove after a simple decorative technique. This

[2] See pp. 261–7.

often became precious and mannered, with its weakness for lilies, hearts and embossed metal.

Here and there a church built in the 'nineties broke away from the wearisome monotony of the later Gothic Revival. S. Aidan's, Leeds (1894), designed by R. J. Johnson and W. S. Hicks, is one of them. Planned on the lines of a late Roman basilica, it contains furnishings of unusual richness, including the canopied pulpit, gigantic font and carved choir stalls, not forgetting the vast litany-desk on wheels. The walls of the apsidal chancel are decorated with mosaics by Frank Brangwyn. Everything in this church is on a big scale, evocative of the wealth of the Yorkshire churchpeople, who erected this building as a memorial to Bishop Woodford.

Somewhat similar in style, but not so overpowering in opulent display, was S. Agatha's, Portsmouth, designed by J. Henry Ball and opened in 1895. It was an Italian Romanesque variety of the Christian basilica. A low alabaster screen divided the nave from the chancel. Within the apse, above the high altar, was a stately baldachin. Robert Radclyffe Dolling, the incumbent of the parish, which was the Winchester College Mission, wanted to create a church with fittings suited for Anglo-Catholic worship 'on more unconventional and less artificial lines than those generally recommended by the commercial purveyors of ecclesiastical goods to whom the clergy have resort. . . . Having got hold of real artists to work for him, he knew how to trust them, and to uphold them by his sympathetic encouragement.' [3]

Heywood Sumner, who had designed the capitals of some of the granite or alabaster columns in the nave, was then asked to carry out decorations in mosaic and sgraffito in the Lady Chapel. This famous craftsman also covered the chancel arch with bold and striking decoration. He treated the apse in the same manner. Until the Second World War S. Agatha's, Portsmouth, remained unrivalled as an example of a revived Early Christian basilica. The altars, litany desk and the Stations of the Cross, and every other ornament expressed the best taste of the 'nineties. Since the war, this church has been turned into an Admiralty warehouse. The Lady Chapel was demolished in 1964. Future generations will be unable to study some of the finest ecclesiastical *décor* in Britain. Neither will they be reminded how Anglican church furnishings, even in the 'nineties, were still subject to the theological opinions of bishops. Father Dolling preferred to resign his Portsmouth living rather than remove a third altar in the nave, to which Dr. Randall Davidson, Bishop of Winchester, objected, because it was used primarily for 'Masses for the Dead.'

In the most unlikely places, often designed by forgotten architects, are churches with furnishings of a quite different quality. Hidden away in the Braes of Glenlivet in Banffshire is the Catholic church of Our Lady of Perpetual Succour (1897–1908). Its architect, Archibald MacPherson, had moments of real genius. Here the stencil decorations of the walls and ceiling could hardly have been bettered by J. F. Bentley or by G. F. Bodley. MacPherson was never afraid of colour. Other

[3] Chas. E. Osborne, *The Life of Father Dolling* (New edition, 1905), p. 130.

examples of his work can be found in the church of Our Lady and S. Ninian, Bannockburn, Stirlingshire (begun in 1898), also at Musselburgh, which is rather later.

It is impossible to calculate how many acres of oak trees (home-grown and foreign) must have been used in churches in England, Wales and Scotland during the past hundred years. There has been an almost Druid-like veneration for this wood among architects, clergymen and craftsmen. A conviction grew up that it is sacrilege to paint wood, especially in churches. The earlier Victorians adored shiny varnish, but their children and grandchildren preferred it fumed, plain or latterly pickled. Bentley, Bodley and George Gilbert Scott, Jnr., who had realized the beauty of painted house furniture from William Morris, had the courage to shock conventions in the eighteen-sixties by introducing painted wooden panelling, screens, choir-stalls, pulpits, font-covers, etc., into some of their churches, but they had not many imitators, until Charles Nicholson came along in the 'nineties and experimented with brighter shades than those fancied by Bentley and Bodley, both of whom went in for half-tones and steered clear of primary colours. It was not until after the First World War that these began to appear in churches. Even the sugary pastel shades so popular among the pioneers of the *Art Nouveau* movement towards the end of the century, were rarely used in church decoration. They were felt to be frivolous and not sufficiently 'religious.' They may have reminded people of the iced cakes in tea shops. Comper's painted screens and pulpits (see pp. 280–7) hardly come into the picture, because they belonged to a different world. Only much later was his work imitated. It was generally held that all colour in a church must be quiet and subdued. Anything garish was regarded as vulgar, and not conducive to the right spirit of devotion. This did not wholly apply to stained glass windows, although the 'greenery-yallery' tones of Kempe's glass was what were preferred in more cultured circles.

Anglican altar-frontals, curtains, pulpit-falls, vestments, and even alms-bags, continued to be made of subdued colours throughout the late Victorian era, no matter how rich and costly the materials, and the embroidery with which they were adorned. The ideal aimed at was the atmosphere of a Burne-Jones' painting—a dim twilight world which had no relation to ordinary humdrum life.

Many learned books published in the eighteen-nineties helped to spread knowledge of the history of Christian worship. The Henry Bradshaw Society was founded in 1890, and by the end of a decade had printed many medieval liturgical MSS. with profuse introductions and notes. Then came the Plainsong and Medieval Music Society, which issued adaptations of pre-Reformation chant to Anglican forms of worship. To encourage the practical study of ceremonial, or the arrangement of churches, their furniture and ornaments, in accordance with the rubrics of the Book of Common Prayer, the Alcuin Club was founded in the eighteen-nineties. Another body which helped to awaken a great interest in medieval church furnishings was the S. Paul's Ecclesiological Society—the name of the Ecclesiological Society at one stage of its existence.

S

According to the late Abbot Cabrol of Farnborough Abbey, the average English Catholic of this period was not interested in the liturgy, and did not even understand the meaning of the word. The Abbot wrote: 'If I ask a Catholic who comes to church what is the Sunday, or what is the liturgical season, he seldom knows.' Hence the apparent indifference to church furnishings, ornaments and decorations among English Catholics towards the close of the nineteenth century. It would be safe to say that such works as Duchesne's *Origènes du culte chrétien* (1888), Battifol's *Histoire du breviaire romain* (1893), or Cabrol's *Livre de la Prière antique* (1900) found more Anglican than Catholic readers.

The average English Catholic of the eighteen-nineties, if he had heard of the conversion of the famous French novelist Joris Karl Huysmans, almost at the same time as the appearance of the *Yellow Book,* did not find much to rouse his enthusiasm in the trilogy *En route* (1895), *La Cathédrale* (1898) and *L'Oblat* (1903), yet these three more or less autobiographical stories did more to create interest in medieval church furnishings and liturgical worship than any of the more learned books which appeared about the same time.[4]

One hardly dare think what Huysmans would have thought about the many Catholic churches, most situated in the industrial Lowlands of Scotland, which were designed by the firm of Pugin and Pugin between 1880 and 1910. His language would have been even more abusive than it was in *Les foules de Lourdes.* Yet these churches deserve careful study, because their furnishings and decorations are fascinating examples of a sort of Rococo Gothic Revival. It is extraordinary to think that most of them were contemporary with Bodley's refined creations, or with the Glasgow School of Art and the interiors of Miss Cranston's restaurants in the same city. All that is in common between Charles Rennie Mackintosh's delicately bizarre *art nouveau décor* and Peter Paul Pugin's highly stylized robust English Decorated Gothic, is that both are now curious period pieces.

Nearly all 'P.P.P.'s' interiors, usually of warm red sandstone with stone dressings, are filled with highly varnished pitch-pine or oak pews. More often than not there is an ornate communion rail of marble, stone or lacquered brass. The altars conform to a fixed type. They are constructed of Caen stone and polished marble, including columns suggestive of turned-out tins of luncheon-meat. Each has a stone or marble reredos, ornamented with a profusion of columns, crockets, pinnacles and delicate tracery. Deeply embedded in two or three gradines on the high altar is the tabernacle, generally with a jewel-encrusted brass door. Above the tabernacle there is usually an elaborate throne for exposition, decorated with adoring angels, and surmounted by a tall crocketed spire. The polished parquet or marble floor of the sanctuary often features glazed porcelain pots in which are palms, aspidistras or rubber plants. The windows with their Decorated Gothic tracery are filled with richly coloured stained glass. The walls and ceilings of many of the sanctuaries, generally apsidal, are decorated with stencilling, gleaming with gold-leaf and

---

[4] The influence of Huysmans on the early phases of the modern liturgical movement is stressed by Dom Olivier Rousseau, o.s.b., in his *Histoire du Mouvement Liturgique* (Paris, 1945), pp. 183–5.

colour. Most of the Peter Paul Pugin pulpits are of carved stone or oak. The large confessional-boxes tend to be of varnished pitchpine, and are thoroughly functional. To the student of church furnishing and decoration these churches may yet become as important as the Baroque interiors of Bavaria and Austria, or even the more fantastic Baroque of Latin America. They are best described as the sunset swan-song of the Gothic Revival in Britain. P.P.P. evolved a style of his own,[5] which owed something to his more famous father.

There was a great harmony between the furnishings of the average country church in England of the eighteen-nineties and those of the adjacent rectory or vicarage. Some of these clerical residences, built after the middle of the century, are splendid examples of Gothic Revival. Like the church interiors, they convey an atmosphere of plain living and high thinking, combined with considerable comfort.

The details of the incumbent's study, or more familiarly the den, are almost invariably the same—a Gothic grate behind a club fender. Around the walls hang, as Mr. Lancaster points out, 'groups of long vanished rugger players, beside the pipe-rack on the mantelpiece, Arundel prints in ecclesiastical mounts, hanging between faded sepia photographs of Greek temples and Swiss mountains, a Gothic bookcase with dusty rows of Paley's Evidences and brown-backed volumes of the Badminton Library—all these changeless and inevitable. Likewise a little model of the leaning tower of Pisa, a lump of stone from the Acropolis, whiskered ecclesiastics in Oxford frames, and a large bow-window looking on to the garden dark with laurels.'[6] More likely than not the W.C. has a narrow lancet window with diamond-shaped panes, possibly stained glass to ensure greater privacy.

The late Gothic Revival atmosphere of the drawing-room was often helped by a Morris wallpaper and tapestry curtains from the same firm. One was almost certain to find one or two copies of Italian Madonnas or some more Arundel prints in gilt frames; but the more artistically-minded parsons' wives and daughters of the eighteen-nineties preferred sepia photographs of paintings by Sir Edward Burne-Jones or Mr. Watts, in wide frames of dark-stained oak.

Mr. Lancaster maintains that this style of interior decoration 'may perhaps be thought to represent, as does no other Victorian style, all that was best in that great age.' It deserves careful study, because it explains so much in the furnishing and decoration of country churches. The two go hand in hand; there is no conflict between them. The country vicarage or rectory was the counterpart of the church. Lastly the Victorian ballads sung in the drawing-room had much in common with

[5] e.g. S. Francis Xavier, Carfin (1882); S.-Francis, Glasgow (1882–96); S. Margaret, Kinning Park, Glasgow (1883); Holy Family, Mossend (1884); S. Margaret, Johnstone (1883); Benedictine Convent, Dumfries (1884); S. Michael, Linlithgow (1888); Convent of Faithful Companions of Jesus, Paisley (1889); S. Mary, Paisley (1889); S. Peter's College, Bearsden (1892); S. Bridget, Bailleston (1893); Holy Family, Kirkintilloch (1893); S. Agnes, Lambhill, Glasgow (1894); S. Gregory, Preshome, Banffshire (new sanctuary 1896); S. John, Portugal Street, Glasgow (1897); S. Patrick, Dundee (1898); S. Patrick, Anderston, Glasgow (1897); S. Patrick, Shieldmuir, Wishaw (1898); Our Lady of Good Aid—now the Cathedral—Motherwell (1900); S. Peter, Partick, Glasgow (1903); Holy Redeemer, Clydebank (1903); S. Mary, Stirling (1905); S. Joseph, Blantyre (1905); All Saints', Airdrie (1905); S. Patrick, Shotts (1905); Holy Cross, Crosshill, Glasgow (1911); S. Patrick, Dumbarton (1903).

[6] *Homes Sweet Homes* (1939), n. 48 'Anglican.'

some of the tunes in *Hymns Ancient and Modern,* or with the simple anthems rendered by the village choir of men and maidens on the greater festivals, when the church was still as lavishly decorated with greenery and flowers as it had been half a century before.

Trying to fit the bits and pieces of the ecclesiastical *décor* of the eighteen-nineties with contemporary secular life is like painting a surrealist painting. Rood screens by Bentley or Bodley went with ladies in 'bicycle suits' (vulgarly known as 'bloomers') pedalling around Battersea Park. Few Anglican bishops had yet dared to don mitres, but 'matinée hats' of vast size often blocked the view of altars and pulpits at Mattins or Mass, just as they hid the stage of a theatre. Unfortunately for worshippers just behind them, such hats could not be removed in church. 'Problem Plays,' such as Pinero's *The Notorious Mrs. Ebbsmith,* were fashionable, though the average churchman probably preferred the simple fun of the newly produced farce *Charley's Aunt!*

The picture becomes even more bizarre if one visualizes drawings by Aubrey Beardsley or Charles Ricketts, or some of Whistler's *Nocturnes* decorating the interior of one of Fellowes Prynne's churches. How far removed from each other were the dull furnishings designed by Arthur Blomfield or James Brooks with the sparkling epigrams of Oscar Wilde, with which they were contemporary. Mr. Cutts' typical communion table belongs to another world to that of Sargent's painting *Carmencita.* Peter Paul Pugin's wedding-cake Catholic altars may have had a little more affinity with the 'Living Pictures' (otherwise 'Animated Photographs') shown on the screen at the Empire Music Hall, because both sparkled and flashed. But the more one compares secular and ecclesiastical art, the more apparent it becomes how great was the gulf between religion and everyday life in the eighteen-nineties.

The Episcopalian churches of the United States are, in some ways, a better hunting ground for students of ecclesiastical good taste in the latter years of the century than those of England. North America evolved its own version of Gothic Revival in church furnishings and decorations. Examples of it can be found which are wonderful period pieces, worthy of preservation. Or if a change of fashion insists on their removal, some of these altars should be preserved in folk-museums.

In New York City, for example, there is the William B. Astor memorial high altar in Trinity Church, designed by Frederick C. Withers; also the smaller reredos designed by the same architect in Trinity Chapel. Both are reminiscent of the work of Sir George Gilbert Scott in England. Mr. Withers was the architect of a similar Caen stone much crocketed and pinnacled altar in the Church of the Transfiguration. Another stone sideboard altar and reredos combined is the high altar of S. Ignatius', New York, designed by Kivas Tully in 1886. The persistence of this fashion can be seen in Henry Vaughan's altar in the Constable Chapel of the Church of the Incarnation, New York, erected in 1903. Bishop Grafton of Fond du Lac was not far wrong when he said that R. Geissler's reredos in the Church of S. Edward the Martyr 'marks a new stage in the progressive development of ecclesiastical art.' There is an *art-nouveau* rococo quality about this Gothic carving. Another kind of 'queerness,' and an urge to be original, is noticeable in photographs of William Halsey Wood's stone and marble altar and reredos in the Church of Zion and S. Timothy, New York City (1892).

The altar and reredos in the Chapel of the General Theological Seminary, designed by Charles C. Haight in 1888, suggest a Scott or Street inspiration; whereas Louis C. Tiffany's elaborate mosaic reredos and altar, exhibited at the World's Columbian Exposition in 1893, and re-erected in the Cathedral of S. John the Divine, New York, has a certain flavour of what Sedding had been striving after in England. Here was one of the first complete break-aways from the sterility of the Gothic Revival.

One of the most awe-inspiring altars inserted into Episcopalian churches towards the close of the century was that of the Cathedral of S. John, Quincy, Illinois. The usual Cram, Goodhue and Ferguson carved oak reredos was not quite the right sort of framing for the sentimental paintings of angels and saints by the Revd. Johannes A. Oertel of Washington, D.C., who was then regarded as having 'the spirit of the old masters and whose canvasses enrich many of our churches.' But the Quincy altar was nothing when compared to the one designed by William Halsey Wood for S. Michael and All Angels, Anniston, Illinois, the date of which is 1888. The seven round alabaster turrets, which cannot decide whether they are medieval Gothic or Mexican Baroque, are crowned by seven alabaster angels. Another priceless period piece was produced in Illinois—the high altar of the Church of the Ascension, Chicago (1893), designed by Edward J. N. Stent of New York. The photograph shows above the mosaic tabernacle door a lofty stone and marble canopied exposition throne. Gazing towards the throne are two large alabaster angels. In addition to the six big candlesticks arranged on tiers of gradines, there are over fifty smaller candles on branches. The correct 'Catholic' note is provided by the deep lace draped over the top of the long marble altar.

A curious feature of many High Churches of the 'eighties and 'nineties is their stressing of their Catholicism by the height of their reredoses and the candles. Typical is the high altar of the Church of the Advent, Boston, Mass. A contemporary photograph records six candlesticks placed on top of the original stone reredos designed by John H. Sturgis, to which was added a stone screen with open tracery, designed by Harold Peto, of London. Although a relief of the Crucifixion formed part of the original reredos, it was felt necessary to insert a movable crucifix in the exposition throne of the upper reredos. Looking rather lost, two large candlesticks rest on the one gradine. Here we find the then fashionable seven lamps hanging before the altar. During the 'nineties they were regarded as essential furnishings for almost every Anglo-Catholic church in Britain. Was it in emulation of the silver altar which had been erected in S. Bartholomew's, Brighton, that another and even richer one found its way into S. Mark's, Philadelphia, as the Wanamaker

277

Memorial? The latter was made by Barkentin and Krall, London. It contains 144 small figures of saints in niches.

To-day the once greatly admired late Gothic Revival altars, reredoses, pulpits, fonts and choir stalls designed in North America by Henry Vaughan; Cram, Goodhue and Ferguson; George T. Pearson, Henry Randall; Francis R. Allen— to mention some of the architects—are regarded indulgently as curios and relegated to the status of museum pieces.[7]

[7] See pp. 300–1.

CHAPTER XXVII

SIR JOHN NINIAN COMPER
BEAUTY BY EXCLUSION AND INCLUSION

IT was in 1893 that an event took place which was to have an almost revolutionary effect on church furnishings, although it is improbable that anybody realized it at the time. A certain young architect, aged twenty-nine—John Ninian Comper— who had been articled to the firm of Bodley and Garner, had been studying the illuminated pages of medieval manuscripts in the British Museum; not for ecclesiological purposes, but for their beauty. 'It was at the time of a chance acquaintance with the Secretary of the Society of S. Osmund,' he tells us, 'whose interpretation of medieval altars in practice was disputed on the strength of these pictures.' The Secretary therefore asked Mr. Comper to give a lecture to the Society. His paper was read in the Church House, London, early in 1893. It was re-read, first before the Aberdeen Ecclesiological Society, and secondly in S. Paul's Cathedral, London, on November 29th of that same year. In 1894 Dr. Wickham Legg published the paper in *Some Principles and Services of the Prayer Book historically treated,* when the title was abbreviated to *The English Altar and its surroundings.* Later on it reappeared in the Transactions of the S. Paul's Ecclesiological Society, under the original title of *Further Thoughts on the English Altar, or Practical Considerations on the Planning of a Modern Church.*[1]

Since the death of Augustus Welby Pugin in 1852 it would be true to say that no English architect tried to reproduce the traditional form of the medieval altar, however keen he was on medieval architecture. Ignorance of pre-Reformation church furnishings was widespread. It was not until 1890, when Mr. J. T. Micklethwaite read a paper entitled *The Ornaments of the Rubric* before the S. Paul's Ecclesiological Society, that any serious interest began to be taken in them.

In 1893 young Comper was invited by the Revd. W. M. Tatham, Vicar of Cantley, near Doncaster, to refurnish the little church of S. Mary, which had been 'restored' almost out of recognition by Sir Gilbert Scott. Here Comper put into practice the principles laid down in the paper he had read to the Society of S. Osmund. The Cantley altar, with its four posts, dossal and riddels, standing in front of a low-down east window, became the prototype of thousands of similar altars which have been erected in the past half century.

[1] A revised and enlarged edition was printed by W. Heffer and Sons, Cambridge, in 1933.

It was unfortunate that Comper used the expression 'English Altar,' for, as he later pointed out, 'neither riddels nor posts are a necessary adjunct of the English altar and it is a misnomer to call them "English" in that sense.' Very few illuminated manuscripts depict altars in England with side curtains. The traditional and practical point of greatest importance about the altar posts is that they are a relic of the ciborium or baldachin of an earlier period.

It is worth quoting Comper's opinions on the type of altar he is supposed to have invented or revived. 'A likeness used scoffingly to be found in the "English Altar" to the four-post bed; but in truth a likeness in some of its more recent examples may be found much more to a box-bed, so complete is the sense of shutting in. The hangings are sometimes arranged under a returned cornice tight against the ends of the altar and give the sense of a permanently closed structure. Dr. Creighton, when Bishop of Peterborough, once said, in sympathy with the attempt to reform, "in my young days altars were like dining-room sideboards but now they are like drawing-room mantelpieces." The box-bed was as yet to come and, as often as not, it has preserved the worst feature of the drawing-room mantelpiece in the flower vases which offend ecclesiastical rule even more by standing on the altar itself than they used to do when on a shelf. It is not the high reredos—which has the precedent of many of our medieval choirs and of Spain and of the German triptychs—that is necessarily the offender, though it was greatly attacked, but it is the narrowness and cramping of the altar itself, and this cramping is now being done in another way. We want neither a sideboard, nor a mantelpiece, nor a box-bed, but the table and altar of sacrifice, both of which should stand as much as possible in the open.' [2]

When the chancel of Cantley church was refurnished in 1893, it was a complete contrast to any church in Britain—Anglican or Catholic—almost all of which displayed either a 'dining-room sideboard' or 'drawing-room mantelpiece' in one form or another. Some of them were wooden, others were of carved stone or marble. One or more gradines, i.e. shelves, were regarded as an essential feature to every altar. Some architects, including Bodley, had started to erect sham tabernacles in the middle of the gradines, on which rested the altar cross. The fashion had been started of testers which projected only a foot or two from the top of the reredos, and covered nothing, not even the tops of the candles. Side curtains, invariably sticking out at an angle of 45 degrees, and serving no practical purpose, were another popular addition. But at Cantley the riddel posts supported gilded angels, holding tall tapers. There was a canopy or tester completely covering the altar. From it was suspended a white-veiled pyx for the reservation of the Consecrated Elements—the almost universal method employed in England before the Reformation, and unique in an Anglican parish church at that date.

Between 1893 and about 1907 Comper designed many more altars reminiscent of Cantley. In 1895 he transformed the crypt chapel at Street's church of S. Mary Magdalene, Paddington, into a sumptuous late medieval dream-world, where the

[2] *Further Thoughts on the English Altar,* etc. (Cambridge, 1933), p. 38.

wealth of gilded decoration is almost overpowering. Both here and at S. Mary's, Egmanton, Nottinghamshire (1897), suspended pyxes for reservation were inserted above the altars. Of Egmanton Dr. Pevsner writes: 'There is no denying the fact, Comper's screen, organ-case and pulpit make the church. As a piece of reconstruction the screen with its rood and rood-canopy is admirable, and as pieces of a medieval revival organ-case and pulpit are admirable too. But as pieces of contemporary art they are of course all valueless.' [3] Still these furnishings do reflect a change of ecclesiastical taste; it is odd to recall that they belong to the same year as Queen Victoria's Diamond Jubilee.

In 1897 Comper's furnishings in Hansom's Lady Chapel at Downside Abbey, near Bath, were completed. It pleased him that this was 'one of the first unchallenged acceptances of "the English Altar," ' and that every new altar in the great church was designed more or less in conformity with it. He wrote: 'This is an important witness to a fact which is far too much forgotten, viz. that union between what is really English and really Roman there is no difference. It is a happy bond of union with Rome which no political or dogmatic difference can break'— an eirenic statement typical of Comper's mentality.[4]

There is little difference in the altar and other furnishings and ornaments of the Lady Chapel at Downside Abbey, and those of the Chapel of the Convent of the Holy Name, Malvern Link, also S. Margaret's, Braemar, Aberdeenshire, both erected in 1898.

It was the opening of S. Cyprian's, Dorset Square, London, in 1903 that finally established the reputation of the architect. Here for the first time Comper designed a large parish church according to his rigid principles, regardless of cost. The most striking feature of the interior is the lofty rood-screen (a riot of gilded and painted carved woodwork and tracery) which extends right across the nave and aisles. Above the rood, high up in the ceiling, is the traditional medieval 'Majesty,' the image of our Lord enthroned in glory. The exceptionally long high altar occupies the entire width of the great window above it. There are riddel posts with gilded angels, and a low painted dossal. The choir was placed in the rood gallery. Another novelty was making the levels of the chancel and chapels as low as possible; the three altars are in fact not raised above eye level. Finally there were no fixed seats, only chairs, which during the week were removed, so that most of the polished parquet flooring was left bare. Nobody had ever seen anything like S. Cyprian's. It was far too novel to start a wholesale change in church furnishings, but it exercised an indirect influence for many years.

Although it might not be suspected at first sight, the furnishings and ornaments of this exteriorly uninviting red brick church near the Clarence Gate of Regent's Park evoke memories of the second year of the reign of Edward VII. A brief decade of dazzling seasons had been started, which in their splendour were to recall

---

[3] *Nottinghamshire* (The Buildings of England: Penguin Books, 1951), p. 65.
[4] *Further Thoughts on the English Altar*, p. 30.

if not recapture the days of Louis Philippe and of the Second Empire. 'At the court drawing-rooms,' as Cecil Beaton describes, 'ladies with Prince of Wales feathers in their hair wore trains that swept for many yards the floor.' The over-powering richness of Comper's ecclesiastical *décor*, even if late medieval in inspiration, was as opulent as the setting of Edwardian dinner parties, where 'the masterpiece of decoration, most usually sweet peas, was saved for the centre of the dining-table, which would be dotted with olives, salted almonds, sugared green peppermints and chocolates in cut-glass bowls or silver dishes.'[5] Pious Anglo-Catholic ladies of the upper middle class or the nobility drove to S. Cyprian's on Sunday mornings in hansoms or the new taxi-cabs—a few in their own electric broughams. Their bosoms were 'laced into corsets that gave them pouter-pigeon bosoms and protruding posteriors. Perched on their heads, and elevated by a little roll just inside the crown, were hats which had grown as frivolous as the milliner's trade could make them—enormous galleons of grey velvet with vast grey plumes of ostrich feathers sweeping upwards and outwards, or they would be trimmed with artificial flowers and fruit.'[6]

In a curious way the typical Comper church interior of the mid-Edwardian era recalls the distorting mirror of Ronald Firbank's fantastic imagination. A mock medieval paraphrase of *Caprice* would be an apt summing up of S. Cyprian's, Clarence Gate, and other churches which followed it. Of Firbank's prose style Sir Osbert Sitwell once wrote: 'Just as in the autumn the silver cobwebs lightly cover the trees with a fine mist of impalpable beauty, so a similar highly stylized but intangible loveliness hung over every page, while wit ran, round and under-neath each word.' With certain reservations this might be said of Comper's exquisite pastiches in church furnishing and decoration, which were contemporary with Firbank's world.

Throughout the reign of Edward VII Comper went on refurnishing churches and building a few new ones, all of which in their own way reflected a note of sparkling luxury—evocative of *pêche Melba*, elaborate feminine coiffures and boudoirs filled with bric-à-brac. More and more Anglo-Catholic clergymen were employing him, if they could afford to. In 1906 he created the exquisite chapel at S. John's Hospital, Cowley S. John, Oxford, for the All Saints' Sisterhood. On a smaller scale it reflected the same world as did S. Cyprian's of which Dr. Nikolaus Pevsner says: 'If there must be medieval imitation in the twentieth century, it is here unquestionably done with joy and care. Beyond that appreciation can hardly go. There is no reason for the excesses of praise lavished on Comper's church furnish-ings by those who confound æsthetic with religious emotions.'[7]

By this time Comper had begun to be dissatisfied with his own work. He tells us that he underwent a sudden æsthetic 'conversion' in North Africa. The sources of beauty are universal, he realized, and that unity must be achieved by the

---

[5] *The Glass of Fashion* (1954), p. 6.
[6] ibid., p. 7.
[7] *London except the Cities of London and Westminster* (The Buildings of England, Penguin Books, 1952), p. 329.

S. ANDREW'S EPISCOPALIAN CATHEDRAL, ABERDEEN
(J. N. Comper, 1940)
The end of an epoch. Neo-Classic baldachin erected during the
first year of the Second World War

inclusion of all styles and periods. Moreover his ideas were being copied by other
architects; he had no exclusive rights of the misnamed 'English Altar.' Since 1899
Dr. Wickham Legg, the editor of Mowbray's *English Churchman's Kalendar*, had
been illustrating its front page with a photograph of some altar designed according
to the principles laid down in Comper's paper of 1893. These Kalendars and
Percy Dearmer's *Parson's Handbook*, of which more will be said in the next
chapter, helped to popularize a new fashion in church furnishings and ornaments
in circles far outside that of a small ecclesiological society.

Comper's own work acquired the quality of expensive caviare, costly chocolates, or glacé pears and imported greengages. He lived apart from the outside world in his secluded 'Gothick' house on Beulah Hill, near the Crystal Palace. Here or in his studio on Knight's Hill he designed churches, altars, screens, pulpits, font-covers and more stained glass. A Renaissance note which had first appeared in the tall font cover at S. Cyprian's, Clarence Gate, as far back as 1903, was strongly marked seven years later in the furnishings of Wimborne S. Giles, Dorset, but mixed up with late Gothic elements. In 1912 the new high altar, screen and Lady altar in the Grosvenor Chapel, Mayfair, London, showed the extent of Comper's conversion to Classic styles. At the same time he was designing church furniture and ornaments reminiscent of the eighteen-nineties, e.g. the altar screen at Wymondham, Norfolk (1913); S. Michael, Newquay, Cornwall (1911); the Heritage Craft Schools' Chapel, Chailey, Sussex (1913); and the Stanton Chantry in S. Alban's, Holborn, London (1917).

Almost the first of his Classical baldachins was erected in Bedford's 1822–4 Greek Doric church of S. John's, Waterloo Road, London, destroyed during the Second World War. Three years later, in 1927, it was repeated with slight variations in his own new chapel at All Saints' Convent, London Colney, Hertfordshire. The tall golden columns shine like polished brass. On them are painted little flowers. The baldachin has a crocketed ogee top, and the whole conception is a fascinating combination of the Italian Renaissance with late English Gothic. It is a galaxy of gold and colour, standing out in strong contrast to the all-white interior of the chapel. Other variations of this baldachin were designed later on, notably for Temple Moore's chapel of Pusey House, Oxford, in 1937.

Two years before this Comper evolved the first example of another type of baldachin, better described as an Early Christian ciborium, for the chapel of the House of Prayer, Burnham, Buckinghamshire. It was repeated in more ornate form in S. Philip's, Cosham, Portsmouth (1937); S. Andrew's Episcopal Cathedral, Aberdeen (1941); and elsewhere, usually with a suspended veiled pyx for reservation.

The genius of Comper is best studied in the furnishings and ornaments of S. Mary's, Wellingborough, Northamptonshire; a large church begun in 1906, and not fully completed until nearly forty years later.

The interior of this Perpendicular Gothic church contains examples of almost every known style of European architecture. The nave has ornate lierne vaulting with pendants. The octagonal orange-yellow ironstone columns have the Greek *entasis,* and the same fluting as those in the Parthenon at Athens, but the capitals and bases are *sui generis.* A lofty rood-screen separating the nave from the chancel has mouldings and acanthus scrolls on its traceries, taken direct from ancient Greece, though the general design is as much Italian as English. The wrought iron parclose screens are obviously Spanish Renaissance in inspiration. The chancel is a step lower than the nave—an unusual feature. The high altar stands beneath a sumptuous Classical baldachin, and behind it is a large east window with intricate Perpendicular tracery, and some of Comper's finest painted glass. The Jesus Chapel

S. MARY'S, WELLINGBOROUGH (J. M. Comper)
'Beauty by inclusion.' Classical baldachin in English Perpendicular
setting, *c.* 1911

—the northmost of the five aisles—was built first, and its furnishings are severely
late medieval Gothic. Photographs can give only a feeble impression of the
gorgeous interior. The brilliant gold and colour decoration is rendered still more
vivid by contrast with the white walls, lit up by the sun pouring through the
large windows which, even where filled with stained glass, do not exclude the
light. The whole thing is a brilliant *pastiche*.

Comper's work is found all over Britain; his output has been enormous since
he designed the western chapel at his father's church of S. Margaret's, Aberdeen,
in 1889. This was followed two years later by the chapel for the Community of
S. Margaret in the same city, with its replica of the late medieval Scottish 'Sacra-

ment House,' i.e. an aumbry or cupboard in the north wall of the sanctuary for the reservation of the consecrated elements.

It was Comper who spread reservation among Anglicans; a custom which existed only in a few chapels of sisterhoods before the eighteen-nineties. The first revival of the medieval 'suspended tabernacle' or hanging pyx was in 1893, when Comper designed one for the Clergy House Chapel of S. Matthew's, Westminster. To quote his own words: 'It remained for twenty years or more when it was replaced, as were also the nearly contemporary hanging tabernacles at S. Mary Magdalene's, Paddington (1895) and S. Mary's, Egmanton (about 1896), by an unnecessary and inaccurate following of the ordinary modern Roman use. More happily the second of the restored hanging tabernacles, namely of 1895, still remains in use at Cantley; and later examples are two very simple forms, one in the chapel of the Wantage Sisters at Spelthorne S. Mary and one at S. Pancras Church at Bagborough (Somerset). Richer vessels are in the chapel of the Sisters of the Holy Name at Malvern Link and the Grosvenor Chapel in London. In the last instance and in the Conventual Church of the All Saints' Sisters near St. Albans, the tabernacle is suspended from a crook in the French manner.' [8]

The suspended tabernacle which Comper designed for the then Anglican Benedictines of Caldey Island in 1910 has had a curious history. After the reconciliation of most of the community with the Roman Church in 1913 the triple crown and pyx were returned to the donor who handed them over to the newly established Anglican Benedictine monastery at Pershore. But they soon wanted an ordinary Roman tabernacle on the altar, so Bishop Frere installed it in his cathedral at Truro. On his resignation of the see in 1935 the suspended tabernacle passed to the Community of the Resurrection at Mirfield, because the new bishop, Dr. Hunkin, did not approve of Reservation. To-day it hangs above the altar in the chapel of the University Hostel of the Resurrection at Leeds. In 1940 Comper provided another triple crown and tabernacle for suspension from the ceiling of the ciborium of the high altar of S. Andrew's (Episcopal Cathedral, Aberdeen).[9]

Amongst the later examples of Comper's tabernacles is the solid silver *turris* nine feet high, above the high altar of Butterfield's All Saints', Margaret Street. A miniature lift, worked by electricity, was placed in the upper story of the silver steeple, within which the actual tabernacle was drawn up. But fashion is fleeting, and for some years this novel method of reservation was given up. A small veiled tabernacle was placed on the altar in the north aisle, for what were regarded as practical reasons, but probably rather from an urge for stricter conformity with Roman canon law.

[8] ibid., p. 47. What Comper describes as 'an unnecessary and inaccurate following of the ordinary modern Roman use' resulted in the removal of the suspended pyx from the chapel of the All Saints' Sisters at London Colney, and a small domed tabernacle being placed on the high altar. More recently the same has been done at S. Mary's Convent, Wantage, where the veiled aumbry has given place to a similar tabernacle on Comper's high altar in the main chapel.

[9] 'According to long existing custom in the Scottish Church, the Presbyter may reserve so much of the consecrated Gifts as may be required for the Communion of the Sick and others who could not be present at the celebration in church. All that remaineth of the Holy Sacrament, and is not so required, the Presbyter and such other of the communicants as he shall then call unto him shall, after the Blessing, reverently eat and drink' (General Rubric in the *Scottish Book of Common Prayer*, Edinburgh 1929).

To the general public Comper is perhaps better known as a glass painter. Examples of his windows are to be found all over Britain, and as far afield as China, South Africa and North America. His windows are characterized by a lavish use of clear translucent glass. Some of his best work can be seen in Westminster Abbey, where in 1931 he also furnished the Warriors' Chapel. He also designed many vestments and frontals, most of them for Anglican churches and cathedrals, although one magnificent set of vestments was made for Notre Dame, Paris. In France, too, there is a replica of his statue of S. Joan of Arc in Winchester Cathedral, adorning the parish church at Domrémy where she was born.

John Ninian Comper—he was knighted at the age of eighty-six in 1950— always stood apart from his fellow church architects, a mysterious and elusive figure difficult to place in any category. *The Times Literary Supplement* rightly commented: 'His work is distinguished by its remarkable sense of scale, and its colours—rose-pink predominating, white walls, golden woodwork—the whole effect of a transparency of coloured richness to which his many imitators cannot attain. . . . In all of his works the altar is his chief concern—how best to show the altar, how to lead the eye to it through colour and light, how to bend the knee to it through scale, how to humble the heart to it through beauty of design, how to give it worthy ornaments. . . . His work is simple in its elaboration, because wholly subordinated to the purpose of a Catholic church—the worship of the Incarnate Son of God in the sacraments.' [10]

The work of this architect, who died in 1962, has been imitated by many younger men, most of whom were at one time his pupils. Among them are his son, J. S. Comper, Geoffrey and Christopher Webb, Martin Travers, F. E. Howard and W. H. Randoll Blacking. Sometimes the imitation is so meticulous that it is almost impossible to be sure if the work is by the master or the disciple. Nevertheless there is usually an undefinable quality in Comper's church furnishings and ornaments which not even his closest admirers have been able to capture.

[10] April 27th, 1951.

CHAPTER XXVIII

EDWARDIAN ECCLESIASTICAL AESTHETICS

THE church furnishings of the Edwardian era must be seen against the background of fashions in dress and in domestic *décor* with which they were contemporary. The first decade of this century was felt to be a brave new world in which the younger generation was waging war against the general stuffiness and smugness of the Victorians. Both secular and ecclesiastical fashions were full of violent contrasts. Some churches look little different to those designed in the eighteen-eighties, just as did the furnishings of many Edwardian drawing-rooms. But there are exceptions where we find the urge to return to simplicity, and to break away from superfluous ornamentation by designings from basic forms. The trumpet shaped skirts of the eighteen-nineties, with the ample bust and huge hats, soft materials, bead and sequin embroidery, cobweb lace insertions and artificial flowers, did not give way to the hobble skirt until about 1910. Victorian Gothic Revival in church furnishings took even longer to die. 'The Merry Widow,' as dressed by Lily Elsie at Daly's Theatre in 1909, was the ideal of many a pious worshipper in the churches of the pre-1914 epoch. Churches. like houses, were still overcrowded and over-dressed.

An important source of reference to the furnishings and ornaments of Anglican churches in the reign of Edward VII are the three volumes of the *Report of the Royal Commission on Ecclesiastical Discipline,* published in 1906. A large number of churches were visited, and the answers to the questions put to the witnesses (even if they often display an incredible ignorance of ritual and ceremonial), together with the various appendices and the more serious contributions by eminent liturgists, make up a significant *corpus.* It is possible to identify the churches in England sixty years ago in which could be found vestments, altar lights, a sanctus bell, a confessional, censers, aumbries or tabernacles, Stations of the Cross, statues, pictures or crucifixes, and many other ornaments—legal and illegal.

It was in 1864, so it is believed, that eucharistic vestments were first adopted in any London church—S. Mary Magdalene, Munster Square. This example was soon followed by a few other churches, e.g. S. Alban's, Holborn; S. Michael's, Shoreditch; S. Matthias', Stoke Newington; Christ Church, Clapham; and S. Ethelburga's, Bishopsgate. By 1906 there appeared to be 113 churches in the Diocese of London, and thirty-seven in the Diocese of Rochester (which at that date included most of

London south of the Thames) where vestments were worn. Most of the churches reported on had two altar candlesticks, but a fair number preferred to follow the modern Roman rule of six lights on the high altar.

'Ecclesiastical Repositories' had found many purchasers of sanctus bells or gongs

'CORRECT' HIGH ALTAR IN A 'HIGH' CHURCH (*c.* 1900)
Sham tabernacles, high gradines, towering candles, riddel-curtains (sticking out from the wall) and slightly projecting testers were much in vogue at this period. Lace often added a pretty finish to altar cloths

all over England, but there was not an equal demand for thuribles. Since the burning of incense was first revived at S. Mary Magdalene's, Munster Square, at Easter 1859, about thirty churches in the Diocese of London had followed the example. Thuribles were not in use in more than half a dozen London churches south of the Thames. In the strongly Protestant Diocese of Liverpool only one church burned incense; and only one in the Diocese of Manchester, although in the Diocese of

289

T

Birmingham there were four. Every church that claimed to be Anglo-Catholic had a set of Stations of the Cross around its walls.

The witnesses reported a number of altars with tabernacles, but they were not certain if they were actually used for reservation. Probably many so-called tabernacles were merely the fashionable ornamented box structure on which rested the altar cross. Only two churches in the Diocese of London in 1906 had 'public reservation'—S. Columba's, Haggerston, and S. Cuthbert's, Philbeach Gardens. In the Diocese of Rochester there were two churches where reservation was 'probable,' but not certain. Little demand was evinced by Anglican clergymen for tabernacle safes. It was rare to come across a chancel with an aumbry in the north wall; still less a real tabernacle in use, either on the high altar or in a side chapel.

A single joiner, employed by the Provinces of Canterbury and York, could not have earned his living by making confessional boxes sixty years ago. In the very few Anglican churches where confessions were heard openly, a curtain usually divided the priest from the penitent, and in some places even that was regarded as too risky. A chair and a prie-dieu had to suffice. Statues were a different matter, and judging from the 1906 *Report* quite a number of churches had images of our Lady, but few of any other saints. Most of these statues were bought at Roman Catholic shops, at home and abroad, but Mowbray and Co., as well as one or two other Anglican firms kept a stock—plain or coloured—from which customers could choose what they fancied. To find a statue carved by a real craftsman was a rare event. It seldom occurred to any cleryman to commission a professional artist to paint an altar-piece or a picture to adorn a church.

Very few such Anglo-Catholic churches existed in the Edwardian era. There were many large towns where they did not exist. More common were the strongholds of militant Protestantism, in which the furnishings and decorations created a very different atmosphere from those lonely outposts of extreme Anglo-Catholicism. It was common to find the pews of these Evangelical interiors provided with iron or brass umbrella holders, with a white enamelled dish at the bottom (vaguely suggestive of spittoons, in the choir stalls of many an Italian church) to catch the drips. These umbrella holders and drip-catchers were screwed on to the sides of the pews, and created quite a decorative effect looking up the centre aisle, which, very frequently, was carpeted with brown coconut matting. Choir stalls in the chancel were often occupied on Sundays by female choristers as well as men and boys. The old idea that it was 'Romish' to wear a surplice in the pulpit had almost been forgotten. By the first decade of the century the clergy of Evangelical churches had abandoned their black Geneva gowns, though they went in for black scarves or stoles instead of coloured ones. Texts in large Gothic lettering were a popular form of decoration, and were painted around the walls, arches and cornices.

The communion table—never referred to as the altar—was a real oak table, either left bare or vested in a stiff frontal of crimson cloth, sometimes embroidered with lilies or passion flowers, but seldom with a cross. At either end were two large hassocks or specially designed kneelers, because standing or kneeling in front of the communion table was regarded as the first step towards Ritualism and Rome; just as were brass flower vases placed on or above the table. The only ornament permitted was a much more liturgical brass alms dish, which rested against the reredos, if there was one. The latter generally took the form of Gothic arches, with the Commandments, Lord's Prayer and the Creed painted in the

The 'North End' continued to be perpetrated in a limited number of Anglican Communion tables, in spite of the 'Catholic Movement'

panels. A white linen cloth was spread over the table only when the Communion was to be administered, very much as is the custom in the Good Friday liturgy in the Roman rite. Little did these Evangelical clergymen suspect that, half a century later, the 'Romans' would be adopting many of the ceremonial details which they regarded as the hall-mark of Protestantism, including 'evening communion services' and altars stripped of everything when not actually in use. Stained glass, often a combination of pink, pale maroon, buff and greeny-blue, went with such churches, but windows with figures that did not encourage mariolatry or the superstitious veneration of saints were admitted.

A minor accessory that began to add a note of colour to the pews or chairs of most Anglo-Catholic churches after 1906 was the bright green-bound *English Hymnal,* but in Evanglical interiors it was still the more sombre coloured *Hymnal Companion* that lay about with the Bibles and Prayer Books. Elsewhere one noticed

S. ANNE'S CATHEDRAL, LEEDS (J. H. Eastwood, 1902). *Art nouveau* Gothic

the dark-blue covered *Hymns Ancient and Modern,* which for many years remained part of the *décor* in 'moderate' churches.

Looking back half a century it has to be admitted that most church furnishings of the Edwardian era were as unexciting as the majority of domestic furnishings and decorations. The quality of craftsmanship was sound enough, but the designs tend to be dull and repetitive. Ecclesiastical circles hardly noticed the *Art Nouveau* movement, which caused such a sensation in the Paris Exhibition of 1900.

Still examples of what were then regarded as eccentricities can be found here and there. One of the earliest is S. John's Roman Catholic Church, Portobello, Edinburgh, designed by J. T. Walford in 1896. Here the influence of Glasgow fashions evolved by Charles Rennie Mackintosh (1868–1928), as well as those of French and Belgian 'modernists' can be detected in the fittings and decorations. '*Art Nouveau* Gothic Revival' also found expression in J. H. Eastwood's Catholic Cathedral of S. Anne, Leeds (1902). Its furnishings are all original in style and detail, even if they have a vague flavour of John Dando Sedding and his partner, Henry Wilson. This Cathedral is a remarkable Edwardian period piece.

Far more startling to contemporary ideas was S. Mary the Virgin, Great Warley, Essex, designed by Harrison Townsend in 1904. Its furnishings are as bizarre as the building itself, which is reminiscent of the same architect's Whitechapel Art Gallery (1899) and the Horniman Museum, Forest Hill (1902) The panelled walls feature lilies in their design. What Mr. Goodhart-Rendel calls 'stylisation florale' was one of the characteristics of the *Art Nouveau* protagonists.

So the chancel screen displays a luxuriant growth of rose trees, with angels and birds nestling beneath the branches. The screen and two standing bronze angels were carried out by Sir William Reynolds Stephens also the pulpit and reading desk. The stained glass in the three-light east window was designed by Heywood Sumner. The carved reredos, electric light fittings and choir stalls were inspired by Harrison Townsend. When they were inserted half a century ago they were the *dernier cri* of the *avant garde*.

Harrison Townsend's little church of S. Martin, Wonersh, Surrey, is of rather later date, and is not so startling as S. Mary's, Great Warley. The chancel screen shows Jacobean influence. The upper part is gilded, and the lower part painted dark green. Mrs. Lea-Merritt painted the frescoes. The walls are lined with bands of light and dark alabaster, conveying the impression of a *de luxe* bathroom. The iron work, painted reredos and other furnishings are all *art nouveau* in style.

We find the 'Simple Life' school style, derived from William Morris, and developed by the Art Workers' Guild, in Kempley Church, Gloucestershire, designed by A. Randall Wells about the same time. Here was one of the few attempts to encourage rural craftsmanship. All the work was carried out without a contractor, the labour being mainly local. Ernest Gimson, whose hand-made furniture was soon bought up by the intelligentsia, made the candelabra and a pair of iron candlesticks. All the woodwork was made by local joiners. The village painters decorated the chancel beam in Chinese vermilion, ruby madder, golden ochre, chrome green, permanent blue and indigo. The figures of the rood beam were carved by David Gibb, the only ships' figurehead carver left in London. But the Bishop of Gloucester maintained that these 'idols' might lead to superstitious abuses and ordered their removal, with the tester over the altar. He allowed Ernest Barnsley's oak lectern to remain.

A more sophisticated 'art and crafty' church is S. Christopher's, Haslemere, Surrey, designed by Charles Spooner, who had individual craftsmen to do the furnishings. The oak altar, carved by Romney Green, was provided with riddel curtains of red silk damask, lined with copper coloured silk. These were hand-woven by Luther Hooper. The wall hangings were woven by William Morris and Co. Mrs. Spooner did some paintings on the reredos. The candlesticks, and the pulpit (English oak, steel and leather) all express the spirit of plain living and high thinking. They evoke memories of illustrations in the olive green covered issues of *The Studio* during the first decade of this century.

Something of the same atmosphere can be found in Arthur Bartlett's church at Dodford, Worcestershire. Here the rood-beam cross was made by Amy Walford in metal and enamels. The beam itself was of silver hardwood, with emblems of gilded lime tree. There were modelled plaster panels in the soffits of the arches representing the produce of the district. Most of the parishioners earned their living by market gardening. William Lethaby's All Saints', Brockhampton, Herefordshire (1902) is another Edwardian church in which the 'Simple Life Movement' was expressed in its 'arty crafty' furnishings.

S. Andrew's, Roker, Co. Durham, designed by E. S. Prior in 1906, also belongs to the 'Simple Life' school of English architecture, of which Charles A. Voysey (1857–1941) was the chief exponent. Dr. Pevsner observes: 'the building is a model of how personality can be combined with just enough adherence to tradition to make it acceptable for a church.' [1]

The furnishings are all original. The font was carved by Randall Wells; the altar, processional cross and lectern were made by Ernest Gimson; and the dedication stones carved by Eric Gill. The reredos above the high altar is a Morris and Co. tapestry designed by Burne-Jones. The chancel carpet was also supplied by Morris. The stained glass in the neo-Perpendicular east window came from the studio of H. A. Payne at Birmingham. Here at Roker is a splendid church with fittings and ornaments which are a lasting memorial to the Arts and Crafts movement.

Another church deserves mention as displaying a similar quality to that of S. Andrew, Roker—Goathland, Yorkshire. It was designed by W. H. Brierley, and is natural and unassuming, so much a part of the country-side, that questions of traditionalism and modernity do not arise.

As the reign of Edward VII passed by, dress became more and more luxurious, as did the interiors of fashionable houses. By 1907 lustrous satins consorted with shimmering brocades and soft velvets. An effect of general fluffiness was achieved by lace trimmed sleeves, collars, bodices and petticoats, offset by extremely tight corsets. Neither can we forget the frilly parasols, feather boas, long gloves and, above all, the veils with which all respectable ladies still hid their faces out of doors.

---

[1] *County Durham* (The Buildings of England: Penguin Books, 1953), p. 197.

One of the best specimens of church furnishing at this time is the interdenominational Christ Church, Port Sunlight, Cheshire, erected at fabulous cost by Lever Brothers Ltd., and designed by William and Segar Owen in a late Perpendicular style. The overpowering richness of the machine-made furnishings have to be seen to be believed. The profits derived from soap have their lasting memorial in the organ case, choir stalls, communion table, reredos, pulpit, reading desk, Sicilian marble paving and stained glass. They represent Edwardian opulence to perfection. Perhaps Lever Bros. Ltd. tried to put the Church of England in its place by showing what nonconformists could do if they had the money!

Different again is the triptych reredos which E. P. Warren got Anning Bell and Dacres Adam to design, carve and paint for his church of S. Peter, Lowestoft, which is very arty-crafty. There is another triptych reredos above the altar of Walter Tapper's little church of the Ascension, Malvern Link, Worcestershire, of about the same date. This was painted by Sister Catherine Ruth of the All Saints' Community. The figures on the rood-beam came from Ober-Ammergau. The black and white marble paving, with the grey marble font and its copper cover, create a very chaste effect. The highly decorative sanctuary lamps, and the wrought iron chancel screen with its six carved angels, are a throw back to the world of the Gothic Revival.

S. Jude's, Hampstead Garden Suburb, designed by Lutyens, and opened in 1910, is a magnificent Edwardian period piece; the spiritual centre of this fifty year old experiment in the breaking down of class distinctions by new housing schemes. The tunnel-like domed interior contains a wonderful collection of gay furnishings, the wilful naughtiness of which was quite in keeping with the emancipated outlook of the people who lived in the hand-made red brick houses designed by Raymond Unwin, Baillie Scott, Guy Dawber, Morley Horder, Geoffrey Lucas and Crickmer—all of whom were then regarded as the last word of fashion. Gorgeous is the best word to use for the painted ornaments and decorations; which, for the most part, recall the favourite reds, greens and orange used by Sir Frank Brangwyn.

Architects in the first decade of this century who were tired of Gothic Revival, sometimes designed churches which looked curiously alien to their surroundings. E. S. Prior and Arthur Grove decided that an Early Christian basilica, adorned with Byzantine trimmings, would go well with the red brick villas set in the pine woods of Parkstone, Dorset. Within the apsidal sanctuary of S. Osmund's, they erected a ciborium, inspired by that of San Clemente in Rome.

Giles Gilbert Scott tried hard to break away from stylism in 1906 when he designed the Roman Catholic Church of the Annunciation, Bournemouth, with its curved steps leading up to the sanctuary, placed under the tower, and the bare painted altar, with its long-shaped tabernacle set into a low gradine, backed by a tall dossal. But this young architect had been drawn back into Gothic Revivalism with Liverpool Cathedral. Its Lady Chapel, the first portion to be built, was opened in June 1910. The great triptych reredos above the long communion table, the richly carved stalls and other woodwork and the marble paving, carry on the Bodley tradition. A similar flamboyant treatment of Gothic is to be found in his Catholic church of S. Joseph, Sheringham (1908), where the lofty painted reredos and hanging rood deserve mention.

'Restful and refined' is the best description of the furnishings in all Temple Moore's churches erected in the first decade of this century.[2] He carried on where Bodley left off. We find much the same feeling in W. E. Tower's reredos and rood screen at the Convent of the Holy Cross, Haywards Heath, Sussex (1902). The urge to copy late medieval models is apparent in Edmund Sedding's rood screen at S. Crantock, Cornwall, and in Hastwell Grayson's chancel screen in Tranmere Church, Cheshire.

By contrast there are the traditional Renaissance furnishings of Beresford Pite's new chancel at Clapham Parish Church, and Mervyn Macartney's rich reredos in the Chapel of SS. Michael and George in S. Paul's Cathedral. John Belcher designed the right period furnishings for his new Church of Holy Trinity, Kingsway.

'Dull' is the only word for Sir Aston Webb's fittings in the chapel of the Royal Naval College at Dartmouth. The same has to be said of the stuff inserted in Sir Thomas Jackson's neo-Byzantine-English Perpendicular chapel at Giggleswick School, Yorkshire; and those designed by Briggs and Partners for the Bluecoat Hospital chapel, Liverpool.

'Edwardian Evangelicanism' found expression in Godfrey Pinkerton's communion table and neo-Jacobean reredos in S. Mary's, Summerstown, London. Here the architect had to plan for the 'North End' being observed. No cross was permitted, and the panels of the reredos contain the Ten Commandments, and the Creed. A low gradine was allowed for two brass flower-vases.

A curious treatment of the east end of a chancel was that made by A. Winter Rose at Bramfield, Suffolk. Here a small communion table was dwarfed by ornate stone carving, with large statues of saints on either side of it.

There were many churches built between 1900 and 1910 but few stand out in retrospect. Both Roman Catholic and Anglican places of worship display the same refined mediocrity. They probably expressed the average outlook of the people who frequented the churches. Their interest therefore is more social than æsthetic. Wood, iron, brass, stone, marble and stained glass immortalize a particular epoch, to-day almost forgotten.

Of the Roman Catholic churches of the period, Classic furnishings are to be found in those designed by J. Kelly, e.g. S. Patrick, Soho Square, W.1; Our Lady of Grace, Chiswick (1904); S. Vincent de Paul, Clapham; and S. Saviour, Lewisham (1909). Then there was F. W. Tasker who, since he designed S. Patrick's, Wapping, in 1879, leaned more towards Italian Renaissance than Gothic. Between 1900 and 1910 he was responsible for several London churches, most of which have seventeenth or eighteenth century period furnishings. So also has F. W. Walter's

---

[2] e.g. All Saints', Tooting Graveney (1905); S. Luke's, Eltham (1906); S. Cuthbert, Middlesbrough (1901); S. Margaret, Leeds (1910).

church of SS. Anselm and Cecilia, Kingsway (1909). Mention should be made of the new Oratory Church at Edgbaston, Birmingham, which contains some ornate furnishings by E. Doran Webb (1909). Similar in style are the altars in S. Aloysius, Garnethill, Glasgow, designed by Charles J. Ménart in 1910.

By way of contrast are the Gothic Revival churches put up by the firm of Pugin and Pugin, which have been described already. About eight of them belong to the first decade of this century.

When Fr. Benedict Williamson started to design altars and baldachins based on the architectural forms of ancient Egypt, most Catholics supposed that this was quite original. Actually this priest architect was inspired directly by the theories of the Benedictine monks of Beuron in Germany, where in the eighteen-seventies [3] an art school had been established. Some of Fr. Williamson's neo-Egyptian furnishings are very bold and effective, e.g. those in S. Ignatius, Stamford Hill (1904); the Lithuanian Church, Hackney Road (1901) and S. Boniface, Tooting (1907). When he reverted to Gothic Revival, as at Slough (1904), or Southwold, Suffolk (1916), he became commonplace.

The furnishings designed by Sir Robert Lorimer for his church of S. Peter, Morningside, Edinburgh, begun in 1906 were very different. Here he supplied an original Baroque marble high altar, with a permanent exposition throne standing on top of a very high gradine. Above it was a painting by Frank Brangwyn. The two side altars were given large framed paintings as reredoses, that of the Sacred Heart by Drummond Young. The Stations of the Cross were specially painted by John Duncan. Much stained glass was done by Maurice Meredith Williams. S. Peter's soon became the most 'modern' and 'artistic' Catholic church in Scotland.[4]

An unusual note of austerity marked the few furnishings of the great red brick church at Quarr Abbey in the Isle of Wight, erected in 1911, and designed by Dom Paul Bellot, O.S.B. Some people felt that it looked more Protestant than Roman.

None of these churches was typical of the normal expression of Roman Catholic worship in Britain, except those designed by Pugin and Pugin. Each in its own way was an attempt to raise the level of ecclesiastical taste. The average church, so far as its furnishings and decorations were concerned, seldom revealed the austerity and simplicity of the early Latin rite, but rather a somewhat debased form of it which resulted from centuries of persecution, particularly in Ireland, from which country the majority of the worshippers or their immediate ancestors belonged. Neither priests nor people saw anything incongruous or undevotional in the brightly coloured plaster statues, or the fussy and over decorated altars with their dominating reredoses. The church interiors were a re-creation of the average domestic background, with Gothic detail to give the necessary symbolism. To persons of refined taste, including the better educated converts from Anglicanism, assisting at Mass or Benediction was more of a penance than anything else. Most of the furnishings were supplied by 'Catholic Repositories,' and these commercial firms set the standard of taste. They knew from long experience what the greater

[3] See p. 257.   [4] See p. 302.

number of their clients demanded. The average Roman Catholic church interior at this period retained the bright, cheerful amosphere of an old-fashioned 'pub,' with the same well polished brass work and general cosiness. Anglican worshippers

BUCKFAST ABBEY—THE LADY CHAPEL (F. A. Walters, 1922)
A late survival of traditional Gothic Revival *décor*

disdained 'pubs,' but quite a number of Anglican church interiors suggest the dignified respectability of a London club.

These Edwardian church interiors must be thought of in relation to vintage motor cars, suffragettes, vegetarians, bridge-parties, the 'Simple Life Movement,' the bare-foot dancing of Maude Allan on the one hand, and 'Rag Time' and the

'Cake Walk' on the other. They belong to the same period as 'Peter Pan' and the craze for the poems of Ella Wheeler Wilcox and Omar Khayyam. Many of the upper classes were deserting their churches, having found Christian Science, 'New Thought,' or Theosophy more soul-satisfying. Church-going ladies wore large hats, adorned with artificial flowers and feathers, perched on top of piled up sumptuous chevelures, and projecting well forward over the face. In summer the sleeves of their silk dresses resembled those of an Anglican bishop's rochet. Draped over their shoulders were feather boas or fur stoles or capes. The necks of the more fashionable male worshippers were encased in high starched collars that stuck into their necks.

In the last year of the reign of Edward VII, a liturgical congress took place, with the encouragement of Cardinal Mercier, at Louvain. This witnessed the birth of the modern 'Liturgical Movement,' whose founder was Dom Lambert Beaudouin, a monk of the Abbey of Mont-César, Louvain. In 1907, three years earlier, Camon Callewaert had formed a liturgical study circle for priests at Bruges. The publication in Belgium of such magazines as *La vie liturgique, Questions liturgiques, L'Artisan Liturgique* and *Liturgische Tijdshrift*—all edited by Benedictine monks—did much to bring about a change in church furnishings and decorations as well as helping to popularize corporate worship. The movement spread to Austria, Germany, France and Holland, and thence to the United States of America, where it was taken up especially by the Benedictines of S. John's Abbey, Collegeville, Minnesota; resulting much later in the publication of the magazine *Orate Fratres,* the title of which in recent years was changed to *Worship.* With Dom Gasper Lefevbre as its leader, the Belgian liturgical movement gained impetus from the Abbey of Saint-André, near Bruges, after the publication of the *Missel quotidien,* since translated into many languages. So far as Great Britain was concerned the progress of the Liturgical Movement was slow.

The sunset phase of Gothic Revival church furnishings cannot be appreciated without a study of North American products, where the *décor* of churches became even more highly stylized than in Britain and on the continent.[5] All religious denominations in North America have in common the fact that they are immigrant bodies, and consequently lack indigenous appreciation of art. Until recently American church furnishings, as well as church architecture were all inspired by memories of buildings in Europe. The vision was a watered down evocation of the past. It was inevitable that Protestant Episcopal Churches in the United States harked back to Britain, and in particular to medieval England.

The firm of Cram, Goodhue and Ferguson designed many costly buildings, mostly for Episcopalians. Ralph Adams Cram possessed an encyclopedic knowledge of medieval architecture, and believed that by reproducing its details and methods

---

[5] Cf. Ralph Adams Cram, *American Churches,* 2 vols., New York, 1915. This monumental work conveys a comprehensive idea of church architecture and furnishings in the United States during the first decade of the present century. It is profusely illustrated.

of construction he was helping his fellow countrymen to appreciate Anglo-Catholic modes of worship. He and his partners also created some splendid Baptist, Presbyterian, Congregationalist and even Unitarian churches which—apart from their furnishings—suggested that they had been planned for the celebration of Mass in its most ornate medieval manner.

Perhaps the most characteristic and certainly the most extravagantly expensive Episcopal church designed by the firm, is S. Thomas's, New York. No other late Gothic Revival church in Europe can rival its *décor*. The font-cover evokes many Bodley designs; the elaborate carvings on the lectern, parclose screens and choir stalls testify to Cram's knowledge of medieval Gothic and his uncanny gift of imitation. Few modern sacristies can boast of such magnificent furniture. The organ screens are a riot of flamboyant Gothic carving. Goodhue was a genius at making drawings of the firm's designs, and his exquisite water-colour of the chancel of S. Thomas's, showing the sunlight casting its rays through stained glass on to the towering reredos, is in itself a vision of the medieval masterpiece which these architects wanted to create in the heart of Manhattan. They aimed to give New York a bigger, costlier reredos than anything to be seen in pre-Reformation English cathedrals.

An equally striking recreation of the Middle Ages in modern America is the Chapel of the Intercession, New York. Here again the influence of Bodley and Garner on Cram, Goodhue and Ferguson is paramount. Thousands of dollars must have been spent on the screens, vast organ case, choir stalls, pulpit, lectern, sedilia and piscina, which display an orgy of late Gothic carving. The high altar has ornate riddel posts and a baldachin. The Lady Chapel contains a richly carved and painted reredos, designed by Bertram G. Goodhue.

Calvary Church, Pittsburgh, is another mock medieval monument by this same firm—a pathetic attempt to reproduce the glories of medieval Europe in twentieth century Pennsylvania. But the seventeen statues of the great reredos above the stone high altar, the rood screen without a rood, and the other costly furnishings belong inseparably to their period and setting. The Chapel of West Point Military Academy, which from the architectural point of view is probably the most striking of all the works of Cram, Goodhue and Ferguson, is another case in point. The two massive and richly carved seven-light candlesticks on either side of the communion table, as well as the dim and mysterious crypt chapel, are nothing except unreal, and it must be confessed, unfunctional Protestant late Gothic Revival dreams, materialized regardless of cost.

The lighting fixtures are often quite original in an *art nouveau* style. These were generally designed by Goodhue, whose style was derived from Henry Wilson and the Arts and Crafts pioneers in England. Otherwise the furnishings left us by this firm are even more incongruous than the costumes worn by the female worshippers. Did the clients or the architects insist on the invariable carved wooden or stone reredos of late English Gothic flavour, with many small statues of saints? They are the focal point of most Cram, Goodhue and Ferguson churches, including the Episcopal cathedrals at Detroit and Halifax, Nova Scotia. Gothic Revival in all its lushness is provided in the choir-stalls, bishop's throne and other furnishings at Detroit. The crucifix and figures of our Lady and S. John on the Halifax rood-screen, very richly carved, are made as inconspicuous as possible for fear of Protestant prejudices.

Among the smaller churches designed by these partners are: All Saints', Dorchester, Mass.; S. Mark, Mount Kisco, New York; S. Luke, New York; and S. Andrew's Chapel, Chicago. They supplied a Spanish Baroque reredos for the Episcopal Cathedral at Havana. Their lesser furnishings and ornaments display a masterly knowledge of Gothic detail, e.g. altar crosses, candlesticks, chalices, alms-basins and boxes, door handles and hinges, locks and keys. Symbolism runs riot with carved or wrought bulls, dragons, lions, panthers, peacocks, pelicans and many other decorative beasts and birds

Henry Vaughan was another American architect who was trying to 'Catholicize' Protestant Episcopalians by offering them mock medieval Gothic furnishings in the Bodley and Garner tradition. Characteristic examples of his choir-stalls, lecterns and lofty reredoses can be found in the chapels of Groton School and S. Paul's School, Concord. There is a rich Puginesque rood screen without a rood in Christ Church, New Haven, Conn. The chapel of the Western Reserve University at Cleveland, Ohio, reveals how far Vaughan had to adapt medieval models to Protestant forms of worship. An even more interesting instance of the adaptation of the styles of the later Middle Ages to the mentality of early twentieth century American Protestantism is in the chapel of the Union Theological Seminary, New York; the work of Allen and Collins. These partners coped more successfully with the same problem in the Skinner Memorial Chapel, Holyoke, Mass.

Watson and Huckel were other architects who designed richly furnished Episcopalian churches, usually in Perpendicular Gothic. S. Mark's, Frankford, Philadelphia, displays an ornate stone pulpit, bishop's throne, high altar, and rood screen—all somewhat cold and lifeless.

Carved stone furnishings of great elaboration are also the chief feature of Christ Church, Norfolk, Virginia, where a rood beam, lacking a figure on the cross, is provided. Charles C. Haight tried to revive Perpendicular Gothic. His furnishings in S. Ignatius', New York, with its carved stone high altar, reredos, and rood beam cannot be described as either original or inspiring.

Even if many of them are crude and garish in their furnishings, the Roman Catholic churches erected during this same period often possess a bold vigour which is lacking in many Episcopalian places of worship. Maginnis, Walsh and Sullivan designed several neo-Byzantine or Renaissance churches in which the altars have a dramatic quality. Typical furnishings by these partners can be studied in Our Lady of the Presentation, Brighton, Mass.; S. Vincent, South Boston, Mass.; S. Joseph, Dayton, Ohio; and S. John, North Cambridge, Mass.

John W. Donohoe was another Catholic architect most of whose furnishings and ornaments were inspired by Byzantine or Romanesque originals. Good examples of them are to be found in S. John Cantius, Northampton, Mass.; Our Lady of

Mount Carmel, Springfield, Mass.; and the Immaculate Conception, West Springfield, Mass.

But by and large a preoccupation with the inessentials of Gothic furnishings, lack of imagination and an excessive facility at *pastiche* vitiate the work of Transatlantic ecclesiastical furnishings in this period.

Many of the churches mentioned in this chapter, besides those erected during the eighteen-nineties, have now been purged of their period furnishings. The reason usually given by those responsible is that one must keep moving with the Liturgical Movement, though what it often amounts to in the long run is an urge to 'keep up with the Joneses.' At S. Peter's, Morningside, Edinburgh (see page 297), Sir Robert Lorimer's Baroque reredos, exposition throne, and six candlesticks (in the same style) were cast out, also other structural elements in the architectural composition. The large painting by Sir Frank Brangwyn which served as the altar-piece was taken down, and at the time of writing its fate hangs in the balance. Something had to be done to fill up the blank space left, so the hanging rood was fixed to the wall. No longer is the high altar vested with frontals, but left nude, so that it is hardly visible from the body of the church, its green marble being the same colour as that of the lower walls of the apse. There are rumours that John Duncan's Stations of the Cross are soon to share the same fate as the above mentioned furnishings, even if he was quite a distinguished member of the Royal Academy.

Unfortunately no Roman Catholic dioceses in Britain have councils for the preservation of churches and their furnishings. The result is that priests are able to do pretty much what they like, granted that their bishops raise no serious objections.

CHAPTER XXIX

THE ALCUIN CLUB, PERCY DEARMER AND 'THE PARSON'S HANDBOOK'

B Y the end of the last century the furnishings and decorations of Anglo-Catholic churches were in a chaotic state. Most architects of the later Gothic Revival had either depended on their imagination, or had sought inspiration from contemporary continental sources, whether or not they were suitable for adaptation to the worship of the Book of Common Prayer. Few clergymen could claim much knowledge of liturgy. The majority had forgotten the principles laid down by the Cambridge Camden Society in the eighteen-forties, or if they remembered them vaguely, felt they were hopelessly out of date. Tractarian fashions were as outmoded as the crinolines with which they were contemporary. The ecclesiastical modes of the eighteen-nineties were as fussy and restless as the fashions favoured by smart women. Anglo-Catholic churches in particular were cluttered up with as many ornaments and knick-knacks as an average drawing-room. The majority of churches in communion with Rome were even more overcrowded, because statues and images were continually added in the hope of encouraging piety. No priest needed permission to change the furnishings of his church, as Anglicans did— although many of the latter risked prosecution for disobedience to this law.

Most Anglican clergymen tried zealously to obey the Rubrick of the *Book of Common Prayer* which reads: '*And here is to be noted, That such Ornaments of the Church, and of the Ministers thereof at all times of their Ministration, shall be retained, and be in use, as were in this Church of England, by the authority of Parliament, in the second year of the reign of King Edward the Sixth.*' The difficulty was, however, that nobody had any clear idea *what* 'ornaments of the Church' were in use in the second year of Edward VI, i.e. between January 28th, 1548 and January 27th, 1549. Everything depended on those decisive twelve months more than three hundred years ago.

After the publication of the first of the Alcuin Club Tracts in 1897 there was no further excuse for ignorance or for defying the authority of Parliament. That same year Mr. Comper brought out a learned but characteristically 'misty' pamphlet entitled *The Reasonableness of the Ornaments Rubric, illustrated by a Comparison of the German and English Altars,* but he was not really interested in Canon Law; the sources of beauty being his chief preoccupation. Very different in tone was

Mr. J. T. Micklethwaite's *The Ornaments of the Rubric.* This Gothic Revival architect was a stickler for the letter of the law. He managed to produce an astonishing collection of furnishings which appeared to be lawful, some of which his readers have never heard of. He explained that the often quoted rubric 'after standing neglected and almost forgotten for two hundred years, has in our time been brought very much into notice, and attempts to obey it have led to extravagances which are not only shocking to persons of refined taste, but sometimes not free from a tendency to suggest false teaching. The science of Ecclesiology, invented about half a century since, at a time of strong religious revival, soon attracted many enthusiastic disciples. But enthusiasm without study could not carry its subject very far. There have been a succession of real students from the beginning, but the sciolists have been the more numerous and perhaps the most aggressive, and when ecclesiological teaching became ecclesiastical practice the influence of the sciolists on its course was by far the greatest.

'The result has been the setting up of the standard called *correctness* which has ruled the planning and the ornaments of churches for many years. *Correctness* has no definite principle underlying it, and it takes little notice of the adaptation of the buildings or their furniture to the uses for which they are intended. Several elements have contributed to its making. Reading had a little to do with it, a superficial knowledge of our own ancient churches rather more, and hints taken from modern practice in foreign churches most of all. These have been combined and modified by a sort of timidity which attempting compromise has often achieved monstrosity.'

Mr. Micklethwaite, with the collaboration of the other members of the Committee of the Alcuin Club, drew up a list of ornaments which could be used without going beyond the Book of Common Prayer. He produced much documentary evidence proving that they were being used in the second year of the reign of Edward VI. His Tract was a masterpiece of historical erudition.

Images and pictures, for instance, could be used for the decoration of churches so long as they 'did not commemorate feigned miracles and were not abused by superstitious practices, but were "for a memorial only." '

He made it quite clear that churches in 1548–9 still retained side altars, which were in regular use, the English form of service being used instead of the Latin. It was quite easy to visualize the sort of altars that existed at the time, and which the rubric still required in the sixtieth year of Queen Victoria, although some of the other members of the Alcuin Club were doubtful if an 'altar shelf' or gradine was lawful, as Mr. Micklethwaite insisted was so. Whether it was advisable to revive the 'Elevation Curtain' was questionable, but 'curtains, riddels or costers' around altars were definitely desirable for strict conformity with the Prayer Book rubric.

Many loyal churchmen were greatly surprised to learn that it was lawful to have a hanging pyx as a method of reserving the consecrated elements. They were more astonished to read that in 1547 there were a few churches in England where there was a 'little coffer' on the high altar for reservation. This suggested that it was not illegal to instal the modern Roman form of tabernacle. As to altar candlesticks, the use of 1548-9 indicated that two lights on the high altar and one on each side altar should be the general rule, but that many more could be used on great festivals.

It is quite certain that in 1897 no Anglican churches possessed all the countless ornaments which Mr. Micklethwaite maintained were lawful, but his long list must have made ritualistic clergymen long for them—including a 'standing pyx,' a 'monstrance or coster,' 'houseling cloths,' 'skep for holy bread,' 'lenten veils,' 'fire-pans,' 'chafing balls,' a 'herse, harrow or Judas candlestick,' not to mention all sorts of accessories required for funerals, baptisms and weddings. All these came within the rubric in question. 'And so, let us use them, and not any novelties, English or foreign, instead of them'—such was the opinion of the learned author of Tract One of the Alcuin Club. He ended with the words: 'The substitution of foreign ornaments is mischievous from the countenance it gives to those who profess to see in the present revival within the Church of England only an imitation of the Church of Rome. And we do not want the things, our own are better.' [1]

What was needed was somebody to popularize these ecclesiological discoveries. The Alcuin Club publications reached only a very limited circle. The average Anglican parish priest had neither time nor inclination to read these precious-looking volumes, mostly printed on hand-made paper. Fortunately the right man turned up at the right moment. Percy Dearmer (1867–1936), having been ordained in 1891, was a curate at S. Mark's Marylebone Road, when Mr. Micklethwaite's *Tract* was published. It seems to have been the eclectic Anglo-Catholic ceremonial at this church which first aroused him to popularize the findings of the Alcuin Club. The first edition of his *Parson's Handbook* appeared in April 1899. A much revised and enlarged edition followed in February 1903, and a sixth edition of even greater bulk and with many more illustrations in 1907.

'The object of this Handbook,' so the Introduction announces, 'is to help, in however humble a way, towards remedying the lamentable confusion, lawlessness and vulgarity which are conspicuous in the Church at this time.' The confusion was due to the want of 'liturgical knowledge among the clergy, and of consistent example among those in authority.' Far more complex causes accounted for the lawlessness, which was 'even greater among those who are often called "moderate," and among those who dislike all ceremonial.' Dearmer was of the opinion that 'the vulgarity in the Church' was due to the alienation of 'those who earn their living by writing and the arts—perhaps the most influential classes in modern society.' Things were no better in France and Belgium. The majority of Anglican clergy had worked on purely commercial lines; 'they are mostly even now content with decoration that is the ridicule of competent artists, or is ignored by them as not being even amusing; and the Church has almost entirely failed to call to her

[1] p. 62. In 1901 Mr. Micklethwaite published a supplement to the third edition of his Tract. In it he made short work of his critics, maintaining that most of them were quite ignorant of the use of the second year of Edward VI.'

U

service the great artists and craftsmen of which the last generation produced so large a number. Her place as patroness of art has been taken by the merchants of Birmingham, Manchester and Liverpool.' Another class was the working class. 'For vulgarity in the long run always means cheapness, and cheapness means the tyranny of the sweater. A modern preacher often stands in a sweated pulpit, wearing a sweated surplice over a cassock that was not produced under fair conditions and, holding a sweated book in one hand, with the other he points to the machine-made cross at the jerry-built altar, and appeals to the sacred principles of mutual sacrifice and love.' Dearmer was convinced that this vulgarity was due as much to the same causes as the confusion and lawlessness—'a failure to recognize the principle of authority; and authority is as necessary in art as it is in religion. Every one does what is right in his own eyes, because we have refused to accept the first principles of the matter, the necessity of wholesome tradition on the one hand and of due deference to the artist's judgment on the other. We do not listen to the artist when he tells us about art, and we are surprised that he does not listen to us when we tell him about religion.'

In a long Introduction Dearmer set forth the doctrines of what was called 'Parson's Handbook' or 'British Museum religion.' He was convinced that the Church of England had its own mind about ritual and ceremonial. 'But whether the ceremonial used is little or much, the services of our Church should at least be conducted on the legitimate lines, if only that they may be freed from what is anomalous, irreverent, tawdry or grotesque.' The frontispiece of the 1907 edition was a pen and ink drawing by Geoffrey Lucas and A. Stratton, showing a chancel furnished with an 'English Altar' which might well have been designed by Ninian Comper. Strange to say, Dearmer never refers to Comper's diligent researches into the history and significance of medieval ceremonial. His two learned publications which had appeared in 1893 and 1897 are not included among the books quoted in *The Parson's Handbook,* the list of which takes up eight closely printed pages.

Anybody who has the time and the patience to wade through the three bulky 'blue books' containing the reports of the 1906 Royal Commission on Ecclesiastical Discipline will have a vivid and detailed picture of Anglican churches half a century ago. Most of the evidence deals with Anglo-Catholic churches in England; some of these witnesses seem to have had uncanny powers of observation, not matched unfortunately by their knowledge of ceremonial. Percy Dearmer was not far wrong about the 'lamentable confusion, lawlessness and vulgarity' which characterized the ceremonial of Anglo-Catholic places of worship in the first decade of this century. He launched a crusade which was to have far greater results than he himself dreamed of at the time. Comper might have become the leader instead of Dearmer, but he was too much of a recluse, and he had no gift for publicity.

Dearmer was justified in saying that the Church of England had neglected the great artists and craftsmen of the last generation. Very few such men were employed on the furnishing and decoration of churches, yet some of them were world famous.

Ernest Gimson was making domestic furniture, noted for its simplicity of form, soundness of construction and the perfect selection of woods. One can picture the sort of sanctuaries and side chapels which *might* have been designed by M. H. Baillie Scott or C. F. Annesley Voysey—chaste and simple. How gay and lively would have been a church furnished and decorated by H. Davis Richter, or other young men then regarded as 'modern.' Gilbert Bayes had, it is true, been commissioned to carve statues for a few churches; and R. Anning Bell designed some mosaics and stained glass in one or two places, but neither of them could have earned a living from ecclesiastical work alone. Walter Crane, the first President of the Arts and Crafts Society, had seldom been allowed to adorn churches with his plaster or gesso reliefs, stained glass, metal work, tiles, pottery and textiles. Alexander Gascoyne and Henry Holiday had been more fortunate. Frank Brangwyn could count two or three churches where his genius for interior decoration had been made use of. Then there was Heywood Sumner, whose only big chances had been at All Saints, Ennismore Gardens and S. Agatha's, Portsmouth (see p. 272). Edward Spencer's metal work had found a place in perhaps half a dozen churches in England, but it paid him better to design radiators for the *Mauretania*. Harold Stabler's metal work and jewelry found buyers all over the world, but neither Catholic nor Anglican priests were employing him to any extent. The same is true of the remarkable metal work of Alexander Fisher. Stained glass of a new and interesting style was being made by many young craftsmen, but most of it went into public buildings and houses, because it was not regarded as sufficiently ecclesiastical or devotional. So were the tapestries and embroideries of Mabel Nicholls, Anne Macbeth and Mrs. E. Reginald Frampton. Never had there been so many first class makers of furniture, interior decorators, sculptors, stone and wood carvers and metal workers working in England. The Church missed a great opportunity in not employing them.

It was in the last weeks of 1900 that Percy Dearmer accepted the living of S. Mary the Virgin, Primrose Hill, London. Now that he had a church of his own, he settled down to an application of the principals of the *Parsons' Handbook*. His red brick church had been built in 1873, and its architect, W. P. Manning, had adopted the popular style of Early French Gothic, with a stone vaulted apse. Within a few years Dearmer had transformed the interior. He began by lowering Bodley's gorgeous triptych reredos above the high altar; removing the gradines and the sham tabernacle in their midst. Harold Stabler supplied the designs for the iron posts between which were now hung riddel curtains and a dorsal. The altar stood out as it had never done before. People got a shock in March 1903 when they first saw the red brick walls and stone vaulting of the sanctuary and choir white-washed. Later on the nave and aisles were whitened. Thus was initiated the fashion for all-white interiors.[2] As time went on more additions were

[2] When Comper's church of S. Cyprian, Clarence Gate, was opened on June 30th that same year the effect of an all-white interior was even more striking, because colour and gilding were not added to the rood-screen until later. Dearmer never tried to emulate the somewhat pedantic anti-

S. MARY'S, PRIMROSE HILL, LONDON (The Lenten Array, 1908)
Typical 'English' altar. Frontal and curtains of brown holland;
the frontal ornamented with red linen *appliqué*. Cross veiled,
and doors of triptych-reredos closed

made to the furnishings. Three silver lamps of Venetian workmanship were
bought. Clement Skilbeck designed two tables of the Ten Commandments which
were placed each side of the chancel arch.

Finally, about 1914, a rood beam was placed across the chancel arch, with the
figures carved by Gilbert Bayes. A wooden corona-lucis—always referred to as
a 'trundle'—designed by Randall Wells, was hung from the rood. The pulpit and

quarianism of the ceremonial favoured in this exquisite church, where the floor was strewn with
flowers and rushes in the medieval manner at the consecration ceremony; the form of service used
following the ancient Pontifical of Egbert as closely as possible.

choir-stalls were adorned with shields painted by the Revd. E. E. Dorling. Dearmer intensely disliked realistic crucifixes. All those in S. Mary's had figures of a vested and crowned Christ.

This transformed interior of S. Mary's, Primrose Hill, may not suggest anything very extraordinary to people to-day, but fifty years ago it was unique in Britain. This was not so much on account of the furnishings as of the way the services were conducted. Here, for the first time, people carried out the *Book of Common Prayer* to the letter, with most elaborate ceremonial which, as Percy Dearmer could prove, was neither illegal nor contrary to episcopal or Privy Council legislation. On Sundays the church was crowded, the congregation drawn from all parts of London. Incense was used generously, but non-ceremonially. During the week the stale fumes of gum olibanum hung around the interior. The vestments worn were full and ample. Percy Dearmer started the fashion of tacking coloured 'apparels' on to albs and amices, so that eventually they were worn in Anglican cathedrals as well as parish churches.

He had not only created a perfect background for the externals of worship by whitewashing the interior of S. Mary's, and calling in the best craftsmen of the day to design the ornaments, but he insisted on good music. The congregation soon grew to love plainchant, and after 1906 they were introduced to the newly published *English Hymnal,* of which he was the chief editor. None of the more popular Victorian hymn-tunes were ever heard at S. Mary's. Dearmer insisted that 'you must give people what is good and they will come to like it.' The fact that the beauty of the setting, ceremonial and music filled the church to capacity at every service on Sundays proved him right.

Dearmer was not guided by personal fancies. The liturgical regime he initiated continued under the next three incumbents who, though very different personalities, altered almost nothing of the Dearmer tradition, a fact perhaps unparalleled in the London Anglo-Catholic churches.

The lead given in ecclesiastical circles by the Alcuin Club, and Percy Dearmer in particular, was followed in domestic furnishings and costume. The younger members of the Primrose Hill congregation were almost certain to be Christian Socialists, and possibly vegetarians. With this went an urge to live in Garden Cities, or quaint little houses of the 'Simple Life' style, designed by architects such as Annesley Voysey or M. H. Baillie Scott, with white rough-cast walls, low rooms, casements with leaded lights, rose pergolas and crazy pavements. If possible the furniture would be hand-made by Ernest Gimson or Ambrose Heal; the crockery 'leadless glaze.' Dearmer and his wife set the pace when they moved into their new vicarage in 1907. The drawing-room had a cream paper with nine tall rose trees blossoming on it. There were curtains of natural glazed holland, and rose-coloured chintzes, with a grass-green carpet. 'Beauty' was taken very seriously, and by it was meant something which harked back to the Pre-Raphaelite tradition, although with a faint whiff of Aubrey Beardsley's guttering black candles, and the distant rumblings of the revolt of women.

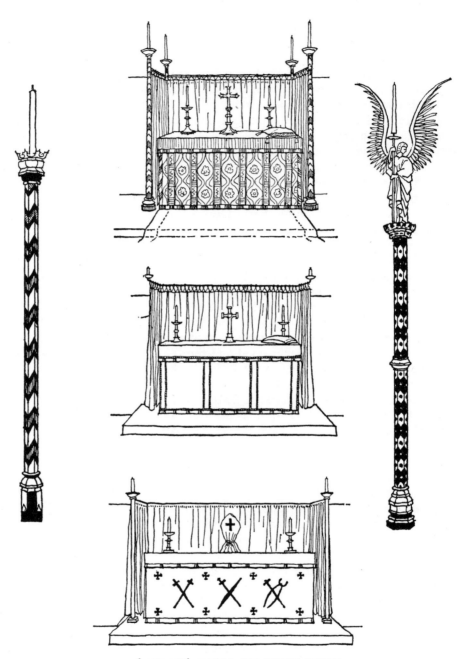

'ENGLISH' ALTARS AND RIDDEL POSTS

310

This revolutionary feeling could be detected in the clothes of the worshippers in churches which were refurnished according to the principles of *The Parson's Handbook.* In a church like S. Mary's, which attracted authors, artists and social reformers, some men defied Sunday conventions by wearing baggy suits of home-spun tweed, shirts with soft collars, and quite probably sandals instead of shoes or boots. Their women-folk tended to look like the models painted by Rossetti or Burne-Jones, and revolted against fashion by discarding corsets. Unlike the more fashionably dressed ladies with their trumpet-shaped skirts and sway-back carriage, they inclined to droop in a willowy manner, although some adopted a masculine costume, with a practical, though still long, serge skirt, starched blouse and high collar. The first decade of the twentieth century was full of contrasts in the costumes of church congregations. It was the end of an epoch, but the second spring was on the way.

By 1912 the Alcuin Club had published twenty volumes in its series of 'Collections,' and nearly a dozen 'Tracts.' All, either directly or indirectly, provided information on the arrangement of churches, their furniture and ornaments, in accordance with the rubrics of the Book of Common Prayer. Just what these rubrics were supposed to involve was shown clearly in the thirteen line drawings by Clement O. Skilbeck which appeared in *Illustrations to the Liturgy* (see p. 318). Percy Dearmer wrote the descriptive notes in a long Introduction. Every altar is provided with a dorsal and riddel curtains. Most of the chancels have screens. The clergy wear eucharistic vestments of the correct 1548 shape. The servers are vested in girded albs and amices, both adorned with apparels. The choir men and boys are clothed in the long surplices. The frontispiece shows the furnishings of the principal altar of S. John's, Newcastle-upon-Tyne, designed by Sir Charles Nicholson, Bart. Here can be seen the intention of the Alcuin Club to refurnish every Anglican place of worship on 1548 lines. No deviations from this line were permitted.

As Nan Dearmer says in her *Life* of husband, Percy's 'influence was immeasurable and the teaching of the *Parson's Handbook* and the example set at S. Mary's had wider results than he ever suspected. The outcome of what he did at Primrose Hill has had a great effect on churches and cathedrals as a whole. To take a few examples from externals. The "English Altar" in its various forms has been recovered as the normal thing. When Percy went to Primrose Hill it was rare indeed to see an altar without a gradine or vases of flowers or one with the lights placed directly upon it, and with a cushion for the book instead of a hideous and clumsy desk. All the essentials of the altar for which he worked are now the correct official practice in the Church of England. The restoration of the choir habit of the clergy, which had come down unbroken from early post-Reformation times to the Victorian era, was due to Percy. So was the use of the "Lenten Array," and the more graceful form of vestments.

'None-the-less the average Anglo-Catholic of to-day, asked how far Percy's work had influenced Ritualism in England, would probably say that any such influence was local and transitory, so that it is the more interesting to note that while the Anglo-Catholic party has rejected the results of liturgical scholarship in favour of copying Rome, the Roman Church itself (never wholly without it) now welcomes scholarship and is influenced by it. The wheel has come full circle and if Percy's work has been rejected by the official Anglo-Catholics because they tried to copy Rome, the Rome they tried to copy is now following, not Percy of course, but the very same liturgical principles for which he stood. His influence reached the "broad" churches and also some "low" churches, giving an added dignity to the service even in places where ceremonial of any kind would not be approved.' [3]

Percy Dearmer gave up his work at Primrose Hill in 1916, but not before he had ensured the spread of the *Parson's Handbook* principles in church furnishings. Shortly before he went to S. Mary's in 1901 he had launched the S. Dunstan's Society which made surplices, albs, hoods and vestments according to approved patterns. By 1912 he and his friends decided that something larger was needed. Many were members of the Alcuin Club, the object of which was to encourage the practical study of ceremonial, the arrangement of churches, their furniture and ornaments in accordance with the rubrics of the *Book of Common Prayer;* strict obedience to which was the guiding principle of the work of the club. A centre was now wanted in London where those interested in the 'English Use' could be shown the actual ornaments of the Church of England specified in the *Parson's Handbook,* and also to recommend artists and craftsmen who would carry out work in accordance with the English tradition.

So it was that the Warham Guild was established. From the first it had help from various liturgical and other experts, including the late Dr. F. E. Brightman, Dr. Hermitage Day, Dr. F. E. Lacey, the Revd. E. E. Dorling, Mr. Kruger Gray, Fr. Walter Frere, c.r., Dr. F. C. Eeles, and many others. These gave valuable advice with regard to the designs and shapes of various ornaments, and helped in other ways to ensure that the work of the Guild should be worthy of the best traditions of pre- and post-Reformation in England. They continued their influence and assistance until their death, and the last member of the original Advisory Committee, Dr. F. C. Eeles, died in 1954.

Many other artists and architects worked in connection with the Warham Guild. Among them have been F. E. Howard, Geoffrey Lucas, W. H. Randoll Blacking, Ellery Anderson, Martin Travers and Christopher Webb. Examples of their work, carried out in association with the Guild, can be found in cathedrals and churches all over England.[4]

[3] *The Life of Percy Dearmer* (1940), pp. 115–16.
[4] The following were some of the high lights of the Warham Guild's work previous to the Second World War: Capetown Cathedral (high altar and hanging rood); S. John's, Red Lion Square, London (high altar, side chapel and hanging pyx); Westminster Abbey (frontals, copes, etc.); Maidstone Parish Church, Kent (high altar); S. Gabriel's, Swansea (reredos, choir stalls, altar rail); Lahore Cathedral, India (reredos for chapel); S. Peter's, Streatham (pulpit); Jurby, Isle of Man (reredos and tester); Valetta (Anglican) Cathedral, Malta (side altar); Anglican Cathedral, Montreal (stone reredos); Merrow, Surrey (reredos); Princes Risborough, Bucks (high altar and Lady Chapel reredos); Wookey Hole, Somerset (entire sanctuary refurnished). Many churches in Britain and abroad contain stained glass supplied by the Guild.

The work of the Guild was at first confined to Britain, but gradually it spread overseas, where countless churches, both in the Commonwealth and the United States, have been equipped with every type of ornament covered by the Ornaments Rubric of the Prayer Book. In addition Percy Dearmer has left his mark upon almost every cathedral in England.

Soon after the first edition of the *Parson's Handbook* came Mowbray's *English Churchman's Kalendar,* which for the past half century has continued to popularize the type of furnishings and decorations advocated by Percy Dearmer and the Warham Guild by its illustrations of altars, pulpits, fonts, vestments and other ecclesiastical ornaments. From time to time the Guild produced booklets and leaflets, all well written and illustrated. A glance through the 1932 *Warham Guild Handbook,* which is almost a condensed and up-to-date version of Pugin's *Glossary,* helps us to see the sort of goods which were being designed and made a quarter of a century ago. The many photographs show rich frontals, altars with riddels and dossals, servers vested in apparelled albs or sleeveless rochets, clergymen in flowing surplices, chasubles and tunicles, embroidered banners, rood screens and rood beams, carved and gilded altar crosses and candlesticks, aumbries, fonts and lecterns, chalices and ciboria, censers, sanctuary lamps, double-pyxes and sick communion vessels, stained glass and much else. The Warham Guild believed in advertising, and catered for both rich and poor. A thirty-page *Economy Leaflet,* published about 1930, helped to dispel the belief that poverty involved tawdriness. Everything put on to the market by the Warham Guild has always been of the highest quality. Most of the goods sold have had a definite medieval flavour. Some critics might be tempted to describe them as 'sham antiques.' Very few of the furnishings have been influenced by contemporary movements in art. Since their functional purpose has been to go with the 'English Use,' perhaps it is well that they have always been so completely English in their inspiration. To the present generation their charm lies in the fact that they are invariably such perfect period pieces of ecclesiastical fashions which became the *dernier cri* about half a century ago. They represent the best ecclesiastical taste of the Edwardian and Georgian eras, which has managed to survive in Anglican circles until the present day.

Many years after Percy Dearmer had given up parish work, and held the post of Professor of Ecclesiastical Art and Lecturer in Art at King's College, London, he was still convinced that the 'English Altar' was the only type which was lawful in Anglican churches. But by the nineteen-twenties he maintained with even greater conviction that 'they are really Catholic altars—the type which, in more than one form, persisted from early times over the whole Church, and only succumbed two centuries after the Renaissance had begun, to the Baroque influence of the Counter-Reformation.' [5] That was the real difficulty—Dearmer had no use for Counter-Reformation Catholicity in either doctrine or worship. Fundamentally he was a Protestant, with a Lutheran temperament. His detestation of everything 'Romish' increased as he grew older.

On the other hand he was not far wrong in his belief that an 'English Altar is

[5] *Some English Altars* (Warham Guild Publications, No. 23).

equally admirable in a great cathedral or for places where an altar is temporarily set up.' 'It is also forced upon us,' he wrote wisely, '(unless we do violence to all architectural principles) by our old parish churches, just because they were built for [this type of altar], and their low east window requires a reredos not more than about three feet high.'

F. E. Howard's high altar and highly decorated reredos, riddel posts and angels, in S. Mary's, Atherstone, show how the five-light Perpendicular east window forms a perfect whole with the low structure beneath it. Again, how admirable is the effect of the side altar with its simple reredos in a decorated frame, with riddel rods, candle sconces and a frontal adorned with narrow orphreys in the Church of S. Peter-ad-Vincula, Coggeshall, Essex. For the rest, no matter where one finds these English altars, they tend to become monotonous : the same ingredients are used up again and again. In some places, e.g. at Southwell Minster, the dorsal and riddels are omitted, and it is quite a relief not to find them. The same fabrics, the same fringes, became almost an article of faith. They were safe—and could be used with impunity. Variety was achieved in Lent, when altars had to be vested with rough white linen, often appliquéd or stencilled with red crosses or other emblems, such being the medieval custom in England. Veils of the same material formed part of the 'Lenten Array' for crosses, pictures and images which are not of an architectural character.

Dearmer's greatest chance came when he supervised the transformation of the Eccleston Square Congregational Chapel into the Guildhouse. This interdenominational place of worship was opened in the late autumn of 1920, mainly because no Anglican bishop was prepared to allow Miss Maude Royden to preach in any parish church or cathedral. She records that while she 'was groaning over the ugliness of the building which was to become the Guildhouse, Percy was delighting in its goodness! He pointed out that it *was* good—honest and well-built, no sham Gothic, no shoddy work. The painting and "decoration," we agreed, were hideous. He applied his favourite remedy—whitewash—and the place was transformed. He gave us, on this background of white, brilliant colours. The great lanterns, the pulpit cushions, the stewards' blue cassocks, all were joyful and full of colour.' [6] The converted nonconformist meeting-house in Pimlico became almost as gay as the harem of Scheherazade as devised by Bakst in the Russian ballet produced by Diaghilev.

About six years later Dearmer had another opportunity to play about with colours. Canon Dwelly took his advice on the choristers' cassocks, vergers' gowns and various cloaks of many shades and hues worn on processional occasions in the Anglican cathedral at Liverpool. The colours were carefully chosen to go with the dull red sandstone interior of Sir Giles Gilbert Scott's building. Even the surplices were made of unbleached linen for the same reason.

Mr. D. L. Murray sees Dearmer as 'one of the finer representatives of that superb Victorian romanticism which believed that the Church could, if only loyal to its

[6] *Life of Percy Dearmer*, p. 242.

principles, effect the social regeneration of England and the banishment of Victorian stuffiness and ugliness from modern life—almost within a generation. . . . I should imagine there were no "Percy Dearmerites" when he died; he was the leader, I suppose, of no group, even the smallest; yet the Church (and the religious world outside it) may one day rediscover his books for the reconciling wisdom and the profound simplicity they contain.' [7] When he refurnished and redecorated a place of worship himself, the result was always about as perfect as it could be, but most of his disciples lacked this genius. Their imitations of the Master's work are often piteous to behold. D. L. Murray, who first became acquainted with S. Mary's, Primrose Hill, in 1905, maintains that Dearmer's 'passion for the beauty of medievalism stamped itself on his labour as a ritualist—I never knew him at all fair to the beauty of the *baroque*—but you could not make a universal connoisseur out of such a positive personality, and the point is that his minute ceremonial research was directed by a large vision, the holiness of beauty serving the beauty of holiness.' [8]

[7] ibid., pp. 269–70.
[8] ibid., p. 138.

CHAPTER XXX

BACK TO BAROQUE

THE SOCIETY OF SS. PETER AND PAUL

THE *Parson's Handbook* was regarded by extreme Anglo-Catholics as little short of heresy. By 1910 it was felt that something must be done about it. After all Edward VII was on the throne, not Edward VI. On the other hand, Gothic Revival was quite *demodé*. More progressive Anglo-Catholics were convinced that a well organized crusade should be instituted against the principles of the Alcuin Club. Ceremonial development would after all have taken place in the English Church as on the continent of Europe had it not been for the atrophying effect of Protestantism. On February 24th, 1911, a meeting of prominent Anglo-Catholics at the Medici Society in London decided to form a body to act as a counterblast to so-called 'British Museum Religion.' The name chosen was 'The Society of SS. Peter and Paul.' Mr. Samuel Gurney agreed to act as honorary secretary, and it was he, with the help of Maurice Child (then a curate at S. Andrew, Haverstock Hill), who started things off. Much assistance was given in the first years by Vincent Baker before he was reconciled with the Roman Church, and joined the London Oratory. Among prominent helpers were Ronald and Wilfrid Knox, N. P. Williams, Cyril Howell (the rector of S. Mary's, Graham Street), and the Duke of Argyll.

Looking back on the first years of the S.S.P.P. Mgr. Ronald Knox wrote that the founders did not intend it to be 'a return to the past, but as a resumption of arrested development.' In other words, the object of the Society was not to return to the pre-Reformation period, but to advance towards what the Church might have been if the Reformation, in its more destructive aspects, had never occurred.

The S.S.P.P. planned firstly to print and publish liturgical books of all kinds—missals, office and choir books, rituals containing the occasional offices. It was to be to the Catholic Revival in England what Pustet and Desclée had been on the Continent. All this would 'lead on, in God's good time, to Corporate Reunion with the Catholic Churches of Eastern and Western Christendom'—so stated an article in the June 1912 issue of *Pax,* the quarterly review of the then Anglican Benedictines of Caldey Island. Most of these young Anglo-Catholics agreed that Britons should become familiar with Benediction, the Rosary, and other popular devotions of the Latin rite. Since the Church of England was part of the Western Patriarchate, even if out of communion with the Holy See, ceremonial innovations ought to be based on the use of the present day Church of Rome rather than on archæological research and antiquarian fancies. The two Provinces of Canterbury and York must transform their ritual and ceremonial to that of the other Provinces of the Western Patriarchate. The Church of England was in a state of revolution, and

SOCIETY OF S·S· PETER & PAUL

The ideal aimed at was to transform the externals of Anglican worship into the closest possible resemblance of those of seventeenth and eighteenth century Continental Catholicism

Anglican worship must be brought into line with that of the Church of Rome. The ideal was to create an unEnglish and Continental atmosphere.

Advertisements inserted in *The Church Times* for a firm selling 'Lambeth Frankincense' or 'Ridley and Latimer Votive-Candle Stands' produced little results. Bishops, deans, canons and other dignitaries found 'Disculus' on the right way to celebrate Low Mass most provocative. Neither could they agree with what 'Anglicanus' wrote about some 'important liturgical questions.'

The S.S.P.P. soon found offices of its own, and to create the right period ethos a Baroque *décor* was insisted on. Objects of piety were scattered among the books and pamphlets. Geoffrey Heald, who was a curate at All Saints', Margaret Street, from 1916 to 1928 ransacked the back streets of Soho to find furniture of the Baroque or Rococo styles. Candlesticks, lamps and crucifixes were bought for a song and quickly sold at a profit. The firm of Louis Grossé was kept busy making cheap vestments of Italian, Spanish or French shape, which were the only types recognized by the Society. The Art and Book Company, with its shop opposite

'BACK TO BAROQUE' 'CORRECT' S.S.P.P. ALTAR
(*c.* 1920)

Westminster Cathedral, probably made more money by selling antique monstrances, thuribles, tabernacles, crucifixes, statues, chalices and fiddle-back vestments to Anglo-Catholic clergymen than to the clientele for which the company expected to cater. Even a Roman '*ombrellino*' found an occasional Anglican purchaser—a vital item for any church where the local ordinary forbade a tabernacle and insisted on an aumbry, if he were prepared to sanction any method of reservation.

Clement Skilbeck's *Illustrations of the Liturgy* (Alcuin Club Collections XIX) appeared in 1916. It depicted 'the celebration of the Holy Communion in a parish church' according to the rulings of *The Parson's Handbook.* Percy Dearmer contributed a long Introduction entitled 'The Present Opportunity.' Four years later the S.S.P.P. retaliated. A young artist, Martin Travers, had broken away from the medievalism of his master, Ninian Comper, and showed a rare facility for playing about with Baroque and Rococo ornament. His drawings in *Pictures of the English Liturgy—Low Mass* depicted a priest vested in ultra-Italian fashions, celebrating Mass at a Baroque altar, with his server wearing a cotta instead of a flowing surplice, or an apparelled alb and amice. It was obvious that this book was intended as a counterblast to Percy Dearmer because its Introduction was entitled 'The Lost Opportunity.' In 1922 the S.S.P.P. brought out a companion volume with drawings by Martin Travers showing the celebration of High Mass. Each picture displays a different type of Baroque or Rococo altar. One of them shows High Mass with a monstrance enthroned beneath a canopy supported by fat cherubs. Beneath another altar is an immense Renaissance reliquary, while a third drawing has an altar with riddel posts of seventeenth century style, and a Rococo image of the Madonna above the low reredos.

Adrian Fortescue's *Ceremonies of the Roman Rite Described,* published in 1917, gave the S.S.P.P. an authoritative guide for the refurnishing of Anglican cathedrals and churches in accordance with the Decrees of the Sacred Congregation of Rites, the rubrics of Roman liturgical manuals, and the new Code of Canon Law of the Latin Church.

The Back to Baroque movement was contemporary with a similar change in domestic *décor.* Osbert Lancaster points out 'Curzon Street Baroque,' which set the tone in house furnishings towards the end of the First World War, always had a markedly ecclesiastical note. Its sources were the churches of Italy, and to a lesser degree of Spain and Southern Germany. 'Forests of twisted baroque candlesticks, willingly surrendered by countless Italian padres (in exchange for the wherewithal with which to purchase up-to-date machine-turned electroliers), old leather-bound hymn books cunningly hollowed out to receive cigarettes, and exuberant prie-dieux ingeniously transformed into receptacles for gramophone records,' all formed an essential part of 'Curzon Street Baroque.' Not only 'little Fabergé knick-knacks and Dresden shepherdesses' were cast out of Anglo-Catholic churches and the boudoirs and drawing-rooms of Belgravia and Mayfair; more often the rejected junk was of Gothic Revival. In more than one incense-laden Anglican Papalist place of worship imitation medieval ornaments were 'finally routed by a noble army of martyrs from the Salzkammergut whose plaster writhings were rendered properly decorative by a liberal application of irridescent paint,' just as was done in the homes of the 'Bright Young Things' of the early nineteen-twenties.[1]

This new Baroque and Rococo belong to the period of cloche-hats, Russian boots, bobbed-hair, and the disappearance of the female waist-line. Skirts ending at the knees went with fiddle-back chasubles of about the same length in the

[1] Osbert Lancaster, *Homes Sweet Homes,* p. 64.

more extreme Anglo-Catholic churches. Both produced a similar tubular effect. Cottas became even shorter by way of protest to the long and flowing surplices favoured by the Alcuin Club and *Parson's Handbook* school of *couturières*. A cotta was not really 'correct' unless its lower part consisted of several inches of lace, and it must not be deeper than the average male waist-line. Albs too resembled Victorian lace curtains in all S.S.P.P. approved churches.

1924 saw the climax of Baroque and Rococo in Anglican Papalist churches. Both 'Curzon Street' and Anglo-Catholic Baroque belonged to the same age as *The Co-optimists* at the Palace Theatre, Nikita Balieff's *Chauve Souris* at the Strand Theatre, the Diaghilev Russian Ballet at the Coliseum, and the earlier C. B. Cochran revues at the London Pavilion. The eighteenth century costumes and scenery shown at the Lyric Theatre, Hammersmith, first in *The Beggar's Opera,* and subsequently in *The Duenna,* may have inspired the refurnishings of more than one church. There was much in common between the fashions popularized by Nigel Playfair in the theatre and those propagated by the S.S.P.P. in churches.

One of the earliest transformation scenes effected on S.S.P.P. principles was at S. Michael's, Plymouth, after Maurice Child found himself in charge of this church about 1913. He erected two altars which might have been transported from Central or South America. Never before had such an exotic display of

S. AUGUSTINE'S, QUEEN'S GATE, LONDON
W. Butterfield's Gothic Revival church with Southern Baroque
reredos by Martin Travers (1928)

Baroque and Rococo been seen in an Anglican church.[2] Not long after this the
interior of S. Thomas's, Oxford, was completely refurnished in the post-Tridentine
manner. The Gothic Revival fittings designed by Butterfield, Street and Skidmore
about 1850, also later decorations by Kempe, were removed. When almost every
trace of Tractarian 'correctness' had been obliterated by 1917, this little church was

---

[2] It was against this background that Ronald Knox was roused to write *Reunion All Round*
(1914), and other satires aimed at the inconsistencies of Anglicanism.

X

astonishingly like some of those medieval churches in France or Belgium which retained their seventeenth or eighteenth century furnishings and ornaments.

In 1920 Roger Wodehouse, who had been a curate at S. Thomas's for six years, became vicar of S. Paul's, Oxford. Few churches in Britain offered a better chance to the S.S.P.P. than this classical building designed by H. J. Underwood in 1836, with its later apsidal chancel. A tabernacle and throne were added to the high altar, the side altars draped with lace and adorned with artificial flowers, reliquaries, etc; and several shrines erected. Very few visitors would have guessed that S. Paul's was in communion with Canterbury. It looked far more 'Roman' than any of the Roman churches in Oxford.

Another strong supporter of the S.S.P.P. was Humphrey Whitby, who succeeded Cyril Howell as vicar of S. Mary's, Graham Street, London, in 1916. Martin Travers designed an Italian Baroque gilt wooden *retablo* for the high altar in this rather dull church, but his scheme for the complete refurnishing of the interior was never completed, except for some of the shrines and statues.

About 1928 Travers got the chance of a lifetime when Carrick Deacon, rector of Butterfield's 1865–71 church of S. Augustine, Queen's Gate, London, commissioned him to obliterate most if not all of its Gothic Revival atmosphere.

A wildly Baroque *retablo,* evocative of Spain or Latin America, filled up most of the east wall behind the high altar. Butterfield's strident polychrome brick work disappeared beneath off-white distemper. The rest of the furnishings introduced were reminiscent of those of the nearby Oratorian Church of the Immaculate Heart of Mary.

One wonders what Sir George Gilbert Scott would have felt about the transformation of the interior of S. Matthew's, Westminster, which he designed about 1849. Bodley had provided a metal screen with a wooden loft in 1893; also one of his characteristic triptych reredoses. But after Martin Travers had been called in to design a gilt wooden Baroque tabernacle for the high altar, an extra side altar, and one or two shrines, the Anglican Papalist atmosphere of this Gothic Revival church became far more pronounced. The total effect, surprisingly enough, is quite pleasing.

Similar transformation scenes took place in some of the Brighton strongholds of extreme Anglo-Catholicism. Vast sums must have been spent in the effort to make Somers Clarke's red brick interior of S. Martin's (1875) less English. A huge marble holy-water stoop, with a statuette of S. John the Baptist, competed with the original Sussex marble font, adorned with agates. The focal point of the interior became the richly carved and gilded Baroque tabernacle, above which rose up the great reredos of elaborate Gothic design. The ornaments and decorations of the Lady Chapel helped to create the illusion of being in Italy. Confessional boxes placed in the aisles completed the thoroughly un-Anglican *décor*.

So violent was the reaction against everything medieval among most Anglican Papalists that a Baroque frame had to be provided for the early Burne-Jones' painted reredos above the high altar of Carpenter's Decorated Gothic interior of S. Paul's, Brighton. Baroque candlesticks and a tabernacle also helped to give the sanctuary a more ultramontane atmosphere.

The furnishings of E. Scott's immensely lofty brick church of S. Bartholomew, Brighton, opened in 1874, had always been eclectic and somewhat bizarre. Here the *art nouveau* of the eighteen-nineties mingles quite happily with later Baroque fittings. What with the tremendous marble-faced baldachin over the high altar, the rails of gilded metal, the silver Lady altar, the shrines in recesses of the walls, and the large confessional boxes with domed roofs, it is extraordinary to reflect that this famous church is under the jurisdiction of the Bishop of Chichester.

A visitor who wanders round S. Andrew's, Worthing, might easily suppose that Sir Arthur Blomfield's red brick Gothic Revival church had been reconciled with the Roman Catholic diocese of Southwark. Here again are numerous altars draped with lace and Baroque ornaments. The nearby 'Roman' church, in which some of the altars have riddels and dossals, is far more English in its furnishings.

One of the happiest examples of the urge to refurnish Anglican places of worship in accordance with the decrees of the Sacred Congregation of Rites is Wren's church of S. Magnus the Martyr, Low Thames Street, London. The Classic interior is now an 'inexplicable splendour of Ionian white and gold.' [3] Even Wren himself might admit that the transformation of the interior to resemble a late seventeenth century Catholic church gives it a distinction it may have lacked when it was erected between 1671 and 1705.

S. Magnus's is one of Martin Travers' best refurnishings. His work can also be studied at Compton Beauchamp, near Shrivenham, Berkshire, where he was employed by Mr. Samuel Gurney, the first secretary of the S.S.P.P. The little medieval church is a riot of Baroque—high altar, domed tabernacle, font-cover, rood and side altars. Travers did altars in the same style at Ashbury and Cricklade, both in this neighbourhood. When the Anglican Benedictines became the owners of Nashdom, the Renaissance mansion designed by Sir Edwin Lutyens, Travers was the obvious architect to transform the ballroom into the main chapel, which he provided with a sarcophagus shaped high altar.

The new Church of the Good Shepherd, Carshalton, Surrey, erected in 1930, proved that he had gradually evolved his own personal style of Baroque. Emmanuel Church, Leyton (1935), and the Holy Redeemer, Streatham Vale (1931), both showed that he was capable of adapting Baroque to Evangelical principles. Neither of these churches required candlesticks for the communion tables.

In some of the Gothic Revival churches the urge to give their interiors a more continental look, led to the demolition of rood screens or rood-beams. S. Stephen's, Clewer, Windsor, is a case in point. S.S.P.P. fashions were not confined to the south of England. They can be seen in the more recent furnishings of Street's church of S. Margaret, Prince's Road, Liverpool; also in Bodley's S. John the Baptist, Tue Brook, now part of Liverpool. S. Michael's, Hill Square, Edinburgh, is almost a museum of now faded Baroque furnishings. Joseph Peacock's dull Gothic Revival church of S. Stephen, South Kensington (1865), was lavishly provided with Baroque bric-à-brac.

Most of these interiors take one back to the world of Max Reinhardt's production

---

[3] E. and W. Wayland Young, *Old London Churches* (1909), p. 97.

COMPTON BEAUCHAMP, BERKS
Baroque furnishings by Martin Travers, 1928

of *The Miracle* at Olympia; the music of George Gershwin, the fashion drawings of Cecil Beaton; the first dramatic successes of Noel Coward; the acting of Beatrice Lillie and Gertrude Lawrence; and much else that was significant in that strange restless post First World War decade.

Between 1920 and 1930 a succession of Anglo-Catholic Congresses up and down England, accompanied by Priests' Conventions, and smaller gatherings of clergy and laity, helped to popularize Baroque and Rococo furnishings and decorations among those members of the Church of England who prayed for reunion with Rome. By 1922 the S.S.P.P. catalogues were advertising more than three hundred tracts and leaflets, all of which aimed at familiarizing Anglicans with continental modes of spirituality and worship. Liturgical books, translated and slightly adapted from those of the Roman rite, were on sale, so that it was easy enough to know what

THE HOLY HOUSE, WALSINGHAM (1931)
This Anglican shrine in Norfolk recreates the atmosphere of the *Santa Casa* at Loreto

to do at Exposition and Benediction, or how to carry out the Roman ceremonies of Holy Week, Ash Wednesday, Candlemas and Corpus Christi. At the S.S.P.P. shop you could buy candlesticks, crucifixes, chalices, vestments, monstrances, statues, rosaries, etc., etc.—all guaranteed Catholic in the Roman sense, and as un-English as were the furnishings of a Curzon Street Baroque boudoir.

The ultramontane transformation of Sir Walter Tapper's Church of the Annunciation, erected in 1913, in the best Bodley tradition, was done with impeccable taste. The lofty Gothic chancel screen and rood-beam were both retained, as was Bewsey's immense painted and gilded triptych reredos above the high altar. Six splendid Baroque candlesticks and a large crucifix stand directly on the mensa, together with a veiled domed tabernacle. Votive candle-stands, hanging lamps, chubby Baroque cherubs, and the right amount of flower vases create the setting for the crowned statue of our Lady, draped with old lace. Æsthetically there is much to be said for this famous stronghold of extreme Anglican Papalism in the West End of London.

Anglican Papalist activities are to be found in abundance at Walsingham. In 1921 when the Revd. A. Hope Patten was appointed to the living, he began to transform the large medieval parish church into a replica of its French or Belgian opposite number. So numerous became the shrines, reliquaries, pictures, statues, banners, lamps and other *objets de piété,* most of which evoked the seventeenth and eighteenth centuries, that no uninitiated visitor would have guessed that this overcrowded church was Anglican. The total effect was reminiscent of those illustrations in *L'Art Sacré* which depict French churches before they have been stripped of accumulated *bric-à-brac.*

It was inevitable that loyal Protestants should object. In 1931 the College of the Guardians of the Sanctuary of Our Lady of Walsingham, founded that year, decided to erect a National Shrine of Mary on private property in the village. During the next eight years Messrs. Milner and Craze supervised the furnishing and decoration of this building. Here in what is known as 'England's Nazareth' can be found some of the most characteristic examples of the 'Back to Baroque' movement.

In the centre of the church, which has fifteen altars in honour of the mysteries of the Rosary, stands a replica of the Holy House of Loreto. The dim, dark interior of the *santa casa,* heavy with the fumes of stale incense, guttering votive candles, and the oil of flickering hanging lamps, captures the Italian atmosphere. Norfolk is forgotten. *Ex voto* tablets, and offerings left by grateful pilgrims, encrust the bare stone walls. Above the lace-draped altar is a Madonna, vested in a richly jewelled and embroidered cope, and wearing an ornate crown. The Reformation might indeed have never taken place.[4]

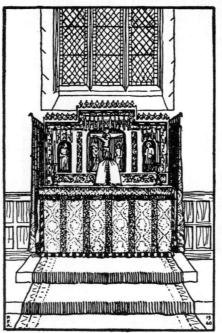

THE SLIPPER CHAPEL, WALSINGHAM (1933)
Compare the 'English' altar of the Roman Catholic shrine of our Lady with 'ultramontane' *décor* of the Anglican Holy House

The Anglican National Shrine of Our Lady of Walsingham achieved something which even the optimistic founders of the S.S.P.P. could hardly have dreamed of

---

[4] The altar was simplified some years ago according to the designs of the late Sir Ninian Comper.

in 1911. Here is the supreme monument of the 'Back to Baroque' movement. An equally curious phenomenon is that the furnishings of the Roman Catholic shrine of our Lady of the medieval Slipper Chapel convey the impression of being strongly influenced by the antiquarian researches of the Alcuin Club, if not directly by Percy Dearmer's *Parson's Handbook*. Little could be more ironic.

This curious phase of Anglo-Catholic church furnishing and decoration occurred between 1912 and 1940 It was the most aggressive effort made in a hundred years to force people to worship in a setting which was completely out of tune with their daily life. In this sense the 'Back to Baroque' movement was not only unreal but unhealthy. There is a theatrical quality about most of these furnishings. They look best under artificial light, like stage scenery. It is seldom that the altars, tabernacles, reredoses, font-covers, shrines, exposition-thrones, etc., will stand close inspection. In some instances they are badly made and show dishonest craftsmanship. No doubt it was great fun shocking Protestant-minded bishops, rural deans, archdeacons and the more conservative clergy and laity with these often merely superficial evocations of Counter-Reformation Bavaria, Austria, Italy, Spain or Latin America. To-day many of these twentieth century imitations of late seventeenth or eighteenth century furnishings look sadly dated. The gold leaf (often varnished silver-leaf for cheapness) has grown dim after forty years' exposure. Black Madonnas vested in richly embroidered copes and jewelled crowns have ceased to be exciting. To the present generation the typical S.S.P.P. interior *décor* is just an amusing period piece, with the same sort of appeal as *The Boy Friend*. Bobbed hair and baroque ornament, chubby cherubs and the Charleston—all these are nostalgic memories of the middle-aged persons or objects of the gentle ridicule of the younger generation, which appears to demand more convincing proofs of Catholicity than decadent continental fashions in church furnishing and ceremonial.[5]

[5] The urge to obey the latest rules of the Roman Sacred Congregation of Rites among the *avant garde* Anglican Papalists, and to be loyal to the Holy Father, is likely to result in a nation-wide crusade involving casting out Baroque and Rococo furnishings. It is to be hoped that the Council for the Care of Churches will manage to save some of the more outstanding examples of this now unfashionable style of *décor* before, e.g., the Priests' Sodality of the Precious Blood and the Society of the Holy Cross, issue orders that altars of post-Tridentine design must be replaced by kitchen tables, to enable the celebrant to face the people during the celebration of the 'Western Rite.' Already brass eagle lecterns are being brought back and polished up so that the Epistle and Gospel can be read from them instead of the Lessons at Mattins and Evensong.

_____

CHAPTER XXXI

CHAOTIC ECLECTICISM

THE END OF AN ERA

THANKS to *The Architectural Review* (July 1927) which featured several articles on contemporary church building, with many illustrations, it is fairly easy to recapture the fashions which were in vogue during the first decade after the First World War.[1]

Eric Gill's article on church furniture gets down to the root of the matter. He points out that 'furniture is anything necessary and useful wherewith a building is furnished, and an article on the subject should be equally necessary and useful to those who have in hand or in mind the business of furnishing. What should be said to such persons? It seems to me that the very first thing to be said is that as we now live in the midst of an industrial system, and as there is a fundamental and necessary incompatibility between industrialism and any religion which involves the worship of God, therefore the products of industrialism are unsuitable for the furnishing of churches.' Having defined exactly what he means by industrialism, he adds that so far as churches are concerned it 'may be pictured in the mind as that row of Jewish shops at Lourdes wherein they sell rosaries and medals for Catholics.' He asks whether, when the industrial world is triumphant, there will be any need for churches, or church furniture. But 'what are we to do while we are still half throttled by the commercialism which is the basis of industrialism to-day? I believe there is an easy solution to this one, too. The answer is: What you don't need, go without, and what you do need, get good. But two questions are here urgent. What *do* we need, and what *is* good? We must answer these at all costs. The first is really simple. What we need is what authority prescribes, and authority, having much sense, prescribes very little. "Stations of the Cross," for instance, are by no means necessary, and even where there seems a necessity for that "devotion" authority prescribes merely wooden crosses, fourteen in number, and nothing more at all. In Catholic churches you *must* have a crucifix on the altar (and you must have an altar), but any uneducated child can make a good crucifix, which is more than a limited liability company can do. Indeed, the only difficulty

_____

[1] The articles were 'Church Plan in England' (The Editor); 'Art and Religion' (Percy Dearmer); 'Our Churches' (The Very Revd. Hewlett Johnson); 'Old Standards and Modern Problems'; 'Public School Chapels' (The Headmaster of Charterhouse); 'New Lamps for Old—Symbols and Ceremonies of Toc H' (Barclay Baron); 'Church Furniture' (Eric Gill).

is finding the authority, and some three hundred and forty million Christians find no difficulty even in that! The only difficulty is in doing what he says.'

In 1927 it was hard to make architects and clergymen see that it was unreasonable 'to have sham Gothic or sham Byzantine or sham any other kind of furniture.' Gill pointed out a number of other things which were unreasonable, but thirty years ago not many people would accept his basic principles. He ended his long article, asking: 'Shall we get beautiful churches and church furniture by thus pursuing the rule of reason? God knows. At any rate, we should avoid present vulgarities and inanities; and the field of fancy, having lain fallow for a generation, will perhaps bear a better crop later on.'

Percy Dearmer, who by 1927 had become an extreme 'Modern Churchman,' busy promoting the League of Arts, pleaded for a sound philosophy of æsthetic, and deplored the lack of a theology of beauty. He shocked many orthodox Anglicans by maintaining that such ugly things as 'sin,' 'hell' and the mortification of the flesh were merely medieval superstitions. Yet he was confident that 'the bishops and clergy are for the moment in advance of their congregations; and at the same time the younger generation has been so repelled by the mixture of dreariness and sentimentality in the churches and chapels that they have been keeping outside. Hence a general confusion and many difficulties.' Like Eric Gill, he believed that the root of bad furnishings in churches could be traced to the Industrial Revolution.

Hewlett Johnson, then Dean of Manchester, to-day better known as the 'Red Dean' of Canterbury, was all out for more colour in church furnishings, yet 'with great cool spaces, with whitened walls, with windows through which one could see the trees and fields and clouds, enlivened here and there with a splash of colour, or a patch of heraldry.' He pleaded for furniture that should be sparing— an 'altar rich in hangings set on riddels, broad and majestic in its form, but severe in its splendid restraint. . . . Flowers should stand in glass vases upon the altar or in great bowls on the floor beside it; or on a low stand by the chancel steps. And there should be flowers in the porch to welcome me. . . . The few lamps, ceremonial or otherwise, should be largely conceived and hung by great cords from the roof. . . . The pulpit should rise all alone unjostled by any seats, and the font in splendid isolation should face the altar from the west, with its own rich cover nobly hung by a great chain or cord from the roof. Nor should it lack homely and intimate touches. Round the empty aisles there would be chapels or corners for special purposes, and the children should not be forgotten. But the main impression should be that of space, broken only by a few significant and exquisitely beautiful things; and every detail of the church, from the latch on the door to the buffet beneath my feet, should bespeak a care and a thought and a beauty worthy of God's House. Such a church, with its impalpable air of freshness and vitality would recall us time and again to meditation and refreshment. And with infinite variations of these churches, scattered throughout the land, in every degree of enrichment or simplification, but all conceived and executed in the big manner, the earnest ministers and parish priests would be twice armed for their difficult task.'

There can be little doubt that when he wrote this Dean Hewlett Johnson was thinking of the big medieval parish church at Thaxted in Essex. Here the Revd. Conrad Noel had whitewashed the interior, taken away all but the major furnishings and, among other minor objects of piety, had hung up the red flag with its sickle, symbolic of spiritual union with Soviet Russia! Not many Anglican parsons had the courage of Conrad Noel, and few were brave enough to recreate great cool spaces so as to give splendid isolation to the font, pulpit and altars. One of the few

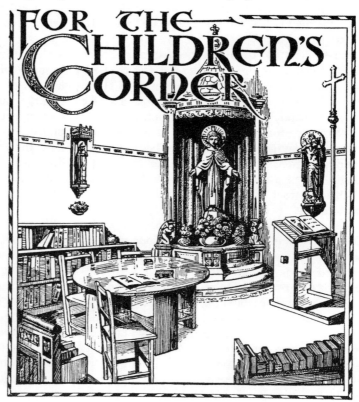

'Children's Corners' became the rage in Anglican churches after the First World War

medieval country churches where the pews were removed and the interior treated in a similar manner was South Creake, Norfolk.

The Dean's remark that 'the children should not be forgotten,' and that there should be 'chapels or corners for special purposes,' is a reminder of the so-called 'Children's Corners,' which became so popular in Anglican churches during the decade after the First World War. The fashion spread like wild-fire, and certain firms of church furnishers specialized in catering for the demand. Tiny tables and chairs were mass produced. Hangings of a rather sickly shade of blue were almost obligatory, likewise framed reproductions of water colours by Miss Margaret Tarrant, generally with plenty of rabbits and birds in the foreground. Lots of little flower vases and statues of the Christ Child, his Mother Mary, and very often S. Francis of Assisi (because he loved animals) were part of the *décor* of a typical Children's Corner. So too were low oak shelves, filled with illustrated books. The strange thing was—and still is—that in spite of the multiplication of Children's Corners from one end of Britain to another, they never appear to be used. In some churches they are neglected and dusty; elsewhere they have been dismantled in recent years. Perhaps in matters of taste, the child is indeed father to the man.

Christmas Cribs, and later on 'Easter Gardens,' became popular in Anglican churches after the First World War. These temporary furnishings are not confined to Anglo-Catholic places of worship; they are to be found in the most moderate of country parish churches. The old fear of the worship of graven images is a thing of the past.

By 1927 people felt that ecclesiastical art was less vulgar than during the late Victorian period. An anonymous writer in *The Architectural Review* (July 1927) said: 'For many years the Church of England, the owner of by far the greatest mass of artistic treasure in the country, has been regarded as the patroness of the dullest and worst kind of shop material. During the generation before the war, few churches or church ornaments were produced which any artistically interested person would have troubled to go to see. And how many ugly tablets, dull windows and common-place fittings were turned out!'

Thanks to the Diocesan Committees composed of cultured clerics and laymen it had been possible to check the flow of 'offensive furniture,' and gradually to make people employ competent designers. War was waged against those Philistines who chose what they fancied from catalogues to disfigure their church. The Diocesan Committees were being broadminded and approved of any sound work. The problems which had to be solved were many and difficult, because fashions in ceremonial were not stable, and it was still not always easy to know what was forbidden by law.

The same writer continued: 'If there be some who would ask for more originality and more strikingly modern work, let them take a wide view of the whole situation, and compare the examples given with (1) the average continental church fittings; (2) the average here in England, say, in the 'nineties or even before the war. More important still, let them find out from the Diocesan Advisory Committees on the one hand, or from disgruntled Philistines in the suburbs on the other, something about the vast number of unworthy "ornaments" of all kinds which have not been allowed to encumber our churches, and see if the gradual growth of affairs during the last decade, even with all its deficiencies, is not a very real and a very great achievement to the credit of the Church of to-day.'

It is interesting to look back thirty years and study what was then accepted as

Change of fashion in a typical country church, 1870 and 1940

good taste.' Sir Giles Gilbert Scott's altars and reredoses get top priority. These may be seen in S. Joseph's, Sheringham, Norfolk; Liverpool Cathedral; the Lady Chapel of the Assumption, Northfleet, Kent; and the War Memorial Chapel at Ampleforth Abbey, York. All are exquisite examples of late Gothic Revival carving, which perpetuate the Bodley tradition.

Sir Robert Lorimer comes next with the woodwork in his War Memorial Chapel at Rossall School, Lancashire; also pulpits and lecterns designed by him for the Episcopalian church at Pittenweem, Fife, and elsewhere. An example of Robert Thompson's now famous woodcarving—one of the outstanding features of the new choir of Ampleforth Abbey—is given in a photograph of the Selwyn Memorial choir stalls at Uppingham School, designed by W. G. Newton.

Charles Spooner's always refined church furnishings find a place, with photographs of an altar at S. Anselm's, Hatch End, Middlesex, and a lectern at S. Michael's, Little Ilford, Essex; the former carved by J. Armitage and the latter by A. Robinson. The only fitting which shows any definitely 'modern' feeling is the kneeler for S. Andrew's Chapel in Westminster Cathedral; designed by Sidney Barnsley and carried out by W. H. Berry. Sir Walter Tapper's altars in the three War Memorial chapels of York Minster, also the wrought iron screens, designed to go with them, are in the Renaissance style.

Good metal work of original character was being designed thirty years ago by several architects and craftsmen, particularly Hubert Worthington, Alan Durst and Edward Spencer. The altar and processional crosses made by the two last were

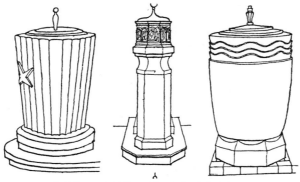

FONTS OF THE NINETEEN-THIRTIES

a considerable improvement on those supplied by commercial firms.

For the rest, old and new churches up and down the country were having their interiors whitewashed, and wherever possible the original nineteenth century communion tables and reredoses were being replaced by 'English Altars,' vested in frontals, and provided with a dossal and riddels. People of good taste had begun to appreciate eighteenth century art, as adapted by Lovat Fraser in his costumes and scenery for *The Beggar's Opera,* but the nineteenth century was still too near their own day for them to take an objective view (as we are now beginning to do) of Victoriana.

Refined austerity might be said to be the predominant note in English ecclesiastical 'good taste' during the thirties of the present century. Fonts, for instance, were as plain as the designer could make them, and so were the majority of font-covers. Typical examples are those at S. Luke, Benchill, Manchester (Taylor and Young, 1939); S. Thomas, Hanwell (E. Maufe, 1933); S. John, Beckenham (Pite and Fairweather, 1933); S. Gabriel, Walsall (Lavender and Twentyman, 1939); and S. Hugh, Old Bromby, Lincs. (L. Bond, 1930).

Here and there a chancel screen was still erected in an Anglican church. In All Saints, Dormanstown, Middlesbrough (1932) Leslie T. Moore inserted a typical medieval rood screen and loft, which would have delighted A. W. Pugin. This same architect, two years later, provided S. Oswald's, Grove Hill, Middlesbrough, with a more open chancel screen and other woodwork fittings of late medieval inspiration. Edwin F. Reynolds designed a sort of neo-Byzantine screen to divide the nave and chancel of S. Mary's, Pype Hayes, Birmingham (1930). The open chancel screen and other furnishings of the Church of the Holy Spirit, Harlescott, Shrewsbury (1936) are almost a throw-back to the *art nouveau* work of Charles Rennie Mackintosh—graceful and slightly precious. The note of refined simplicity is strongly marked in the open screen in the Church of the Ascension, Hanger Hill, Ealing, designed by the Hon. John Seely and Paul Paget in 1939. An original rood screen was designed by Bernard Miller and carved by Alan Durst for the medieval interior of Woodchurch, Cheshire. It is 'modern' in spirit, yet essentially in the old tradition.

Sir Charles Nicholson designed some neo-Jacobean rood screen. Harold S. Rogers provided one, at the cost of Lord Nuffield, for S. Luke's, Cowley, Oxford. Rood-beams ceased to be popular, but they turned up from time to time. Harold Gibbons designed a Gothic one for S. Mary's, Kenton, Middlesex, in 1936; and Edmund Oakley added a Classic rood cross in S. George's East Boldon, Co. Durham (1933).

Choir stalls varied considerably in style. Jacobean was adopted by Isaac Taylor and Cecil Young at S. Gabriel's, Prestwich, Manchester, in 1930; and by Sir Charles Nicholson in most of his churches; also by S. E. Dykes-Bower in All Saints', Hockerill (1936). In the majority of Anglican churches the choir was still placed in the chancel, but one exception is at the John Keble Memorial Church, Mill Hill, London, where D. F. Martin-Smith arranged the choir in front of the nave, with the organ in a west gallery.

Pulpits varied from Gothic to neo-Byzantine. In some churches two Early Christian *ambones* were introduced instead of a pulpit, e.g. at S. Wilfrid's, Halton, Leeds, designed by A. Randall Wells in 1938.

The position of the main altar in Anglican churches was no longer invariably shoved up against the east wall of the chancel. At S. Wilfrid's, Brighton (1933) H. S. Goodhart-Rendel put the plain stone high altar (without gradines and six tall candlesticks) several feet from the east wall. J. Harold Gibbons erected the high altars of S. Francis, Bournemouth (1930) and S. Francis, Gladstone Park (1933) in the centre of each church, with chapels behind them. So did W. H. R. Blacking in S. Mary's, Littlehampton, Sussex (1935).

A proof of the pervasive influence of *Parson's Handbook* is found in the number of altars with riddel posts and curtains, designed by numerous architects.[2] By 1940 the so-called 'English Altar' had found its way into churches from one end of

---

[2] e.g. S. Thomas, Hanwell (E. Maufe, 1933); All Saints, Thames Ditton (E. Maufe, 1930); S. Gabriel, Prestwich (Taylor and Young, 1934); S. Francis, Petts Wood (G. Mullins, 1935); S. Alban, North Harrow (A. Kenyon, 1932); Keble Memorial, Mill Hill (D. F. Martin-Smith, 1936); and almost every church by Sir Charles Nicholson.

JOHN KEBLE CHURCH, MILL HILL (D. Martin Smith, 1936)
'English' altar in contemporary setting

Britain to the other, though the treatment varied considerably. Largely due to
Geoffrey Webb's book *The Liturgical Altar* (1938) what had been regarded
hitherto as an exclusively Anglican type of furnishing began to be inserted in a
fair number of Catholic churches.

The baldachin or ciborium had never been really popular either with Catholic
or Anglican architects during the nineteenth century. Between 1910 and 1940

335

several Anglican churches were given a baldachin over their high altars, the designs of which ranged from medieval Gothic to Modernistic.[3]

It might well be that the splendid baldachin over the high altar of Westminster Cathedral (see p. 266) encouraged other architects to insert them in Catholic churches. F. X. Velade designed an extremely original domed baldachin for S. Matthew's, Clubmoor, Liverpool, and a modernistic tester for S. Monica's, Bootle, towards the end of the nineteen-thirties. Reginald Fairlie provided a

BRAINTREE, ESSEX (Geoffrey Webb, 1940)
'English' altar adapted to the Roman rite

wooden one with an embossed leather pyramidical top in the Blessed Sacrament Chapel of Fort Augustus Abbey towards the end of the First World War. At Fort William he designed a wrought iron baldachin for the Catholic church he erected there in the 'thirties. Geoffrey Webb designed simple wooden ciboria for his churches at Seaford, Sussex, in 1933, and seven years later at Braintree, Essex. J. Arnold Crush added flat topped baldachins to the furnishings of the still incomplete new church at Douai Abbey, Berkshire, about 1933, and in the oratory of Fisher House, Cambridge.

[3] e.g. S. Anselm, Kennington (Adashead and-Ramsey, 1933); S. Francis, Bournemouth (J. Harold Gibbons, 1930); All Saints, Hockerill (Dykes-Bower, 1936); S. Mary, Kenton (J. Harold Gibbons, 1936); S. Alban, Hull (Milner and Craze, 1936); S. George, East Boldon (E. Oakley—semi-circular—1933). The various ciboria designed by J. N. Comper are mentioned on p. 284.

East windows became very unpopular; the theory being that they diverted the light from the high altar. An immensely tall reredos, either of carved wood or some rich fabric, could be found in most churches. Sir Giles Gilbert Scott inserted carved oak reredoses, sometimes gilded, into most of his Anglican and Catholic churches, although he provided a species of stone Gothic ciboria for the double high altar in the new church at Ampleforth Abbey.[4]

Utterly unique furnishings are to be found in the chapel of the House of the Sacred Mission, Kelham, Nottinghamshire, which were carried out by the architect, Charles Clayton Thompson in 1927. A dramatic touch is the bridge-like brick rood-beam which spans the sanctuary arch, with a group of figures carved by Sargent Jagger, the sculptor of the Artillery Memorial at Hyde Park Corner, London. This rood is the antithesis of those exquisite medieval re-creations of Sir Ninian Comper

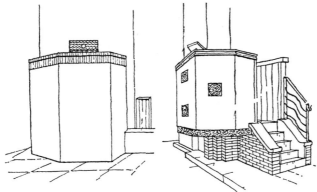

PULPITS OF THE NINETEEN-THIRTIES

—it is realistic and virile, yet poignant with emotion. The big plain altar, with no gradine, stands out against the dull dark blue background of the apse. The two altar and two standard candlesticks are black ebony and silver. The altar cross in enamels was designed by Alexander Fisher. The three sanctuary lamps, suspended from the rood arch, are of original design, with scarlet tassels attached. All these furnishings are reflected in the highly polished black squared flooring. The bare orange-red brick walls of rough texture form the general background for the fittings of this unique interior.

As we have pointed out already, ecclesiastical good taste often mirrors contemporary domestic furnishings and dress. This is certainly true of the inter-war period, when the 'straight-line' was all the rage. Women tried to look like tubes, without hips or breasts. Skirts ended either just below or above the knees. A boyish 'bob' or an 'Eton crop' was still fashionable. Straight lines, plain materials and the elimination of details typified interior furnishings and decoration. By 1930 a change was setting in. Hair was allowed to grow; evening dresses became longer. Curves appeared again. About the same time an 'all white' craze began. Furniture

[4] It does not cover the altar, and is more like an open screen surmounting it.

337

Y

was bleached, pickled or scraped. The sugary magentas and pinks, and the strident yellows and orange of the nineteen-twenties were superseded by white walls, white rugs and white covers for chairs and sofas. Gilt was transformed into silver wherever possible. Where an alternative to white was required only pale almond greens, greys and soft buffs were permitted. All these found their way into churches as well as houses. So did the many new materials which were being invented. But fashion is always fleeting. The Regency note which crept into domestic furnishings during the middle 'thirties can be detected in several churches of the same date, if only in the use of black, gold and stripes of vivid colours, and a certain eclecticism in the decorations. Yet at the same time these churches go with the contemporary materials, such as nylon and perlon. Some have a sort of plywood 'new look.'

Just as many old-fashioned houses still retained their Victorian furniture and ornaments, so a few churches up and down England had been untouched by the changes of ecclesiastical fashions. They were mostly strongholds of extreme Evangelicalism. More often than not they were situated in the industrial towns, or in the once fashionable watering places. One of the best examples which survived until the Second World War was S. John's, Portsea, thus described by Mr. John Betjeman.

'A forest of woodwork of excellent joinery; round the walls above, tier the empty galleries, with hard but seemly seats for the poorer people; below and level with our shoulders the box pews for the gentry, with their doors which shut with a loud smack. High above the pews is the double decker pulpit with the clerk's desk beneath. And at the end of the church the holy table, carefully removed from the wall so as to conform with Protestant doctrine, encircled by simple communion rails. Look up at the white plaster ceiling pleasantly moulded. The incumbent enters. He is wearing the black gown, just as his predecessors of one hundred and fifty years ago. The congregation, which can only be seen when it stands above the grained oak fastness, is small and bleak . . .' [5]

New materials brought about a change in church decorations, but not so much as in houses and public buildings. Ecclesiastical taste is always behind secular fashions. Asphalt and concrete came into greater use. Glass was being manufactured in larger sheets. There was coloured opaque sheet glass for wall linings. No longer did architects and craftsmen have to limit themselves to iron, steel, brass, copper, bronze and silver. New alloys were being invented for decorative purposes. Aluminium started to be used instead of iron and ordinary bronze. Then came chromium plating. Wood, marble, glass, pottery and certain other materials could be replaced by plastics. What was the use of spending money on solid wood for panelling when plywoods could create the same effect at half the cost? High gloss paints were being put on to the market, and were far better for use in town churches, since they were washable. Spray painting took far less time than covering

[5] *Ghastly Good Taste* (1933), p. 79.

large areas with a brush. It was stupid to spend money on parquet floors or marble pavements for churches, when rubber or cork were both cleaner and almost noise-less. Since building costs rose steadily year after year, why use quarried stone, when for many purposes the greatly improved artificial stone looked almost as good? There was also a far greater range of timber imported from abroad, which could be used for both joinery and veneering. Some of it was much less expensive than oak.

The inter-war period was one of rapid transition in decoration and furniture. In churches, as in houses and public buildings, there was a greater mingling of permanent materials, and a tendency to aim at transitory effects with new materials. Tubular steel furniture was introduced and even found its way into churches. Both Renaissance and Gothic Revival buildings, when these traditional styles were still used by architects, lost most of their decorated mouldings and embellishments. The urge towards 'functionalism,' which was a sort of narrow puritanism, and part of the cynical intellectual outlook of most of this period, was strongly marked in the furnishings of some churches; oddly enough combined with a new sort of romanticism. As the inter-war period passed by designers gradually abandoned eclecticism, and sought to achieve attractive relationships of colour, shape and material alone.[6]

But when all is said and done, it is very difficult to sum up the characteristics of church furnishings and decorations between 1920 and 1940. Fashions were seldom stable or uniform. On the one hand there were imitation Gothic or Baroque altars, pulpits, font covers, etc.; on the other, streamlined furniture which would have looked equally at home in, say, the Bexhill Pavilion, designed by Mendelsohn and Chermayeff in the late 'twenties, or the new Shakespeare Memorial theatre at Stratford-on-Avon, or in any typical cinema or cocktail bar.

By 1930 a few of the younger architects had realized that church furnishing in Britain was out of date compared with the Continent. They were turning their eyes to Sweden and discussing the gay and striking ecclesiastical *décor* created in Lutheran churches by Ivar Tengbom, Knut Nordenskjöld and Sigfrid Ericson. The fittings of most English churches were dull indeed compared with those designed in Germany by Otto Bartning, Fritz Fuchsenberger, Hans Herkomer, Martin Weber, Dominic Bohm, Albert Bosslet and Clement Holzmeister. Why was there no one at home to evolve original altars and pulpits like Karl Moser and Fernand Dumas in Switzerland? English ecclesiastical taste was hardly likely to find favour with the work of such Frenchmen as Paul Tournon or A. and G. Perret, although some English church furnishing still compared favourably with its continental equivalents.

It was high time to improve the furnishing of Catholic places of worship. In 1933 Geoffrey Webb and Philip Lindsey Clarke formed an inner circle of the

---

[6] Cf. Bruce Allsopp, *Decoration and Furniture*, Vol. I, *The English Tradition* (1952), p. 215 *et seq.*

Guild of Catholic Artists, known as the Company of S. Joseph. This company, which never numbered more than a dozen members, was closely associated with the Benedictines of Prinknash Abbey. A few exhibitions were held in London, but this little group, whose purpose was the regular study of liturgical rules, rubrics and decrees so far as they affected the furnishings and decorations of churches, ceased to function towards the end of the 'thirties.

More successful was the Liturgical Arts Society in North America. This came into being in 1926–7 when a small group of architects began to discuss how to

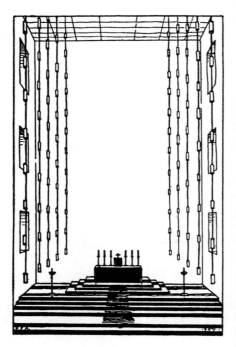

GERMAN AUSTERITY, 1930

improve ecclesiastical taste. Meetings were held at Portsmouth Priory, Rhode Island, where the Benedictine monks of the English Congregation were sympathetic and encouraging. A national quarterly magazine was launched. Under the name of *Liturgical Arts* it has done much to influence fashions in church furnishings. This trans-Atlantic movement aimed 'to create a climate in which all the different elements can collaborate in producing an art worthy of the spirit of the Church.' The Society has tried for the past twenty-five years to encourage a spirit of co-operation between all those factors of the processes of construction and decoration which are favourable to truly creative work. From its foundation the Liturgical Arts Society has seldom dogmatized on schools or types of art, or attached itself to any one style; after all the Pope himself has never attempted to do so. It has encouraged architects and craftsmen to choose and act within normal limits. It has aimed at developing a world perspective of liturgical art, based on a profound study of ancient traditions, and at the same time to keep abreast of new movements in all parts of the world, so that American Catholics can make their special contribution to the art of the Universal Church.

But the influence of the Liturgical Arts Society was limited to a comparatively small circle, and in the nineteen-thirties not many people read its magazine. Similar publications on the Continent were equally restricted.

Dr. Andrew L. Drummond's historical and constructive study, *The Church Architecture of Protestantism*, appeared in 1934. It made it clear that no Lutherans or Calvinists were afraid of richly decorated churches. The many photographs reproduced reveal a startling contrast between the older 'meeting houses' of what are styled Nonconformist sects in England and some of the splendid Baptist,

Many Scottish Presbyterian and English nonconformist places of worship were replanned and refurnished in this manner from about the turn of the century.

Congregational, Methodist, Presbyterian and Unitarian churches in the United States, Germany and even Scotland. Some of them were so ornately furnished and decorated that at a first glance they might have been mistaken for Catholic. Even more astonishing was the revival among Protestants of the mid-Victorian Anglican passion for Christian symbolism, though reinterpreted in the light of modern aspirations. Some of the communion tables illustrated in Dr. Drummond's book display crosses and even candlesticks. They look as if the ministers who used them for the not very frequent administrations of the Lord's Supper wanted to feel that they were 'saying Mass.' So by the nineteen-thirties the former distinction between

341

the furnishings of Catholic and Protestant churches was becoming less marked largely because of an ever increasing comprehensiveness in the doctrines preached from the pulpits of the latter. The fittings of many of these new buildings suggested that it is possible to be 'Catholic' without being in communion with either the Roman or any of the Eastern Churches, or for that matter with Canterbury.

The furnishings and decorations of the Jesuits' chapel in Campion Hall, Oxford, designed by Sir Edwin Lutyens, created much interest. Among them were Stations of the Cross painted by Frank Brangwyn, and stone carvings by Eric Gill. The amusing juxtaposition of modern furnishings and Baroque antiques found in J. E. Dixon-Spain's new Catholic church of S. Joan of Arc, Farnham, Surrey (1930) was all in keeping with the eclectic taste of the early 'thirties. E. Bower Norris was regarded as one of the most original architects of the moment; quite prepared to go all out 'modernistic' in the Catholic churches at Wythenshawe, Manchester, and North Walsham, Norfolk, or to turn to Portuguese Baroque for the inspiration of the altars in SS. Peter and Paul, New Brighton, Cheshire (1933). He could ring the changes with neo-Byzantine when wanted, as in Blackburn.

Eric Gill had reached the peak of his fame by the early 'thirties. His stone carvings were to be found in more and more churches—Catholic and Anglican—including small statues in the new chapel of Blackfriars, Oxford; S. Patrick's, Dumbarton; Rossall School Chapel; and Ratcliffe College, Leicestershire. His pupils and disciples were turning out work in a similar style; among them being Laurence and Joseph Cribb, Antony Foster, Dom Hubert Van Zeller of Downside Abbey, Fr. O'Mally, of the Institute of Charity, and Fr. Aelred Whitacre, O.P. Other Catholic sculptors making a name for themselves were Philip Lindsey Clark and Julian Allan. No longer was it necessary to depend on 'Catholic Repositories' for statues to put up in churches.

Miss Joan Morris, who edited an illustrated magazine, *Art Notes,* waged war against *bon-dieuserie,* and tried to inculcate a higher tone of artistic appreciation among the Catholic bishops and clergy. She also painted altar pieces with a distinct modern flavour. Similar paintings were being done occasionally by Dame Werburgh Welch, a nun of Stanbrook Abbey. Dom Theodore Baily of Prinknash Abbey was painting imitation Russian ikons, but did not find a market for many of them. Neither did Geoffrey Houghton-Brown for his religious paintings. On the whole taste remained fairly conservative.

Mosaic became popular for lining the walls of sanctuaries; largely due to the influence of Westminster Cathedral. Gabriel Pippet covered the walls of the Catholic church at Droitwich, Worcestershire, with neo-Byzantine mosaics. The firm of Oppenheimer and Co. supplied gorgeous mosaics for several churches designed by E. Bower Norris, and for others in Ireland.

Stained glass underwent a change. Weird figures, evocative of those in Aubrey Beardsley's drawings, appeared in the windows designed by Harry Clarke of Dublin. His colours were richer than anything which had been seen before. Douglas Strachan was adding some splendid windows to many churches in Scotland; including those of the National War Memorial in Edinburgh; and King's College Chapel, Aberdeen. The Ninian Comper tradition in stained glass was being per-petuated by Christopher and Geoffrey Webb; but another of his pupils, Martin Travers, was fast evolving a style of his own, and breaking away from late medieval English glass, although retaining much clear glass as a background for his figures. From time to time Sir Frank Brang-wyn designed some gorgeous windows, e.g. those in the Protestant cathedral in Belfast.

Good and original metal work was being made between the two world wars by such craftsmen as Omar Ramsden, Harold Stabler, Geoffrey Hart, Dunstan Pruden and the Broms-grove Guild. Buckfast Abbey was given some magnificent candelabra designed by Benno Elkan, who made some equally original candle-sticks for the chapel of New College, Oxford.

However, very little of the church furnish-ings and decorations in Britain between the two wars was as revolutionary as those on the Continent.

From time to time during the nineteen-thirties an architect would try to be 'clever' or 'amusing' when designing church furnishings —by way of protest against the commercial firms, who knew from long experience exactly what appealed to the customer.

S. HUGH,
OLD BROMBY
(Lawrence
Bond, 1938)

JOHN KEBLE
CHURCH,
MILL HILL
(D. F. Martin-
Smith, 1937)

When Isaac Taylor and Cecil Young designed S. Paul's, Blackley, Lancashire, in 1933 they let themselves go on the furniture. The two altar candlesticks stand on slightly projecting ends of the tall gradine. There is a similar kind of square shaped pedestal in the centre of the gradine from which rises a twisted Baroque column (about six feet in height), the cross standing on top of it. Typical of their period are the furnishings of S. Faith's, Lee-on-the-Solent, Hampshire, designed by the Hon. John Seely and Paul Paget in 1933. The choir stalls, made of un-polished English cedar of lebanon, were highly original. So was the altar, with its tall narrow dossal behind, and the odd-shaped sanctuary lamp.

Messrs. Welch, Cachemaille-Day and Lander were the most revolutionary ecclesi-astical architects during this period. In S. Nicholas, Burnage, Manchester (1932) the font has a base of ordinary bricks arranged in a circular zig-zag pattern, support-ing a stone bowl. The screen is built up of oak slats, gilded outside and painted

S. SAVIOUR, ELTHAM (Welch, Cachemaille-Day and Lander, 1931)
The streamlined furnishings represent similar fashions in domestic *décor*
and clothes

vermilion inside, with gilded lacquer on white metal leaf. There is a figure of the
Christ Child by Donald Hastings. The pulpit and reading desk were also of
ordinary brick. The choir was placed in a west gallery. The communion rails are
vaguely Jacobean in design. Behind a long 'English Altar' is a brick wall, and
above it a simple iron screen, with a chapel in the apsidal east end, approached by
steps on either side of the sanctuary. The colours everywhere make the interior of
this church a bright spot in Manchester.

The following year these same architects created even greater astonishment at

S. Saviour's, Eltham, London—an austerely simple brick church of no known period. The focal point of the interior is a life-sized stone statue of Christ standing on a pedestal behind the long high altar; like the one at Burnage correctly vested with a frontal. Above the entrance to the sanctuary hangs an immense decorated cross.

In 1937 came N. F. Cachemaille-Day's star-shaped church of S. Michael and All Angels at Wythenshawe, Manchester. The oak furniture is fumed to a dark brown colour. The ceiling panels and upper parts of the walls are painted blue. The electric lighting is mainly from a large central chandelier of gilded wood and metal. The choir is placed between the congregation and the main altar; the latter, without a gradine, standing out at the angular east end with large windows formed of brick and concrete tracery, and filled with stained glass of brilliant hues, mainly blue.

Furnishings of an equally original character designed by this architect can be found in S. Barnabas, Tuffley, Gloucestershire (1939); S. Laurence, Barkingside, Essex (1939); S. Paul, Ruislip Manor, Middlesex (1936); S. Edmund, Chingford, Essex (1939); and S. Anselm, Belmont, Middlesex (1940).

S. Luke's, Benchill, Manchesteer (1939) contains some very modernistic fittings, designed by Messrs. Taylor and Young. Most of the woodwork is left in natural colour, as was fashionable at this period. The focal point of the interior is a large square shaped panel filling up most of the east wall, with two angels in low relief, and a seated Christ surrounded by gilded Baroque rays. The large plain altar cross conveys the impression that it is standing on a sham square-shaped tabernacle. In S. Gabriel's, Walsall (1939), Messrs. Lavender and Twentyman placed a very tall and narrow plain cross on the rough cast wall above the simple high altar. Richard Nickson provided two similar crosses (the one behind the altar of the Lady Chapel being a window) in S. Chad's, Bolton, Lancashire (1937).

The craze for vivid colour effects in interior decoration comes out strongly in Bernard A. Miller's churches of S. Christopher, Withington, Manchester (1935); S. Christopher, Norris Green, Liverpool (1931); and S. Columba, Anfield, Liverpool (1932). On entering the first of these churches the eye rests on the gorgeously painted reredos which rises up from the top of the altar to the level of the roof. An unusual feature here is placing the semi-circular baptistery towards the east end of the south aisle. The choir is arranged between the nave seats and the chancel, with two low ambones instead of a pulpit and reading desk.

The furnishings of F. X. Velarde's Anglican church of S. Gabriel, Blackburn, were equally gay and colourful, even if old-fashioned people felt that they were more suited to a cocktail bar. He was still more revolutionary a year or two later when he designed the interior fittings of the Catholic church of S. Monica, Bootle, Liverpool (1936).

But such furnishings were the exception rather than the rule in both Anglican and Catholic places of worship. The majority of architects had to cater for less emancipated tastes. Martin Travers was still turning out Baroque altars, e.g. at S. Mary, Liss, Hampshire (1931) and S. Dionis, Fulham (1934). Up and down

S. LUKE'S, BENCHILL (Taylor & Young, 1939) 'Modernistic Baroque'

the country W. H. Randoll Blacking was carrying on the Comper and Dearmer tradition with English altars. So were Christopher Webb, Harold S. Rogers, E. Ellery Anderson and F. E. Howard.

Sir Charles Nicholson belonged to the same school, and examples of his charming but conservative pulpits, screens and altars can be studied in such churches as S. Alban, Copnor, Portsmouth (1914); S. Dunstan, Bellingham, Kent (1925); S. Mary, Frinton-on-Sea, Essex (1928); S. Elizabeth, Becontree, Essex (1932); Holy Cross, Airedale, Yorkshire (1932); S. Laurence, Eastcote, Middlesex (1932); All Saints, Hillingdon, Middlesex (1932); S. Peter, Morden, Surrey (1932–4); Chelmsford and Portsmouth cathedrals (1923 and later). The same Jacobean

s. CHAD, BOLTON, LANCS (Richard Nickson, 1937)
Striving after originality in decoration, but traditional Anglican
plan of chancel

feeling which was to be found in most of his earlier churches persists, with
certain modifications in the subsequent furnishings and decorations.

Sir Charles Nicholson, like Sir George Gilbert Scott during the middle of the
last century, became the really representative Anglican architect of the first three
decades of the present century. He designed furnishings which were both traditional and refined. The faint period flavour about them was inoffensive, and the use
of colour was in keeping with contemporary 'good taste.' A church designed and
furnished by Sir Charles always provided the right background for the services
of the *Book of Common Prayer*, carried out with loyal but rich Catholic ceremonial.

None of his churches show a papalist influence, as do those transformed by Martin Travers. A typical Charles Nicholson interior reflects the spirit of the Caroline Divines. Both Archbishop Laud and Bishop Andrewes would feel quite at home in them. A similar Jacobean or Caroline note is very marked in the screens, etc., designed by W. H. R. Blacking, e.g. S. Mary's, Littlehampton, Sussex (1935).

Liverpool Cathedral provides numerous examples of Sir Giles Gilbert Scott's sophisticated late Gothic Revival furnishings. The font (of Lunel Rubane marble from near Nimes in France, surrounded by other marbles on which are portrayed fishes swimming through the waves of the sea) has an enormous cover of oak, of medieval type. It stands beneath an elaborately carved oak canopy. The pulpit and choir stalls are equally rich. The immense carved stone reredos above the high altar is picked out with gold leaf. Less ornate are the altars and furnishings in the War Memorial Transept and the Chapel of the Holy Spirit, but in each case no money has been spared on the work. An unusual piece of furniture is the oak catafalque to hold the casket of ashes after cremation. Over the catafalque hangs a folded red and gold pall, which blends with the altar frontal and the dull red stone of the high altar reredos. Four massive candlesticks have been designed to stand around the catafalque, which (so the Cathedral Guidebook tells us) 'is an experimental way of meeting the mental needs of the occasion. There is a dignity of art and human proportion about it. Designer and craftsman have combined to do symbolically what we pray that God in fact will do, clothe the Departed in His creative and immortal artistry.'

The consecration of the cathedral and the opening of the chancel and the first set of transepts took place on July 19th, 1924. Not every one admires the stupendously rich furnishings of this great modern cathedral. There are some who feel they are an almost perfect example of what Mr. John Betjeman calls 'Ghastly Good Taste'! Every detail of the furnishings of Liverpool Cathedral reflects in some curious manner the evolution of ecclesiastical fashions in the past hundred years. They are the end of the story: it would be impossible to repeat it or to rewrite it in a slightly different manner. Here at Liverpool one can detect the remote sources—the teachings of the Cambridge Camden Society as to what was 'correct' and 'incorrect.' One realizes that all these highly stylized *objets d'art* can be traced back to A. W. Pugin, by way of Bodley, Pearson, Street, and the architect's own grandfather, the immortal Sir George Gilbert Scott.

Perhaps the greatest change in the furnishings of Anglican churches between the two wars was in the multiplication of aumbries for the reservation of the consecrated elements, in spite of many bishops banning them. In many Anglican Catholic churches it was common enough to find a lamp burning before a white curtained cupboard, usually inserted into the wall of a side chapel, but sometimes into the north wall of the sanctuary. Such bishops who did give permission for reservation invariably insisted on an aumbry rather than a tabernacle, feeling that the former was less 'Roman,' and not so likely to lead to superstitious

S. MONICA'S, BOOTLE (F. X. Velarde, 1936)
'Modernistic' Roman Catholic altar and reredos

abuses. However the erudite Dom Gregory Dix, in his little book entitled *A Detection of Aumbries,* managed to prove fairly conclusively that tabernacles on the altar were part and parcel of the rather exotic eucharistic cultus that was such a feature of 'Nordic Catholicism' before the Reformation, whereas aumbries belonged to the dignified austerity of the Roman rite. It upset the theories of the episcopate to learn that in Italy the change from the aumbry to the tabernacle did not take place generally until after the Reformation. Not many Anglo-Catholic churches adopted the suspended pyx, the use of which was introduced by Ninian Comper in 1893 (see p. 280). The revival of this medieval mode of reservation, almost universal in England previous to the middle of the sixteenth century, was soon discovered to be inconvenient. Since many of the more papalist-minded incumbents wanted to

ANGLICAN AUMBRIES
(W. H. R. Blacking)   (H. S. Rogers)

encourage post-Tridentine devotion to 'The Prisoner in the Tabernacle' they generally avoided aumbries, regarding them as slightly Protestant.

It has been borne in on me that ecclesiastical fashions are thoroughly paradoxical. At the same time as Anglican Papalists began to put tabernacles on to the high altars of their churches, the *avant-garde* of Roman liturgists abroad had started to get rid of them wherever possible; regretting that modern Canon Law lays down that reservation must be in a metal safe fixed to the altar, and wishful that sooner or later permission would be granted for a return to the more primitive aumbry. This went with the fashion for central altars and celebrating Mass facing the people, which are dealt with in the epilogue.

Since 1783, when it was founded at Bruges, the firm of Louis Grossé Ltd. has been famous of the high quality of its vestments, altar frontals, etc. The two present directors of the London headquarters are the great-great-grandsons of the Belgian founder. They carry on the traditions of past generations, and examples of their work can be found in many Catholic and Anglican sacristies.

Good vestments and ecclesiastical embroidery have been produced by the two Anglican communities of the Sisters of Bethany, Lloyd Square, London, and the Society of S. Margaret, East Grinstead; usually in the Gothic Revival manner. The German Congregation of the Sisters of the Poor Child Jesus, who opened a convent at Southam, Warwickshire, in the 'seventies, have also been famous for their embroidery and vestment making. The London firm of Watts and Co., founded in the 'seventies, supplied the frontals, curtains, hangings, etc., for most of the churches designed by Bodley and Garner. The rich materials, seldom of primary colours, but quiet half-tones, evoke the fashionable shades of the Æsthetic Movement of the 'eighties.

By the nineteen-thirties flowing unlined vestments, made of handmade silk, had begun to supersede so-called Gothic vestments. At first their use was confined almost entirely to some of the older Catholic religious orders. The Benedictine monks of Prinknash Abbey specialized in them, and helped to spread the fashion. Most of the really advanced Anglo-Catholic churches stuck to vestments of Roman or Spanish shape, as being more 'Catholic.'

The firm of John Hardman and Co. of Birmingham, established in 1838, traces its origin to a small shop in Paradise Street, Birmingham, which manufactured any small article of an ornamental nature, e.g. buckles, ink-stands, snuff-boxes and candlesticks. After the French Revolution when it became difficult to obtain religious articles from abroad, Mr. Hardman senior decided to turn his attention to the manufacture of such objects. His son happened to meet Augustus Welby Pugin, and was so fascinated by his enthusiasm for medieval art, that Mr. Hardman was persuaded to start a metal and glass works to carry out Pugin's designs. A band of artists was brought together and the making of church plate and stained glass windows was begun. The first window the firm carried out was for Ushaw College. The cartoons were drawn at Pugin's house at Ramsgate, the master being helped by his then eleven year-old son, Edward, and John Hardman junior. Orders multiplied and more lads from Birmingham were added to the Ramsgate staff. It was the Great Exhibition of 1851 (see p. 79) that did most to advertise the metal work and stained glass of Hardman and Co. After that the firm never looked back. Most of the cathedrals and many of the important parish churches in England, contain stained glass windows; in addition to those in Catholic college chapels, churches and seminaries.

Some of the most outstanding windows in Anglican places of worship are the west windows and aisles at Tewkesbury Abbey; the west window at Worcester Cathedral; the east and west windows at Bury St. Edmunds; the east window in Carlisle Cathedral; and a complete series at Newbury Parish Church, Berkshire. Among the Catholic work the following places might be mentioned: the cathedrals of Birmingham, Plymouth, Northampton and Lancaster; S. John's, Norwich, and S. Mary's, Derby; and many more at Ushaw, Upholland, Oscott and Ware among the seminary chapels. Abroad there are windows in Sydney, Melbourne and Perth Catholic cathedrals, and many more in the U.S.A. At one time or another Hardman and Co. have carried out decoration schemes in one form or another, murals, etc. for hundreds of Catholic churches—the earlier ones very elaborate, the more recent with greater restraint. Even to-day the work produced by this firm retains something of its quiet, good, solid Victorian quality. The actual craftsmanship is usually impeccable.

J. Wippell and Co. of Exeter is an even older established firm of church furnishers and decorators. Its work has been confined almost entirely to Anglican and Nonconformist places of worship. Until fairly recently most of the designs were characterized by a somewhat rigid adherence to not very exciting Gothic Revival traditions; but before the last war this firm started to emulate the style of furnishings carried out under the auspices of the Warham Guild (see p. 312), including 'English altars.'

The Art and Book Shop, under the shadow of Westminster Cathedral, has had a tradition, ever since its establishment, for religious works of art, mainly in the Baroque and Rococo styles. Having found that there was a demand for real or sham antiques of the seventeenth and eighteenth centuries, this firm has continued to supply them, without venturing into fresh fields or pastures new.

The firm of Campbell Smith and Co., established in 1873, has carried out a considerable amount of church decoration since that date, far too numerous to mention in detail. Its own workmen have been employed on the redecoration of countless Anglican and Roman Catholic places of worship, throughout the length and breadth of Britain.

In more recent times the Faith Craft-Works, connected with the Anglican Society of the Faith, founded in 1905, have carried out the furnishings of several cathedrals and many more parish churches; in many cases from the designs of artists employed by Faith Craft-Works. They made the impressive altar at the Church Union's Centenary Congress in the Albert Hall in 1958.

Wood and stone carvings for churches have been provided by such firms as Boulton and Sons (Cheltenham), Earley and Co. (Dublin), Hammer and Co. (Harringay, London), Alberti Ltd. (Manchester), and Maile and Son (London). A. R. Mowbray and Co. have specialized in woodwork of a traditional character (mainly Gothic) for Anglican churches. Vanpoulles Ltd. (London), established half a century ago, have supplied innumerable Roman Catholic churches with every type of furniture, ornament and vestment. Hayes and Finch Ltd., better known as candlemakers, have also done a considerable amount of church furnishings over a long period; mainly for Roman Catholic places of worship. The same applied to the now defunct firm of Francis Tucker and Co., established in 1730 for making church candles.

F. Osborne and Co., with a tradition going back many centuries, have a worldwide fame as artists and craftsmen in church plate and metal work of all descriptions. Fenning and Co. (London) and L. Oppenheimer Ltd. (Manchester) have both carried out much mosaic and marble decoration in the past fifty years. Laverty and Sons (Leeds) have provided many Roman Catholic churches with plate and metal work, in addition to what are known as 'objects of devotion.' This list of firms which have catered for every fashion in church furnishing and decoration in the period covered by this book is by no means complete, but it includes the names of those which are better known.

Between the two world wars fashions in church furnishings in North America underwent little change, and for the most part were based on the same traditional ideas as those in Britain. On the other hand, throughout the nineteen-thirties Catholic churches here and there began to be influenced by what was known as the 'Liturgical Movement.' Architects and priests tried to insert altars which were rubrically 'correct,' and this striving was much helped by the Liturgical Arts Society.

Very little new ground was broken, and George I. Lovatt's Church of the Holy Child, North Philadelphia, proves how the more artistically-minded Catholic clergy and layfolk were unable to see how illogical it was to build a large church in a blending of French Romanesque architecture, and to insist that every detail of its furnishings was covered with neo-Norman ornament. No expense was spared on the stone font, pulpit and altars, or the splendid repoussé lead doors. The stone reredos above the high altar with an exposition throne is decorated with conventional Romanesque stone carving.

Carlton Strong's Church of the Sacred Heart, Pittsburgh, more or less contemporary with the former, was a refreshing contrast; full of interesting and original neo-Gothic furnishings, all designed and carried out by real craftsmen even if in a late medieval manner. The holy-water stoops, carvings in wood and stone, the polychromed rood-beams and baldachin, all struck a new note.

A similar urge to ensure liturgical correctness in Catholic church furnishings was evident in Wilfrid E. Anthony's designs for S. Catherine of Sienna, New York —a modern Gothic brick church. Here the influence of Sir Ninian Comper and the Alcuin Club reached North America. The altars are gorgeous with gold leaf and colour on their delicate wood-carving. The high altar was given riddel posts. Another New York church built about the same time which showed that a small section of American Catholics studied the Alcuin Club publications—even Dr. Percy Dearmer's *Parson's Handbook*—is S. Vincent Ferrer's. The high altar has no gradine, and is provided with a tester, dossal and riddel curtains. Above the veiled tabernacle is a curious umbrella-shaped canopy, strongly reminiscent of Comper's hanging pyx in the chapel of the Anglican Convent of the Holy Name, Malvern Link, Worcestershire. Riddels, dossals and testers, such as were becoming more and more fashionable in Anglican churches in England, also found their way into Carlton Strong's Catholic church of Our Lady of Sorrow, Johnston, Pennsylvania, in the nineteen-thirties. Many of the churches which were remodelled under the direction of the Liturgical Arts Society featured these medieval furnishings. Even the firm of Rambusch—'Designers, Decorators and Craftsmen'—found that it was profitable to recommend liturgical 'correctness' to their clients, for whom they supplied many costly pulpits, screens, altars, reredoses and baldachins—all carried out in Byzantine, Baroque, Gothic (of any period), Romanesque or Renaissance as desired. This craze for recreating past periods of architectural styles across the Atlantic reached its peak in George I. Lovatt's S. Michael's Chapel at Torresdale, Pennsylvania, which was a wonderful replica of an Early Christian basilica—complete with a confessio and a ciborium over the high altar. Unfortunately there was no body of a martyr to be venerated by pilgrims, so there was no *raison d'être* for this confessio: its interest was purely antiquarian.

z

How attractive 'period styles' could be made was proved by many of the altars and reredoses designed by Miss Charlton Fortune and the Monterey Guild. The latter remodelled a number of Catholic churches. Worthy of mention are Miss Fortune's altar and triptych in the chapel of the Dominican Convent, San Rafael, California; also Ross Montgomery's Spanish Baroque furnishings in Our Lady of Mount Carmel, Montecito, California.

Many pastors who could afford the cost erected sumptuous baldachins over the high altars of their churches—Byzantine, Romanesque, Gothic or Renaissance. Veiled tabernacles became fairly common, but not frontals. Throughout the nineteen-thirties there was little or no evidence in the length and breadth of the North American continent that architects and church furnishers realized that a revolution had taken place on the continent of Europe. The repercussions of the new movement in Germany, France, Switzerland and Holland left very few marks in American church planning and furnishing. The more cultured clergy and laity of all Christian denominations were still seeking their inspiration in the remote past and not in the present. The externals of public worship were completely divorced from ordinary life.

But here and there, and usually in the most unlikely places, the dry bones were being made to live. S. Peter's Chapel, Montclair, New Jersey, designed for a negro Catholic congregation, broke new ground towards the close of this decade. Every detail of the furnishings showed the inspiration and craftsmanship of the individual responsible—the bronze doors, statues, lighting fixtures, wooden holy-water stoops, the carved and polychromed wooden altar and candlesticks, also the Stations of the Cross painted on the lower part of the windows. An even greater note of austerity and a breaking away from traditional styles was apparent in the remodelled church of S. Francis of Assisi, Portland, Oregon. The striking and costly bronze Gothic baldachin, designed by Maginnis and Walsh for S. Patrick's Cathedral, New York, shortly before the Second World War, sums up the taste of the more artistic and liturgical-minded American Catholics throughout the nineteen-thirties.

No better way to appreciate the extraordinary and eclectic nature of church furnishings, ornaments and decorations during the nineteen-thirties can be found than to study the 770 illustrations (a veritable ecclesiastical chamber of horrors) in Dom Roulin's monumental volume, entitled *Nos Eglises,* published at Paris in 1938. Some of the French and Belgian furnishings are wildly extravagant—*art nouveau* gone mad. Elsewhere Gothic is seen to have reached intriguing depths of decadence.

Canon Arnaud d'Agnel has left us a happier impression of the same period in his *L'Art Religieux Moderne,* published at Grenoble in 1936. The superb illustrations record impressive work in France, Holland, Belgium, Germany, Switzerland and Sweden. In this book there is a sense of a 'second Spring,' and not merely the end of an interminable autumn.

Perhaps we are still too close to the pre-war decade to take an objective view of its church furnishings, both at home and abroad, but after a lapse of twenty years most of the architects and craftsmen remind us of the children and 'storm-tossed sailors' mentioned by S. Paul in the Epistle to the Ephesians—'driven before the wind of each new doctrine that human subtlety, human skill in fabricating lies, may propound.' [7] It cannot be said that they were 'always humble, always gentle; —patient too, in bearing with one another's faults, as charity bids; eager to preserve that unity the Spirit gives, whose bond is peace.' [8] Each architect and craftsman may have 'received his own special grace, dealt out to him by Christ's gift,' but few, if any, had 'realized their common unity through faith in the Son of God, and fuller knowledge of him.' [9]

[7] Knox version, Chap. 4: 14.
[8] ibid., 4: 2.
[9] ibid., 4: 12.

THE WHEEL COMES FULL CIRCLE

S. BONAVENTURE remarks in his *Itinerarius Mentis in Deum* that 'the nature of God is a circle of which the centre is everywhere and the circumference is nowhere.' In a sense this is true of the furnishings and decorations of churches. The wheel has come full circle in the course of the last hundred years. This phenomenon, so far as ecclesiastical *décor* is concerned, is quite in keeping with the subtle and shifting nature of every fashion in every age. The pioneers revive the fashions of the past, with slight adaptations. There is nothing, or nearly nothing, new under the sun.

From the middle of the sixteenth century both Catholics and Protestants were trying to achieve closer participation of the laity in public worship by developing a room-plan of church. The Jesuits helped to popularize open churches, designed so that the congregation had an unbroken view of the high altar. Sir Christopher Wren, having studied such churches on the continent of Europe, stated that his aim was to produce a building in which everybody could conveniently see and hear the minister during any part of the service. There was no liturgical purpose for screens in what Wren called 'auditory churches.'[1] The room-plan of church held its own among Catholics and Protestants until the Gothic Revival when, as I have tried to show earlier, a sense of mystery in worship pervaded all. 'Auditory churches' were quite out of date. To be really 'okay' both Catholic and Anglican places of worship required a mock-medieval rood-screen. All furnishings and ornaments had to be based on the Middle Ages. A 'dim religious light' was vital for real devotion.

Between 1840 and 1940 the circle has been completed. To-day we have got back to the 'auditory church' of Sir Christopher Wren and his followers. The reasons for this change of fashion can be found in various factors—social and economic as well as liturgical. The 'thirties, as I have shown, was a challenging period for architects, church furnishers and decorators. Increasing costs of construction and higher wages for labour had enforced economy on both client and designer. Almost the only solution of the problems was by way of simplicity and the elimination of the fake trimmings of the past. There was no longer money to

---

[1] Cf. G. W. O. Addleshaw and F. Etchells, *The Architectural Setting of Anglican Worship* (1948), pp. 52, 54, 59, 60.

copy the glories of Early Christian, Byzantine, Romanesque, Gothic or Renaissance architecture. The majority of the clergy, architects and church furnishers, however, were still 'haunted by a nostalgia for an imagined past, with consequent disregard for the needs of their times.' [2]

Chaotic is the best word that sums up ecclesiastical *décor* in the nineteen-thirties. It had become all topsy-turvy, and the prevalent trends are difficult if not impossible to interpret. Yet just such an *omnium gatherum* was a real expression of the spirit of the age. The only solution was a return to the basic principles of Christian worship.

The first thing was to transform the faithful from 'silent onlookers' (Pius XI) to active participators in the offering; the individual worshippers were to join with the priest to form one community united by the sacrifice. Church architecture must subserve this developing community of the altar, 'providing it with an environment in which each person should be in contact with each other, and all with the altar, participating visually and orally, unhindered, in the sacrifice of the Mass.' [3] The 'all-seeing principle of worship' is the direct antithesis of the views of Augustus Welby Pugin in his *Treatise on Chancel Screens and Rood Lofts; their Antiquity, Use, and Symbolic Signification*, first published in 1851.[4]

The transformation of the typical Gothic Revival or neo-Byzantine or pseudo-Renaissance church of the late nineteenth century church into what became known as the 'liturgical church' started on the continent, and went through several phases. 'Liturgy and architecture had first to make mental contact with each other and clarify their mutual relationship. Practice and theory were each dependent upon the other, finally coalescing in such a way as to make it impossible for the historian to distinguish clearly between the different contributions to the common work.' [5] Among the many prophets who arose to spread new ideas on church planning and furnishing were Alexandre Cingera in Switzerland, Romano Guardini and the Benedictine monks of Maria Laach in Germany, Pius Parsch and Joseph Jungmann, S.J., in Austria, also the French Dominicans, under the leadership of Father Pie Régamey.

The first of the new type of church was Notre Dame de Raincy, outside Paris, designed by Auguste Perret as early as 1923. Many churches of the same character followed in Switzerland and Germany, e.g. S. Anthony, Basle, designed by Karl Moser in 1927; the Blessed Sacrament at Aachen, built by Rudolf Schwarz in 1930; and S. Engelbert in Riehl (Cologne) which Dominikus Böhm created in 1932. Then architects began to break away from the traditional position of the altar at the east end of the building.

Anton Henze has evolved a theory that 'the history of art in the West has shown

[2] Maurice Lavanoux. Preface to the American edition of *Contemporary Church Art* by Anton Henze and Theodor Filthaut (New York, 1956), p. 9.
[3] ibid., p. 21.
[4] See p. 41.
[5] ibid., p. 21.

BUCCLEUCH CHURCH, EDINBURGH
Typical late nineteenth century Presbyterian lay-out

that in every period church architecture has represented a sublimation of the building characteristic of the ruling class of the period. The great cathedrals of the twelfth and thirteenth centuries do not continue to be the dour, fortress-like royal towers but reveal themselves as castles of God, on the same ample scale as the contemporary castle of the Emperor and the knights, and so setting the sacral crown upon that golden age of the West. The city church of the Renaissance is in no way reminiscent of a Gothic castle but of the palaces of those men who set the tone of the age; and the Baroque period—despite undertones of apparent historicism—not only built new churches in its own style but was very ready to cover the interiors of old ones with its own lavish decorations.' [6] This German authority on the history of architecture visualizes the leading class of the present day as homeless technical and industrial workers; the characteristic building, the 'Tent of Labour'—a tent-like steel-frame structure, deriving its forms from industrial architecture. He would have us see the Christian church as the 'Tent of God,' symbolizing 'Christ our Brother and Redeemer,' just as the earliest Christian places of worship typified 'Christ in the guise of a Roman emperor.' [7] Unlike Eric Gill he accepts industrialism within the framework of Church worship.

So churches became proletarian in their plan and furnishing, taking on the character of the industrial architecture around them. Their purpose was practical rather than symbolical: to unite the congregation as closely as possible with what is going on at the altar. 'There is nothing strange in the fact that we can see the aspirations of our time mirrored in its church architecture: its longing for primitive, authentic reality, for genuine simplicity, for community, for brightness and lightness, for open space and ordered clarity and the warmth and intimacy of a safe shelter.' [8]

On the continent a few central altars had been erected in churches in the late nineteen-twenties, but it was not until 1935 that the first example of them appeared in England, when Mgr. John O'Connor (Chesterton's 'Father Brown') started the fashion at the Church of the First Martyrs, Bradford.

Writing to Graham Carey (January 16th, 1936), Eric Gill said: 'Yes, it is true that Fr. O'Connor recently built a round church (actually it is octagonal, but it comes to the same thing in practice). The altar is right in the middle, and the result, as you may guess, is very remarkable. The sacrifice is offered not only for the people, but by them and in the midst of them. . . . Actually it is not a very notable piece of building.' [9]

Eric Gill, having seen the octagonal church at Bradford, with its central altar, became enthusiastic for this then novel idea of plan. The immediate result was a lecture given to the boys of Blundell's School, Tiverton, Devonshire, early in 1938, which was reprinted in *Sacred and Secular* (1940), under the title of 'Mass for the Masses.' In September 1938 Gill 'got a job to build a real Church with a central altar and all.' It was at Gorleston-on-Sea, Suffolk. He wrote to Graham Carey: 'It is an interesting plan with crossed arches to make an octagonal central space. . . . The church will be very plain and small—no ornaments except perhaps a figure of S. Peter on the outside and a large Crucifix hanging over the altar.' [10] Two Catholic churches in England, each with a central altar, were built before the outbreak of the Second World War.

Central altars became almost an obsession with Eric Gill. He wrote: 'There is

---

[6] *Kirchliche Kunst der Gegenwart* (American translation, *Contemporary Church Art*, New York, 1957, p. 41).
[7] ibid., p. 40.
[8] ibid., p. 51.
[9] *Letters of Eric Gill*, edited by Walter Shewring (1947), p. 351.
[10] ibid., pp. 408–9.

CHURCH OF THE FIRST MARTYRS, BRADFORD, YORKS (1935)
The first church in Britain designed with a central altar.
It is interesting to note that this Roman Catholic return to
Early Christian austerity was contemporary with the Baroque
and Rococo gorgeousness of the Anglican 'Holy House' at
Walsingham (see p. 325)

nothing in the nature of an altar that implies that it should be anywhere but in the
middle. It began as a table around which people sat and partook of the consecrated bread and wine. It remains that thing. . . . To revive the liturgy it is first
necessary to disinter it. It is buried at present beneath a load of medieval and post-
medieval custom. The divorce between the clergy and the people, between the
people and the altar, has become as wide as the distinction between the artist and
the factory-hand, the responsible human worker on the one hand and the irrespon-
sible tool on the other. . . . The altar is the centre of the church; it is indeed
the church. . . .' Like some of his contemporary Catholics on the continent of
Europe, Gill became absolutely convinced that in the course of centuries 'a monstrous division between the place of the altar and the rest of the church' had been

360

created. He wrote: 'The sanctuary is ruled off as being not merely a holy place but a mysterious place—a place in which only professional feet may tread, a place in which the laity can only enter, more or less timidly, when they go up to receive Communion.' Gill's supposed anti-clericalism horrified the more conservative priests. He wanted to 'bring God again among men,' and to do away, so to say, with 'the whole caboodle of pharisaic ceremonies and mystogism.' So he concluded: *'The altar must be brought back again into the middle of our churches,* in the middle of the congregation, surrounded by the people—and the word surrounded must be taken literally. It is essential that the people should be on all sides, in front and behind. The Holy Sacrifice must be offered thus, and in relation to this nothing else matters.'

'The choir, the vestments and the stained glass windows, the carvings, the paintings and the statues, all are so much frippery compared with the altar and the service of the altar.' Gill added that all these ornaments 'are not the product of the people's hands, they are for the most part mere merchandise, stuff produced like everything else not for any use, holy or unholy, but for profit. Away with them—or if that be too difficult for our feebleness, at least let us disregard them; for merely to remove frippery, to wallow in an orgy of good taste is not itself of any value at all. The only important thing and the only thing that matters is to bring the altar to the people. It is like the cry "back to the land," which means back to the people, back to humanity, and in this connection we must add, back to Christianity, back to the Incarnation.'

Towards the end of the nineteen-thirties liturgical pioneers in France, Belgium, Holland, Germany and Austria were expressing very much the same opinions as those of Eric Gill in England. So the new movement in the planning and furnishing of Catholic churches gained momentum. The pendulum had swung from one end to the other. All those rigid principles set forth by Pugin and the ecclesiologists in the eighteen-forties and -fifties were thrown overboard. The reversal was complete.

The supper room at Jerusalem became the pattern for the perfect Christian church, as being its origin and prototype for all time. Architects and priests, having digested the two volumes of *Der christliche Altar,* written by Fr. J. Braun, S.J., and first published at Munich in 1924, were filled with an urge to get back to a primitive type of holy table free from all unnecessary accretions, from which even the cross and candlesticks were excluded until the Middle Ages. Fr. Braun, with tremendous erudition, had left no room for doubt that the ideal altar must be placed in a position where it can be seen by all, and that it is 'most fitting, most beautiful, and also most traditional' if the Eucharistic table of the sacrificial community is placed in such a position that it can be freely approached on all sides.

So started the fashion for celebrating Mass facing the people, and with it came the desire to remove the tabernacle from the high altar where it prevented the congregation from getting an unbroken view of the priest's hands.[11] Iconoclasm spread like wild-fire in France. Every young priest who was caught up in the movement for popularizing the liturgy, wasted no time in erecting at least a temporary altar in the middle of the church, where the Sunday Masses were celebrated, usually facing the people. Elsewhere the original high altar in the chancel was pulled down. Sometimes a simple stone holy table was substituted, but not always.

MASS FACING THE PEOPLE
A revival of early Christian simplicity in Roman Catholic externals of worship

Once the custom of communicating the laity from hosts consecrated during the Mass, instead of from the reserved Sacrament in the tabernacle, became the general rule in churches where the Liturgical Movement had won the day, priests could see no reason for retaining a tabernacle on a main altar. So especially in France and Germany there were a few churches in which the Blessed Sacrament was reserved

[11] What became known as the 'Parish and People' movement helped to spread the same ideas in the Church of England. It was felt that a sense of corporate liturgical worship such as existed in the Early Christian Church must be developed. The Revd. Basil Minchin set forth these ideas in *The Celebration of the Eucharist Facing the People* (1st edition, 1954). The leaders of the liturgical movement among the Reformed Churches on the continent of Europe are seeking after very much the same type of 'living worship,' envisaged by Pius XII in his Encyclical Letter 'Mediator Dei' (1947). Several new Anglican churches have been designed with central altars, and almost as bare of decoration as the latest Catholic churches in France and Germany.

on a small altar erected where the original altar stood, i.e. behind the new high altar more or less in the middle of the church. Elsewhere, in accordance with one of the earlier methods of reservation, although contrary to the prescriptions of modern Canon Law, there was a reversal to an aumbry set in a wall. Shrines and votive candle-stands were cast out. Statues were banished. Polychrome decorations on walls were hidden under a coating of whitewash, or the walls scraped of layers of paint.

By 1940 a few of the more revolutionary leaders of the Liturgical Movement on the continent of Europe had achieved a state of almost complete 'nudism' so far as altars were concerned. The altar was left quite bare except for Mass. A cross and candlesticks were placed on it only when required by the rubrics of the Missal. In a few churches they were stood on the floor, around the altar. If a cross and candlesticks still remained permanent ornaments, then they were made as small and as inconspicuous as possible. Fiddle-back vestments of Baroque or Rococo style were taboo, and had to be replaced by plain and ample chasubles and dalmatics, evocative of the cloak that S. Paul left behind at Troas.

Within a year of the outbreak of the Second World War, the liturgical movement, especially in France, went underground, not from choice but from sheer necessity. Since 1934 the Abbé Godin, who had been one of the most active promoters of the Young Christian Workers, had been collecting material about the general indifference to religion which would form the basis of his *France, Pays de Mission?* published in 1944, leading to the formation of the first group of 'priest-workers.' Cardinal Suhard, the Archbishop of Paris, was not the only member of the French hierarchy who felt that to rechristianize the proletariat the methods of the first century of the Christian era must be revived. So urgent was it to bring the Mass to the pagan or semi-pagan masses, and rather in the form of a communal meal than of a sacrifice carried out with dignified ceremonial, that in places where there were not enough churches, it should be celebrated in the homes of the poor, even on kitchen tables.

So started yet another fashion in church furnishings, based on a return to the age of the Catacombs, and those far off times when small groups of persecuted Christians around the Mediterranean broke bread behind the locked doors of private houses.

The experiences of priests who found themselves prisoners of war, lacking most of the rubrical essentials for celebrating Mass, also helped to create a new conception of the liturgical movement, including a complete indifference to the traditional furnishing and decoration of churches. Having been obliged to celebrate Mass without vestments or a proper chalice, some of these priests began to ask themselves whether such externals of worship were really helpful as aids to devotion. They hoped that when peace was restored to a war-ravaged world, the Congregation of Rites would see its way to grant a permissive use for Mass being celebrated in lounge suits; preferably dungarees as being more symbolic of 'Christ the Workman.'

Such opinions were strongly criticized by liturgists of more balanced views. For example, Fr. H. A. Reinhold pointed out that the central-altar enthusiasts who became very vocal by 1952, were deficient in their knowledge of history. He wrote that Eric Gill and many continental pioneers of the liturgical movement had 'taken the word *"circumstantes"* literally and without distinction. In the first place: this term does not occur in a prescriptive rubric, nor is it directive. Secondly: its interpretation may refer to clergy as well as people. Thirdly: it has never been taken literally, in the sense that the faithful must surround the altar.

'The rubrics (and common sense) require that the priest faces the people, when he greets them (*Dominus vobiscum*). He can do this either when he stands behind the altar (*more Romano*), or by turning round (the present custom). This rubric would be completely senseless if the priest were in the centre of the congregation.' [12]

Fr. Reinhold, and most liturgical scholars would agree with him, reminded his readers that there are many reasons, hierarchical and dynamic, for having the Christian altar 'opposite' the people, and that there are almost equally strong reasons for the celebrant standing with his back to the congregation as facing them. Moreover, 'There is no historical precedent for central altars; the few examples are either only apparently centralized (Hagia Sofia, San Vitale, Aix-la-Chapelle), or converted Mausolea (Santa Costanza), or chapels of a romantic community (Templars), not parishes.' [13]

But by the end of the Second World War, and during the years that followed it, some of the more reckless leaders of the liturgical movement on the continent of Europe, had ceased to bother about rubrics. Their ideal church furnishings consisted of a plain wooden table, set in the midst of an upper room, and nothing else for preference, except perhaps an inconspicuous cupboard fixed to one of the walls in which the Blessed Sacrament was reserved. One or two dumpy candlesticks might stand on the holy table during the celebration of Mass (generally in the evening), but they were usually removed afterwards. To create the ethos akin to that of the catacombs, it was preferable for the congregation to stand or sit on the floor.

Revolutionary customs on these lines were being introduced into parish churches here and there. They were denounced strongly by Pope Pius XII in his Encyclical Letter *'Mediator Dei'* (1947). The Pope stated categorically that private individuals have no authority in liturgical matters, and that it rests with the Sovereign Pontiff alone to 'permit or establish any liturgical practice, to introduce or approve new rites, or to make any changes in them he considers necessary.' He denounced certain unauthorized innovations in public worship of which he had heard, and continued:

'The liturgy of the early ages is worthy of veneration; but an ancient custom is not to be considered better, either in itself or in relation to later times and circum-

[12] *Speaking of Liturgical Architecture* (Notre Dame, Indiana), p. 6.
[13] ibid., p. 7.

stances, just because it has the flavour of antiquity. More recent liturgical rites are also worthy of reverence and respect, because they too have been introduced under the guidance of the Holy Ghost, who is with the Church in all ages even to the consummation of the world. These too are means which the august Bride of Christ uses to stimulate and foster the holiness of men.

'To go back in mind and heart to the sources of antiquity of sacred liturgy is wise and praiseworthy. The study of liturgical origins enables us to understand better the significance of festivals and the meaning of liturgical formulas and ceremonies. But the desire to restore everything indiscriminately to its ancient condition is neither wise nor praiseworthy. It would be wrong, for example, to want the altar restored to its ancient form of table; to want black eliminated from the liturgical colours, and pictures and statues excluded from our churches; to require crucifixes that do not represent the bitter sufferings of the divine Redeemer; to condemn polyphonic chants, even though they conform to the regulations of the Apostolic See.' [14] Indeed, the Pope went so far as to describe the attempts being made to revive 'archæologism' as 'a wicked movement, that tends to paralyse the sanctifying and salutary action by which the liturgy leads the children of adoption on the path to their heavenly Father,' He ended this chapter of the Encyclical Letter with the warning: 'Let nobody take it upon himself to make his own rules and impose them upon others'; telling bishops that they were to use their authority 'even with salutary severity, if necessary'—to put a stop to dangerous novelties in church planning and furnishing.[15]

Fashions, especially ecclesiastical ones, are nothing if not paradoxical. While Catholic churches on the continent of Europe were growing more and more like Calvinist places of worship, nonconformists were hurrying in a Papalist direction. In some Scottish Presbyterian kirks the communion tables were shoved back against the east wall, and vested with richly embroidered frontals. Long after flower vases had been removed from the altars of Anglican churches under the influence of Percy Dearmer, Presbyterian and Nonconformist ministers began to encourage a cultus of the goddess Flora. Groups of pious ladies—floral confraternities—were formed to attend to the flower vases on the communion tables. In some of the larger places of worship of the Established Church of Scotland, e.g. the medieval cathedrals or collegiate churches, side chapels were arranged, usually with a small table vested with a frontal, sometimes with hassocks or stools at either end, thus imitating the traditional 'Low Church' Anglican 'Use.' The more courageous Presbyterian ministers even dared to put wooden or brass crosses on their communion tables, just when many Catholic priests were trying to find valid reasons for removing them. The Iona Community had a sort of wooden pylon made, on which to stand a large silver cross behind the great marble high altar of the medieval Abbey Church. Some Presbyterian ministers may have wished they could introduce eucharistic vestments, but a fair number compromised by pulpit-falls and

[14] ibid., Chapter V, Section 65.
[15] ibid., Chapter V, Section 68.

book-markers of the liturgical colours, usually those of the Roman rite, of the seasons of the Christian year. In the United States the practice of furnishing Baptist, Congregational, Methodist, Presbyterian and even Unitarian places of worship with altars and reredoses, usually copied from medieval Gothic examples, continued. In the Catholic church, where the modern Liturgical Movement had been introduced, the aim was a reversal to the Puritan tradition of the eighteenth or early nineteenth century 'meeting house.'

Once the Battle of Britain started in the summer of 1940, there was no time to think about fashions of church furnishing and decoration. Many a pulpit, altar, reredos and font was reduced to dust and ashes. This widespread destruction of churches and their *décor* may have helped to make people realize how transient and ephemeral are ecclesiastical fashions, like all others. Cecil Beaton wrote: 'Interior decoration, like ladies' fashions, has run a restless and everlasting gamut since the first cave man brought a rock into his cave to sit upon; like fashion, any voyage to the interior is fraught with peril between the Scylla of antique and the Charybdis of an operating room sterility. . . . Fashion is the subtle and shifting expression of every age. It would be foolish to expect our social mirror to always send back the same image. The important thing, in the last analysis, is whether the image really corresponds to what we feel ourselves to be.' [16]

Looking back over a hundred years on the ecclesiastical *décor* dealt with in these pages, let us treat its many phases with the respect they deserve. We have no right to dismiss the taste of our parents and grandparents, even if we cannot help being amused at it sometimes. Our grandchildren are likely to be equally ribald about our supposed 'good taste' and enlightened ideas. No better ending for this study of church decoration can be found than an observation by Fr. H. A. Reinhold.

'We see that all these styles were children of their own day. None of their forms are ours. We have concrete, steel, wood compositions, brick, stone, glass of all kinds, plastic material, reverse-cycle heat and radiant heat. We can no longer identify the minority, called Christendom, and split into schisms, with the Kingdom of God on earth. We live in a new atmosphere, a secularist atmosphere, even though our society still calls itself Christian.

'We are not the Church of early persecutions, nor the queen of creation as in the Middle Ages, nor the guarantor of order as in the bourgeois period. The divine Presence, the permanent Parousia, made by the liturgy, is again, in a new way, a mustard seed and a leaven. For this our architects must find as good an expression in our language of form, as our fathers did in theirs.' [17]

This chronicle of ecclesiastical fashions between 1840 and 1940 may help to convince the reader of the truth of the words of the writer of Ecclesiastes: 'The thing that hath been, it is that which shall be; and that which is done is that

[16] *The Glass of Fashion* (1954), pp. 212 and 337.
[17] op. cit., p. 32.

which shall be done; and there is no new thing under the sun. Is there any thing whereof it may be said, See this is new? it hath been already of old time, which was before us' (vv. 9, 10).

Again, when one thinks of all the changes in the styles of church furnishing and decoration during the century which have been studied in these pages, how true it is (as the Preacher reminds us) that 'the sun also ariseth, and the sun goeth down, and hasteth to his place where he arose. The wind goeth toward the south, and turneth about unto the north: it whirleth about continually, and the wind returneth again according to his circuits' (vv. 5, 6). In the long run it is safer not to dogmatize about ecclesiastical *décor*. Our problem, what is good or bad, is no less ultimate than Pilate's, 'What is truth?'

FINIS

BIBLIOGRAPHY

Place of publication: London (unless otherwise stated)

Addleshaw, G. W. O., and Etchells, F. *The Architectural Setting of Anglican Worship* (1948).
Anglo-Catholic Congress Reports (1920–30).
Anson, Peter F. *Churches, their Plan and Furnishings* (Milwaukee, 1948).
— *The Call of the Cloister* (1955).
— 'Catholic Church Buildings in Scotland from the Reformation until the outbreak of the First World War, 1560–1914' (article in *The Innes Review*, 1954).
— 'Sir John Ninian Comper,' in *Transactions of the Scottish Ecclesiological Society*, 1950.
Art Journal. Illustrated Catalogue: The Industry of all Nations (Great Exhibition, Hyde Park, London, 1851).
— *Illustrated Catalogue of the International Exhibition of 1862.*

Baker, Joseph Ellis. *The Novel and the Oxford Movement* (Princeton, 1932).
Barbier de Montaut. *Traité pratique de la Construction de l'ameublement et de la décoration des églises* (Paris, Vol. I 1885, Vol. II 1899).
Barr, James. *Anglican Church Architecture* (Oxford, 1842).
Barry, Alfred, *Life and Work of Sir Charles Barry* (1867).
Bartoli, L. *L'Arte nella Casa di Dio* (Roma, 1950).
Beaton, Cecil. *The Glass of Fashion* (1954).
Bennett, Frederick. *The Story of W. J. E. Bennett* (1909).
Benson, A. C. *Life of Edward White Benson*, 2 vols. (1899).
Betjeman, John. *Ghastly Good Taste* (1933).
— *First and Last Loves* (1952).
— 'A note on J. N. Comper,' article in *Architectural Review* (February 1939).
— *Collins Guide to English Parish Churches* (1958).
— and Piper, J. *Murray's Berkshire* (1949).
— and Clarke, B. F. L. *British Churches* (1963).
Blacking, W. H. R. *The Arrangement and Furnishing of a Church* (1954).
Blencowe, Miss. *Church Embroidery* (c. 1850).
Blomfield, Sir Reginald. *Memorials of an Architect* (1932).
Bond, Francis. *Screens and Galleries in English Churches* (Oxford, 1908).
— *The Chancel in English Churches* (Oxford, 1916).
Bond, F. B., and Camm, O.S.B., Bede. *Rood Screens and Rood Lofts*, 2 vols. (1909).
Bonney, H. K. *Bonney's Church Notes, being Notes on the Churches in the Archdeaconry of Lincoln.* Edited by N. S. Harding (Lincoln, 1937).
Bouyer, Louis. *Life and Liturgy* (1956).
Bowen, W. E. *Contemporary Ritualism* (1902).
Brandreth, H. R. T. *Dr. Lee of Lambeth* (1951).
Brannach, Frank. *Church Architecture* (Milwaukee, 1932).
Braun, S. J. Joseph. *Die Liturgische Gewandung in Occident und Orient* (Freiburg, 1907).
— *Der Christliche Altar*, 2 vols. (Munich, 1924).
Briggs, Martin S. *Goths and Vandals* (1952).
— *Puritan Architecture* (1946).
Briggs, R. J. E. *History of S. John's, Torquay* (Torquay, 1930).
Broderick, Robert C. *Historic Churches of the United States* (New York, 1958).
Brown, F. C. *Modern English Churches* (Cleveland, Ohio, 1927).
Bumpus, T. Francis. *London Churches Ancient and Modern*. Second series: *Classical and Modern* (n.d.).

Cabrol, O.S.B., Fernand. *Dictionnaire d'Archéologie et Liturgie* (Paris, 1924–54).
Cachemaille-Day, N. F. 'Ecclesiastical Architecture in the Present Age,' in *Journal R.I.B.A.* LX, 825–38.

Cambridge Camden Society. *Hints for the Practical Study of Ecclesiastical Architecture* (1839).
— *A Few Words to Church Builders* (1841).
— *A Few Words to Churchwardens on Churches and Church Ornaments, suited to town and manufacturing districts.* Parts I and II (1844, 1851).
— *Church Enlargement and Church Arrangement* (1842).
— *Hints to Workmen engaged on Churches* (1844).
— *Twenty-three Reasons for Getting Rid of Church Pues* (1843).
Caroe, A. R. D. *Old Churches and Modern Craftmanship* (1949).
Carpenter, S. C. *Church and People, 1789–1889* (1933).
Casagrande, *L'Arte a servizio della Chiesa* (Turin, 1931).
Cazenove, J. G. *An Account of the Collegiate Church and College in the Isle of Cumbrae* (Edinburgh, 1872).
Central Council for the Care of Churches. Annual reports (under various titles).
— *Building New Churches* (1962).
— *New Churches,* exhibition catalogue (1963).
Church Association. *Illegal Ritual in the Church of England* (1899).
Church Congress Exhibitions Catalogues.
Church Craft League Reports.
Clark, Kenneth. *The Gothic Revival, an Essay in the History of Taste* (New York, 1928).
Clarke, Basil, F. L. *The Church Builders of the 19th Century* (1938).
— *Anglican Cathedrals outside the British Isles* (1958).
— *My Parish Church* (1943).
Clarke, C. P. S. *The Oxford Movement and After* (1932).
Close, Francis (later Dean of Carlisle). *Church Architecture, Scripturally Considered from the Earliest Ages to the Present Time* (1844).
— *The Restoration of Churches is the Restoration of Popery, proved and illustrated from the Authentic Publications of the Cambridge Camden Society* (Cheltenham, 1844).
Codex Juris Canonici. Liber II, De rebus, Parts I and II (Roma, 1917).
Collins, H. E. *The Church Edifice and its Appointments* (Philadelphia 1932; n. ed. 1940; rev. 1953);
Comper, Sir John Ninian. *Further Thoughts on the English Altar, or Practical Considerations on the Planning of a Modern Church* (Cambridge, 1933).
— *Of the Christian Altar and the Buildings which contain it* (1950).
— *On the atmosphere of a Church* (1947).
Cope, Gilbert. *Symbolism in the Bible and the Church* (1959).
— ed. *Making the Building Serve the Liturgy* (1962).
— *Ecclesiology Then and Now* (1963).
Cornish, E. W. *History of the English Church in the Nineteenth Century.* 2 vols. (1910).
Costantini, Celso (Cardinal). *Arte Sacra e Novecentesimo* (Roma, 1935).
— *L'Istruzione de S'Officio sull' Arte Sacra* (Roma, 1952).
— *Nozioni d'Arte per il Clero* (Roma, 1909).
Cox, Edward Young. *The Art of Garnishing Churches at Christmas and other Festivals* (1st ed. 1868; 2nd ed. 1871).
Cox, J. C. *English Church Fittings, Furniture and Accessories* (Oxford, 1933).
— *Pulpits, Lecterns and Organs in English Churches* (Oxford, 1915).
Cram, Ralph Adams (introduction by). *American Churches.* 2 vols. (New York, 1915).
— *Church Building* (3rd. ed., New York, 1924).
Cutts, Edward L. *Church Furniture and Decoration* (1854).

d'Agnel, G. Arnauld. *L'Art Religieux Moderne* (Grenoble, 1931).
Dale, J. D. Hilarius. *The Sacristan's Manual* (1854; 2nd ed. 1860).
Davies, J. G. *The Architectural Setting of Baptism* (1962).
Dean, Beryl. *Church Needlework* (1961).
Dearmer, Nan. *The Life of Percy Dearmer* (1940).
Dearmer, Percy. *The Parson's Handbook* (1899; revised and enlarged 1903; 6th ed. with additional matter, 1907, Oxford).
— *Art and Religion* (1923).
— *A Short Handbook of Public Worship* (Oxford, 1931).
Dearmer, Percy. *Fifty Pictures of Gothic Altars* (Alcuin Club, 1910).
— *The Art of Public Worship* (1919).
— *The Ornaments of the Minister* (1920).

A*

De Mille, G. E. *The Catholic Movement in the American Episcopal Church* (2nd ed. Philadelphia, 1950).
Dictionary of National Biography, and *Supplements* (1882–1921).
Distel, W. *Protestantischer Kirchen seit 1900 in Deutschland* (Leipzig, 1903).
Dix, Gregory. *A Detection of Aumbries* (1942).
— *The Shape of the Liturgy* (1945).
Drummond, Arthur Landale. *The Church Architecture of Protestantism* (Edinburgh, 1934).
— 'The Architectural Interest of English Meeting Houses' in *Journal R.I.B.A.,* XLV, 909–17.
[Drummond, Henry.] *The Principles of Ecclesiastical Buildings and Ornaments* (1851).
Duret, D. *Mobilier, vases, objets et vêtements liturgiques* (Paris, 1922).

Eastlake, Charles. *The History of the Gothic Revival* (1872).
Ecclesiastical Discipline, Report of the Royal Commission on, 3 vols. (1906).
Ecclesiological Society. *History of Christian Altars* (1847).
— *Instrumenta Ecclesiastica,* 2 vols. (1847, 1856).
Eden, F. C. *The Organ* (Church Building Society leaflet, n.d.).
Edgell, G. H. *The American Architecture of To-day* (New York).
Eeles, Francis C. *Traditional Ceremonial and Customs connected with the Scottish Liturgy* (Alcuin Club Collections, XVII, 1910).
— 'The Anglican Tradition, Ornaments and Fittings,' in *Post War Church Buildings* (1947).
Elliott-Binns, L. E. *Religion in the Victorian Era* (1936).
Ernest Gimson, his Life and Work (1924).

Farleigh, John. *The Creative Craftsman* (1950).
Ferrey, Benjamin. *Recollections of A. N. Welby Pugin and his father Augustus Pugin* (1861).
Ferriday, Peter, ed. *Victorian Architecture* (1963).
Fifty Modern Churches. Inc. Church Building Society (1947).
Fleetwood-Hesketh, Peter. *Murray's Lancashire architectural guide* (1955).
Forse, E. J. G. *Ceremonial Curiosities* (1936).
Fortescue, Adrian, and O'Connell, J. B. *The Ceremonies of the Roman Rite Described* (1946).
Freeman, Andrew. *Church Organs and Organ Cases.*
Frere, Walter Howard. *Principles of Religious Ceremonial* (1928).
Fritsch, K. E. O. *Der Kirchenbau des Protestantismus von der Reformation vis zur Gegenwart* (Berlin, 1893).

Geldart, Ernest. The Art of Garnishing Churches (1882).
— *A Manuel of Church Decoration and Symbolism* (Oxford, 1899).
Gieselmenn, R., and Aebli, W. *Kirchenbau* (1960).
Gill, Eric. *Art Nonsense* (1929).
— *Beauty Looks after Herself* (1933).
— *Letters of* (ed. by Walter Shewring) (1947).
— *Sacred and Secular* (1940).
Glendinning, F. J., ed. *The Church and the Arts* (1960).
Goodhart-Rendel, H. S. *English Architecture since the Regency* (1953).
Gough Michael. *The Early Christians* (1960).
Gresley, William. *Bernard Leslie, or a Tale of the Last Ten Years* (1842; 2nd ed. part. 1859).
Gurlitt, C. *Kirchen* (Stuttgart, 1906).

Hammond, P. *Guide to Modern French Churches* (1959).
— *Liturgy and Architecture* (1960).
— ed. *Towards a New Church Architecture* (1962).
Hay, George. *The Architecture of Scottish Post-Reformation Churches, 1560–1843* (Oxford, 1957).
Hebert, Gabriel. *Liturgy and Society* (1935).
Henze, Anton. *Kirchliche der Gegenwart* (Rechlinghausen, 1954). American translation by Cecily Hastings—*Contemporary Church Art*—ed. by Maurice Lavanoux (New York, 1956; London, 1957).
Hierurgia Anglicana: Documents and Extracts Illustrative of the Ceremonial of the Anglican Church after the Reformation. Edited by the Ecclesiological Society (1848). Revised and enlarged by Vernon Staley, 3 vols. (1902).

Hitchcock, Henry Russell. *Early Victorian Architecture in Britain,* 2 vols. (New Haven, 1954).
— *Architecture: 19th and 20th Centuries* (Pelican History of Art, 1958).
Hope, A. J. B. Beresford. *Worship in the Church of England* (1874).
— *The English Cathedral of the 19th Century* (1861).
Hope, W. H. St. John. *English Altars* (Alcuin Club Collections, 1899).

Jebb, John. *Three Lectures on the Cathedral Service in the Church of England* (Leeds, 1845).
Jenner, Henry L. *Of Flowers as Employed in the Adornment of Churches* (1847).
Jones, R. P. *Nonconformist Church Architecture* (1914).
Jungmann, S.J., Joseph. *Missarum Solemnia* (Vienna, 1949). American translation *The Mass of the Roman Rite,* 2 vols. (New York, 1951).

Kelly, Bernard W. *Historical Notes on English Catholic Missions* (1907).
Kidder Smith, G. E. *The New Churches of Europe* (1964).
King, Georgiana G. *George Edmund Street—unpublished Note Books and reprinted papers* (1916).

Lancaster, Osbert. *Homes Sweet Homes* (1939).
Laver, James. *Taste and Fashion* (1945).
Law, H. W. and Irene, *The Book of the Beresford Hopes* (1925).
Leatherbarrow, J. Stanley. *Victorian Period Piece* (1954).
Lee, F. G. *The Directorium Anglicanum* (2nd ed. edited by F.G.L. 1865; 4th ed. 1879); see Purchas, James.
— *A Glossary of Liturgical and Ecclesiastical Terms* (1877).
— *A Dictionary of Ritual and other Ecclesiastical Terms,* Part I (1871).
Legg. J. Wickham. *English Church Life from the Reformation to the Tractarian Movement* (1914).
Lethaby, W. A. *Philip Webb and his Work* (1935).
l'Hôpital, Winefride de. *Westminster Cathedral and its Architect,* 2 vols. (1919).
Lickford, J. Malcolm. *The Catholic Apostolic Church, Gordon Square, London* (1935).
Liddon, H. P. *Life of Edward Bouverie Pusey,* 4 vols. (1893–4).
Lindsay, Ian G. *The Scottish Parish Kirk* (1960).
Littledale, R. F. *North Side of the Altar* (1865).
Lough, H. G. *The Influence of John Mason Neale* (1962).

MacDonald Sinclair, W. 'New Church Work in Great Warley' in *Architectural Journal* (1905, pp. 64–77).
Mackeson, C. *Guide to the Churches of London and its Suburbs* (1889 and 1884–5).
Mackmurdo, A. H., ed. *Selwyn Image Letters* (1932).
Maguire, R., and Murray, K., *Modern Churches in the World* (1965).
Malherbe. *Le Mobilier Liturgique* (Luttre, 1927).
Marklande, J. H. *Remarks on English Churches* (1842).
Martin, W. W. *Ecclesiastical Architecture* (Cincinnati, 1899).
Maskell, H. Parr. *Hints on Building a Church* (1905).
Maskell, W. *Monumenta Ritualia Ecclesiae Anglicanae,* 3 vols. (1846–7).
Mathew, David. *Catholicism in England* (1936).
Matthews, W. R. *History of S. Paul's Cathedral* (1957).
Maufe, Edward. *Modern Church Architecture* (1948).
Maughan, H. Hamilton. *Wagner of Brighton* (1949).
Mellor, Richard. *Modern Church Design* (1948).
Micklethwaite, J. T. *The Ornaments of the Rubrics* (Alcuin Club Collections, 1901).
— *Modern Parish Churches.*
— *Occasional Notes on Church Furniture and Arrangements* (new ed. 1908).
Mills, Edward D. *The Modern Church* (1956).
Morris, Joan. *Modern Sacred Art* (1938).
Munier, A. *L'Eglise à notre epoque,* 3 vols. (Bruges, 1925–6).
— *Un projet d'Eglise au XXe siècle* (1933).
Muthesius, H. *Die neuere Kirchliche Baukunst in England* (Berlin, 1901).

Neale, John Mason. *Hierologus. A Church Tour through England and Wales.*
— *The History of Pues* (1843). (See Cambridge Camden Society publications.)
— and Webb, Benjamin. *The Symbolism of Churches and Church Ornaments. A Translation of the 1st Book of the Rationale Divinorum Officiorum by William Durnandus* (1845, new ed. 1893).

New Churches Illustrated. Incorporated Church Building Society (1936).

Newman, J. H. *Loss and Gain* (1848).

Nicholson, Sir Charles, Bart., and Spooner, Charles. *Recent English Ecclesiastical Architecture* (n.d.).

Nicholson, Sir Charles, Bart. *The Planning and Arrangement of a Church and its Furniture* (Inc. Church Building Society leaflet, n.d.).

O'Connell, J. *Directions for the Use of Altar Societies and Architects* (1936)
— *Church Building and Furnishing* (1955).

Ollard, S. L. *The Anglo-Catholic Revival* (1925).

Osborne, Chas. B. *Life of Father Dolling* (new ed. 1905).

Overton, J. H. *The English Church in the 19th Century* (1894).

Paget, Francis. *S. Antholin's* (1841).
— *Milford Malvoisin, or Pews and Pewholders* (1842).

Paley, F. A. *The Church Restorers. A Tale Treating of Ancient and Modern Art and Church Decoration* (1845).

Paton, D. M., ed. *The Parish Communion To-day* (1962)..

Perry, T. W. *Lawful Church Ornaments* (1857).

Pevsner, Nikolaus, *The Buildings of England* (Penguin Books. 27 vols. since 1951).

Phillips, C. S., and others. *Walter Howard Frere, Bishop of Truro* (1947).

Pichard, Joseph. *Les Eglises Nouvelles à travers le Monde* (1960).

Pilkington, Rinaldo. *Le Chiesa e il suo arredamento* (Turin, 1931).

Pinnock, W. H. *Laws and Usages of the Church of England ornaments and goods of the Church* (1855).

Poole, G. A. *Appropriate Character of Church Architecture* (Leeds and London, 1842).

Port, M. H. *Six Hundred New Churches: A Study of the Church Building Commission 1818–56* (1961).

Pugin, Augustus Welby. *Gothic Furniture in the style of the 15th century* (1836).
— *A Treatise of Chancel Screens and Rood Lofts, Their Antiquity, Use, and Symbolic Signification* (1851).
— *An Apology for a work entitled 'Contrasts' . . . followed by 'Some Observations on the State of the Arts in England'* (1837).
— *Contrasts; or a parallel between the noble edifices of the 14th and 15th centuries and similar buildings of the present day; showing the present decay of taste* (1836; enlarged ed. 1841);
— *Designs for gold and silversmiths* (1836).
— *Designs for Iron and Brass Work in the style of the XV and XVI centuries* (1836).
— *Floriated Ornament* (1849, new ed. 1875).
— *Glossary of Ecclesiastical Ornament and Costume* (1844; 2nd ed. revised and enlarged by Bernard Smith, 1846; 3rd ed. 1868).
— *Pugin's Ornaments of the XV and XVI centuries* (1904).
— *The Present State of Ecclesiastical Architecture in England* (1843).
— *The True Principles of Pointed or Christian Architecture* (1841). French ed. *Les Vrais Principes de l'Architec-Ogivales ou Chrétienne* (Bruges, 1850).

Pullan, R. P. *Architectural Designs of William Burges* (1887).

Purcell, E. S. *Life and Letters of Ambrose Phillipps de Lisle,* 2 vols. (1900).

Purchas, James, *The Directorium Anglicanum* (1st ed. 1859).

Quennell, P. *Victorian Panorama* (1937).

Régamey, P. R., O. P. *L'Art Sacré au XXe siècle* (Paris, 1952).

Reinhold, H. A. *Speaking of Liturgical Architecture* (Notre Dame, Indiana, 1952).

Ritual, 1st Report on the Royal Commission on (1867); *2nd Report* (1868).

Rogers, Harold S. *Fittings and Ornaments of Churches* (C.C.C.C. Occasional Leaflet, n. 34).

Rohault de Fleury. *La Messe,* 7 vols. (Paris, 1883–9).

Roulin, E., O.S.B., *Vêtements et Vesture* (Paris, 1931).
— *Nos Eglises* (Paris, 1938).

Rousseau, Olivier, O.S.B. *L'Histoire du Mouvement Liturgique* (Paris, 1945).

Russell, G. W. E. S. *Alban the Martyr, Holborn* (2nd ed. 1917).

Bibliography

Scott, George Gilbert. *Personal and Professional Recollections* (edited by his son, 1879).
Scott, George Gilbert, Jnr. *An Essay on the History of English Church Architecture* (1881)
Scott, Judith. *The Story of S. Mary Abbot's, Kensington* (1942).
Servettaz, N. *Architectura razionale religiosa* (Milan, 1932).
Sewell, Elizabeth. *Margaret Percival* (1847).
Short, E., ed. *Post-War Church Building* (1947).
Short, E. H. *The House of God* (1926).
Simpson, W. J. S. *The History of the Anglo-Catholic Revival from 1845* (1932).
Sirr, Harry. 'Augustus Welby Pugin: a sketch' (*Journal* R.I.B.A., August 1918).
Skilbeck, Clement O. *Illustrations of the Liturgy* (Alcuin Club Collections, xix, 1912).
Soenens, F. *Les Edifices du Culte* (1923).
Spence, Basil. *Phoenix at Coventry* (1962).
Spicer, Francis H. *Holy Trinity, Sloane Street* (articles in *Parish Magazine*, 1955).
Staley, Vernon. *Ceremonial of the English Church* (2nd ed. Oxford, 1900).
Street, A. E. *Memorials of George Edmund Street* (1888).
Suffling, E. Y. *Church Festival Decorations* (New York, 1907).
Summerson, John. *Heavenly Mansions* (1949).

Tamagnone, G. *Il Decoro della Casa di Dio* (1930).
Tatum, George B., and Bentley, Osmund. *Directions for the Use of Altar Societies and Architects* (revised ed. 1912).
Thiry, Paul. *Churches and Temples* (New York, 1953).
Thurgood, Monica. *Church Embroidery* (*c.* 1850).
Towle, E. A. *John Mason Neale* (1906).
Trappes-Lomax, Michael. *Pugin, a Medieval Victorian* (1932).
Travers, Martin. *Pictures of the English Liturgy* (1916).
— *The Celebration of High Mass* (1922).
Truman, Nevil. *The Care of Churches* (1935).

Vallance, Aymer. *English Church Screens* (1936).
— *The Decorative Art of Burne-Jones* (Arch. Journal Easter Annual, 1899).
Vavasseur-Haegy. *Manuel de Liturgie et Cérémonial*, 2 vols. (1932).
Victoria and Albert Museum, *Catalogue of an Exhibition of Victorian and Edwardian Decorative Art* (1952).
— *Victorian and Edwardian Decorative Art* (Small Picture Book, No. 34, 1952).
Viollet-le-Duc, E. *Dictionnaire raisonnée du mobilier français* (1855–75).
— *Dictionnaire de l'architecture française* (1858–68).

Wainwright, Arthur S. 'The Jewellery of Mr. and Mrs. Arthur Gaskin' in *The Studio*, Vol. LX (1912).
Walcott, Mackenzie E. C. *The Constitutions and Canons Ecclesiastical of the Church of England* (1879).
Walker, Charles. *The Ritual Reason Why* (1st ed. 1866).
Walsh, Walter. *The Secret History of the Oxford Movement* (1897).
Ward, Wilfrid. *The Life and Times of Cardinal Wiseman*, 2 vols. (1912).
Warham Guild Handbook. *Historical and Descriptive Notes on 'Ornaments of the Church and of the Ministers thereof'* (1932).
Warham Guild Leaflets.
    Day, E. Hermitage. *Some Notes on Vestments.*
    — *The Altar according to the English Tradition.*
    Dearmer, Percy. *Monuments and Memorials.*
    — *The Chalice and Paten.*
    Dorling, E. E. *Heraldry as an Element in Church Decoration.*
    Duncan-Jones, A. S., and Dunlop, D. C. *The Aumbry and Hanging Pyx.*
    Eeles, F. C. *The Episcopal Ornaments.*
    Howard, F. E. *The Chancel Screen.*
Warren, Edward. 'Life and Work of G. F. Bodley.' *Journal* R.I.B.A., XVII (1910).
Watkin, E. I. *Catholic Art and Culture* (revised ed. 1947).
Wattjes, J. G. *Moderne Kerken in Europa en America* (Amsterdam, 1931).

Webb, Geoffrey. *The Liturgical Altar* (1939).
Webber, F. R. *The Small Church* (Cleveland, Ohio, 1939).
Weber, E. J. *Catholic Church Building* (1927).
Weinbach, Werner. *Der Barok als Kunst der Gegen Reformation* (Berlin, 1921).
Weingarten, Josef. *Das Kirchliche Kunstegewerbe der Neuzeit* (Innsbruck, Wien, München, 1927).
Weyres, W., Bartning, O., and others. *Kirchen: Handbuch für den Kirchenbau* (1959).
White, James T. *The Cambridge Movement* (1962).
Wigley, G. J. *St. Charles Borromeo's Instructions on Ecclesiastical Building* (1867).
Williamson, Benedict. *How to Build a Church: What to do and what to avoid* (1934).
Wilson, Henry. *Silverwork and Jewellery* (1903).
Wilson, Henry, and Cooper, J. P., ed. *In Memoriam, J. D. Sedding* (1891).
Witte, Robert. *Das Katholische Gotteshaus* (Mainz, 1951).
Wood, Esther. 'Some metalwork by Omar Ramsden and Alwyn Carr,' in *The Studio*, Vol. XXXII (1904), pp. 21–4.
Woodforde, Christopher. *English stained and painted glass* (Oxford, 1954).
Wright, John. *Some notable altars in the Church of England and the American Episcopal Church* (New York, 1908).

Young, E. and W. *Old London Churches* (1956).

PERIODICALS

(*a*) BRITISH

A.A. Journal, The.
Architect and Building News (since 1854).
Architect's Journal (since 1895).
Architectural Review (since 1897).
Architecture Illustrated (1930).
Art Journal (1849–1912).
Art Notes (Oxford, 1936–43).
Art Union (1839–48).
British Architect (1874–1904).
Builder, The (since 1843).
Church Builder (1862–1904).
Churchbuilding (since 1960).
Ecclesiologist, The (1843–61).
English Churchman's Kalendar (since 1899).
Journal of the Royal Institute of British Architects (since 1837).
Royal Academy Illustrated (since 1916).
Studio (since 1893).
Studio Year Book of Decorative Art (since 1906).

(*b*) FOREIGN

Architectural Forum (New York).
Arte Sacra (Turin).
Bulletin Paroissial Liturgique (Abbaye de Sainte-André, Bruges).
Cahiers d'Art Sacré (Paris).
Deutsche Kunst und Dekoration (Darmstadt, 1897–1934).
Die Christliche Kunst (Munich).
Kunst und Kunsthandwerk (Vienna, 1898–1921).
L'Architecture Vivante (Paris).
L'Art d'Eglise (Abbaye de Saint-André, Bruges, since 1950).
L'Art Sacré (Paris).
L'Artisan Liturgique (Abbaye de Saint-André, Bruges, from 1927).
Liturgical Arts (New York, since 1932).
La Maison-Dieu (Paris).
Moderne Stil (Stuttgart, 1899–1904).
Orate Fratres (now *Worship*) (S. John's Abbey, Collegeville, Minn.).

INDEX

INDEX OF PLACES

INDEX OF PERSONS